D0217183

Christianity and Sexuality
in the Early Modern World

Christianity and Sexuality in the Early Modern World: Regulating Desire, Reforming Practice surveys the ways in which Christian ideas and institutions shaped sexual norms and conduct from the time of Luther and Columbus to that of Thomas Jefferson. The book is global in scope and geographic in organization, with chapters on Protestant, Catholic and Orthodox Europe, Latin America, Africa and Asia, and North America. The volume examines the subjects of marriage, divorce, fornication and illegitimacy, clerical sexuality, witchcraft and love magic, homosexuality, and moral crimes.

The book sets its findings within the context of many historical fields – the history of sexuality and the body, women's history, legal, religious, and gay and lesbian history, and colonial studies – and provides readers with an introduction to key theoretical and methodological issues in each of these areas. Each chapter contains three major sections: ideas, institutions, and effects. The first section discusses learned and popular notions of sexuality, both Christian, and, in areas outside Europe, non-Christian. The second section describes the development and operation of institutions established to enforce Christian standards, such as law codes, courts, disciplinary bodies, prisons, and marital regulations. The third section explores the degrees to which such efforts were successful, noting wide variations within and between Christian denominations, and analysing the role played by class and racial differences, family and economic structures, and local traditions in shaping sexual behaviour.

Merry E. Wiesner-Hanks is Professor of History at the University of Wisconsin-Milwaukee and author of *Women and Gender in Early Modern Europe* (Cambridge, 1993).

Christianity and society in the modern world
General editor: Hugh McLeod

Also available:

The Reformation and the visual arts: the Protestant image question in Western and Eastern Europe
Sergiusz Michalski

European religion in the age of great cities
Hugh McLeod

Women and religion in England, 1500–1720
Patricia Crawford

The reformation of ritual: an interpretation of early modern Germany
Susan Karant-Nunn

The Anabaptists
Hans-Jürgen Goertz

Women and religion in early America, 1600–1850: the puritan and evangelical traditions
Marilyn J. Westerkamp

Christianity and Sexuality in the Early Modern World

Regulating Desire, Reforming Practice

Merry E. Wiesner-Hanks

London and New York

First published 2000
by Routledge
11 New Fetter Lane, London EC4P 4EE

Simultaneously published in the USA and Canada
by Routledge
29 West 35th Street, New York, NY 10001

Routledge is an imprint of the Taylor & Francis Group

Typeset in Perpetua by The Florence Group, Stoodleigh, Devon
Printed and bound in Great Britain by
T J International Ltd, Padstow, Cornwall

British Library Cataloguing in Publication Data
A catalogue record for this book is available from the British Library

Library of Congress Cataloging in Publication Data
Wiesner-Hanks, Merry E., 1952–
    Christianity and sexuality in the early modern world:
regulating desire, reforming practice / Merry E. Wiesner-Hanks.
        p. cm. – (Christianity and society in the modern world)
    Includes bibliographical references and index.
    1. Sex – Religious aspects – Christianity. 2. Sex – History.
3. Sex customs – History. I. Title. II. Series.
BT708.W467 1999
261.8′ 357′ 0903–dc21   99-24259
                                        CIP

ISBN 0-415-14433-7 (hbk)
ISBN 0-415-14434-5 (pbk)

In memory of Bob Scribner (1941–1998),
great scholar, great editor, great friend

CONTENTS

ACKNOWLEDGMENTS

In writing any book, an author incurs many debts; in writing this one, which attempts to span the globe, my debts are both enormous and far-flung. Some of these are financial: I would like to thank the John Simon Guggenheim Foundation for its support, which provided me with a year off to research and write, and also the funds to spend part of that year in the Hawaiian sun instead of the Wisconsin mud. Much of my research was accomplished during the year when I held the Association of Marquette University Women (AMUW) Chair in Humanistic Studies, which gave me excellent access to Catholic materials, and I would like to thank AMUW for its support.

More of my debts are intellectual. I would first like to give special thanks to three people: the late Robert Scribner, who as editor of this series first asked me to write something on Christianity and sexuality, taught me (and many others) to see religion as "a matter of continually contested understandings," and did not blanch when I suggested the book be world-wide in perspective; Barbara Andaya, who invited me to be the comparative voice in a workshop on gender in early modern South-east Asia, inspired me to move beyond Europe for this study, and arranged for me to have visiting faculty status at the University of Hawaii; Samantha McLoughlin, my student assistant at Marquette, who bore much of the brunt of my decision to go global and plowed through massive amounts of source materials, including nearly all of the 73 volumes of the *Jesuit Relations,* searching for references to sex and marriage.

Choosing to look at the world rather than my more familiar Europe meant that I had to rely on a vast network of friends and colleagues to advise me. I had already discovered, when writing *Women and Gender in Early Modern Europe,* how gracious people were in sharing their expertise, and for this book I shamelessly turned to an even wider circle. JoAnn McNamara, Susan Stuard, Judith Bennett, Susan Karant-Nunn, Scott Hendrix, Ulinka Rublack, Jeffrey Merrick, Susan Burgess, Eve Levin, Mary Elizabeth Perry, Anne Schutte, Larissa Taylor, Allyson Poska, Linda Hall, Barbara Andaya, Carolyn

Brewer, Ellen Langill, Elizabeth Hitz, Bea Greene, and Linda Kealey all read and commented on drafts of chapters, and my dear friend Gwynne Kennedy read the entire manuscript.

Academic conferences are often described as frivolous junkets at which we hear papers that are better read, drink too much, sleep too little, and eat too well. The last is certainly true – particularly at those conferences fortunate enough to occur in Italy – but the purported uselessness of conferences is vastly overstated. My own thoughts on many of the issues in this book were deepened and broadened by my fellow participants at seven conferences which took place while I was researching and writing this book: "Geschlechterperspektiven in der Frühen Neuzeit" at the University of Frankfurt; "Imaginationen des Anderen" at the Herzog August Bibliothek in Wolfenbüttel (Germany); "Space and Time in Women's Lives in Early Modern Europe" at the Istituto Storico Italo-Germanico in Trento (Italy); "Das Konzept der Ehre in der Frühen Neuzeit" at the Institut für Europäische Kulturgeschichte der Universität Augsburg (Germany); "Political Writings, Political Women: Early Modern Britain in a European Context" at the Folger Institute in Washington, DC; "Engendering the History of Early Modern Southeast Asia," at the University of Hawaii; "Attending to Early Modern Women: Crossing Boundaries" at the University of Maryland-College Park. I would like to thank the organizers of all these conferences for inviting me, and for providing excellent fora where comparative issues could be discussed.

Women's history has taught us that the axes of difference in history may not simply be reduced to race, class, and gender, but are almost too numerous to list. I was faced with a similar conundrum when thinking of all the people with whom I have discussed the issues in these pages over the years and whose thoughts as well as their published works are thus reflected here. I initially planned simply to thank them as a group lest I risk leaving someone out, but then decided that names are important (another insight of women's history). Thus, in addition to the people I have listed already, and with apologies to anyone I may omit, I would like to thank: Darlene Abreu-Ferraira, Margo Anderson, Edward Behrend, Jodi Bilinkoff, Renate Bridenthal, Judith Brown, Martha Carlin, Brenda Child, Elizabeth Cohen, Natalie Zemon Davis, Lisa Di Caprio, Gisela Engel, James Farr, Evelyn Brooks Higginbotham, Fred Hoxic, Grethe Jacobsen, Margaret Jolly, Amy Leonard, Mary Lindemann, Deirdre McChrystal, Jean O'Brien, Beth Plummer, Catherine Pomerleau, Helmut Puff, Elizabeth Rhodes, Diana Robin, Lyndal Roper, Hilda Smith, Ulrike Strasser, B. Ann Tlusty, Gerhild Scholz Williams, Heide Wunder, and Max Yela. Finally, I would like to thank my husband Neil and my sons Kai and Tyr for their patience during the long process of this book, and for sharing in its benefits and its detriments.

INTRODUCTION

INTRODUCTION

A s a historian of a period long ago, I often encounter skepticism about the relevance of my research in the contemporary world. When I began this study, I was struck by how different the responses were to the project. People I met at community meetings, soccer games, or my hair salon were extremely interested, even when I told them the book stops in 1750. I could, of course, attribute this to their "prurient" interests in anything having to do with sex, and see it as proof that the French philosopher, Michel Foucault, and the American radio host, Howard Stern, are right: modern people want to talk about sex more than anything else. But it was not merely the sex part they were interested in, it was also the connection of sex to Christianity, a connection which they saw as both self-evident and extremely relevant.

This book explores how Christian ideas and institutions shaped sexual attitudes and activities from roughly 1500 to 1750, both in Europe and in areas of the world being colonized by European powers. Though in many ways Christian treatment of sex during this period largely continued patterns and practices which had begun centuries earlier, I have chosen to highlight this period, generally termed "early modern," for a number of reasons. The beginning point is quite traditional, and chosen for its significance in the history of Christianity: the splintering of Christianity within Europe at the same time as Christian doctrine was being spread beyond Europe through colonization. Both developments had important implications for Christian ideas about and patterns of sexuality. The ending point acknowledges the rough chronological juncture of three trends: the emergence of secular governments as more authoritative regulators of sexuality than the church in many parts of the world; the onset of a new wave of exploration and colonialism, which brought different issues and colonial powers to the fore; and the beginning of what scholars of sexuality usually call "modern sexuality." That shift in thinking generated new ideas about the body, changes in marriage patterns, new concepts of gender differences, greater symbolic importance attached to sexuality, and new methods of controlling people's sexual lives. Although scholars disagree about exactly when modern sexuality started and how sharply it differed from what came before, the notion of a turning point is nonetheless very powerful. I have therefore chosen to end my study at what most scholars see as the beginning of modern sexuality.

Along with the phrase "early modern," the other words of my title may also need some clarification. I use the term "Christianity" very broadly, for Christianity had an impact on the regulation of sexuality not only through the actions of church officials and the ideas of theologians, but also through the actions and ideas of lay people, from monarchs to ordinary individuals. If individuals or groups described their actions as Christian or held a position of authority within either a Christian denomination or a state where the official religion was Christianity, I include them here. I am not using "Christian" in a moral sense, and some of the attitudes and activities discussed here may be viewed by my contempories – and in fact *were* seen by some early modern people – as being antithetical to what they feel is the true message of Christianity.

"Sexuality" is a more problematic word, because no one in the centuries I am discussing used it. "Sexuality," defined as "the constitution or life of the individual as related to sex" or "the possession or exercise of sexual functions, desires, etc.," first appears in English only in 1800, and its use signals the beginning of "modern sexuality." Because of its recent origin, some historians choose to avoid the word "sexuality" when discussing earlier periods. They note that people in earlier centuries did not think of themselves as having a "sexuality" or classify as sexual things that to us seem obviously to be so. They point out that ancient Greek and medieval Latin did not even have words for "sex" or "sexual." Using a modern category such as "sexuality" to explore the past is not an unacceptable practice, however, because investigations of the past are always informed by present understandings and concerns. Thus the editors of the central journal in the field chose the title *Journal of the History of Sexuality* when it began publication in 1990. I use the word as well, and include in this study topics which the twentieth century considers related to sexuality, even if they were not perceived that way in earlier centuries.

Because exploring all aspects of the relationship between Christianity and sexuality over roughly two and a half centuries throughout the world would be impossible to do in a single book, I have chosen to focus on the ways in which people used Christian ideas and institutions to regulate and shape (or attempt to regulate and shape) sexual norms and conduct. Except for Chapter 1, which traces these issues from the beginning of Christianity to about 1500, the chapters are primarily geographical: Protestant Europe, Catholic and Orthodox Europe, Latin America, Africa and Asia, North America. Each of these chapters surveys learned and popular notions of sexuality, both Christian, and, in areas beyond Europe, non-Christian. They then discuss the development and operation of Christian institutions, such as law codes, courts, prisons, and marital regulations, as well as actual changes in such areas as marriage, divorce, illegitimacy, sanctioned and unsanctioned sexual relations, witchcraft, relations between Christians and non-Christians and between different denominations of Christians, and moral crimes. Though the book is oriented toward intellectual and institutional change and its social consequences, rather than toward social change alone, it should be clear that I do not see Christianity as an abstract force or regulation or as something imposed in a vacuum. The regulated as well as the regulators shaped Christianity's intellectual and institutional structures. As Christianity split into numerous denominations and expanded beyond Europe, the dialectic between official theology and the responses of practitioners grew ever more complex.

General theoretical and historiographical background

This study draws on research and analysis from many fields of history, fields that sometimes overlap or interact synergystically, yet that at other times are hostile to one another. Prime among these is the history of sexuality, which, until recently, was viewed as a questionable or at best marginal area of scholarly inquiry. Vern Bullough, one of the first investigators of medieval sexuality, reports that throughout the 1960s – that decade of the "Sexual Revolution" – his research on such topics as homosexuality, prostitution, and transvestism was rejected by historical journals as unsuitable, while books which avoided any discussion of sex, such as Edith Hamilton's *The Greek Way*, were best-sellers.[1] This attitude began to change in the 1970s for a number of reasons. Historians became more interested in the lives of ordinary people rather than simply political or intellectual elites, and they used methodologies from other disciplines such as anthropology and economics to create what they termed the New Social History. These changes combined with the feminist movement to create an enormous interest in women's history, of which the history of women's bodies and sexual lives was a significant part. The gay liberation movement encouraged both public discussion of sexual matters in general and the study of homosexuality in the past and present.

Like women's history, it challenged the assumption that sexual attitudes and practices or gender roles were "natural" and unchanging.

The denaturalizing of sexuality and gender led some scholars to assert that the body itself has a history: that is, cultural understandings of bodily processes, including sexuality, that shape the way people experience their own bodies have changed over time. This position is often labeled "social constructionist," and its most radical proponents argue that everything is determined by culture. They assert that because the experience of "homosexuals" or "heterosexuals" or even "men" or "women" differs so widely from culture to culture or between classes within one culture, these are simply categories that have no physical basis. What we commonly call "biology," from this perspective, is also a socially and historically variable construct – the word "biology" itself did not appear until 1802, about the same time as "sexuality" – and those who argue for a biological or physiological basis for sexual orientation or gender difference are "essentialists." Many historians of sexuality point out that most types of anatomical and genetic tests currently used by medical researchers to explore gender and sexual differences are not applicable for populations long dead; the exceptions are those few tests which can be performed on skeletal remains. They note that the only thing historians *can* explore about past sexuality is its social construction, its meaning, because that is what the historical record contains.

Interest in the meaning of sexuality also reflects a more general trend in historical studies over the last decade, known as the "linguistic turn" or the New Cultural History. Under the influence of literary and linguistic theory – often loosely termed "deconstruction" or "post-structuralism" – some historians focus their attention on the words of the past rather than on events, individuals, or groups. The most radical proponents of this point of view argue that the only thing we can know in history is words: that is, because historical sources always present a biased and partial picture, we can never really know what actually happened. Historical documents are "constructed," written by particular individuals with particular interests and biases that consciously and unconsciously shape their content. They are thus no different from literary texts, and historians should simply analyze them as texts, elucidating their possible meanings. Historians should not be concerned with searching for "reality," in this viewpoint, both because to do so demonstrates a naive "positivism," and because the language itself determines our understanding of reality. Most historians do not take such an extreme approach, but instead treat their sources as at least partial reflections of some people's reality. They do tend to use a wider range of sources than they did in earlier decades – literary and artistic sources are very much a part of the New Cultural History – and this has dramatically increased the array of sources available for the study of sexuality. In many eras matters relating to sex were much more likely to appear in painting, poetry, and drama than in traditional historical sources such as chronicles.

This strong emphasis on language, or what is often termed "discourse" as it incorporates visual materials such as paintings and film along with written texts, may be found in many areas of historical research at present, but especially in the study of sexuality. This is in large part due to the field's most important theorist, the French philosopher Michel Foucault, who in 1976 began publication of a multivolume *History of Sexuality*, intended to cover the subject in the West from antiquity to the present. Though only three volumes were published before his death in 1984, the first of these, along with Foucault's other works on prisons, insanity, and medicine, greatly influenced later historians.

Foucault argued that the history of sexuality in the West was not characterized by the increasing repression of a free biological drive, but instead by the "transformation of sex into discourse." This process began with the Christian practice of confessing one's sins to a priest, during which first acts and then thoughts and desires had to be described in language. This practice expanded after the Reformation as Catholics required more extensive and frequent confession and Protestants substituted the personal examination of conscience for oral confession to a priest. During the late eighteenth century, Foucault argued, sexuality began to be a matter of concern for authorities outside religious institutions: political authorities tried to encourage steady population growth; educational authorities worried about masturbation and children's sexuality; and medical authorities both identified and pathologized sexual "deviance" and made fertility the most significant aspect of women's lives. Foucault traced this expansion of discourses about sex into the present, when "we talk more about sex than about anything else"[2], and create modern "sexuality" as we now understand the term. Before people learned to talk about sex so thoroughly, there was sex, according to Foucault, but not sexuality. Modern sexuality is closely related to power, not simply the power of authorities to define and regulate it, but also the power inherent in every sexual relationship. This power – in fact, all power, in Foucault's opinion – is intimately related to knowledge and to "the will to know," the original subtitle of the first volume of his *History of Sexuality*.

Historians of sexuality after Foucault have often elaborated on his insights by defining what is specific to modern Western sexuality (many scholars now see the sharpest break with the past as coming in the nineteenth rather than the eighteenth century, with the development of the notion of a "sexual identity"); exploring the mechanisms that define and regulate sexuality; and investigating the ways in which individuals and groups described and understood their sexual lives. Other scholars have pointed out gaps or weaknesses in Foucault's theories, and address issues that he largely ignored, among them women's sexuality, the relationship between race and European notions of sexuality, and the ways in which economic power structures shaped sexual ideas and practices. Historians of religion have gone far beyond his brief discussion of confession to explore the sexual aspects of saints' lives, heresy persecutions, and doctrinal changes.

Along with Foucault, women's studies and feminist theory have made important contributions to the new scholarship on sexuality. Many ideas central to women's studies, such as the arguments that culture shapes sexuality and that sexual relationships are power relationships (captured in the slogan "the personal is political"), not only parallel Foucault's ideas, but, in fact, predate his work on sexuality. Others do not, particularly the emphasis in women's studies on the very different experiences of men and women in history, and on the ways in which societies create gender distinctions between men and women. Feminist analysts point out that Foucault's studies of sexuality are, in fact, studies of *male* sexuality, despite the fact that *female* sexuality has generally been of greater concern to authorities throughout history. They have thus turned their attention both to the construction of female sexuality by intellectual, religious, and political authorities (who were usually men), and to women's understanding of their own bodies and sexual lives.

The study of sexuality within feminist scholarship has produced several areas of sharp controversy. One involves the degree to which the body, sexual desire, and the experience of motherhood can be sources of power for women. Should women celebrate their bodies, the mother–daughter bond, and their sexual feelings, or do these actions overlook differences among women and reinforce the nefarious notion that "biology is destiny"? A second debate concerns pornography and sexual practices such as sado-masochism. Are these necessarily harmful to women, or can there be "feminist" pornography or sado-masochism? Does pornography limit women's civil rights, or is censorship of pornography, like any censorship, ultimately more dangerous than the material it prohibits? A third area of controversy, one which more often draws on historical and religious examples from history and religion than the others, addresses the valuation of sexual activity: Can a life of chastity and celibacy be a freeing option, or is it always an example of repression? Does our contemporary emphasis on finding and expressing one's "sexual identity" lead scholars to misrepresent the lives of women in the past? The fourth area intersects the debate about deconstruction and language: Does the emphasis on discourse in the study of sexuality contribute to the neglect of what most historians view as real events related to sex such as rape or wife-beating which are injurious to women? And finally: How are sexuality and gender related: that is, how do cultural definitions of what it means to be a man or a woman relate to such matters as sexual identity, erotic desire, and sexual activities?

The relationship between gender and sexuality is also a key issue in gay and lesbian studies, an academic discipline originating in the 1970s. At that time, historians of women pointed out that most of the work initially done in the history of homosexuality concerned men (often without stating so explicitly), while historians of homosexuality observed that most research on the history of women dealt with heterosexual women (even more often without stating so explicitly). Since then, lesbian history has developed as a field that draws from both gay and women's studies.

In the early 1990s, cultural theorists combined elements of gay and lesbian studies along with deconstruction to create queer theory. Many of the issues found in the study of sexuality or in feminism also occur in queer theory: To what degree is sexual identity socially constructed? To what extent can sexual or gender identity (or even sex) be intentionally blurred or hidden, making it simply a "performance" rather than part of one's essential nature? To what extent *should* sexuality or gender be blurred? Is an "identity" – or in literary and cultural studies terms a "subjectivity" – a tool of liberation or oppression? In other words, can one work to end discrimination against homosexuals, women, African-Americans or any other group, if one denies that the group has an essential identity, something that makes its members clearly homosexual or women or African-American? Why are identities so often constructed through oppositional pairs, such as men–women, homosexual–heterosexual, black–white?

In the same way as the development of women's history led scholars to start exploring men's experiences in history *as men* (rather than simply as "the history of man" without noticing that their subjects were men), gay and lesbian studies has led a few scholars to explore the historical construction of heterosexuality. Recognizing the contructed nature of heterosexuality has been just as difficult for many historians as recognizing that most history was actually "men's history," however. Eve Sedgwick wryly notes that "making heterosexuality historically visible is difficult because, under its institutional pseudonyms such as Inheritance, Marriage, Dynasty, Domesticity, and Population, heterosexuality has been permitted to masquerade so fully as History itself."[3]

Questions of identity, subjectivity, and the cultural construction of difference have also been central areas of inquiry in colonial studies and its theoretical branch, post-colonial theory. Historical study of Europe's colonies is not new, but until recently it tended to be regarded as separate from the study of Europe, as a kind of "overseas history" with its own trends and patterns, and as affected by, but not influencing, developments in Europe. It has become increasingly clear that the histories of Europe and its colonies – colonies and "metropole" are the common terms – must be meshed. It is also clear that imperial power is explicitly and implicitly linked with sexuality; many recent studies demonstrate how imperial powers shaped cultural constructions of masculinity and femininity and how images of colonial peoples were gendered and sexualized. This work is often interdisciplinary in nature, combining artistic and literary evidence with more traditional historical documents; its emphasis on discourse and representation frequently aligns it with the New Cultural History.

An important theme in much post-colonial theory has been the notion of hegemony, initially developed by the Italian political theorist Antonio Gramsci. Hegemony differs from domination because it involves convincing dominated groups to acquiesce to the desires and systems of the dominators through cultural as well as military and political means. Generally this was accomplished by granting special powers and privileges to some individuals and groups from among the subordinated population, or by convincing them through education or other forms of socialization that the new system was beneficial or preferable. The notion of hegemony explains why small groups of people have been able to maintain control over much larger populations without constant rebellion and protest, though some scholars have argued that the emphasis on hegemony downplays the ability of subjugated peoples to recognize the power realities in which they are enmeshed and to shape their own history.

One group of historians, those associated with the book series Subaltern Studies, has been particularly influential in calling for historical research which focuses on people who have been subordinated by virtue of their race, class, culture, gender, or language. Subaltern Studies (the adjective is drawn from Gramschi's writings) began among South Asian historians, who investigated such topics as Indian peasant revolts and the development of Indian nationalism; it is becoming increasingly influential among historians of other parts of the formerly colonial world, such as Latin America and Africa. Historians of Europe and the United States are also applying insights drawn from Subaltern Studies to their own work, particularly as they investigate "subaltern" groups such as racial and ethnic minorities. They pay special attention to the language of hierarchy and domination, noting that subordinated groups often developed their own distinctive and more liberating meanings for such language in a process the Russian linguist M.M. Bakhtin calls "double-voiced discourse."[4] Thus in the cultural construction of difference and identity, the meanings and implications of words depend on who is using them.

Theory and the early modern period

Many of the issues raised by the newer scholarship on sexuality and colonialism may seem to be quite contemporary and hence anachronistic to early modern Christianity, but they are actually central to understanding both the ways in which Christianity regulated the sexual lives of Europeans and colonial subjects, and the ways in which individual men and women, Christian and non-Christian, responded to and shaped these attempts at regulation. Though they used different terminology, theologians, law-makers, rulers, courts, and private individuals all wrestled with issues of identity and difference in sexual matters: Should a Jew be allowed to marry a Christian, a Protestant a Catholic, a Native American a Spaniard? What were the children of such unions' ethnic, religious, or racial identities? (The answer determined their access to education, property, government positions, and marital partners.) Should everyone marry? Should hermaphrodites (those born with ambiguous genitalia) marry? What about those who vowed to God never to marry: were they holy or misguided? What sexual practices made one a sinner (a common "identity" in Christianity) – prostitution, masturbation, homosexuality, bigamy, premarital sex, lust for one's spouse – and which were the more serious sins?

In addition to questions arising from general theories about sexuality, this study also engages with theoretical issues pertaining directly to the early modern period. One of these is the notion of social discipline, a concept which was developed originally by the German historian Gerhard Oestreich. He and others point out that almost all religious authorities in the early modern period, whether Catholic, Lutheran, Anglican (the Protestant Church in England), or Calvinist, were engaged in a process of social disciplining, by which they mean working with secular political authorities in an attempt to get people to live a proper, godly life. This process began before the Reformation especially in cities, when, as we will see in more detail in Chapter 1, political leaders regulated prostitution, made sodomy a capital crime, and increased the penalties for illegitimacy. After the Reformation, religious and political leaders of all denominations expanded and sharpened their efforts at social discipline, usually combining them with an increased interest in teaching people the basics of their particular version of Christianity, a process known as confessionalization. Officials began to keep registers of marriages, births, baptisms, and deaths, and these records allowed them better to monitor the behavior and status of individuals. They restricted gambling and drinking, increased the punishments for adultery and fornication, forbade certain books and encouraged the reading of others, prohibited popular celebrations (such as Carnival and parish fairs), and preached and published pamphlets against immoral behavior. In England and New England these measures are especially associated with the Puritans, Calvinist-inspired individuals who thought the reforms instituted by the Anglican Church had not gone far enough and who wanted to "purify" the English church of any remaining Catholic practices and immorality.

This process of social disciplining has been linked to, or seen as part of, a more general social change that is often called the "reform of popular culture" or "the reformation of manners." The English historian Peter Burke has described the process of social discipline as a "triumph of Lent," in which popular culture was restricted by moral and clerical reformers bent on making people's behavior more pious, somber, and sober.

While Burke concentrates on external agents of control, the German sociologist Norbert Elias focuses on internal agents: that is, on the ways people internalized more controlled social behavior and habits which they learned from their parents or superiors or from reading books of manners and conduct. Elias traces long-term changes in habits of eating, washing, blowing one's nose, and urinating from the fourteenth century through the nineteenth. He notes that these natural functions were increasingly regarded as inappropriate in public, and that polished manners came to be regarded as a sign both of civility and of civilization. He links this "civilizing process" to changes in the structures of power and state formation in Europe; to Elias, it explains why Europeans by the nineteenth century could view themselves as "civilized" and superior to the "savages" in areas being colonized. Elias's supporters stress that he was critical of such value judgments. A few of his opponents, most prominently the German sociologist Hans Peter Duerr, argue on the contrary that the civilizing process itself is a "myth," that reticence about the public display of nakedness and bodily functions can be found around the world. They point out that taboos about certain behaviors have existed throughout history, and cite the work of Mary Douglas and other cultural anthropologists to support their position.

Elias's main concern is Europe, and, with the exception of research on the New England Puritans, theories about social discipline, the reform of popular culture, and the civilizing process are drawn entirely from studies of Europe. Several theories developed by scholars working in non-European areas during the early modern period have also had an impact on the material treated in this book. Prime among these is the concept that relations between Europeans and non-Europeans were primarily "encounters" rather than discoveries or conquests, with cross-cultural exchanges in terms of material goods and intellectual concepts in both directions. An emphasis on encounters has been particularly prominent in recent scholarship on the Americas, which explores the ways in which indigenous peoples not only reacted to and fought against European ideas and practices, but also transformed them for themselves and for the colonial powers. Because the Americas were colonized at a point when Christian beliefs and institutions were more powerful than they would be later in Europe's history, historians of American colonization pay greater attention to religious ideas and structures than do those studying the British Empire outside North America, and view religion as a central force in the creation of hegemony.

Scholars of cross-cultural encounters during the early modern period increasingly point out that such contacts not only occurred between Europeans and non-Europeans, but also happened between Chinese and South-east Asians or Arabs and Indonesians, for example. In most encounters, people confronted others of different ethnicity, race, language, and religion, and they had to develop ways of understanding this alterity. In no instance was that understanding based simply on actual encounters; it was also shaped by preconceptions about other peoples and about themselves. Some scholars describe this process as "creating the Other" or "constructing the Other" or sometimes even "Othering."

Though confronting or constructing the Other occurred throughout the world and was a many-sided process, European responses to non-Europeans have received the most scholarly attention. The greater availability of source materials from Europeans partly accounts for this emphasis. Europe was also establishing political and economic hegemony over much of the world at this time, so that scholars consider this line of encounter to be the most significant. Some argue, as well, that Europeans both created and utilized more radical distinctions between self and other than other people did.

Studies of European constructions or inventions of the Other include encounters with both the East and the West. Those which focus on European ideas about Asia, such as the works of Edward Said, tend to concentrate on the period since the eighteenth century, whereas those which focus on the New World start, for obvious reasons, with Columbus. European response to the New World was first analyzed by the Mexican historian and philosopher Edmundo O'Gorman, who coined the phrase the "invention of America" to describe the ways in which Columbus's cultural assumptions shaped both his own and subsequent commentators' descriptions of his voyages and the New World. More recently, European writings about the New World have been a central topic for literary critics and historians influenced by theories of the centrality of language. These scholars assert that colonial discourse is so shaped by preconceptions that it can reveal little about the people described; the proper – indeed the only possible – focus of study is simply the discourse itself. Others (myself included) find this approach limiting and unsatisfying, and consider European observations, imperfect and biased as they are, as nonetheless valuable for analyzing other cultures.

The range of approaches informing this book may seem quite dizzying, and it may be tempting here at the outset to try to link all of these various theories, or to claim that they are simply different words to describe the same processes: Is not social discipline really cultural hegemony by another name? Were not prostitutes and homosexuals, like Native Americans and Asians, constructed as the Other? Were not popular beliefs and practices in regard to sexual matters restricted similarly throughout the world? The temptation is especially great because the geographical scope of my study is so large, and the precedent for grand theories regarding sex is so well established; it includes not only Foucault, Aristotle, and Sigmund Freud, but also the latest pop psychology books on gender differences.

I want to resist that temptation, or at least hold my discussion of unifying themes until the conclusion. A stress on commonalities does help to avoid what Edward Said has termed "orientalizing," (making other cultures appear overly exotic and bizarre), but it also risks creating an artificial sameness that renders every other culture more or less like "us." Because most theory about sexuality has been developed in reference to Europe (actually only a small part of Europe, England and France) there is a risk of importing west European theory into areas where it is not appropriate. Thus the chapters which follow each address the same topics – ideas, institutions, effects – but the material they present may be even more dizzying in its variety than the theories discussed in this introduction. I hope this variety reinforces rather than negates the expectations of my friends and neighbors, and that it strengthens their assumptions about the continued importance of connections between Christianity and sex.

Notes

1 Vern Bullough, "Sex in History: A Redux," in Jacqueline Murray and Konrad Eisenbichler, eds, *Desire and Discipline: Sex and Sexuality in the Premodern West* (Toronto: University of Toronto Press, 1996), 4; Edith Hamilton, *The Greek Way* (New York: Norton, 1942 and many reprints).

2 Michel Foucault, *The History of Sexuality I: An Introduction*, trans. Robert Hurley (New York: Random House, 1990), 33 (orig. *L'Histoire de la sexualité 1: La Volonté de savoir* (Paris: Gallimard, 1976)).

3 Eve Sedgwick, "Gender Criticism," in Stephen Greenblatt and Giles Gunn, eds, *Redrawing the Boundaries* (New York: Modern Language Association, 1992), 293.

4 M. M. Bakhtin, *The Dialogic Imagination: Four Essays,* ed. Michael Holquist, trans. Caryl Emerson and Michael Holquist (Austin: University of Texas Press, 1981), 324.

Selected further reading

This book is designed for students and general readers as well as more specialized scholars. Because of its audience, and because the materials for a broad study such as this are so numerous, I have included only English-language works in this and subsequent chapter reading lists. Most of the more specialized works included here will lead interested readers to the appropriate primary and secondary materials in other languages.

A good place to begin for overviews of sexual issues is the work of Vern Bullough, including *Sexual Variance in Society and History* (New York: John Wiley, 1976) and Vern Bullough and Bonnie Bullough, *Sexual Attitudes: Myths and Realities* (New York: Prometheus, 1995). (There are several very dated books titled *Sex in History* which are no longer viewed as authoritative.) For surveys of modern Western sexuality, see Carolyn Dean, *Sexuality and Modern Western Culture* (New York: Twayne, 1996); Jeffrey Weeks, *Sex, Politics, and Society: The Regulation of Sexuality Since 1800* (London: Longmans, 1981); John C. Fout, ed., *Forbidden History: The State, Society, and the Regulation of Sexuality in Modern Europe* (Chicago: University of Chicago Press, 1992); Catherine Gallagher and Thomas Laqueur, eds, *The Making of the Modern Body: Sexuality and Society in the Nineteenth Century* (Berkeley: University of California Press, 1987). The notion of a divide between modern sexuality and earlier ideas can be seen also in the increasing use of the term "premodern" in new collections on sexuality, such as that edited by Murray and Eisenbichler in note 1 above, or Louise Fradenburg and Carla Freccero, eds, *Premodern Sexualities* (New York: Routledge, 1996).

There are countless books which explore issues of Christianity and sexuality in contemporary society, written to provide guidance and advice for clergy and lay people or to address contentious issues such as homosexuality, abortion, or divorce. One of the more academic of these, which does explore historical developments along with contemporary concerns, is Elizabeth Stuart and Adrian Thatcher, eds, *Christian Perspectives on Sexuality and Gender* (Leominster: Gracewing/Grand Rapids: Eerdmans, 1996). Many of the materials included in the section titled "Sexuality, Spirituality, and Power," from Eugenia C. DeLamotte, Natania Meeker, and Jean F. O'Barr, eds, *Women Imagine Change: A Global Anthology of Women's Resistance from 600 BCE to the Present* (New York: Routledge, 1997) are from Christian authors, and the section as a whole provides a good comparison of links between sexuality and spirituality in many religious traditions.

There is an excellent survey of the development of the history of sexuality in the introduction to Domna Stanton, ed., *The Discourses of Sexuality: From Aristotle to AIDS* (Ann Arbor: University of Michigan Press, 1992), and a briefer one in Lawrence Stone, *The Past and the Present Revisited* (London: Routledge, 1987), pp. 344–382. A summary of the new history of the body may be found in the chapter by Roy Porter in Peter Burke, ed., *New Perspectives on Historical Writing* (London: Polity Press, 1991); this book also contains a survey of women's history by Joan Scott. Several other useful essay collections are: Sherry B. Ortner and Harriet Whitehead, *Sexual Meanings: The Cultural Construction of Gender and Sexuality*

(Cambridge: Cambridge University Press, 1981); Pat Caplan, ed., *The Cultural Construction of Sexuality* (London: Tavistock, 1987); Kathy Peiss and Christina Simmons, eds, *Passion and Power: Sexuality in History* (Philadelphia: University of Pennsylvania Press, 1989).

Foucault's impact on the history of the body is explored in several of the essays in Colin Jones and Roy Porter, eds, *Reassessing Foucault: Power, Medicine and the Body* (London: Routledge, 1994), which also contains a select bibliography of recent works on Foucault. Porter also debates Foucault's usefulness in Nikki R. Keddie, ed., *Debating Gender, Debating Sexuality* (New York: New York University Press, 1996), 247–273. Several of the essays in Lynn Hunt, ed., *The New Cultural History* (Berkeley: University of California Press, 1989) discuss the impact of Foucault's thought on history more generally; this collection is also a very helpful introduction to the field of cultural history as a whole. An excellent summary of Foucault's thought is Alan Sheridan, *Michel Foucault: The Will to Truth* (London: Routledge, 1990) and a good collection of his writings is David Couzens Hoy, ed., *Foucault: A Critical Reader* (Oxford: Blackwell, 1986). An insightful discussion of the intersections between Foucault and colonial studies is Ann Laura Stoler, *Race and the Education of Desire: Foucault's* History of Sexuality *and the Colonial Order of Things* (Durham, NC: Duke University Press, 1995).

Discussions of the relationship between Foucault and feminism have been largely in the form of collections of articles, such as Irene Diamond and Lee Quinby, eds, *Feminism and Foucault: Reflections on Resistance* (Boston: Northeastern University Press, 1988); Caroline Ramazanoglu, ed., *Up Against Foucault: Explorations of Some Tensions Between Foucault and Feminism* (New York: Routledge, 1993); Susan Hekman, ed., *Feminist Interpretations of Michel Foucault* (University Park, Pa.: Penn State University Press, 1996). Lois McNay provides a longer analysis in *Foucault and Feminism: Power, Gender and the Self* (Boston: Northeastern University Press, 1993).

Theoretical discussions of the constructed nature of gender and sexual identity include Teresa de Lauretis, *Technologies of Gender* (Bloomington: Indiana University Press, 1987); Judith Butler, *Gender Trouble: Feminism and the Subversion of Identity* (New York: Routledge, 1990) and *Bodies That Matter: On the Discursive Limits of Sex* (New York: Routledge, 1993); Donna Haraway, *Simians, Cyborgs and Women: The Reinvention of Nature* (New York: Routledge, 1991). Two key articles which discuss the use of gender in historical analysis are: Joan Scott, "Gender: A Useful Category of Historical Analysis," *American Historical Review* 91 (1986): 1053–1075 and Gisela Bock, "Women's History and Gender History: Aspects of an International Debate," *Gender and History* 1 (1989): 7–30. The debate within feminism about pornography and sado-masochism is discussed in Carol Vance, ed., *Pleasure and Danger: Exploring Female Sexuality* (New York: Routledge, 1984) and reviewed in B. Ruby Rich, "Feminism and Sexuality in the 1980s," *Feminist Studies* 12 (1986): 525–561.

Important studies of homosexuality over a long period include: David Greenburg, *The Construction of Homosexuality* (Chicago: University of Chicago Press, 1988) which takes a strongly social constructionist position and has a bibliography of more than 100 pages; Martin Duberman, Martha Vicinus, and George

Chauncey, Jr., eds, *Hidden From History: Reclaiming the Gay and Lesbian Past* (London: Meridian, 1989); Jonathon Dollimore, *Sexual Dissidence: Augustine to Wilde, Freud to Foucault* (New York: Oxford University Press, 1991). Edward Stein, ed., *Forms of Desire: Sexual Orientation and the Social Constructionist Controversy* (New York: Garland, 1990) traces the whole social contructionist debate, and Scott Bravman, *Queer Fictions of the Past: History, Culture and Difference* (New York: Cambridge University Press, 1997) looks at the current state of gay and lesbian studies, especially history. The bibliographies which follow each chapter contain additional works on homosexuality relevant to the chapter's focus. On the lack of a discussion of lesbians in a wide range of scholarship see Judith Roof, *A Lure of Knowledge: Lesbian Sexuality and Theory* (New York: Columbia University Press, 1991), and in historical studies in particular see the introduction to Duberman, et al., *Hidden From History*.

The basic works in queer theory include: Eve Sedgwick, *Epistemology of the Closet* (Berkeley: University of California Press, 1990); Julia Epstein and Kristina Straub, eds, *Body Guards: The Cultural Politics of Gender Ambiguity* (New York: Routledge, 1991); a special issue on "Queer Theory: Gay and Lesbian Sexualities," *differences* 3/2 (Summer 1991); Michael Warner, ed., *Fear of a Queer Planet: Queer Politics and Social Theory* (Minneapolis: University of Minnesota Press, 1993); Peggy Phelan, *Unmarked: The Politics of Performance* (New York: Routledge, 1993). For a recent overview designed for students, see, Annamarie Jagose, *Queer Theory: An Introduction* (New York: New York University Press, 1996), and for essays linking feminist and queer theory, see Elizabeth Weed and Naomi Schor, eds, *Feminism Meets Queer Theory* (Bloomington: Indiana University Press, 1997).

Two articles are especially helpful for understanding links between gender and race, and have been widely reprinted in various collections: Tessie Liu, "Teaching the Differences Among Women from a Historical Perspective: Rethinking Race and Gender as Social Categories," *Women's Studies International Forum* 14 (1991): 265–276 and Evelyn Brooks Higginbotham, "African-American Women's History and the Metalanguage of Race," *Signs* 17 (1992): 251–274.

Some of the central works in the theory of race and colonialism are: Henry Louis Gates, Jr., *"Race," Writing, and Difference* (Chicago: University of Chicago Press, 1986); George Mosse, *Toward the Final Solution: A History of European Racism* (Madison: University of Wisconsin Press, 1978); Edward Said, *Orientalism* (New York: Pantheon, 1978) and *Culture and Imperialism* (New York: Knopf, 1993).

Bill Ashcroft, Gareth Griffiths, and Helen Tiffin provide a good introductory survey of the main ideas in post-colonial theory in *The Empire Writes Back: Theory and Practice in Post-colonial Literatures* (London: Routledge, 1989); the same three scholars have also edited a large anthology of articles by many major post-colonial scholars, *The Post-colonial Studies Reader* (London: Routledge, 1995). Two works which bring together feminist and post-colonial analysis are Trin T. Minh-ha, *Woman, Native, Other: Writing Postcoloniality and Feminism* (Bloomington: Indiana University Press, 1989) and Chandra Talpade Mohanty, Ann Russo, and Lourdes Torres, eds, *Third World Women and the Politics of Feminism* (Bloomington: Indiana University Press, 1991).

The work of the Subaltern Studies group may best be seen in its ongoing series of essay collections, *Subaltern Studies*, which began publication in 1982 in

Delhi. Two additional important theoretical works by Indian scholars associated with Subaltern Studies are Partha Chatterjee, *Nationalist Thought and the Colonial World: A Derivative Discourse* (London: Zed, 1986) and Gayatri Chakravorty Spivak, *In Other Worlds: Essays in Cultural Politics* (London and New York: Methuen, 1987). Debates about issues raised by Subaltern Studies may be found in a series of articles by Gyan Prakash, Florencia Mallon, and Frederick Cooper in *The American Historical Review* 99 (1994): 1475–1545 and by Patricia Seed, Hernan Vídal, Walter D. Mignolo, and Roleno Adorno in *Latin American Research Review* 26 (1991): 181–200 and 28 (1993): 113–152.

Most studies of the links between sexuality and empire focus on the British experience in the modern period, including: Ronald Hyam, *Empire and Sexuality: The British Experience* (Manchester: Manchester University Press, 1990); Graham Dawson, *Soldier Heroes: British Adventure, Empire, and the Imaging of Masculinity* (London: Routledge, 1994); Anne McClintock, *Imperial Leather: Race, Gender and Sexuality in the Colonial Contest* (London: Routledge, 1995); Felicity Nussbaum, *Torrid Zones: Maternity, Sexuality and Empire in Eighteenth-century English Narratives* (Baltimore: Johns Hopkins University Press, 1995); Mrinalini Sinha, *Colonial Masculinity: The "Manly Englishman" and the "Effeminate Bengali" in the Late Nineteenth Century* (Manchester: Manchester University Press, 1995); Revathi Krishnaswamy, *Effeminism: The Economy of Colonial Desire* (Ann Arbor: University of Michigan Press, 1998). Gyan Prakash, ed., *After Colonialism: Imperial Histories and Postcolonial Displacements* (Princeton: Princeton University Press, 1995), Lenore Masterson and Margaret Jolly, eds, *Sites of Desire, Economies of Pleasure: Sexualities in Asia and the Pacific* (Chicago: University of Chicago Press, 1997) and Ruth Roach Pierson and Nupur Chaudhuri, eds, *Nation, Empire, Colony: Historicizing Gender and Race* (Indianapolis: Indiana University Press, 1998) include some essays which discuss other colonial powers. See below and the bibliographical essays which follow Chapters 4 and 5 for readings about the colonial Americas.

A good introduction to Antonio Gramschi's notion of hegemony is Joseph V. Femia, *Gramschi's Political Thought: Hegemony, Consciousness and the Revolutionary Process* (Oxford: Clarendon, 1981) or Gramschi's own work, *Selections from the Prison Notebooks of Antonio Gramschi* (New York: International Publishers, 1971). Steve Stern, *Peru's Indian Peoples and the Challenge of Spanish Conquest: Huamanga to 1640* (Madison: University of Wisconsin Press, 1982) discusses hegemony in a colonial Latin American context.

The concept of "social disciplining" was first discussed by the German historian Gerhard Oestreich, and his major work has now been translated into English: *Neostoicism and the Early Modern State* (Cambridge: Cambridge University Press, 1982). Most of the studies of specific areas are in German, to which there is a good bibliography in R. Po-Chia Hsia, *Social Discipline in the Reformation: Central Europe 1550–1750* (London: Routledge, 1989); this book also provides a good overview of the whole issue.

The concept of a reform of popular culture was set out most influentially by Peter Burke, *Popular Culture in Early Modern Europe* (London: Temple Smith, 1978) and Robert Muchembled, *Popular Culture and Elite Culture in France,*

1400–1750 (Baton Rouge: Louisiana State University Press, 1985). Norbert Elias's major work, *The Civilizing Process,* was originally published in German in 1939, but the first English translation of the first volume on manners was not published until 1978 (New York: Urizen Books). A good introduction to his thought is Norbert Elias, *On Civilization, Power, and Knowledge*, eds Stephen Mennell and Johan Goudsblom (Chicago: University of Chicago Press, 1998). His harshest (and longest-standing) critic is Hans-Peter Duerr, who has now completed four volumes of a planned five-volume work entitled *Der Mythos vom Zivilisationsprozeß [The Myth of the Civilization Process]* (Frankfurt: Suhrkamp, 1988–1997). This work concentrates on nakedness, intimacy, rape, and the female breast and has not been translated into English. The classic study of taboos cross-culturally is Mary Douglas, *Purity and Danger: An Analysis of the Concepts of Pollution and Taboo* (New York: Praeger, 1966).

The many works of James Axtell have been especially influential in developing the notion of "encounters" as central to colonial history in North America. See, for example, his *Beyond 1492: Encounters in Colonial North America* (New York: Oxford University Press, 1992) and *The Invasion Within: The Contest of Cultures in Colonial North America* (New York: Oxford University Press, 1985). Colin G. Calloway also has a number of significant books, most recently *New Worlds for All: Indians, Europeans and the Remaking of Early America* (Baltimore: Johns Hopkins University Press, 1997). Both Axtell and Calloway, along with other scholars, use the word "Indians" rather than "Amerindians," "Native Americans," or "First Peoples" when discussing the indigenous residents of the Americas. This usage is also favored by native scholars in their writing and teaching, and I have adopted it here.

Edmundo O'Gorman's pioneering study of European colonial discourse was published in Spanish as *La invención de América; El universalismo de la Cultura del Occidente* (Mexico City: Fondo de Cultura Económica, 1958); an expanded and modified version appeared in English as *The Invention of America: An Inquiry into the Historical Nature of the New World and the Meaning of its History* (Bloomington: Indiana University Press, 1961). In the last several decades, it has been joined by numerous others: Tzvetan Todorov, *The Conquest of America: The Question of the Other,* trans. Richard Howard (New York: Harper and Row, 1984); Peter Hulme, *Colonial Encounters: Europe and the Native Caribbean, 1492–1797* (London: Methuen, 1986); Urs Bitterli, *Cultures in Conflict: Encounters Between European and Non-European Cultures, 1492–1800,* trans. Ritchie Robertson (New York: Polity Press, 1989); Peter Mason, *Deconstructing America: Representations of the Other* (London: Routledge, 1990); Stephen Greenblatt, *Marvelous Possessions: The Wonder of the New World* (Chicago: University of Chicago Press, 1991); Anthony Pagden, *European Encounters with the New World: From Renaissance to Romanticism* (New Haven: Yale, 1993); O.R. Dathorne, *Imagining the World: Mythical Belief versus Reality in Global Encounters* (Westport, Conn.: Bergin and Garvey, 1994) and *Asian Voyages: Two Thousand Years of Constructing the Other* (Westport, Conn.: Bergin and Garvey, 1996); John F. Moffitt and Santiago Sebastián, *O Brave New People: The European Invention of the American Indian* (Albuquerque: University of New Mexico Press, 1996). Encounters with and representations of Africans have been the focus of fewer studies; the best introduction to this issue from a European perspective is Kim F. Hall, *Things of Darkness: Economies of Race and Gender in Early Modern England* (Ithaca: Cornell University Press, 1995) and from an American perspective Winthrop D. Jordan's classic *White Over Black: American Attitudes Toward the Negro, 1550–1812* (Chapel Hill: University of North Carolina Press, 1968).

There are numerous essay collections dealing with colonial encounters, some of which do not include discussion of issues of gender and/or sexuality; a sample of those which do: Francisco Javier Cevallos-Candau, et al., eds, *Coded Encounters: Writing, Gender, and Ethnicity in Colonial Latin America* (Amherst: University of Massachusetts Press, 1994); Stuart Schwarz, ed., *Implicit Understandings: Observing, Reporting and Reflecting on the Encounters between Europeans and Other Peoples in the Early Modern Era* (Cambridge: Cambridge University Press, 1994); Kenneth J. Adrien and Rolena Adorno, eds, *Transatlantic Encounters: Europeans and Andeans in the Sixteenth Century* (Berkeley: University of California Press, 1991).

CHRISTIANITY TO 1500

Fifteenth-century wall painting from the Risinge gamla kyrka in Sweden showing a couple giving each other their hands in marriage, with a priest blessing the union. By this point, a priestly blessing was encouraged but not required for a valid marriage. By permission of Antikvarisk-Topografiska Arkivet, Stockholm.

CHRISTIANITY TO 1500

MANY FACTORS SHAPED ancient and medieval Christian ideas about sex, the institutions that resulted from these ideas and in turn influenced them, and the actual sexual practices of Near Eastern, African, and European Christians. Of these factors, the words of Jesus of Nazareth as recorded in Christian Scriptures were probably the least important, for Jesus seems to have said very little about sex, and his recorded words are contradictory. Jesus describes marriage as ordained by God (Matthew 19: 4–5), yet later in the same discussion appears to approve of those "who have made themselves eunuchs for the sake of the kingdom of heaven" (Matthew 19: 12). He also characterizes those who remained unmarried as "equal to angels . . . and sons of the resurrection" (Luke 20: 36). Jesus clearly opposes adultery and divorce, and seems to have condemned sex with prostitutes, though he made friends with individual prostitutes and shocked priests who challenged him by commenting that repentant prostitutes would get into heaven before they would (Matthew 21: 31–32). While Jesus was himself a man, the centrality of the male disciples may have been less evident during his lifetime than it later became; women were present at many of the key events of his life and were the first to discover the empty tomb after the crucifixion (Mark 16: 1–8).

For New Testament roots of Christian ideas about sex, the letters of Paul and those attributed to Paul are far more important than the Gospels containing the words of Jesus. A convert from Judaism, Paul never met Jesus, but became an important early Christian missionary. His letters to many Christian groups around the Mediterranean became part of Christian Scripture, and his reputation was so great that works probably written by others were also attributed to him. The Epistles of 1 and 2 Timothy and of Titus are now considered by almost all Biblical scholars not to be Paul's words, though they were considered Pauline for most of Christian history. The majority of modern scholars view Ephesians, Colossians and 2 Thessalonians also as deutero-Pauline, that is, as written by someone other than Paul. Many of the most restrictive comments about women in the New Testament occur in these books, and have carried the weight of Paul's authority.

Like all early Christians, Paul expected Jesus to return to earth very soon, and so regarded sex as one of the earthly concerns that should not be important for Christians. To him, the virgin life was best, but if people could not "exercise self-control, they should marry. For it is better to marry than to be aflame with passion" (1 Corinthians 7: 9). Paul warned against those who prohibited marriage and emphasized the importance of spousal love and respect. Like Jesus, Paul opposed divorce, and he even suggested that widows and widowers would be happier if they did not remarry. He condemned all extramarital sex, singling out adulterers and masturbators, along with thieves and drunkards, as people who were unworthy of heaven (1 Corinthians 6: 9). This list also includes words that most historians and many Bible translators interpret as referring to homosexuals, although the original Greek is somewhat ambiguous and has occasioned scholarly controversy. Elsewhere Paul condemns male–male sexual activity (Romans 1: 27) though his parallel condemnation of some female sexual activity (Romans 1: 26) does not explicitly mention lesbianism.

Sexuality in Judaism

Because most Christians came to accept Hebrew Scripture as part of their tradition – designating certain books of the Hebrew Bible the "Old Testament" to parallel specific Christian writings termed the "New Testament" – Jewish writings on sex also influenced the development of Christian thinking. Jewish ideas about human sexuality were rooted in Jewish concepts of the divine. In contrast to other ancient cultures, Judaism held to a strict monotheism, with a God (Yahweh), who was conceptualized as masculine but did not have sexual relations as Greek or Egyptian male deities did. Yahweh's masculinity was affirmed by the words used to describe him – Lord, King, Father – and not by any progeny or penis. His sexuality was thus spiritualized, and human sexual relations, though basically good because they were part of Yahweh's creation, could also be a source of ritual impurity. Nocturnal emissions in men made them and anything they touched unclean, as did menstruation and childbirth in women; sexual relations made both partners impure (Leviticus 12 and 15). Other sexual practices created more than ritual impurity (which was removed by baths or temple sacrifices) and were termed "abominations"; violators were liable to the death penalty. Leviticus 20 specifies as abominations adultery with a married woman, incest with a variety of relatives, bestiality on the part of men or women, and male homosexuality. (Female homosexuality is not mentioned anywhere in the Old Testament, and sexual relations between a married man and an unmarried woman were not considered adultery.)

Despite the ritual impurity it created, sex itself was not regarded as intrinsically evil, and husbands were religiously obligated to have sex with their wives. Women were expected to have sex with their husbands – though not religiously obligated – and the bearing of children was seen in some ways as a religious function, for this would keep Judaism alive. Sexual relations were viewed as an important part of marriage even when procreation was impossible, such as after menopause. As the definition of adultery in Leviticus makes clear, men were free to have sexual relations with concubines, servants, and slaves; polygamous marriage was acceptable and occurred often among Jewish leaders in the Old Testament. In theory, unmarried women were also quite free sexually, for Hebrew Scripture nowhere forbade sex between unmarried individuals, though the harsh treatment of children born out of wedlock undoubtedly acted as a deterrent to such relationships. Prostitution was officially prohibited to Jewish women, but the many references to prostitutes in the Old Testament and other sources indicate that it was tolerated. Prostitution – the usual English translation is "harlotry" – occurs frequently as a metaphor for the Jewish people's turning away from their single god to worship numerous other deities, a usage that equates polytheism with a woman's having many lovers (e.g., Leviticus 20: 5–6; Jeremiah 3). Because many of these deities were the fertility gods and goddesses common to the Israelites' neighbors, their worship sometimes did involve a stress on divine sexuality that was not part of the worship of Yahweh; the prophet Jeremiah condemns this practice as "committing adultery with stone and tree" (Jeremiah 3: 9).

Judaism influenced Christian sexuality not only through the writings of the Old Testament, but also through its actual sexual practices. By the time of Jesus and Paul, most Jewish couples were monogamous, though polygamy was sometimes promoted as an expression of Jewish identity in contrast to the monogamous Romans. Marriage was arranged by the families of the spouses, and involved the transfer of goods or money from the husband's family to the wife's or from the husband to the wife; this would assure her support in the event of his death or divorce. Unilateral divorce on the husband's part was permissible, though community norms frowned on divorce for frivolous reasons. A wife could not divorce her husband, even for desertion, though the desperate situation this created for some women led rabbinical authorities to relax the rules in actuality. Traditionally, Judaism frowned on celibacy – "chastity" is defined in Jewish law as refraining from illicit sexual activities, not from sex itself – and almost all major Jewish thinkers and rabbis were married. In the centuries immediately before the development of Christianity, there was some change in these views, however, and a few Jewish groups such as the Essenes began to advocate abstinence from sexual relations for their members.

Greek and Roman traditions

The Essenes' rejection of sexuality, new to Judaism, came in part from Greek and Roman schools of thought which also influenced Christian ideas directly. Both Plato and Aristotle, the two most important philosophers of ancient Athens, were suspicious of the power of sexual passion, warning that it distracted men from reason and the search for knowledge. They praised a love that was intellectualized and nonsexual, the type of attachment we still term "platonic." (Neither Plato nor Aristotle was concerned about what sex does to women except as this affects men.) Plato developed a dualistic view both of humans and of the world, arguing that the unseen realm of ideas was far superior to the visible material world, and that the human mind or soul was trapped in a material body. This mind–body split did not originate with Plato, but his acceptance and elaboration of it helped to make this concept an important part of Western philosophy from that time on, and led some groups (though not Plato) to reject sexual activity completely. In Aristotle the mind–body split is reflected in the process of procreation (what he termed "generation"), with the male providing the "active principle" and the female simply the "material." (The Greek physician and medical writer Galen disagreed with this formulation, however, and regarded both parents as providing "active principles.") The categories male and female were not completely dichotomous to Aristotle or Plato, however, but part of a hierarchical continuum, what historians have since termed the "one-sex model." Males resulted when conditions during sexual intercourse were optimum, and females when they were somehow faulty, with heat viewed as the most important force in the creation of sexual difference. Because women and men were located along the same continuum, certain women could be more "manly" than some men, and exhibit the qualities that were expected of men such as authority or self-control. Accidents might also cause a woman to turn into a man, with her sexual organs emerging later in life as a boy's did in the womb. (Female sex organs were generally viewed as equivalent to the male's, but simply turned inside out, an idea that lasted well into the seventeenth century.)

Stoic philosophy, which was very influential in Rome, agreed with Plato that sexual passion was disruptive. Stoics viewed sexual relationships as an important area of government concern; they believed that government should oversee the family, which they considered the basis of the social order, as well as other types of sexual activities, in order to promote public order and civic harmony. Stoic opinion on sexual matters was widely held, and Roman lawmakers frequently enacted statutes dealing with sexual offenses. The most serious transgressions were those which might upset the social order: adultery (again applying only to married women); sexual relationships involving young upper-class unmarried women (particularly if the man was from a lower social group); marriages which crossed social boundaries; and rape or abduction of girls or boys.

Most Romans considered marriage a positive good, viewing procreation and the education of children as part of their duty to the state; in fact, Roman law required a man to have children by a legal wife if he wanted to inherit property. Fathers had great power over their children; they could decide whether to accept them into the family at birth and choose who they would marry and whether they could divorce. The Stoic notion that spouses should feel "marital affection" (*affectio maritalis*) toward one another gained popularity in the first and second centuries CE; if this affection was no longer felt, formal divorce or less formal separation could end the marriage. Despite the general support for marriage, some marriages were prohibited – such as those between a free man and a prostitute, an actress, a slave or freed slave, or a woman over fifty years of age – though Roman law recognized concubinage as a formal relationship in those cases or in other cases where the individuals did not wish to marry. Roman concubinage was an alternative to marriage, not an addition to it; Romans were monogamous, and men could have either a wife or a concubine, but not both. Being a concubine was generally regarded as honorable and concubines had some legal rights, though not as many as wives. Slaves were not allowed to marry under Roman law, and relationships which they had with one another created no legally recognized ties.

Roman law increasingly drew a distinction between concubines and prostitutes, who were defined as women or men who were sexually available to a large number of people, whether or not they charged for their services. Though slaves or servants were not to be forced to work as prostitutes, the practice itself was not forbidden, and the pagan religious calendar had special feast days dedicated to female and male prostitutes. Roman literature often celebrated sexual relationships of all types in a way Roman law did not. The only two sexual activities uniformly condemned in literature were men taking the passive role in homosexual acts – viewed as unmanly and unworthy of a Roman citizen, and suitable only for slaves and prostitutes – and women taking the active role, which was seen as usurping a masculine privilege.

The fact that the Romans did not draw a sharp line between heterosexuality and homosexuality may seem unusual to us in the twentieth century when sexual "identity" is considered a key part of one's being, but such attitudes were common in many cultures in the ancient world. Ancient homosexuality in classical Athens has drawn the most scholarly attention. In Athens, part of an adolescent citizen's training in adulthood entailed a hierarchical sexual and tutorial relationship with an older man, who most likely was married and may have had other female sexual partners as well. For Athenians, as for Romans, the key distinction was between active and passive, between penetrator and penetrated, with the latter positions appropriate only for slaves, women, and boys. (There is some dispute about whether penetration was involved in male–male sex involving free men, or whether sex was generally intercrural, that is, between the thighs.) These pederastic relations between adolescents and men were often celebrated in literature and art, in part because the Athenians regarded perfection as possible only in the male. The perfect body was that of the young male, and perfect love that between an adolescent and an older man; this love was supposed to become intellectualized and "platonic" once the adolescent became an adult.

Along with philosophy and law, religion was also connected to sexual issues in ancient Greece and Rome. The classical Mediterranean was home to a wide range of religious beliefs and practices that also influenced sexual issues. These spread from one area to another with the conquests first of Alexander the Great and then of Rome; individuals frequently honored a number of gods and goddesses through rituals and ceremonies, both public and private. Traditional Roman religion was a civic or state religion akin to patriotism, in which honoring the gods was viewed as essential to the health and well-being of the state. Aside from their immortality, Roman gods were just like humans, so that they, too, experienced sexual passion. Male gods acted in ways that would have been unacceptable had they been mortal; stories of seductions and rapes by Zeus (called Jupiter in the Roman pantheon) and other gods and heroes form a central part of classical mythology. Though several of the most important goddesses, such as Athena (Minerva), Hestia (Vesta), and Artemis (Diana), were virgins, no male gods abstained from sexual relationships. Male priests in some Mediterranean religions did abstain, however, and occasionally even castrated themselves for cultic purposes; such religions in general were strongly dualistic, with self-castration regarded as proof of a priest's rejection of the body and devotion to the spirit. These religions, usually termed "mystery religions" because they offered their adherents secret powers or personal immortality, were gaining followers in the Roman Empire at the time of Jesus, even though Roman authorities were often deeply suspicious of them.

Early Christianity

In the first several centuries after Jesus, Christianity was spread by individuals and groups acting as missionaries throughout the Mediterranean area. Early converts developed their own ideas about sex, mixing together the teachings of Jesus and Paul, Jewish writings, Greek and Roman philosophy, non-Christian mystery religions, and other religious traditions in highly individualistic ways. There was no central authority at this period, and even bishops were only loosely in control of beliefs and activities in their dioceses; consequently there was an enormous range of ideas and practices.

The ideas that were most influential in the subsequent development of Christianity were those of literate men who corresponded with and advised converts and who often became officials in the growing church. These men, subsequently termed the Church Fathers, held differing views, although the degree of variation was smaller than among the Christian community as a whole. Many of these men agreed with Clement of Alexandria (ca. 150– ca. 200), who accepted marriage – including its sexual activity – as appropriate for Christians and taught, following the Stoics, that husbands and wives should feel affection for one another: "So there is every reason to marry – for patriotic reasons, for the succession of children, for the fulfillment of the universe. . . For the rest of humankind, marriage finds concord in the experience of pleasure, but the marriage of true lovers of wisdom [i.e., Christians] leads to a concord derived from the Logos [i.e., the Word of God, or Christ]."[1] Many Church leaders gradually came to consider concubinage and the slave relationships in Rome as marriages in terms of sexual morality, and to advocate the rights of all classes of people to marry.

Other early Church Fathers were more ambivalent. Tertullian (ca. 150– ca. 240), himself married and was careful to say that marriages were not prohibited to Christians. Even so, he regarded virginity as preferable; because marriage involved the "commixture of the flesh," it "consists of that which is the essence of fornication." He was particularly opposed to second marriages, which he termed "no other than a species of fornication," and wrote against them in an open letter to his wife and in several other works. Tertullian also railed against women who wore fancy clothing and unmarried women who did not wear veils. For them, he recommended "meanness of appearance, walking around as Eve mourning and repentant, in order that by every garb of penitence she might more fully expiate that which she derives from Eve, – the ignominy, I mean, of the first sin, and the odium (attached to her as the cause) of human perdition."[2]

Sex was not simply a matter for learned treatises during the early centuries of Christianity, although actual practices are harder to trace than theoretical opinions. Sporadic persecution of Christians by Roman authorities led to spectacular martyrdoms, but also led people to conduct many of their ceremonies in private, so that few historical sources remain. Most converts to Christianity or those born into Christian families married, in ceremonies that differed little from those of other Romans. Divorce in the case of adultery was permitted, though remarriage while both original spouses were alive was prohibited, and the remarriage of widows and widowers was frowned upon. It appears that most clergy also married, for the first attempt to prohibit clerical marriage was not made until the early fourth century.

Some converts took another path, however, and rejected the married life which their families expected of them; instead they lived singly or in communities, devoting themselves to contemplation or to the charity which was an important aspect of Christianity from the beginning. Their decision to renounce sexuality, though in one sense a rejection of the body, also paradoxically allowed them to claim their own bodies, to decide for themselves what their bodies would do. Stories circulated about men such as St Anthony (251?–ca. 350), who went out into the Egyptian desert as a hermit and became famous for withstanding sexual temptations, or women such as Mary of Egypt and Thaïs who had been prostitutes but gave up their sinful life for one of Christian devotion and bodily neglect. Women's choice of virginity was seen as especially threatening to the social order, because it put them in opposition to their fathers (and occasionally their husbands) whom they were expected to obey. Some patriotic commentators argued that women's decisions to remain virgins might eventually affect the birth rate, and lead to a decline in the number of Romans at the very moment when the empire was being attacked and infiltrated by members of "less worthy" groups, such as Germanic tribes.

Many accounts of women's martyrdoms stress sexual aspects of their lives in ways that descriptions of male martyrs do not. In women, preservation of their virginity and chastity at all costs is praised as the ultimate sacrifice. Some saints' lives (accounts of saints' lives are called *hagiography*) from this period describe women who cut their hair and dressed as men for much of their lives; only at death was their true sex revealed, with their successful cross-dressing viewed as miraculous rather than scandalous. According to her fifth-century biographer, St Pelagia was both a repentant prostitute and a cross-dresser, originally "bare of head and shoulder and limb, in pomp so splendid . . . so decked that naught could be seen upon her but gold and pearls and precious stones;" she later "lived for these many years shut up and in solitude [as] brother Pelagius, a monk and a eunuch . . . wasted and haggard with fasting." Pelagius died, "and when the good fathers set about anointing the body with myrrh, they found that it was a woman . . . and they cried aloud with a shout, 'Glory to Thee, Lord Christ, who has many treasures on the earth, and not men only, but women also.'"[3] Hagiography cannot be taken as an objective life story, of course, as its purpose is to prove the spiritual merit of an individual, but for that very reason we can tell that Pelagia's biographer approved of her actions.

Though stories of heroic virginity were popular among converts (and remained so for centuries), many church leaders were uncomfortable with such a clear rejection of Roman family models, particularly as they were attempting to make Christianity more socially acceptable. They asserted that women who chose a life of virginity were not to use this as a reason for escaping the normal restrictions on women. They were not to be "virgins in the service of Christ," a title some chose for themselves, but rather, in Tertullian's formulation still in use today, "brides of Christ," that is, dependents in a figurative marital relationship.

The Church after Constantine

During the fourth century, the Emperor Constantine first legalized Christianity and then became a Christian himself, and Christianity gradually became a privileged institution in the Roman system. Christian bishops were given greater power within their dioceses, and Christian ideas came to shape imperial law and judicial practice. Gradually, for example, the informal arrangements of slaves came to be considered marriage, and a blessing by a priest came to be a normal part of Christian wedding ceremonies. Christian emperors extended the rules against the marriage of close relatives, so that people were forced to cast their nets wider for an acceptable marriage partner.

At the same time, the most prominent Church Fathers became stronger proponents of asceticism than those of earlier centuries had been. This fourth-century movement in part grew out of the earlier movement rejecting marriage, as some of its most vocal proponents, such as St Jerome (ca. 347–419/20), the translator of the Bible into Latin, came to embrace ideals of sexual renunciation developed by their wealthy female supporters. Jerome's repeated comments that virginity is gold and marriage silver, or that marriage fills the earth while virginity fills paradise, would not have been unwelcome or novel to the Roman women to whom he directed them. By choosing virginity, in the opinion of Jerome and his patrons, a woman could move up the gender hierarchy: "As long as woman is for birth and children, she is as different from man as body is from soul. But when she wishes to serve Christ more than the world, then she will cease to be a woman and will be called man."[4] This gender transformation was to remain a spiritual one, however, for in contrast to the admirers of cross-dressing saints, Jerome did not approve of women who "change their garb to male attire, cut their hair short and blush to be seen as they were born – women."[5]

Non-Christian ideas about sexuality also shaped the fourth-century ascetic movement; this can be seen most clearly in St Augustine of Hippo (354–430), whose importance in the development of Western Christian thought is second only to Paul's. Augustine, the bishop of the north African city of Hippo during the time when the Roman Empire in the West was slowly disintegrating, came to Christianity somewhat late in life after a career as a teacher of rhetoric. Augustine had always been troubled spiritually, and before he became a Christian he had joined the Manicheans, a dualistic religion begun by the Persian prophet Mani (216–277 C.E.) which combined Christianity, Platonism, Gnosticism, and several other schools of thought. The Manicheans taught that procreation imprisoned the soul, and that sexual desire was also innately evil; the most advanced believers – called the Adepts – were those who could renounce both sexual activity and sexual thoughts. Augustine was never able to reach this stage, but lived with a concubine for many years until he became a Christian.

Though he later attacked Manicheanism viciously, Augustine retained much of its suspicion of both sexual activity and desire when he became a Christian. Sexual desire was the one human craving, in Augustine's view, that overcame both reason and will (a truth made evident to him, as he comments, by the fact that he could not control his erections nor give up his concubine, though he desperately wanted to do so). Desire was the result of human sinfulness and disobedience to God, and hence only God's grace could allow one to overcome it or any other human weakness. Augustine's attitude toward sexuality was thus connected to his very negative view of human nature. In his view, no one after Adam and Eve had free will; original sin was transmitted to all humans through semen emitted in sexual acts motivated by desire, and was thus inescapable. Augustine also saw female subordination as intrinsic to God's original creation, for only men were fully created in the image of God. He considered women intellectually, morally, and even physically inferior: "The body of a man is as superior to that of a woman as the soul is to the body."[6] Their lesser status was to be demonstrated in the only permissible position for intercourse, the woman underneath facing upwards and the man on the top. (This later came to be called the "missionary position.")

Despite his deep suspicion of desire, Augustine viewed marriage more positively than Jerome, and set out what became known as the "three goods" of marriage. These were adopted by most Christian writers after him, including both Catholics and Protestants after the Reformation. To Augustine, marriage was good because it produced children, promoted fidelity between spouses, and provided for a permanent union between two individuals and their families. Divorce was therefore unthinkable, for marriage symbolized Christ's union with the church. Sex within marriage was acceptable as long as the couple desired children and the spouses respected one another. This respect should outweigh lust, for as Jerome warned: "Nothing is filthier than to have sex with your wife as you might do with another woman . . . Every too ardent lover of his own wife is an adulterer."[7] Any coital position or sexual activity that would lessen the chances of, or not allow for, procreation was sinful, another reason for favoring the missionary position, as this was regarded as the most likely to lead to pregnancy. The Church Fathers disagreed about whether a partner seeking sex within marriage for procreation never-theless sinned, but most agreed that the partner agreeing to sex did not; that partner was simply fulfilling the "conjugal debt," an obligation to have sex when one's spouse wanted it. The "conjugal debt" applied to both husbands and wives, though husbands were warned their wives might be reticent about expressing sexual needs and might need some encouragement.

During this period, a few men and women decided to combine marriage and virginity, living in what were termed "chaste" or "spiritual" marriages in which the spouses either rejected sexual activity from the start or else renounced it at some time during the course of the marriage. Though Augustine apparently approved of such marriages, most church leaders did not, stating that the power of sexual desire was so great that no one could live with a spouse without sex. This formal disapproval of chaste marriage – Jerome called women who lived in this way "one-man harlots" – contra-dicted the steady stream of praise for virginity and for overcoming sexual temptation, however, and many accounts of early saints' lives include favor-able discussions of their chaste marriages.

Church policy on sexual and related issues was not simply a matter of learned treatises, but was debated and sometimes decided upon at church councils, meetings of large numbers of bishops and other leaders, and at smaller regional meetings known as synods. Councils and synods also acted as courts, for they heard complaints from individuals and groups about the ideas and activities of other Christians. Their decisions, usually called canons, gradually created a body of church law and rulings on sexual matters. Because Constantine and later rulers in Europe regarded themselves as the head of the church as well as the state, they sometimes attended church councils and in other ways shaped the development of Christian doctrine and law; secular law and church law (known as canon law), though distinct in theory, were very closely related in practice.

Constantine and later emperors sought to restrict the grounds for divorce, and most church leaders followed Augustine in discouraging divorce and subsequent remarriage. Nevertheless, it is clear that many Christians in the centuries after Constantine received official ecclesiastical approval for a divorce and then remarried; many more simply separated in a civil ceremony, declaring divorce by mutual consent. Widows and widowers also remarried, though Augustine and others encouraged them to devote themselves to prayer or charitable activities instead. The issue of clerical marriage was much discussed and debated; although celibacy was suggested as the most appropriate life, it was never required, and most priests continued to be married. Sexual offenses were gradually taken more seriously: in the fourth century imperial decrees forbade any sexual activity between husband and wife which did not involve penetration of the vagina by the penis, and church councils forbade women and men from dressing in the clothes of the other sex; in the fifth century adultery became a crime for men as well as women, with death as the prescribed punishment, although actual penalties were much milder; in the sixth century the emperor Justinian condemned homosexual activity between men in harsh language, and called for the death penalty for all repeat offenders, although again actual cases were rare. Prostitution largely escaped imperial or church prohibition, despite all the denunciations of "harlots," though Justinian did call for punishments of brothel-keepers and pimps; this toleration of prostitution had the backing of Augustine, who regarded prostitution as a necessary evil which should be tolerated to keep "honorable" women and girls safe from male lust.

From the fourth through the sixth centuries, when Christian ideas were slowly shaping imperial policy, the Roman Empire itself was changing. Under Constantine, the empire was divided into two parts, a western part with its capital at Rome and an eastern part whose capital was the old city of Byzantium, which Constantine renamed Constantinople. Gradually the western part of the empire disintegrated politically, because of internal weaknesses and migration and invasion by groups of people coming from northern and central Europe; after the late fifth century there was no longer any Roman Empire in the west, but instead smaller territories ruled by kings and chieftains who gradually came to accept Christianity and blend Christian attitudes toward sex with their own traditions.

The end of the Roman Empire in the west is the conventional dividing line between the ancient period and the Middle Ages, although many historians in recent decades have stressed that the break was not as dramatic as it is usually portrayed and that many institutions – including Christianity – continued unbroken lines of development. Historians of eastern Europe also point out that the eastern part of the empire, usually termed the Byzantine Empire, remained as a governmental unit a thousand years longer than the western empire. Nevertheless, Christianity did change its shape during this period, especially because of divisions among different groups of Christians. Beginning in the seventh century, Islamic forces, adherents of the religion begun in Arabia by Muhammed, took over much of the Near East, north Africa, and most of the Iberian peninsula, cutting off small enclaves of African and Asian Christians from the main body of Christians in Europe. In Europe itself, Christianity became increasingly divided between Latin-speaking Christians in western and central Europe, who came to be termed Roman Catholics, and Greek- (and later Slavonic-) speaking Christians in much of eastern Europe,who came to be called Orthodox, with sexual regulations as well as many other matters separating the two traditions. The remainder of this chapter thus will look first at Roman Catholic Europe in the period roughly 500–1500, and then at Orthodox Europe, with Christians outside of Europe considered in later chapters.

The early Middle Ages in Roman Catholic Europe

The groups of people who migrated into the Roman Empire or lived in what is now western Europe beyond the borders of the old Roman Empire are often referred to as "Germans" and "Celts," but they actually belonged to many different groups who had a variety of sexual customs. (It is difficult to obtain accurate information on Germanic and Celtic customs before contact with the Romans or conversion to Christianity, as most of these people had no written language; available sources are thus the reports of outsiders or laws and literature written much later.) There are a few common elements: marriage was generally monogamous, though powerful men often had more than one wife or a wife and several concubines and mistresses, what anthropologists term "resource polygyny"; the most important part of marriage was consummation, with no formal marriage ceremony required; adultery was strictly a female offense and could be harshly punished, though often it was not; extended families and clans were important social units, with marriage among the powerful considered a means to ally two clans; homosexuality is mentioned in only one Germanic law code, that of the Visigoths in Spain, while literary works provide contradictory attitudes toward homosexuality.

During the fifth through the ninth centuries (a period usually called the early Middle Ages), the peoples of central and northern Europe gradually adopted Roman Christianity, and church leaders attempted to bring together Germanic tradition and Christian teachings. The Germanic Emperor Charlemagne (ruled 771–814) forbade remarriage after divorce, though he did not adhere to this rule in his youth and had a number of concubines in addition to a succession of wives. Archbishop Hincmar of Reims (845–882) was the first to suggest that unconsummated marriages were not fully binding, thereby introducing a concept unknown in the Roman world, though the official church position on the exact requirements for a legal marriage remained ambiguous. Many priests married while others lived with concubines, and reports of an unchaste life were no bar to advancement in the church hierarchy.

During the early Middle Ages several institutions developed within Roman Catholic Christianity that would eventually have a major effect on the regulation of sexuality. Even before the end of the Roman Empire in the west, the bishop of Rome began to build up the power of his office compared with that of all other western bishops, and gradually used the title "Pope" as well as bishop. With the end of the empire, the pope gained even more power by taking over political authority in and around the city of Rome as well as continuing to assert his superior spiritual authority. Popes sent many of the missionaries who converted the Celtic and Germanic peoples, thus building up loyalty between newly converted Christians and the papacy. They slowly transformed the Roman Church into a clear hierarchy ranging from local parish priests up through bishops and archbishops to the pope. Letters from the pope conveying his opinion on various issues (termed *decretals*) joined the decisions of church councils in the western church as part of canon law; some of these letters responded to actual cases brought before him, so the pope, like the councils and synods, also served as a judge. As the church expanded, so did its personnel, all of whom were supported by a variety of fees, taxes, tithes, and direct landownership, so that eventually the church became one of the largest landholders in all of Europe.

At the same time as parishes were established and most of western and central Europe became at least nominally Christian, monasteries were set up where men and women lived according to certain rules which prescribed stricter standards of conduct than those expected of most Christians. Monasteries were in theory for the spiritual elite, and required their residents to be chaste and obedient to a superior, and to devote themselves to spiritual concerns such as prayer, meditation, and copying Christian manuscripts. They thus institutionalized what had been the more individualistic ascetic movement in the early church, and women who chose not to marry, in particular, were expected to join a monastery rather than devise their own pattern of spiritual life. Some of these early medieval monasteries were double-houses, in which men and women lived in separate sections, with both sexes under the direction of an abbess.

The residents of early medieval monasteries often viewed themselves as religious athletes, controlling all of their appetites – for food, drink, and sex – as a sign of their spiritual vigor. They were encouraged to do so by their fellow monastic residents, who by the tenth century were also putting into writing their exhortations to chastity and control. There are only a few extant works of this nature by women religious, such as the plays of Hrosvit of Gandersheim (ca. 930–ca. 990), relating the lives of heroic virgin martyrs in a vigorous and sometimes humorous style. In *Dulcitius,* for example, the soldiers who attempt to strip the valiant virgins before torture find: "We labor in vain; we sweat without gain. Behold, their garments remain on their virginal bodies, sticking to them like skin. But he who ordered us to strip them snores in his seat, and cannot be woken from his sleep."[8] Hagiography from the early Middle Ages describes with approval the tribulations women endured to preserve their virginity, hiding for years in small places or cutting off their noses and lips so that men intent on raping or capturing them would simply kill them instead. Saints' lives were often part of sermons and were frequently depicted in church windows, so that people came to know these stories very well; later they also became popular reading material.

Works written by monks for their monastic brothers are much more numerous than those by female monastics for their sisters, and were circulated more widely. Some of these contain the most harshly anti-sexual comments in Christian literature, and they are also virulently misogynist. Monks who achieved the status of saints are often praised for never looking at a woman or even allowing a woman's shadow to touch them. Same-sex attachments are a lesser theme in this type of literature, with "special friendships" warned against primarily because they created factions and were disruptive of the monastic community. Monks were encouraged to control not only their actions, but also their conscious and unconscious desires; full continence included control over nocturnal emissions, with extreme fasting suggested as an effective technique to accomplish this end.

The idealization of abstinence and the general suspicion of sexual relations and desires in the early Middle Ages were communicated not only to monks, but also to lay people through the practice of confession and penance. In the early church, Christians appear to have confessed their sins publicly in front of all believers, but by the sixth century this practice was replaced by private confession to a priest, who then forgave the sin and set a penance which the believer had to perform. As private penance was introduced, guides were written for priests that set out lists of sins and the penances for each one. These guides, called "penitentials," include many sexual activities among their listed sins, and, though some historians regard the lists primarily as reflecting the imaginations of their clerical authors, most scholars see them as describing what at least some people actually did. Though the penitentials vary, oral sex, incest, adultery, and bestiality generally received the stiffest penance, with sex between two unmarried persons ("simple fornication"), masturbation (termed "fornicating by himself"), and seminal emissions viewed as less serious. Clerics and adults generally received a harsher penalty than the laity and younger people. Heterosexual or homosexual anal intercourse (termed sodomy) generally brought a stiff penance, and a few penitentials specifically condemned sex between women, especially if it involved the use of "instruments." Sexual relations with one's spouse were also to be kept within strict bounds, and were prohibited when the wife was menstruating, pregnant, or nursing a child, and during certain periods in the church calendar, such as Sundays and Fridays and most major saints' days, as well as all of Lent and Advent. This left about fifty days a year when a married couple could legitimately have sexual intercourse, and even this was hemmed in by restrictions as to position (prone, man on top), time of day (night only), and proper dress (at least partially clothed). Following the rules did not free one from ritual defilement, however, for couples were expected to wash after sex before coming to church. Lustful thoughts (termed "adultery in the heart") also merited penance, even if they resulted in no activity, for sinfulness was in one's mind and will as well as one's body. This attention to the individual's mental and moral state also resulted in different penances set for acts which were premeditated, impulsive, accidental, or forced – intentionally seducing someone was far more serious than being swept away by passion or being seduced oneself, though the result was the same.

It is extremely difficult to assess whether the system of penance actually affected sexual behavior in early medieval Europe, for measuring that would require sources such as detailed demographic statistics (to see if there was a dip in birth rates nine months after Lent and Advent, for example) that simply do not exist. Because confession is a private matter, there are no lists of sins *actually* confessed to match those of *possible* sins, nor are there diaries from this period which might indicate whether people really felt guilty as they were supposed to. What is clear is that certain teachings of the Church, especially in regard to marriage, did begin to win acceptance; even at the highest levels, monogamy came to be the established household pattern, and divorce became more difficult. This was also increasingly true for slaves and serfs, with the result that households and families across all social levels came to look more like one another than they had in the Roman Empire.

Reforms of the high Middle Ages

Although the close relationship between church and state that began under Constantine was often beneficial to the church, as it put secular power behind Christian doctrine, it also created problems. By the tenth century, parish priests, bishops, abbots and other church officials were often chosen by secular rulers and nobles, who expected their appointees to follow their wishes.

There were various attempts to reform this situation in the Carolingian period, and beginning in the eleventh century, a broad-ranging movement grew over the next two centuries; it is usually termed the "Gregorian reform" after one of its most vocal proponents, Pope Gregory VII (pontificate 1073–1085). This movement transformed the church into an institution much more free of secular control than it had been earlier, and it brought with it a number of dramatic changes in the regulation of sexuality. Gregory adopted the ideas of a viciously anti-sexual monk, St Peter Damian (1007?–1072), who argued that clerical marriage was heresy, and that priests' wives were "harlots" and their children "bastards." Only if the clergy were freed from the worldly concerns created by families would the church be freed from secular control, argued Damian. In 1059, the church issued a decree ordering clerical celibacy, though officials hesitated to break up existing families. By the next century they were less reluctant, and two church councils (the First and Second Lateran Councils, 1123 and 1139) explicitly forbade all priests to marry and declared marriages which did exist invalid. Reform-minded officials began a campaign against clerical families, driving women and children from their homes. Though there were protests against this change in policy, they were not effective, and clerical celibacy became the policy of the western church from that point on. Other contacts between male clergy and women were also restricted: priests were ordered to live separately from their female relatives, and links between monks and nuns in double monasteries were restricted. The sexuality of female religious was to be controlled primarily by cutting them off from the world, a practice known as enclosure. It became official policy in the papal decree *Periculoso* promulgated in 1298 by Pope Boniface VIII, though was never successfully enforced until centuries later.

The campaign for clerical celibacy extended to homosexual relationships as well. Peter Damian denounced (in graphic detail) varieties of what he termed the "Sodomitic vice," arguing that the destruction of the Biblical cities of Sodom and Gomorrah (interpreted as the result of homosexuality) would be repeated if male homosexual acts were not suppressed. The Third Lateran Council (1179) held that clerics who could not give up homosexual activities were to surrender their clerical status, and laymen were to be excommunicated, that is, cut off from church rituals. After about 1250 secular courts in particular sharpened their penalties. Both church and secular authorities increasingly defined homosexual actions as "crimes against nature," and particularly reprehensible because they did not occur anywhere else in creation. Both church reformers and secular authorities mentioned lesbianism only rarely; because in their minds sex always involved penetration, they had difficulty imagining sex without a penis.

The reform movement also brought changes in the marriages and sexual lives of lay persons. In their efforts to assert the independence and primacy of religious authority, church leaders supported the compilation of collections of canon law, the writing of new laws, and the expansion of the jurisdiction of bishops' and other church courts. This continued over several centuries, and so by the thirteenth century, canon law and church courts controlled almost all aspects of marriage (except for property matters) and sexual conduct, including both civil and criminal issues, which, incidentally, brought the Church a great deal of revenue through fees and fines. Marriage was increasingly defined as a *sacrament,* a ceremony which provided visible evidence of God's grace, and as the expected norm for all lay Christians. Clerical writers disagreed about exactly what made a marriage, with most regarding consent as the only necessary requirement, while others included the presence of a priest or witnesses, consummation, or very specific words of consent to make a marriage fully valid (and thus indissoluble). Weddings did not have to take place in a church; in southern Europe they were usually held at home, whereas in northern Europe they were often held at the church door. Canon lawyers also argued about such issues as whether rapists who persuaded their victims to marry them should be liable for their crime, whether impotence constituted valid grounds for annulling a marriage, how that impotence was to be proved, and how often spouses had the right to demand the "conjugal debt" from each other. Disagreement among authorities and confusion among the laity about church policy on marriage were two main reasons that sexual and marital cases constituted a large percentage of the business of church courts.

Reform measures to increase church power over the laity and centralize papal control within the church led to new types of criminal procedure in church courts. These, like most other medieval courts, had traditionally operated with an accusatory procedure, in which an individual accusing someone of a crime confronted the defendant openly in court, produced witnesses (two were usually required), and then a judge or judges (or occasionally a jury) decided the case. This procedure protected defendants against frivolous cases, a protection extended further by the fact that the accuser had to bear all costs of the case until there was a verdict, and all costs in cases when the verdict went against him or her; a negative verdict might also lead the original defendent to sue the accuser, and this worked as a further deterrent against frivolous cases. Increasingly, however, canon lawyers realized the difficulty of finding two witnesses to certain types of crimes, and saw how reluctant accusers often were to state their case openly in court, so around 1200, they began to devise other sorts of procedures for certain types of cases.

One of these, procedure *per notorium* or *per denunciationem*, authorized a court to proceed against someone whose actions were so notorious that the whole community was aware of them. No accuser was necessary, and witnesses were required to testify only that people generally believed the accused to be guilty and not that they had actually seen the crime. Procedures *per notorium* were often used against priests who lived with a concubine or frequented prostitutes, although many jurists had reservations about such procedures because they left the defendant with little protection and could be based simply on rumors. Defendants had even less protection in a second type of procedure devised initially by Pope Innocent III (pontificate 1198–1216), proceedings *per inquisitionem*. As in proceedings *per notorium,* the inquisitorial process began with a judge's decision to investigate a person suspected of a crime. The judge called witnesses, heard testimony, made a judgement, and passed sentence, thus combining the roles of judge, investigator, and prosecutor in one. The defendant did have the right to answer the general charges and to deny guilt, but in particularly heinous cases judges were allowed to use torture to provoke a confession. The judge determined when a case was heinous and also had great leeway in choosing the appropriate punishment. That could be penance, fines, imprisonment, and excommunication, or the party judged guilty could be handed over to secular authorities for more stringent punishments such as beating and execution. (Medieval church courts themselves did not carry out the death penalty.)

Inquisitorial procedures became the preferred method of handling those accused of what were dubbed "occult crimes," which included both heresy and sex crimes. (The word "occult" comes from the Latin word meaning hidden from sight, and only gradually acquired its current associations with magic and witchcraft.) In the early thirteenth century, the papacy grew increasingly alarmed by the spread of ideas it judged heretical, and it established a formal tribunal, the papal Inquisition, to investigate and try people accused of heresy. Judges were sent to areas of what are now France and Italy, where a dualist group called the Albigensians had won many people from Christianity with vigorous preaching and charismatic leaders. Albigensians preached that the material world was evil, created by a second divine power, and that the body was a prison for the soul. Not surprisingly, they thus rejected reproduction, and were accused by church authorities of engaging in "unnatural" (i.e., non-reproductive) sex; inquisitorial legal proceedings, combined with a military campaign, wiped them out.

Secular authorities also recognized that linking heresy and sexual deviance could be a very effective strategy against their enemies. The most spectacular example was the French King Philip IV's trial of the Knights Templars, a military order which had been founded during the Crusades to fight Muslims, but which had also grown extremely wealthy from its landholding and money-lending. In 1307, Philip arrested about 2,000 Templars in France and used the inquisitorial procedure, including torture, to force them to confess to worshipping Muhammed and the Devil, parodying the mass, and engaging in anal intercourse with one another. He then executed many Templars, confiscated their property, and began to persecute other moneylenders, such as wealthy Jews and Italians. It is impossible to tell whether the Templars did any of the things they were accused of, but "heretic and sodomite" there-after became a standard charge to level at one's political or religious opponents. (This linkage is also the origin of the word "bugger," which comes from "Bulgarian," because Bulgaria was regarded as the home of dualist beliefs such as Albigensianism; it was first used in English in a clearly sexual sense in a 1533 law of Henry VIII.)

Though the Templars most likely never worshipped Muhammed or con-verted to Islam, the Crusades and the reconquest of the Iberian peninsula from the Muslims did mean that Christian authorities in these areas were confronted with issues regarding marriage and other sexual relations between Christians and non-Christians. Canon law prohibited all such relations, and some com-mentators held that a non-Christian who converted, but whose spouse did not, was free to marry a Christian. Penalties for sexual relations between Christians and non-Christians could be severe; laws in some areas prescribed death for both partners, and there are examples of this being carried out in cases involv-ing Christian women and Muslim or Jewish men. The reverse pairing was much less likely to be punished, particularly if it involved Christian men and Muslim women. In the kingdom of Valencia, for example, where there was a significant Muslim population, Christian men apprehended in sexual relations with Muslim women were not penalized, but the women were often enslaved to the crown, which then sold them for cash, gave them to royal favorites, or licensed them as prostitutes. Nobles and occasionally even monks profited from this system, ordering Muslim women under their jurisdiction to have sex with them and then denouncing them for miscegenation so they could receive them as slaves; the crown altered the law slightly to prevent such glaring abuses, but did not revoke it.

Dramatic prosecutions such as those of the Knights Templars occurred only rarely; most church court business was much more prosaic, involving questions of how closely related two individuals who intended to marry or who had married were, whether a promise of marriage in front of one's friends in a tavern involved the proper words of consent and was thus a marriage (such cases generally were brought by a pregnant woman), or whether consent had been freely given or been gained by force or threats of force, or whether someone had been correct in calling a neighbor a slut or a bastard. In such matters, church courts paid attention not only to what had happened, the "facts" of the case, but also to what the parties intended. They thus brought into western criminal law a notion deriving from the church's ritual of penance – that the mental and moral state of an offender determined the level of guilt and appropriate punishment. This idea is now fully engrained in most secular law codes, where, for example, the punishment for premeditated murder is very different from that for killing someone in a road accident. Thus much of the business of church courts involved an examination of conscience on the part of the parties concerned: Did you think you were married when you had sex with him? Did you mean to force her into marriage, and if not, why were you carrying a stick? Did you know she was your cousin but decided to marry her anyway? Did you know it was wrong to marry again when you were not sure your first husband was dead? Punishments were set according to the nature of the specific crime and the attitude of the defendant. They could involve fines, exclusion from church rituals, or rituals of humiliation, such as walking around the church carrying a candle.

Church courts thus not only penalized actions in the Middle Ages, but also shaped conscience. The church accomplished this objective through a variety of other means as well. The Fourth Lateran Council (1215) commanded all Christians to make a complete confession at least once a year, preceded by an examination of conscience in which they were to pay special attention to those sins judged "mortal," that is, those which, if unconfessed, would make them liable to damnation. Sexual actions and thoughts were prominent among the mortal sins, although theologians differed about the precise dividing line between mortal and venial (lesser) sins in matters of sexuality.

Sermons were also an increasingly important means of communicating church teachings about sex. Though church services continued to be held in Latin – a language which by the Middle Ages was no longer spoken in Europe outside of university or ecclesiastical circles – beginning in the thirteenth century several new religious orders were founded which preached in the languages that people spoke. Prime among these orders were the Dominicans, founded by St Dominic (1170?–1221), who was sent by Pope Innocent III to preach to the Albigensians. (The timing and circumstances of their founding and their dedication to spreading correct doctrine resulted in the Dominicans becoming the order principally in charge of the Inquisition.) Dominicans and members of other religious orders such as the Franciscans often went from town to town gathering large crowds to hear their sermons, which they delivered in market places as well as churches. The sermons of the most popular preachers were later written down and copies made for others to use; sermon collections are thus a good source for the teachings on sex that people heard regularly. What they heard were frequent denunciations of harlots and adulterers, attacks on lascivious monks and adulterous wives, and other condemnations of a range of sexual sins. St Vincent Ferrer (1350–1419), for example, a Dominican preacher who travelled widely in Spain, France, and Italy, thundered, "Today the law is not obeyed. [Christian men] want to taste everything: Muslims and Jews, animals, men with men; there is no limit."[9] Along with such attacks, sermon audiences also heard glorifications of heterosexual marital love, which was praised as a model of the love between God and humanity, central to the divine plan for the world and thus "natural." (The link between human and divine love was also becoming increasingly popular in secular chivalric romances at the same time, though these stories often focus more on extramarital love.)

The Dominican order dedicated itself to study and teaching as well as to preaching, and many of the most prominent Christian theologians in the Middle Ages were Dominicans. Theological discussions of sexuality did not end with Augustine, and in the thirteenth century they were given added impetus in the course of attempts to integrate the ideas of Aristotle with Christian teachings by philosophers termed *scholastics*. These efforts at synthesis appear especially in the writings of St Thomas Aquinas (1225–1274), a Dominican who was not very popular in his own time but whose philosophical system was later declared the official philosophy of the Roman Catholic Church. Though much of Aristotelian and Christian thought is difficult to reconcile – Aristotle does not believe in the immortality of the individual soul, for example – in terms of sexuality they were compatible and largely reinforced one another. Aquinas and most of the scholastics viewed sexual desire as both sinful and irrational, dangerous to the spirit, and – an idea picked up from Greek and Roman medical theory – particularly dangerous to the male body.

The scholastics believed women had a stronger sex drive than men as well as a lesser capacity for reason; both made them, in Aquinas's words, "naturally subject to man." Aquinas accepted Aristotle's idea that in procreation "the active power of generation belongs to the male sex, and the passive power to the female," but rejected his view that women were misbegotten men; he and the other scholastics viewed the creation of women as part of God's plan, though they were often puzzled by God's motives.[10] Because procreation seemed the most obvious explanation to them, Aquinas and other scholastics condemned contraception, whether attempted physically through coitus interruptus (defined as a "sin against nature") or chemically through herbs and drugs. Their notion of contraception extended through the first few months of pregnancy. Not until the fetus quickened (that is, until the mother felt movement) did it acquire a soul, and only after quickening was ending a pregnancy regarded as abortion. (This opinion lasted for centuries, for it was only in 1869 that Pope Pius IX declared that ensoulment begins at conception.)

The scholastics' admissions that women were created by God and that heterosexual love was acceptable and "natural" were accompanied by a strong emphasis on the divinely ordained and "natural" inequality between men and women. Any attempt to overcome this inequality was regarded as both unnatural and unChristian, particularly if men sank to the level of women. Except during plays and festivals, men who dressed as women were suspected of trying to gain sexual access to women. Men who became sexually aroused too often and too easily, especially if this led to intercourse, were not regarded as manly and macho as they often are in contemporary culture, but as feminine because they were ruled by their bodies to an unacceptable degree. In the western Church, eunuchs were prohibited from becoming priests because they were not fully men; the practice of intentionally castrating boys or adult men to serve as administrators or servants declined. (Castration continued to be used occasionally as punishment for crimes such as homosexuality and rape, and in the sixteenth century men who had been castrated as boys – whose voices thus did not change – began to perform in Italian and Spanish church choirs.)

At the same time as the scholastics were emphasizing reason as the best way to know God, other Christian thinkers were developing a mystical path to understanding that involved the body as well as the mind. Literature written by mystics often portrays union with God in very sensual and bodily terms, as tasting or kissing God, bathing in Christ's blood or becoming one with God. Though most mystical visions were not sexual, some male mystics envisioned their souls as feminine, uniting with Christ as a bride with a bridegroom in language full of sexual imagery, or they described the body of Christ in female terms, as Jesus who "suckles us with his blessed breast." Female mystics often identified with the Virgin Mary, and saw visions of her which were graphically physical, as is this one by St Bridget of Sweden (1303–1373) : "The Virgin Mary appeared again to me, in the same place, and said . . . I showed you . . . the way I was standing when I gave birth to my son, you still should know for sure that I stood and gave birth such as you have seen it now – my knees were bent and I was alone in the stable, praying." [11] Statues of Mary portrayed her as a nursing mother whose body opened up to reveal the Trinity. By bridging body and soul, mysticism thus provided a kind of counter-discourse within Christianity to the much more common disparagement of the body and the senses.

The later Middle Ages in Roman Catholic Europe

This emphasis on the sensual and corporal aspects of love for God was accompanied in the fourteenth and fifteenth centuries (a period conventionally called the "later Middle Ages") by a de-emphasis on physical virginity as central to sainthood for women. Many of the late medieval female saints were wives and mothers who chose a life of "spiritual virginity" after their husbands died, or convinced their husbands to abstain from sex, reviving the practice of chaste marriage begun in the early church. (A few male saints also lived in chaste marriages, although in general aspects of sexuality were far less important in the lives of male saints.) The most spectacular examples of such spiritual virgins were not contemporary women, however, but the repentant prostitutes of the early Church, whose lives were frequently described in sermons and plays and depicted in paintings and sculpture during the late Middle Ages. Prime among these was Mary Magdalene, a figure who in Catholic Christianity combined three different New Testament women and about whom an enormous number of legends grew up. Though in the New Testament she was simply described as a woman possessed by a demon which Jesus exorcized, the story developed that she was a beautiful wealthy woman who was promiscuous sexually, but who abandoned her previous life on meeting Christ. Among the miracles attributed to her was spectacular hair growth; this occurred when she gave up her fancy clothes, and thus she is often depicted wearing only her hair. (This story is also told about the repentant prostitute Mary of Egypt.) Mary Magdalene was the most popular saint after the Virgin Mary in the Middle Ages, although, like the Virgin, she provided an ambiguous message about female sexuality, and by extension male sexuality as well; yes, it was possible for someone who had been sexually active to be saved, but only by renouncing sexual desire and activity.

Real prostitutes, as opposed to those of tradition and legend, were not made saints in the later Middle Ages, but in this period prostitution was more open and treated more tolerantly than it had been earlier or would be later. Prostitution developed in Europe in the twelfth century along with the growth of cities and a larger cash economy, and by the later Middle Ages, most towns and cities had opened official municipal houses of prostitution or designated certain parts of the city as places in which prostitution would be tolerated. Women selling sex outside these areas would be ordered to move, as cities attempted to make a sharper distinction between respectable, married women and "common women" who distributed their sexual favors more widely. Government authorities, including church authorities in cities ruled by bishops or the pope, taxed prostitutes or brothel managers, and they passed regulations which attempted to guard the safety of the brothels' residents and their customers; in some parts of Europe religious organizations such as monasteries and the groups which governed cathedrals (termed cathedral chapters) also owned the brothels. Generally the establishment of a brothel happened with little fanfare, but there were occasional references to St Augustine's view of prostitution as a necessary evil. Italian city officials noted that recruiting female prostitutes might encourage young men into acceptable heterosexual activity and away from homosexual liaisons. During the thirteenth century a special religious order had been set up for repentent prostitutes – named, not surprisingly, the Order of St Mary Magdalene – which established houses in a number of cities, but by the fifteenth century the movement to reform prostitutes lost its steam. Officially brothels in most parts of Europe were closed to priests, Jews, and married men, though usually this ban was enforced only in the case of Jews; priests who openly visited brothels were occasionally reprimanded by the church, but rarely received any more severe punishment. In parts of Europe with significant numbers of Muslims, Christian prostitutes were prohibited from having Muslim patrons and were exempt from severe penalties only if they could prove they did not know the religious affiliation of their customers.

The public and clerical acceptance of municipal prostitution in the fourteenth and fifteenth centuries did not result from a change of heart about sexual desire – sex was still regarded as polluting and sinful – but from a sort of resigned acceptance of its power. This attitude also affected the treatment of clerics who continued their relationships with women, for though they were forbidden to marry, many priests lived in stable relationships with concubines and children or had casual relationships with many women. Church councils and synods set stringent punishments for clerical concubinage and fornication, but local church authorities generally enforced these only in cases which involved public scandal, such as rape or abduction. A similar pattern emerged in cases of divorce and separation; church courts allowed separation for reasons not specified in canon law – including cruelty, mistreatment, drunkenness, and financial irresponsibility – although they consented to a true divorce with rights of remarriage only on very rare occasions. While fornication between unmarried persons was officially prohibited, actual prosecutions are very rare, and confessors reported that most of their parishioners did not consider fornication a sin worthy of penance, much less a crime.

During the later Middle Ages secular courts run by cities, kings, and nobles became more active in handling marriage issues and sexual offenses, though church courts also continued to hear a large number of cases. (The decision about exactly who had jurisdiction over what types of cases was often a matter of dispute, with plaintiffs often choosing whichever type of court they felt would give them a sympathetic judgment.) Secular courts took particular interest in cases in which an actual crime was involved, such as rape, abduction, or adultery, or where property was at stake, such as disputes over dowries. City governments also passed draconian laws about certain types of sexual behavior: sex between Christians and non-Christians merited death by burning alive in some Italian cities, as did certain types of homosexual acts. The enforcement of these statutes tended to be sporadic and localized, however, and some scholars have noted that male homosexual networks developed in Italian and perhaps other cities at this time. During periods of enforcement punishment could be severe, however, with death sentences actually carried out and not simply threatened.

By the late Middle Ages, secular authorities were generally no less concerned than church leaders with trying to make people's sexual and marital lives follow a prescribed pattern. In fact, they could be even *more* rigorous. In 1484, for example, the city council of Cologne asked priests hearing confessions there to reveal the extent of those involving sodomy; most of the priests were reluctant to reply, and appear not to have shared the council's concerns about the presence of sodomites. In many places city authorities barred illegitimate children from membership in craft guilds or city govern-ment and refused to recognize the church's right to confer legitimacy. Occupational groups such as craft and journeymen's guilds also became increasingly moralistic in the later Middle Ages. They denied membership to those born too soon after their parents' wedding (canonical authorities gener-ally recommended that all children born to married women be considered legitimate, no matter when that marriage had occurred), and by the early sixteenth century ejected those known to frequent prostitutes. They enforced their views through formal actions such as banning individuals from working, and also through informal means, such as public insults or rumors. Sometimes these cases ended up in church or secular courts, as when the person accused of immoral acts attempted to clear his or her name, usually by finding a number of people to testify to his or her good character, a process known as *compurgation*. The medieval courts which dealt with slander and rumor provide a good source for the epithets people called one another and can give insight into popular ideas about sexuality. Women were almost always called something sexual, usually a variant of "whore," while men were called names related to their honesty, such as "thief," or to the sexual actions of the women with whom they were involved, such as "whoreson," "whore-master," or "cuckold." In certain circles "sodomite" was also a common term of abuse, often – as earlier in the twelfth century – used against religious or political enemies; the term frequently appears, for example, in slanderous poetry about *converso* officials in Spain. (*Conversos* were Jews who had converted to Christianity, often to avoid forced emigration.)

Thus by the end of the Middle Ages in Roman Catholic Europe, ambivalence about sexuality was not limited to monks, but could be found among lay people as well. This ambivalence came from many sources: pagan traditions, Christian teachings, and secular concerns about the ways in which sexual desire and activities could disrupt public order, sensible business practices, and proper family hierarchy. Even before the Reformation, it was clear, particularly to urban dwellers, that God would look favorably on those places that assured a moral and upright life among their citizens, and that the rewards for such a life were not simply in the hereafter but also in the here and now.

Orthodox Europe

Regulation of sexuality in eastern Europe during the Middle Ages followed a slightly different path than that in western and central Europe, in large part because the political and institutional situation was very different. As in Roman Catholic Europe, Orthodox societies recognized distinct spheres of influence for church and state and had separate codes of law and courts of law for each. The Byzantine ideal was harmony (*symphonia*) between Church and state; the church defended the faith and the Christian people spiritually, and the state defended them physically. The Byzantine tradition accorded the emperor a special role ideologically and administratively, holding that the emperor ruled the earthly kingdom in the way that Christ ruled the heavenly kingdom. In practical terms the emperor presided at the church councils that formed the apex of Orthodox church structure, and often had the final say in who became patriarch – the title of the bishop of Constantinople. The church councils, composed of all Orthodox bishops who were willing and able to attend periodic meetings, set dogma and general policy. Unlike the Roman Catholic pope, the patriarch was merely the first among equals, and had little more than moral suasion to exercise over other bishops, especially outside the boundaries of the Byzantine Empire. The heads of the Orthodox Churches in Bulgaria, Serbia, and Russia, titled in various periods as "metropolitan" or "patriarch," generally sought pro-forma confirmation of their appointment from the patriarch of Constantinople, but operated autonomously in their decision making. The lack of a unified code of canon law, a single administrative structure, and even a single language of operation (Greek, Syriac, and Slavonic were all in use) allowed for considerable local autonomy and diversity in Orthodox practices.

Though the final, formal break between Orthodoxy and Roman Catholicism did not occur until 1054, eastern and western Christianity were already distinct enough in the fourth century that the thought of St Augustine had little impact on Orthodox ideas about sexuality. Augustine's linkage of sexual intercourse and original sin and his concept of the "conjugal debt" were never accepted in the Orthodox East, though this did not mean that the eastern church had more favorable views on sex. The most important of the Greek Church Fathers and Bishop of Antioch, St John Chrysostom (ca. 347–407), was ascetic in his own habits and extremely moralistic, frequently preaching against what he viewed as the decadence of the emperor's court and warning against anything that led even to thoughts of sex, such as theater, dancing, or artistic representations of the human body. Though he did not regard original sin as transmitted through sexual intercourse (the Orthodox Church tended to pay less attention to original sin in general than the Catholic Church), he did see sex as the disgraceful result of Adam's and Eve's disobedience and commented that: "The passions in fact are all dishonorable."[12] Those who had given in to sexual desire and married should never marry again if their spouse died, according to Chrysostom, but spend their remaining years in prayer and penance.

Chrysostom was particularly disturbed by homosexual acts and wrote more about homosexuality than any other Church Father. What bothered him most was that sex between males upset gender norms, "for I maintain that not only are you made [by it] into a woman, but you also cease to be a man." As we saw earlier, women who became men by remaining virgins were praiseworthy to St Jerome, but men who became women were, for Chrysostom, "demented . . . noxious . . . worthy of being driven out and stoned . . . changed from men not into dogs but into a much more loathsome animal than this." In the same sermon, Chrysostom made a few veiled references to sex between women as unnatural and a disease.

Chrysostom's hostility to sexuality and the body comes very close to that of dualist groups such as the Manicheans, but he ultimately and grudgingly accepted marital sex and procreation as necessary. Later Byzantine writers were more moderate, viewing marriage as a positive good and the ideal life as one not of virginity, but of loyalty and attachment to one's spouse. A few went so far as to approve of sexual pleasure, as long as the parties were married. This endorsement of marriage extended in some degree to the clergy, for married men could become priests. Acceptance of clerical marriage was limited to those already in their first marriage, however, for a widowed priest was forbidden to remarry if he wanted to remain a priest, and a man who was unmarried when ordained was expected to remain so. Married priests also could not become bishops. Monks and nuns in the Orthodox Church were expected to be unmarried, though married persons could also enter monasteries with their spouse's approval. Many who lived there were widows or widowers who entered monasteries late in life, rather than life-long celibates. Upper-class widows and, more rarely, unmarried daughters regarded the establishment of a convent as the perfect way to demonstrate both their devotion and authority, and joint monasteries in which abbesses had authority over both women and men persisted in the east, despite official prohibitions. Along with its acceptance of clerical marriage, the Eastern Church also accepted eunuchs as priests; though Byzantine emperors forbade castration, the practice continued, and there were enough eunuch priests available in Byzantium for the founders of some convents to require all clergy who had contact with their nuns to be eunuchs. (Eunuchs were not used in this capacity among the Slavs; priests there who ministered to convents were supposed to be married men, though often they were not.)

As in the Western Church, church courts developed within Orthodoxy to handle marriage and sexual cases, although there was even more diversity in their rulings than in the west. After the ninth century, Orthodoxy generally required an ecclesiastical ceremony for a marriage to be valid, with consent of both the parents and the couple viewed as desirable. In Slavic areas, marriages among the elite involved a ceremony in church as well as elaborate rituals at home, though for the peasants church weddings were not common until later. In some countries consent of the parents alone was enough for first marriages, and consent of the couple enough for subsequent marriages. Unions between close relatives were prohibited, as were those with relatives of godparents. Second marriages were frowned upon, with the parties required to do penance before the ceremony; some laws prohibited third or fourth marriages altogether, although demographic realities such as early death and frequent widowhood meant that dispensations to overcome this prohibition were sought and often granted. Because nobody – neither parish priests nor state officials – kept records of births, marriages, and baptisms, observance of the restrictions on consanguinity could not be enforced with any regularity, except among the aristocracy, whose bloodlines were common knowledge. Should political ambitions dictate, noble families could generally persuade clerics to overlook violations of the canons.

Grounds for divorce were gradually extended in Orthodox countries. A husband could divorce his wife for adultery or for going to places of ill repute such as horseraces or bathhouses; if the divorce was granted, he received the right to remarry, whereas the wife could be confined to a convent, although usually she was not. Adultery by a husband was not grounds for divorce – it was not technically "adultery," but rather fornication – but courts did permit divorce in cases where the adultery was blatant and upset community standards; in such cases wives were allowed to remarry. Serious physical abuse, abandonment, impotence, and barrenness were all grounds for divorce; in all of these instances, remarriage was usually permitted. This meant that the Eastern Church, though it disapproved of remarriage after the death of a spouse, actually offered more opportunities for unhappy spouses to separate and start a new marriage than did the Western Church. In addition, if a spouse wished to terminate a marriage in order to take monastic vows, the other spouse was expected to agree to it and to promise not to remarry. In actuality, unhappy wives sometimes used the convent as a respectable escape from their marriages, and unhappy husbands hounded or forced their wives to enter; in such cases, the prohibition on remarriage was generally ignored.

Orthodox teachings generally matched Roman Catholic teachings about the limits of sexual activity within marriage – it was to be restricted to certain times and certain positions, and never to involve hindrances to procreation, so contraception was forbidden. Outside of marriage all sexual activity was sin, though there were gradations of sinfulness according to canon law. Unmarried men were rarely punished for fornication unless it involved an upper-class woman or a young girl. Rape was punishable by mutilation in Byzantium and the Balkans or by the rapist being forced to marry his victim; in Russia, rape was punishable by fines. Taking its cue from Chrysostom, Byzantine law set severe penalties for homosexual acts, including death, castration, and imprisonment, though there is little evidence that such penalties were actually carried out. Slavic law was milder, regarding male homosexual acts as no worse than adultery, and often as a minor transgression; secular governments in Slavic lands also did not outlaw homosexual relations as western governments did, but treated them simply as a violation of church law.

The Slavic treatment of homosexual acts was not motivated by liberality on sexual matters, but by an extremely negative opinion of all sexual relations. Particularly in Russia, Orthodox didactic tracts cast all sexual relations as unnatural and desire as coming from the Devil. Church officials communicated these attitudes to the laity through confession, sermons, and stories about saints, all of which described sex as a sin and praised virginity and chastity. In contrast to Roman Catholic theory in which consummation was an important part of marriage and each spouse owed the other the conjugal debt, in Russia the best marriage was an unconsummated one. This belief led to a motif common in Russian saints' lives, that of a saint being conceived of a pious and abstinent mother, and born of a miracle rather than normal marital intercourse. It also led to the popular idea that Jesus was born out of Mary's ear, not polluting himself with passage through the birth canal. Children were viewed as the result of God's will rather than of intercourse, and the failure to conceive was taken as a sign of God's disfavor. Menstruation thus marked a woman, and menstruating women could not enter churches or take communion; women were also expected to do penance if they miscarried. Whether people actually accepted church teachings is difficult to ascertain, for while penitentials and church law set out official church positions, they do not give insight into how faithfully people followed church prescriptions. Letters written on birchbark which have survived from medieval Russia do contain occasional expressions of passionate love between individuals, so that church teachings about sexuality and the body were in some cases clearly not internalized.

Because neither the Renaissance nor the Protestant Reformation had a direct effect on Russia, the period around 1500 did not mark a break in Russian Orthodoxy; not until the reign of Tsar Peter the Great (reigned 1682–1725) was there a major alteration in church structure. The fifteenth century was significant for Greek Orthodoxy, however, for throughout the century the Byzantine Empire gradually shrank under the military pressure of the Ottoman Turks; in 1453 the Turks conquered Constantinople and the Byzantine Empire officially ceased to exist. The patriarch of Constantinople was given civil and religious jurisdiction over all the Orthodox within the Ottoman Empire, so that church courts continued to operate, but these were now within a Muslim state. Orthodox attitudes toward and treatment of marriage and sexual issues could not help but be influenced by this situation, as we will see in Chapter 3.

Notes

1 Clement of Alexandria, *Stromateis*, trans. John Ferguson (Washington, DC: Catholic University of America Press, 1991), 251, 253.

2 Tertullian, "On Exhortation to Chasitity" and "On the Apparel of Women," trans. S. Thelwall, in Alexander Roberts and James Donaldson, eds, *The Ante-Nicene Fathers* (Grand Rapids, Mich.: Wm. B. Eerdmans, 1951), Vol. 2, 55, 23.

3 The Life of Saint Pelagia the Harlot, in Ross S. Kraemer, *Maenads, Martyrs, Matrons, Monastics: A Sourcebook on Women's Religions in the Greco-Roman World* (Philadelphia: Fortress Press, 1988), 317, 323, 324.

4 St Jerome, *Commentaries on the Letter to the Ephesians,* book 16, cited in Vern Bullough, *Sexual Variance in Society and History* (Chicago: University of Chicago Press: 1976), 365.

5 St Jerome, *The Letters of St Jerome,* trans. C. Mierow, *Ancient Christian Writers* (Westminster, Md.: Newman Press, 1946), Vol. 1, letter 22, 162.

6 Augustine, *Contra Mendacium*, 7.10, quoted in John Boswell, *Christianity, Social Tolerance and Homosexuality: Gay People in Western Europe from the Beginning of the Christian Era to the Fourteenth Century* (Chicago: University of Chicago Press, 1981), 157.

7 Jerome, *Adversus Jovinianum* 1.49, quoted in James A. Brundage, *Law, Sex, and Christian Society in Medieval Europe* (Chicago: University of Chicago Press, 1987), 90–1.

8 Hrosvit of Gandersheim, *Dulcitius,* translated and quoted in Katharina M. Wilson, *Medieval Women Writers* (Athens: University of Georgia Press, 1984), 56.

9 St Vincent Ferrer, *Sermons,* translated and quoted in David Nirenberg, *Communities of Violence: Persecution of Minorities in the Middle Ages* (Princeton: Princeton University Press, 1996), 142.

10 Thomas Aquinas, *Summa Theologica*, trans. Fathers of the English Dominican Province (London: Burns, Oates and Washbourne, 1914), Part 1, Question 96, Article 3 and Part 1, Question 92, Article 1, reprinted in Elizabeth Clark and Herbert Richardson, eds, *Women and Religion: A Feminist Sourcebook of Christian Thought* (New York: Harper and Row, 1977), 87, 88.

11 Bridget of Sweden, *Revelationes* 7.22, translated and quoted in Katharina M. Wilson, *Medieval Women Writers* (Athens: University of Georgia Press, 1984), 345.

12 The three quotations are from St John Chrysostom, Commentary on Romans, Homily 4, translated in Boswell, *Christianity*, 359–362.

Selected further reading

Because this chapter covers such an enormous span of time, the works available for further reading are practically limitless. Good places to start for bibliographical suggestions arranged by topic are Michael M. Sheehan, *Family and Marriage in Medieval Europe: A Working Bibliography* (Toronto: Medieval Studies Committee, 1984); Joyce E. Salisbury, *Medieval Sexuality: A Research Guide* (New York: Garland, 1990); Vern L. Bullough and James A. Brundage, *Handbook of Medieval Sexuality* (New York: Garland, 1996). Vern and Bonnie Bullough have also edited two topical surveys which include the period discussed in this chapter as well as later developments: *Cross-Dressing, Sex, and Gender* (Philadelphia: University of Pennsylvania Press, 1993) and *Sexual Attitudes: Myths and Realities* (New York: Prometheus Books, 1995). For another wide-ranging study, see Jean-Louis Flandrin, *Sex in the Western World: The Development of Attitudes and Behaviors*, trans. Sue Collins (Chur, Switzerland: Harwood Academic, 1991).

One of the most thought-provoking discussions of sexuality in Judaism is Howard Eilberg-Schwartz, *God's Phallus* (Boston: Beacon Press, 1994). See also David Biale, *Eros and the Jews from Biblical Israel to Contemporary America* (New York: Basic Books, 1992); Judith Baskin, *Jewish Women in Historical Perspective* (Detroit: Wayne State University Press, 1991); Daniel Boyarin, *Carnal Israel: Reading Sex in Talmudic Culture* (Berkeley: University of California Press, 1993); Michael L. Satlow, *Tasting the Dish: Rabbinic Rhetorics of Sexuality* (Atlanta: Scholar's Press, 1995); Howard Eilberg-Schwartz, ed., *People of the Body: Jews and Judaism from an Embodied Perspective* (Binghamton: SUNY Press, 1992). For Jewish law see: Louis Epstein, *Marriage Laws in the Bible and the Talmud* (Cambridge, Mass.: Harvard University Press, 1942) and *Sex Laws and Customs in Judaism* (New York: Ktav Publishing House, 1948); Rachel Biale, *Women in Jewish Law: An Exploration of Women's Issues in Halakhic Sources* (New York: Schocken, 1984).

The literature on sex and marriage in the ancient world is vast and growing constantly. Several good collections and studies are: David M. Halperin, John J. Winkler, and Froma I. Zeitlin, eds, *Before Sexuality: The Construction of Erotic Experience in the Ancient Greek World* (Princeton: Princeton University Press, 1990);

Eva Keuls, *The Reign of the Phallus: Sexual Politics in Ancient Athens* (New York: Harper and Row, 1985); John J. Winkler, *The Constraints of Desire: The Anthropology of Sex and Gender in Ancient Greece* (New York: Routledge, 1990); Beryl Rawson, ed., *Marriage, Divorce and Children in Ancient Rome* (New York: Oxford University Press, 1991); Susan Treggiari, *Roman Marriage* (New York: Oxford University Press, 1991). For works which compare pagan and Christian ideas, see Kate Cooper, *The Virgin and the Bride: Idealized Womanhood in Late Antiquity* (Cambridge, Mass.: Harvard University Press, 1996); Aline Rouselle, *Porneia: On Desire and the Body in Antiquity*, trans. Felicia Pheasant (Oxford: Basil Blackwell, 1988); Deborah Sawyer, *Women and Religion in the First Christian Centuries* (London: Routledge, 1996); Bernadette J. Brooton, *Love Between Women: Early Christian Responses to Female Homoeroticism* (Chicago: University of Chicago Press, 1996).

For overviews of early Christian attitudes on specific topics, see Eric Fuchs, *Sexual Desire and Love: Origins and History of the Christian Ethic of Sexuality and Marriage*, trans. Marsha Daigle (New York: Seabury Press, 1983); Robin Scroggs, *The New Testament and Homosexuality* (Philadelphia: Fortress Press, 1983); Wayne A. Meeks, *The Origins of Christian Morality* (New Haven: Yale University Press, 1994); Peter Brown, *The Body and Society: Men, Women and Sexual Renunciation in Early Christianity* (New York: Columbia University Press, 1988).

For overviews of certain topics which span the ancient and medieval period, see: Frank Bottomley, *Attitudes to the Body in Western Christendom* (London: Lepus Books, 1979); André Burguière, Christiane Klapisch-Zuber, Martine Segalen, and Françoise Zonabend, eds, *A History of the Family. Vol. I: Distant Worlds, Ancient Worlds* (Cambridge, Mass.: Harvard University Press, 1996); David Herlihy, *Medieval Households* (Cambridge, Mass.: Harvard University Press, 1985); Margaret R. Miles, *Carnal Knowing: Female Nakedness and Religious Meaning in the Christian West* (Boston: Beacon Press, 1989). Ross Kraemer, *Maenads* (note 3) is a wonderful collection of original sources in translation about women and religion in the ancient world, including pagan, Jewish, and Christian material.

For the ideas and influence of Augustine, see: Kari Elisabeth Børresen, *Subordination and Equivalence: The Nature and Role of Women in Augustine and Thomas Aquinas* (Washington, DC: University Press of America, 1981); Margaret R. Miles, *Augustine on the Body*, American Academy of Religion Dissertation Series, no. 31 (Missoula, Mont.: Scholars' Press, 1979); Elaine Pagels, *Adam, Eve, and the Serpent* (New York: Random House, 1988).

Ancient and medieval church attitudes toward contraception have been covered thoroughly in John T. Noonan, *Contraception: A History of Its Treatment by the Catholic Theologians and Canonists* (New York: New American Library, 1965), which also covers the period up to its date of publication. See also John M. Riddle, *Contraception and Abortion from the Ancient World to the Renaissance* (Cambridge, Mass.: Harvard University Press, 1992) and Angus McLaren, *A History of Contraception from Antiquity to the Present Day* (Oxford: Basil Blackwell, 1990), which come to very different conclusions about the effectiveness of contraceptive techniques before the eighteenth century.

Christian attitudes toward homosexuality in the ancient and medieval period have been hotly debated since the publication of John Boswell's *Christianity, Social*

Tolerance and Homosexuality cited in note 6 above. His more recent book, *Same-sex Unions in Pre-modern Europe* (New York: Villard Books, 1994), which argues that there were Christian ceremonies blessing same-sex unions in the eastern Church, was highly criticized. A summary of this criticism from the point of view of scholars hostile to Boswell and a survey of all recent scholarship is Warren Johansson and Willam A. Percy, "Homosexuality," in Bullough and Brundage, *Handbook of Medieval Sexuality* , 155–189. Two works which predate Boswell but are still useful are: Derrick Sherwin Bailey, *Homosexuality and the Western Christian Tradition* (London: Longmans, 1955) and Michael Goodich, *The Unmentionable Vice: Homosexuality in the Later Medieval Period* (Santa Barbara, Calif.: ABC-Clio, 1979). Two recent studies are: Mark D. Jordan, *The Invention of Sodomy in Christian Theology* (Chicago: University of Chicago Press, 1997) and Helmut Puff, "Localizing Sodomy: The 'Priest and Sodomite' in Pre-Reformation Germany and Switzerland," *Journal of the History of Sexuality* 8 (1997): 165–195. Homosexuality in Italian cities of the later Renaissance is discussed in: Guido Ruggiero, *Boundaries of Eros: Sex Crime and Sexuality in Renaissance Venice* (Oxford: Oxford University Press, 1985) and Michael Rocke, *Friendly Affection, Nefarious Vices: Homosexuality, Male Culture and the Policing of Sex in Renaissance Florence* (Oxford: Oxford University Press, 1995) and in an eastern city in Barisa Krekic, "'Abominandum crimen': Punishment of Homosexuals in Renaissance Dubrovnik," *Viator* 18 (1987): 337–345. There are many fewer works specifically on lesbianism; the best survey of this literature is Jacqueline Murray's essay, "Twice Marginal and Twice Invisible: Lesbians in the Middle Ages," in Bullough and Brundage, *Handbook of Medieval Sexuality,* 191–222.

On women's actions and ideas about gender in early Christianity, see Joyce Salisbury, *Church Fathers, Independent Virgins* (New York: Verso, 1991); JoAnn McNamara, *A New Song: Celibate Women in the First Three Christian Centuries* (New York: Haworth Press, 1983); Elizabeth Clark, *Ascetic Piety and Women's Faith* (Lewiston, Maine: Edwin Mellen, 1988); David M. Scholer, ed., *Women in Early Christianity* (New York: Garland Press, 1993).

For the early Middle Ages, see Suzanne Wemple, *Women in Frankish Society*: *Marriage and the Cloister, 500 to 900* (Philadelphia: University of Pennsylvania Press, 1981); Pierre Payer, *Sex and the Penitentials: The Development of a Sexual Code, 550–1150* (Toronto: University of Toronto Press, 1984); Mary Condren, *The Serpent and the Goddess: Women, Religion and Power in Celtic Ireland* (San Franciso: Harper and Row, 1989); Paul Veyne, ed., *A History of Private Life I: From Pagan Rome to Byzantium*, trans. Arthur Goldhammer (Cambridge, Mass.: Harvard University Press, 1987); Jane Tibbetts Schulenburg, *Forgetful of their Sex: Female Sanctity and Society, ca. 500–1100* (Chicago: University of Chicago Press, 1998).

There is an enormous amount of literature on sex and western Christianity during the high and late Middle Ages; the bibliographies and research guides noted above provide good entries into it. Some good general essay collections are: Vern L. Bullough and James A. Brundage, eds, *Sexual Practices and the Medieval Church* (Buffalo, NY: Prometheus Books, 1982); Joyce Salisbury, ed., *Sex in the Middle Ages: A Book of Essays* (New York: Garland, 1991); Clare Lees, ed., *Medieval*

Masculinities: Regarding Men in the Middle Ages (Minneapolis: University of Minnesota Press, 1994); Karma Lochrie, Peggy McCracken, and James A. Schulz, eds, *Constructing Medieval Sexuality* (Minneapolis: University of Minnesota Press, 1996) and the collections by Murray/Eisenbichler and Fradenburg/Freccero noted in the Introduction. Recent studies of specific issues include: Pierre Payer, *The Bridling of Desire: Views of Sex in the Later Middle Ages* (Toronto: University of Toronto Press, 1993); Christopher N.L. Brooke, *The Medieval Idea of Marriage* (Oxford: Clarendon Press, 1994); Dyan Eliott, *Spiritual Marriage: Sexual Abstinence in Medieval Wedlock* (Princeton: Princeton University Press, 1993); George Duby, *Love and Marriage in the Middle Ages*, trans. Jane Dunnett (Chicago: University of Chicago Press, 1994); John Baldwin, *The Language of Sex: Five Voices from Northern France around 1200* (Chicago: University of Chicago Press, 1994); Valerie Hotchkiss, *Clothes Make the Man: Female Cross-Dressing in Medieval Europe* (New York: Garland, 1996).

The most important work regarding canon law and sex is James A. Brundage, *Law, Sex, and Christian Society in Medieval Europe* (Chicago: University of Chicago Press, 1987). Brundage has also written a concise history of the development of canon law, *Medieval Canon Law* (London: Longman, 1995) and many of his most important articles have been collected in *Sex, Law and Marriage in the Middle Ages* (London: Variorum, 1993). For detailed analysis of the canonists on the issue of women's enclosure, see Elizabeth Makowski, *Canon Law and Cloistered Women: Periculoso and Its Commentators 1298–1545* (Washington, DC: Catholic University of America Press, 1997). On the actual workings of church courts, see Richard Helmholz, *Marriage Litigation in Medieval England* (Cambridge: Cambridge University Press, 1974); Richard M. Wunderli, *London Church Courts and Society on the Eve of the Reformation* (Cambridge, Mass.: Harvard University Press, 1981); Michael M. Sheehan, *Marriage, Family and Law in Medieval Europe: Collected Studies,* ed. James K. Farge (Toronto: University of Toronto Press, 1996). Sheehan and others have addressed issues regarding the relationship between canon law and medieval European marital patterns in "Legal Systems and Family Systems: Jack Goody Revisited," in *Continuity and Change* 6:3 (1991): 293–364. Their essays generally criticize a widely debated thesis put forward by the anthropologist Jack Goody in *The Development of the Family and Marriage in Europe* (Cambridge: Cambridge University Press, 1983), which proposes the church encouraged a larger circle of prohibited marriage partners in order to break apart large landed families who had often intermarried, thus making them more likely to give their land and wealth to the church.

On sexual relations between Christians and non-Christians, see James Brundage, "Intermarriage between Christians and Jews in Medieval Canon Law," *Jewish History* 3 (1988): 25–40 and "Prostitution, Miscegenation and Sexual Purity in the First Crusade," in P. Edbury, ed., *Crusade and Settlement* (Cardiff: University College Cardiff Press, 1985), 57–65; Mark Meyerson, *The Muslims of Valencia in the Age of Fernando and Isabel: Between Coexistence and Crusade* (Berkeley: University of California Press, 1991), 221–223, 250–251; John Boswell, *The Royal Treasure: Muslim Communities under the Crown of Aragon in the Fourteenth Century* (New Haven: Yale University Press, 1977), 344–353; Nirenberg, *Communities* (note 9).

On prostitution, see: Leah Lydia Otis, *Prostitution in Medieval Society: The History of an Urban Institution in Languedoc* (Chicago: University of Chicago Press, 1985); Jacques Rossiaud, *Medieval Prostitution,* trans. Lydia G. Cochrane (Oxford: Basil Blackwell, 1988); Ruth Mazo Karras, *Common Women: Prostitution and Sexuality in Medieval England* (New York: Oxford University Press, 1996). Karras's book in particular analyzes prostitution from the point of view of attitudes toward female sexuality in general. For Muslim prostitution in Christian Spain, see Mark D. Meyerson, "Prostitution of Muslim Women in the Kingdom of Valencia: Religious and Sexual Discrimination in a Medieval Plural Society," in M. Chiat and Katherine Reyerson, eds, *The Medieval Mediterranean: Cross-Cultural Contacts* (St Cloud, Minn.: North Star Press of St Cloud, 1988), 87–96.

Two studies which relate medieval treatment restrictions of sexuality to other types of marginalization are: R.I. Moore, *The Formation of a Persecuting Society: Power and Deviance in Western Europe, 950–1250* (Oxford: Basil Blackwell, 1987) and Jeffrey Richards, *Sex, Dissidence and Damnation: Minority Groups in the Middle Ages* (London: Routledge, 1990). For studies of related issue which have implications for the control of sexuality in western Europe, see: Georges Duby, ed., *A History of Private Life: II: Revelations of the Medieval World*, trans. Arthur Goldhammer (Cambridge, Mass.: Harvard University Press, 1988); Joan Cadden, *Meanings of Sex Differences in the Middle Ages: Medicine, Science, and Culture* (Cambridge: Cambridge University Press, 1993); Caroline Walker Bynum, *Jesus as Mother: Studies in the Spirituality of the High Middle Ages* (Berkeley: University of California Press, 1982) and *Fragmentation and Redemption: Essays on Gender and the Human Body in Medieval Religion* (New York: Zone Books, 1991); Thomas N. Tentler, *Sin and Confession on the Eve of the Reformation* (Princeton: Princeton University Press, 1977); JoAnn Kay McNamara, *Sisters in Arms: Catholic Nuns Through Two Millennia* (Cambridge: Harvard University Press, 1996).

Sexuality in Byzantium and in Eastern Orthodoxy has just begun to be studied, and there are very few works available in any language. In English they include: Eve Levin, *Sex and Society in the World of the Orthodox Slavs, 900–1700* (Ithaca: Cornell University Press, 1989) and "Sexual Vocabulary in Medieval Russia," in Jane T. Costlow, Stephanie Sandler, and Judith Vowles, eds, *Sexuality and the Body in Russian Culture* (Stanford: Stanford University Press, 1993), 41–52; Angeliki E. Laiou, *Gender, Society, and Economic Life in Byzantium* (London: Variorum, 1992) and *Consent and Coercion to Sex and Marriage in Ancient and Medieval Societies* (Washington DC: Dumbarton Oaks Resarch Library, 1993). Byzantine eunuchs are discussed in Peter Brown, *Body and Society,* Kathryn M. Ringrose, "Living in the Shadows: Eunuchs and Gender in Byzantium," in Gilbert Herdt, ed., *Third Sex, Third Gender: Beyond Sexual Dimorphism in Culture and History* (New York: Zone Books, 1994), 85–110 and Shaun F. Tougher, "Byzantine Eunuchs: An Overview," in Liz James, ed., *Women, Men and Eunuchs: Gender in Byzantium* (London: Routledge, 1997), 168–184; this last collection also has articles which touch on other aspects of Byzantine sexuality. A recent survey of Russian women's history includes discussion of sexual issues: Natalia Pushkareva, *Women in Russian History: From the Tenth to the Twentieth Century,* trans. Eve Levin (Armonk, NY: M.E. Sharpe, 1997).

Woodcut illustration of the Whore of Babylon riding the seven-headed beast, from the Revelation to John 17, in a 1522 New Testament translated by Martin Luther. The illustration is from the workshop of Lucas Cranach, and links sexuality, the end of the world, and the papacy by depicting the Whore of Babylon in a papal tiara carrying a chalice.

PROTESTANTISM IN EUROPE

PROTESTANTISM IN EUROPE

DURING THE LATER Middle Ages, a number of groups and individuals increasingly criticized many aspects of western Christianity, including doctrines they judged to have no Biblical basis, institutions such as the papacy or church courts, the tax collection methods and fiscal policies of the church, the ways in which priests and higher officials were chosen, and the worldliness and morals of priests, monks, nuns, bishops, and the pope. Various measures were suggested to reform institutions, improve clerical education and behavior, and even alter basic doctrines, and occasionally these reform efforts were successful on a local level; in several instances reform movements led to dissident groups breaking with the Roman Church.

All of this dissatisfaction did not lead to dramatic changes in the structure of western Christianity, however, until about 1520, when the criticisms of Martin Luther, a professor of theology at the university of Wittenberg in Germany, sparked a widespread revolt against the Roman Church. Luther and other thinkers in German-speaking Europe, such as Ulrich Zwingli at Zurich in Switzerland, rejected many basic doctrines of the medieval church, such as the importance of good works, the authority of the papacy, and the importance of tradition. Their ideas were attractive to a large number of intellectual and political leaders, who broke with the Roman Church and established their own local churches, churches which came to be labeled "Protestant" after a 1529 document issued by princes who followed Luther protesting an order that they give up their religious innovations.

Protestant ideas spread beyond Germany, and by the 1530s much of northern Europe, including England and the Scandinavian countries, had broken with Catholicism. The Reformation in England initially came about because of personal and dynastic issues involving King Henry VIII, but eventually England adopted doctrines and institutions that were similar to those of Lutheran Germany and Scandinavia. In the 1530s, the ideas of John Calvin, the Protestant reformer of Geneva in Switzerland, began to spread to France and eastern Europe, and significant Protestant minorities developed in France, Hungary, and Poland. Calvin's ideas also influenced John Knox, the reformer in Scotland, and Scotland adopted a Calvinist version of Protestantism in the 1550s, which Scottish settlers took to Ireland later in the century. During these decades a great many other individuals and groups developed their own versions of Christianity, some of which included radical doctrines such as communal ownership of property or a rejection of infant baptism; both Catholics and more conservative Lutherans and Calvinists opposed these radicals and at times suppressed and persecuted them, cooperating with secular authorities, who saw them as a threat to political and social order.

The Protestant Reformation was not simply a theological movement, however, but also one which involved political, economic, and social issues. Many of the leaders who accepted Lutheran or Calvinist teachings did so in part out of desires to end the economic and political power of the papacy in their territories, or, in Germany, to oppose the power of the Holy Roman Emperor, who remained a Catholic. Peasants in Germany in the 1520s attached Lutheran demands for the local election of clergy and preaching the "pure Gospel" to their economic grievances, and were bitter when Luther opposed them in the subsequent Peasants' War. Nobles in France who accepted Calvinism saw this as a way to combat the power of the monarchy as well as the papacy, and Henry VIII clearly recognized that a confiscation of church property in England would swell the royal treasury.

Along with power and money, sex was an integral part of the Protestant Reformation from its beginning. One of Luther's earliest treatises attacked the value of vows of celibacy, and argued that marriage was the best Christian life; Luther followed his words by deeds and in 1525 married a nun who had fled her convent, Katherine von Bora. Both Zwingli and Calvin regarded the regulation of sexual activities as just as important as the regulation of doctrine, and established special courts to handle marriage and morals cases, which came to have wide powers; the motto of one of these courts was "discipline is the sinews of the church."[1] Many of the radical groups developed distinctive ideas of the proper sexual life for their members, and punished those who did not follow their rules with complete social ostracism, termed shunning or banning. Since Protestant theology expected good works as the fruit of saving faith, one's sexual activities – and those of one's neighbors – continued to be important in God's eyes, and order and morality were a mark of divine favor.

In a number of matters regarding sexuality, Protestants did not break sharply with medieval tradition. They differed little from Catholics in regard to basic concepts such as the roots and proper consequences of gender differences, or the differences between "natural" and "unnatural" sexual practices. Though Luther flamboyantly rejected canon law – publicly burning canon law books before the students of the University of Wittenberg at one point – it eventually formed the legal basis of much Protestant law regarding marriage and sex. Breaking with tradition in terms of the power of the papacy or the meaning of key rituals turned out to be easier than breaking with tradition in terms of sexual and gender relations. Protestants also did not reject, and in some cases strengthened, the intellectual authority of early Church Fathers such as Augustine who had been most influential in establishing western Christian hostility to, or ambivalence about, sexuality. Both Protestants and Catholics tried and executed thousands of people, mostly women, for witchcraft during the early modern period, a panic resulting in part from notions of human and demonic sexuality shared by most people.

This Protestant continuity with medieval Catholicism, combined with the actions of the Catholic Church after the Protestant Reformation, has led some scholars of sex in post-Reformation Europe to emphasize the similarities rather than differences among Christian demoninations. The processes of social disciplining and confessionalization discussed in the Introduction included Catholic, Lutheran, Anglican, and Calvinist authorities, who generally worked with secular political authorities in an attempt to teach people the basics of their version of Christianity and get them to live a pious and moral life.

The recent scholarly emphasis on the similarities between Protestants and Catholics in the twin processes of social disciplining and confessionalization is in part a reaction against older scholarship which highlighted denominational differences. In part it is also a result of the passage of time since the Reformation, for in hindsight long-term continuities become more visible. Despite similarities and continuities between Protestants and Catholics, however, and also despite wide variety among Protestants in regard to certain aspects of sexuality, Protestant ideas and institutions did differ from those of Catholic and Orthodox Europe. This chapter thus looks only at Protestant Europe, that is, at England, Scotland, and Scandinavia, along with parts of Germany, Switzerland, France, and the Low Countries. Changes within Catholicism in regard to sexuality after the Protestant Reformation were to some degree a response to Protestantism, so Catholicism, along with Orthodoxy (which saw less dramatic change in this period as it did not experience a Reformation) is the focus of the following chapter.

Protestant ideas

The Protestant Reformation is no longer told as the story of Martin Luther standing alone against the world, but Luther's ideas are still central to an understanding of basic Protestant concepts, because his writings were so influential and voluminous. This is particularly true for his ideas about sexuality, for Luther wrote and spoke about sex and related issues such as marriage and women continually throughout his long career. Because he said so much, however, his words often appear contradictory, and there is sharp debate among scholars about how to interpret them.

About some things there is little disagreement. Luther was faithful to Augustine's idea of the link between original sin and sexual desire, but saw desire as so powerful that the truly chaste life was impossible for all but a handful of individuals. Thus the best Christian life was not one which fruitlessly attempted ascetic celibacy, but one in which sexual activity was channeled into marriage. Marriage was not a sacrament – Luther was adamant that it conferred no special grace – but it was the ideal state for almost everyone. Thus the restrictions on marriage which had developed in the Middle Ages should be done away with, and everyone should marry, the earlier after puberty the better. Because sexual desire was natural and created by God, it was a central part of marriage, and marriages in which it could not be satisfied – such as those to impotent persons – were not truly marriages. The centrality of sex to marriage led Luther to advocate divorce in the case of impotence, adultery, desertion, absolute incompatibility, or the refusal of a spouse to have sex; reconciliation was preferable, but if this could not be effected, the innocent party should be granted a divorce with the right to remarry. An even better solution might be bigamy, which Luther recommended as a solution to the marital difficulties of both King Henry VIII of England and Philip of Hesse, a prominent Protestant nobleman. Luther's advocacy of bigamy grew out of his harsh condemnation of all sex outside of marriage, including prostitution, one of the few issues on which he explicitly broke with Augustine. (Many people were scandalized by this advocacy, and actual bigamists were harshly punished throughout Europe.)

Those who view Luther in a positive light point out that his championing of marriage and denial of the value of celibacy raised the status of married people – the vast majority of the population – and made them no longer second-class Christians. For Luther, marital sex was a positive good in itself and not simply because it led to procreation; sex increased affection between spouses, and promoted harmony in domestic life. Refusal to have sexual relations within marriage constituted grounds for divorce, and "although Christian married folk should not permit themselves to be governed by their bodies in the passion of lust . . . neither should [they] pay attention to holy days or work days, or other physical considerations."[2]

Those who view Luther in a negative light point out that this emphasis on marriage may have led to greater suspicion of unmarried persons – always a significant minority in Europe – and particularly of unmarried women, whom he and many other sixteenth-century commentators saw as tempting men to give in to sexual desire:

> For girls, too, are aware of this evil [lust] and if they spend time in the company of young men, they turn the hearts of these young men in various directions to entice them to love, especially if the youths are outstanding because of their good looks and strength of body. Therefore it is often more difficult for the latter to with-stand such enticements than to resist their own lusts.[3]

Though marriage was not a sacrament for Luther and other Protestants, it was the cornerstone of society, the institution on which all other institutions were based. As such, it was not to be entered into lightly. Most Protestant thinkers regarded the consent of parents and a public ceremony as required for a valid marriage, and broke with Catholic doctrine that the consent of the parties alone could be sufficient. Weddings themselves were to be celebrated solemnly and reverently, without wild drinking or jokes and rituals which celebrated and satirized the sexual aspects of marriage. Though Luther himself blessed several wedding beds, this practice was generally discouraged by Protestants, as were "superstitious" practices involving fertility, such as throwing grain or untying knots. (Tying knots was a common magical practice thought to create impotence in men.) Joint prayer should replace friendly toasting and singing as the final activity of the spouses before entering the marriage bed for the first time. After the wedding, the couple should settle into quiet domesticity, with the husband the clear household head, exercising authority over his wife, children, and servants. In this role as the head of society's smallest unit of government (later Puritan Protestants termed the household the "little commonwealth"), men were guided by a flood of literature describing the ideal male head of household (termed in German *Hausväterliteratur*) which poured from the pens of Protestant pastors.

Calvin agreed with Luther in simultaneously rejecting the sacramentality of marriage and praising its God-given nature, although he was more guarded than Luther on the virtue of marital sex; married persons should "be recalled to measure and modesty so as not to wallow in extreme lewdness," an idea which later English Puritans referred to as "matrimonial chastity."[4] The Puritan writer Robert Cleaver warned of the consequences of such behavior:

Christians therefore must know that when men and women raging with boiling lust meet together as brute beasts, having no other respect than to satisfy their carnal concupiscence, when they make no conscience to sanctify the marital bed with prayer, when they have no care to increase the church of Christ . . . it is the just judgment of God to send them either monsters or fools, or else such as . . . one most wicked, graceless and profane persons.[5]

As Cleaver makes clear, though procreation was not the only reason for marital sex, in no case should partners practice active contraception; Calvin agreed, terming coitus interruptus "monstrous" in his commentary on Genesis. Calvin condemned those who sought to impose on marriage restrictions that had no Biblical base and accepted divorce in cases of adultery (he saw desertion as a type of adultery), though he advocated attempts at reconciliation first. Like Luther, he based his acceptance of divorce on the words of Jesus in Matthew (19: 9 and 4: 26, "Every one who divorces his wife, except on the ground of adultery, makes her an adultress"). He also stringently opposed all extra-marital sex, though his language in regard to prostitution is milder than Luther's; while Luther termed prostitutes "stinking . . . tools of the devil", Calvin thought they might be useful as negative examples for pious Christians who might be inspired after seeing prostitutes to reform their own lives.

Luther, Zwingli, Calvin, and Knox, along with a number of other reformers throughout Europe, are usually termed "magisterials" because they believed that the church should work with the state and its officials. ("Magistrates" was the common term for rulers and officials of all types.) As noted above, the Protestant Reformation also had a radical wing, individuals and groups who taught that church and state should be separate and that individuals should be free to follow whatever religious ideas they chose. These radical groups, most of which were quite small, developed widely differing ideas on a number of things, but they generally rejected anything they claimed was not Biblical. Thus marriage was not a sacrament to the radicals – some of them rejected the idea of sacraments completely – but many of them placed more emphasis on its spiritual nature than Luther had. Marriage was a covenant – a contract – between a man and a woman based on their membership in the body of believers, and thus was linked to their redemption. Because of this the group as a whole or at least its leaders should have a say in marital choice, broadening the circle of consent far beyond the parental consent required by the magisterials.

The relationship between this marital covenant and the covenant believers had with Christ was a tricky one, however, for radicals who were sometimes confronted with the very real problem of one spouse deciding to leave the group or not living up to expected standards of behavior while the other was faithful. Did a spouse's deviation, either in terms of conduct or doctrine, give the other spouse the right of divorce? This was a question which the magisterials had also addressed, and their answer had been uniformly no – even if a spouse became a Muslim or a Jew (to say nothing of a different denomination of Christian) all one could do was pray and attempt to convert him or her. Some of the radicals, however, used Paul's words in Corinthians to advocate divorce of non-believers, a position termed the Pauline Privilege. (1 Corinthians 7: 15: "But if the unbelieving partner desires to separate, let it be so; in such a case the brother or sister is not bound.")

This divorce was to be followed by a quick remarriage to a believer, however, a policy which in one case led to enforced polygamy. In 1534–1535, a group of Anabaptist radicals assumed power in the German city of Münster. Large numbers of Lutheran and Calvinist men left the city, leaving their wives to guard their possessions, and more Anabaptist women than men immigrated. The city's religious leaders decided that God's command to be fruitful and multiply justified polygamy and ordered all women to marry Anabaptists, nullifying earlier marriages; those who resisted were imprisoned and some executed, as was a woman who proposed a corresponding polyandry. The Münsterites emphasized the importance of the male seed in procreation – an idea they linked to their understanding of the nature of Christ which denied that Mary had any role in creating even his human nature – and of male dominance on earth; in the words of Bernhard Rothmann, one of their leaders, "God wants to create something new on earth, the men shall no longer be as women [effeminate] . . . so here among us he put all women in obedience to men, so that all of them, young and old, must let themselves be ruled by men according to God's word."[6]

A few of the radical groups spiritualized sexuality along with marriage, emphasizing the goodness of all aspects of human sexuality, including the sexual organs and intercourse. A small German group called the Dreamers, for example, saw intercourse simply as obedience to God's command to "be fruitful and multiply," rather than linking it to disobedience and sin. In the eighteenth century, the Moravians sang hymns to Jesus' penis and Mary's breasts and uterus; their idea of Mary's role differed sharply from that of the Münsterites. The leader of the Moravians, Count Nikolaus Zinzendorf (1700–1760), defended their hymns by asserting that shame about Jesus' or Mary's sexual organs was a denial of the full humanity of Christ. (The relationship between the divine and human natures in Christ was hotly debated in the early church, with the final decision that Christ was both fully human and fully divine; this doctrine of the Incarnation was accepted in Orthodoxy and Roman Catholicism, and by most Protestants.)

Although most radical groups, including the Moravians, developed stringent sexual and moral rules for their members, there were also a few who regarded the Christian message as giving them an inner light which freed them from existing religious and secular law. This position, termed *antinomianism*, occasionally led groups such as the Ranters in seventeenth-century England to proclaim "What act soever is done by thee in light and love, is light and lovely, though it be that act called adultery . . . No matter what Scripture, saints, or churches say, if that within thee do not condemn thee, thou shalt not be condemned."[7] It only very rarely led to any long-term sexual experimentation or break with traditional marriage patterns in Europe, though radical groups which developed slightly later in North America did institute major changes, as we will see in Chapter 6. In Europe the few sexual deviations of the radicals were primarily significant for the propaganda material they provided for both Catholics and magisterial Protestants. The single incident at Münster, for example, was used for decades as a justification for grisly torture and executions of radicals of all types, and groups such as the Ranters caused those in power in England during the Civil War period to pass stringent laws about adultery, profanity, and religious nonconformity.

Protestant institutions

It was not only the threat of the radicals that evoked harsh response on the part of magisterial reformers, but the failings of their own parishioners and neighbors. Luther's very early writings emphasize the need to throw off the shackles of canon law (it is at this point that he burned law books), but by 1525 it was clear to him and other reformers that simply preaching the Gospel was not going to get people to change their ways or create a godly society. The reformers advocated the establishment of courts which would regulate marriage and morals, wrote ordinances regulating marriage and other matters of sexual conduct, and worked closely with the secular rulers in their area, whether city councils or princes. In order to make sure the ordinances were being followed and determine what other measures were necessary, church and state officials often conducted joint investigations termed visitations, in which they questioned pastors, teachers, and lay people about their religious and moral life. These institutions and activities reflected the values and aims of both religious and political elites, each of which regarded marriage and moral order *(Zucht)* as essential to a stable society.

The first Protestant court was the marriage court *(Ehegericht)* in Zurich, established by Zwingli in 1525, which served as a model for similar courts in many other Swiss and German cities. In Zurich and elsewhere, some of the judges were clergy and some of them were members of the city council;

none were professional jurists. Most cases were brought by private parties, with the judges gathering evidence and examining witnesses, and then arriving at a decision by majority vote. In their early years, the majority of cases in Protestant marriage courts involved disputed marriage agreements, and most plaintiffs were unmarried women who wanted to enforce a marital agreement. In making their decisions, judges slowly applied the new Protestant ideas about marriage: Was there parental consent? Did the wedding take place in a church? Were there witnesses? They also no longer applied the canonical impediments which rendered certain marriages invalid in Catholicism, such as spiritual consanguinity and a previous agreement to marry someone else.

Though the new courts in Zurich and elsewhere were called "marriage courts," and cases involving marriage formed the bulk of their business, they also began to hear cases involving other matters which had been heard by Catholic church courts before the Reformation. These included such subjects as gambling, non-attendance at church, blasphemy, and sexual matters not involving marriage such as fornication and prostitution. In some areas, officials recognized from the beginning that the new courts would have a broader purview than simply marriage, and so used other titles for them, such as consistory. Secular rulers such as those in Saxony and Württemberg in Germany appointed consistories made up of clergy, lay officials, and sometimes professional lawyers. In some areas, such as the city of Strasbourg, the city council refused to allow the clergy to have a voice in these courts, transforming the handling of marriage and morals into a secular matter as early as the sixteenth century. (Strasbourg did allow ministers publicly to shame those they judged guilty of moral lapses.)

The most famous Protestant consistory was that established in Geneva under Calvin's leadership in 1541. Even before the Reformation, the city council of Geneva had jurisdiction over morals cases, though the court of Geneva's bishop could overturn its decisions. The bishop was deposed in the process of the Reformation, but Calvin insisted that a body of both clergy and laymen be established as the guarantor of morals and doctrine, and that it have the power to excommunicate, in other words to cut people off from the church community and ban them from all church services, including burial. The Genevan consistory was made up of the city's pastors and twelve lay elders chosen annually by the city's voters from a list approved by the ministers. The formal charge to its members was to "oversee the life of everyone, admonish amicably those whom they see to be in error or living a disordered life, and, where it is required, enjoin fraternal correction."[8] That "fraternal correction" ranged from scoldings to excommunication; in serious cases the offender could be turned over to the city council, which could use torture and had a wider range of punishments, including execution. (This practice of handing serious offenders over to secular authorities for punishment was generally followed by all religious courts, including the Inquisition, as we will see in the next chapter.) Each of the elders was in charge of one specific district of the city, and could require those suspected of moral infractions or doctrinal deviation to appear before the consistory. Thus cases were not limited to those brought by the parties involved, and included blasphemy, divorce, Catholic practices, magic, witchcraft, heresy, and sodomy. In this it differed little from Lutheran consistories; what made it distinctive was the amount of independent power held by the pastors, and the level of its activities. One estimate finds that in 1569 one out of every fifteen adults in Geneva was ordered to appear before the consistory.

As Calvinism spread into France, Germany, Scotland, the Low Countries, and northern Ireland, ordinances were adopted regulating marriage for Calvinist Protestants and consistories were established to oversee doctrine and morals, which followed various patterns in terms of appointment and membership. In many parts of Germany the consistory was appointed by the ruler, just as Lutheran consistories were, with the pastors and lay members serving only as long as the ruler approved. In France, the Low Countries, and some parts of Germany, the consistories were made up of pastors and elected lay elders – as in Geneva – but they often did not have the power to excommunicate and had to rely on voluntary compliance. In many of these areas, only a part of the population was Calvinist, so that the consistory did not have jurisdiction over the whole population as it did in Geneva, but only over church members. Consistories outside of Geneva were often arranged in a hierarchy, ranging from those with jurisdiction over only a single congregation to those with jurisdiction over a larger area (often called a synod, presbytery, or classis) which also served as a court of appeal; in some areas, such as Scotland and northern Ireland, there was also a national body which served as the ultimate court of appeal. These courts heard a wide range of cases and their focus varied over the years, but in general between 30 and 80 percent of their cases involved sex. Offenders were required to confess openly before the consistory, and often before their home congregations as well; those who professed innocence were rare, and were generally subject to elaborate oaths of compurgation before the court or the entire congregation.

Calvinist consistories everywhere vied with secular courts in asserting jurisdiction over certain types of cases, particularly those that involved property or serious crimes; their authority slowly diminished in many places during the seventeenth century. In Scotland, for example, secular commissary courts increasingly heard marriage and divorce cases, with church courts only providing advice. Though this might seem a clear example of secularization, it was balanced in many places by the criminalization of religious offenses. Again using Scotland as an example, though the Scots Parliament in 1560 refused to adopt the whole Calvinist Book of Discipline as the law of the land, over the next century or so because of the influence of church leaders, incest, witchcraft, and adultery were made capital crimes, and blasphemy and doing anything on Sunday except going to church were made illegal. (Traces of the last restriction may still be seen in Sunday closing laws which are part of many secular law codes.) Secular courts throughout Protestant Europe imposed punishments for ecclesiastical offenses such as blasphemy, and used methods of punishment for many offenses that were outgrowths of religious rituals of confession, although increasingly punitive in nature; malefactors had to sit on "stools of repentence" listening to sermons directed at them, apologize and confess before their congregations as well as the court, or wear special signs or garments that proclaimed their status as both sinner and law-breaker.

Most Protestant areas, whether Lutheran or Calvinist, went through at least a brief period of disorder and uncertainty during which the authority of the old bishop's courts was no longer accepted, but no new institutions had yet been established. In some areas, such as Scandinavia, this could last for decades. This did not happen in England, where the church courts were not disbanded when Henry VIII broke with the papacy, but simply continued as bodies for which the ultimate authority was the king rather than the pope. Because most of the English clergy became Protestant when their king did, many of the men who had been judges in church courts before the Reformation stayed on. England also explicitly retained canon law, slowly reforming it to fit with royal wishes and English statutes. English ecclesiastical courts ranged from local to national, with the Courts of High Commission run by England's two archbishops given the power to fine and imprison as well as impose religious sanctions such as excommunication. In London, the governors of Christ's and Bridewell Hospitals, which housed illegitimate children and the poor, heard cases involving sexual offenses; the governors handled all types of cases they felt had something to do with poverty, such as instances of prostitution and fornication, and thus had wide powers over all Londoners, not simply the poor. Ecclesiastical courts, along with other church institutions, were disbanded during the period of the Civil War and re-established with the Restoration in 1660, but they lost some of their control over sexual matters to secular courts at that time; when Christian denominations other than the Church of England were granted limited toleration in 1688, the power of ecclesiastical courts was further eroded.

The many radical Protestant groups which grew in early modern Europe also developed institutions to regulate the sexual and moral behavior of their members. In some cases these were bodies of elders to whom accusations were made or who ferreted out wrongdoing themselves, and in some cases the disciplinary body was the entire group or its male members. The Society of Friends (the Quakers), begun in seventeenth-century England by George Fox, developed the most distinctive institution, a women's meeting which oversaw the readiness of candidates for marriage, upheld the maintenance of decorous standards of dress, and at times ruled on other moral issues. The delegates to a Quaker women's meeting in Ireland in 1677, for example, investigated whether any young women "live by themselves which may give occasion of liberty and looseness."[9] Because radical groups such as the Quakers were never an official state church, the strictest punishment they could mete out was expulsion from the group, which was generally reserved only for serious offenses such as adultery or marriage out of the group.

Courts, consistories, and congregations are generally viewed as the main institutions of social discipline and the regulation of sexuality in Protestant Europe during this period, but it is important to recognize that less formal institutions also shaped people's attitudes and behavior. Protestants used some of the same means that had been available to the medieval church to spread their message, such as sermons and plays, and in Lutheran areas artwork and music. In addition, they had a tool not available for most of the Middle Ages: the printing press with movable metal type, which was developed in Germany about 1450. Protestant reformers used the printing press to spread their ideas on all issues; the works of major and minor reformers went through many editions so that thousands of copies were available. Well over half of the materials printed in the sixteenth century, and nearly half of those in the seventeenth century, were religious. Indeed, some scholars argue that the Reformation would not have been successful had there not been the printing press.

From the beginning, Protestant materials were not limited to theological discussions for scholars, but included illustrated single-sheet broadsides (similar to posters), small paperback pamphlets, and cheap – sometimes pirated – copies of sermons, lectures, guides, and stories. In many of these materials, Protestant ideas about the importance of marriage and moral conduct were communicated in simple language with colorful examples and visual illustrations. Stories of heroic virgins were replaced by those of girls who accepted their parents' choice of husband; woodcuts of ascetic hermits overcoming the temptations of lust were replaced by those of pious families praying at dinner, with the mother and girls on one side of the table and the father and boys on the other. In the "housefather books," male heads of household were encouraged to read the Bible and other devotional literature out loud to their wives, children, and servants, so that even those who could not read could receive religious and moral teachings through printed books.

Girls had books written just for them, such as *The Little Flower Wreath of Honor for Christian Girls* or *The Mirror of Virtue for Christian Maidens,* which explicitly encouraged proper morality and sexual behavior.

Books and other printed materials might be read at home, but they could also be found in Protestant primary and secondary schools, which served as important agents of instilling moral discipline and confessional conformity. Though education was nowhere universal, slowly an increasingly large share of the population in Protestant Europe attended school, at least for long enough to be able to read. The primary school curriculum was based on the catechism, which taught basic Christian beliefs, and emphasized morality more than intellectual endeavors, especially for girls. In the words of a school ordinance from Luther's Wittenberg in 1533, the aim of girls' education was to "habituate girls to the catechism, to the psalms, to honorable behavior and Christian virtue, and especially to prayer, so that they may grow up to be Christian and praiseworthy matrons and housekeepers."[10] The aim of boys' education was fairly similar, except for the very few boys who would go on to a secondary and university education (an opportunity not open to girls). Thus from a very young age – at home from their fathers and at school from their teachers – Protestant children and young people were taught the new ideals of marital chastity and sexual morality.

It is of course very difficult to say how well people learned these new ideals, though there is some evidence that they did internalize them. In a few areas, especially among urban Calvinists, church members pressured the consistory to be *more* active than it was, reporting cases of immoral conduct rather than waiting for an elder or visitation to discover them. Specific complaints of neighbors and more general gossip and rumors identifying deviance often preceded official investigations. Though some of these cases may have resulted from people using consistories to settle old scores, they also reflect an acceptance of what had been taught. This learning was never enough to satisfy religious authorities, however, which is why agents of discipline such as consistories and courts were necessary.

Effects of Protestantism

Internalization is just one aspect of the impact of Protestant ideas and institutions that is difficult to trace. In some cases this is because the records are too sparse, but more often it is because they are too full. The records of many church courts, visitation teams, and consistories are extant, but because each of these often dealt with only a small geographic area generalizations can be difficult. This becomes even more problematic when we want to go beyond a simple tracing of trends to understanding the possible reasons for these trends, because each particular jurisdiction was enmeshed in specific political, economic, and social circumstances, all of which could have an influence on the regulation of sexuality. The personal circumstances of rulers – their desire for an heir or their own sexual behavior – also played a role, as did the aims of individual judges or reformers who were sometimes obsessed with certain issues, such as sodomy, witchcraft, or illegitimate births. The sheer volume of court records can also mislead us into thinking we have the whole picture, when what we have, of course, is a picture of activities early modern Protestant authorities judged somehow deviant, written in the language and from the perspective of those authorities. Despite these problems, however, there are certain trends we can trace in the Protestant regulation of sexuality.

Marriage

One of the most immediately visible changes brought by the Protestant Reformation was clerical marriage. Though some late medieval priests had concubines or short-term sexual relationships with women – despite all the attempts of the church at reform – this was still very different from having a wife. Almost all of the continental Protestant reformers married, some, such as Luther, to former nuns. A few of them, such as Andreas von Karlstadt, argued that the clergy should be compelled to marry, though Luther never went this far. In England, the situation was somewhat different, for clerical marriage did not enjoy as much support as it did on the continent. Neither Henry VIII nor Elizabeth I was in favor of clerical marriage, and people sometimes refused to take communion from married clergy. Elizabeth did not recognize the marriages of bishops, and their wives and children were left in a very tenuous position.

On the continent this change happened so quickly that it was often difficult for people to accept the woman and children living in the pastor's house as his legitimate wife and children. Some pastors' wives were still jeered at as "priests' whores," and they had to create a respectable role for themselves, though they had no official position in the new Protestant Churches. They did this largely – and quite successfully, within a generation or so – by being models of wifely obedience and Christian charity, attempting to make their households into the type of orderly "little commonwealths" that their husbands were urging on their congregations in sermons. Whereas priests' concubines had generally been from a lower social class, by the second generation Protestant pastors had little difficulty in finding wives from among the same social class as themselves, a trend which further aided the acceptance of clerical marriage. Maintaining an orderly household was just as important for

Protestant pastors as teaching and preaching correct doctrine, with visitation teams and other officials investigating charges of sexual improprieties or moral laxness just as thoroughly as charges of incorrect doctrine.

Pastoral households were not the only ones scrutinized for moral failings, as church and state authorities attempted to make their vision of orderly households a reality. Orderly households required a proper foundation, so consistories and courts paid great attention to the wedding ceremony and agreements surrounding the wedding. A wedding without parental consent, a public ceremony, or the blessing of a pastor was not simply frowned upon or officially prohibited, as it was before the Reformation; it was not a wedding and did not create a marriage. Until this ceremony, increasingly held inside the church rather than in front of it, couples had no right to engage in sexual intercourse, even if they were formally engaged or had held a private ceremony marking their consent.

This emphasis on the public nature of marriage was not completely new – a public ceremony with a priest had been recommended at least since the Fourth Lateran Council in 1215 – but the vigor of its enforcement was. In England, large numbers of couples were hauled before church courts in the sixteenth century for not solemnizing their engagements with a wedding, and in Germany, laws were passed against secret "dark-corner marriages" (*Winkelehen*).

Parental consent was another key issue. In the 1562 and 1563 marriage ordinances of the Palatinate in Germany, any marriage of a minor without parental approval was "void, invalid and nonbinding," and the man involved condemned as "a marriage-thief [*ehe Dieb*] [who] has dishonestly stolen her, contrary to God and His Word"; those who assisted such couples were to be considered kidnappers and "immediately imprisoned and, according to the nature of their offense, punished without mercy by imprisonment, fine, or banishment."[11] The 1653 Marriage Act passed in England during the Civil War also made parental consent obligatory for minors, although this law was rendered null when the monarchy was restored in 1660. Even children who were no longer minors were occasionally punished for marrying or entering into an engagement without the approval of their fathers, although courts also very occasionally punished fathers for forcing or attempting to force their children into unwanted marriages.

Some of these cases setting parents against children were quite spectacular, with children – especially daughters – physically locked up by their parents to prevent their marrying unacceptable partners. Such cases have provided evidence in an ongoing debate among historians of the early modern family about the balance between family pressure and personal sentiment in spousal choice. The actual number of cases is very small, however, leading many scholars to conclude that the majority of young people seem to have at least accepted the spouse their parents chose for them, or chosen one themselves who was not objectionable to the family.

Parents and family were not the only ones with a voice in one's choice of spouse, however, for authorities often forbade those living within their jurisdictions to marry certain types of people, to marry without their permission, and sometimes to marry at all. Many of these prohibitions predate the Reformation by centuries, for feudal lords in many parts of Europe controlled the marriages of their serfs – or required serfs to pay a fine if they wanted to choose their own spouse – and cities forbade the marriages of servants and the poor as well as those between citizens and non-citizens. Soldiers were often required to obtain the permission of their commander before marrying, and local women were prohibited from marrying soldiers. Underlying many of these restrictions was a desire to prohibit marriages between those perceived to be unequal, whether that inequality was the result of age, wealth, or social status, and to prevent marriages which might produce children dependent on public welfare. Marriages between non-equals were also the target of public rituals of disapproval termed *charivaris*, in which the spouses were insulted and pelted with food, indicating that this was a matter of popular, as well as official, concern.

With the Reformation, a new form of difference received official and popular attention – religious allegiance. Authorities in many areas prohibited their citizens from marrying those of different denominations, although sometimes they made distinctions on the basis of gender. In 1631, for example, the Strasbourg city council, which was Lutheran, considered whether citizens should lose their citizenship if they married Calvinists. It decided that a man would not "because he can probably draw his spouse away from her false religion and bring her on the correct path," though he would have to pay a fine for "bringing an unacceptable person into the city." A woman who married a Calvinist would lose her citizenship, however, "because she would let herself easily be led into error in religion by her husband and be led astray."[12] Reviving decrees that had first been issued as part of the Statutes of Kilkenny in 1366 – designed at that point to keep the Gaelic and Norman populations of Ireland apart – the Irish parliament in 1697 decreed that any Protestant heiress who married a Catholic would lose her property to her Protestant next of kin. Her marriage would be considered treasonous if her husband had not signed the Oath of Succession in support of the English rulers of Ireland.

Despite these prohibitions, however, mixed marriages continued to occur, particularly in areas where Catholics and Protestants lived in close proximity to one another. And despite their disagreements about marriage, both

Protestant and Catholic authorities agreed to recognize the marriage cere-monies of other denominations, a policy which sometimes led people to move until they could find a priest or pastor who would agree to marry them, whatever their own religious convictions were. (This acceptance of marriage across political jurisdictions continues today, which is why couples in the United States travel to certain places for "quicky" marriages and divorces and why proposals to permit homosexual marriage in any one state are viewed with such interest or alarm in other states.)

Once a marriage had taken place, the key aim of religious and political authorities was to keep the couple together. They generally did not inter-vene in any disputes between spouses unless they created public scandal or repeatedly disturbed the neighbors, and attempted reconciliation first for serious cases. These efforts at reconciliation included horrendous cases of domestic violence, in which one spouse – almost always the wife – accused the other of beatings with sticks or tools, brutal kicking, stabbing, or stran-gling. The accused spouse was usually simply admonished to behave better, and only on a third or fourth court appearance might stricter punishment be set. Courts generally held that a husband had the right to beat his wife in order to correct her behavior as long as this was not extreme, with a common standard being that he did not draw blood, or the diameter of the stick he used did not exceed that of his thumb. (This is the origin of the term "rule of thumb.") If the wife had left the household she was ordered to return, though there are cases in many jurisdictions where this eventually led to a wife's death at the hands of her husband. The reverse situation, in which a wife killed her husband, was very rare, but the few cases that did occur fascinated people and were often retold many times in illustrated pamphlets and broadsheets.

Wives were more often charged with scolding and verbally abusing their husbands than abusing them physically, with patterns developing like that in a London household in which,

> he has given her . . . one or two blows with the back of his hand
> upon her cheek by the provocation of the same Margaret [the
> wife] who upon some fault that this respondent [the husband] has
> found with her hath most uncharitably and beyond the bounds of
> modesty called this respondent rogue, rascal, whorehunter,
> thief.[13]

Verbal abuse was punished with fines and public shaming, with special bridles, iron collars and masks, and ducking stools used on women accused of such behavior. Women who slandered people other than their husbands were also punished in this way, with cases of slander forming a large part of the business of many courts. Terms of slander and verbal defamation were highly gender-specific and sexualized; women were almost always called some variant of "whore" and men something which either impugned their own honesty such as "thief" or attacked the sexual honor of their female family members, such as "whoreson" or "cuckold."

Accusations of adultery were taken far more seriously than those of domestic violence or slander, because adultery directly challenged the central link between marriage and procreation as well as impugning male honor. Many legal codes, including the criminal code of the Holy Roman Empire of 1532, the *Carolina Constitutio Criminalis*, defined adultery as a capital offense, and in a few cases individuals were indeed executed for adultery. In 1508 in Nuremberg, for example, a married woman was burned alive for adultery with several partners, and in 1527 in Zittau a woman was drowned for adultery with sixty-three men. During the early 1560s, though there was no provision for the death penalty in the city ordinances of Geneva, several people were executed for adultery, including two men who were beheaded. (The normal method of execution for female adulterers in Geneva, as elsewhere, was drowning.) In many of these Geneva cases the accused were tortured until they confessed, and in most of them additional charges were involved, such as blasphemy, theft, bigamy, and prostitution. This was also the situation elsewhere, for adulterers were generally punished with fines, prison sentences, corporal punishment or banishment; only when their cases involved multiple partners, public scandal, or incest were they executed. The status of the offender generally determined the punishment, with wealthier individuals being fined and told to return to their spouses and poorer ones being banished. Punishments also often involved public shaming; offenders were sentenced to sit in the stocks or on the "stool of correction," or to wear a large stone attached to a choker in a procession or around the market-place.

Social status clearly influenced the investigation and punishment in adultery cases, and gender played a role as well. In contrast to many medieval law codes, sexual relationships between a married man and an unmarried woman were defined as adultery in most sixteenth-century codes, and, as we have seen above, men were actually tried and punished. An adultery law passed in Geneva in 1566 (*after* the executions discussed above) was totally egalitarian in cases of double adultery (in which both parties were married), calling for death for both. On the other hand, adultery by a married man with a single woman did not threaten the family and lineage in the way that adultery by a married woman did, for it could not bring the child of another man into a family. The horror with which authorities viewed this prospect is seen in the double standard which many areas established in adultery law. In the

1566 Genevan law, an adulterous married man and his lover were to be punished by twelve days in prison, but an adulterous married woman to be executed; in the 1650 Adultery Act in England, adultery was made a capital offense for a married woman and her partner, but was punished only by three months' imprisonment for a married man. In Geneva, the punishment set for the lover of a married woman explicitly links considerations of gender and class, for he was to be whipped and banished unless he was a servant, in which case he was to be whipped and executed. Husbands clearly recognized – and shared in – the values of the courts on this issue, for their justifications for severe violence often involve not simply their wife's scolding, but her adulterous or flirtatious behavior.

Divorce

In almost all Protestant areas, the ultimate solution for cases of domestic discord or other serious marital problems was divorce. Following the ideas of their reformers, Swiss, German, Scottish, Scandinavian, and French Protestant marital courts allowed divorce for adultery and impotence, and sometimes for contracting a contagious disease, malicious desertion, conviction for a capital crime, or deadly assault. Some of them allowed both parties to marry again, and some only the innocent. Though a difference in religious beliefs alone never justified divorce, when it was accompanied by a spouse's desertion or refusal to move with the other spouse, divorces were occasionally granted. In 1531 in Zurich for example, a man whose wife had left him and their seven children to join a radical group (telling him "she wished to be obedient to God, and not to the earthly authorities") was granted a divorce, as was an Italian nobleman who became Protestant and migrated to Geneva but whose wife refused to follow him.[14]

This dramatic change in marital law had less than dramatic results, however, at least judging by sheer numbers. In contrast to today, when divorce is a large part of all civil legal procedures, Protestant marriage courts heard very few divorce cases. The cathedral court of Stavanger in Norway, for example, which had jurisdiction over a huge area, granted only 18 divorces during the period between 1571 and 1596, and the city of Geneva only three between 1559 and 1569. In many jurisdictions the annual divorce rate hovered around 0.02 per 1,000 population, and even cities which were hotbeds of divorce by early modern standards, such as Basel, had a divorce rate of only 0.57 per 1,000 for the period 1525–1592, about one-eighth of that of the United States in the 1990s. (The 1993 US divorce rate was 4.7 per 1,000.)

These tiny numbers resulted from a variety of factors. Marriage was the cornerstone of society not only in theory, but also in economic and social reality, and the consequences of divorce could be disastrous. Most spouses, along with most authorities, thus saw it only as a desperate last resort, once all avenues of reconciliation had been exhausted. Even then petitions for divorce might not be granted; in relatively liberal Basel during the period between 1550 and 1592, for example, about half of the cases for divorce heard by the marriage court were denied. The most acceptable grounds for divorce – adultery or desertion – involved the criminalization of one of the spouses, who would be liable for other penalties and who might not be able to marry again. In many jurisdictions the person bringing the suit also had to prove total innocence, not only in terms of his or her own sexual conduct, but also in terms of collusion with the guilty spouse; charging a spouse with adultery to escape an unwanted marriage – a common practice in the United States before the introduction of no-fault divorce laws – was, in the eyes of authorities, to be prevented at all costs. Judges were also on the look-out for collusion in divorce cases based on impotence or desertion, and almost always called for a waiting period during which further attempts at sexual intercourse (in the case of impotence) or at contacting the spouse (in the case of desertion) were mandatory.

The situation in England and Ireland was different from that in other Protestant countries, for the Anglican and Anglo-Irish Churches rejected divorce and continued to assert the indissolubility of marriage. They did allow legal separations (separations *a mensa et thoro* – from bed and board) as the medieval church had, but these were not true divorces as neither of the spouses could remarry; even separations were allowed only for adultery and life-threatening cruelty. The Anglican rejection of divorce led England to be one of the first areas of Europe to develop a totally secular divorce process; beginning in 1670, divorces for adultery were granted by Act of Parliament, a procedure that remained the only avenue for divorce in England until 1857. These Acts were very rare – there were only 16 during the period 1670–1749 – and almost all granted to men; of the total of 325 acts during the period 1670–1857, only four went to women.

Secular divorce proceedings were not limited to England, however, but began about the same time in Lutheran Sweden, where they could be granted by royal dispensation. Church courts in Sweden allowed divorce for adultery and desertion, but the king also began to grant a few divorces for ill-treatment, drunkenness, and severe incompatibility. The number of these was extremely limited, but it marks the first time that grounds other than those mentioned in the Bible were actually used as a justification for divorce, rather than simply discussed as a possibility. Gradually this idea spread to other Protestant areas, such as Prussia and areas under Prussian domination such as Neuchâtel in Switzerland, where first rulers and then consistories began granting a few divorces for cruelty, insanity, banishment, and (in a handful of cases) incompatibility. This liberalization of divorce was always on a case-by-case basis and in many areas it preceded any change in marital law, which still gave only adultery and desertion as allowable grounds. It was part of a gradual secularization of the control of marriage, but it was clearly, though regretfully, accepted by many church officials as well. The Protestant assertion that the best life was one of spousal companionship and marital chastity brought with it a recognition that if these were impossible, the only thing to do was to end that marriage and try again.

Though possible for Protestants, divorce remained difficult and expensive, and many people used other less formal avenues of ending unwanted marriages. They simply moved apart, though this was prohibited by church and state authorities, or one deserted the other, which was particularly common among the poor. In certain parts of Europe popular rituals developed to undo a marriage in the minds of the community, especially if there had not been a formal church wedding to begin with. In parts of England, Wales, and North America, for example, couples jumped over a broom to indicate they were married, and then backwards over the broom if they discovered within a year they could not live together. Occasionally English-speaking areas also saw wife sales, in which a wife was led with a rope around her neck by her husband to a market or fair, and then auctioned off to the highest bidder, who had sometimes been decided upon in advance and was occasionally her lover in an adulterous relationship. The government tried to stop the practice, but the number of known instances – and probably many more went unrecorded – exceeded the number of divorces granted by Parliament. Though such popular rituals of divorce were nowhere accepted by Protestant authorities, Catholic observers occasionally used them to argue against any liberalization of divorce, as one French commentator noted: "Such is the result of schismatic and heretical doctrines of marriage, and this is proved by the fact that in Catholic Ireland, which is ruled by the same government, and under the same civil law as Great Britain, such revolting sales have never been witnessed."[15]

Fornication and illegitimacy

While divorces and wife sales were colorful and scandalous – and so often the subject of popular pamphlets, ballads, and later novels such as *The Mayor of Casterbridge* – the vast majority of cases involving sexual conduct heard by Protestant courts concerned premarital intercourse, usually termed fornication. This emphasis was in part the result of differences between popular and official understandings of the marriage process; while church and state authorities regarded a marriage as complete only after the church ceremony, many people, especially in rural areas, viewed a formal engagement or the signing of a marriage contract as the point at which sexual intercourse was allowable. Thus many of the cases of fornication were actually between individuals who intended to marry or who were in fact married by the time the case came to court. Historians of England have found that between one-fifth and one-half of brides were pregnant upon marriage in the sixteenth and seventeenth centuries, and up to one-half in the eighteenth. This was also the case in Norway, where almost half of first children were born within eight months of marriage.

If the pregnancy was evident before the formal wedding and both parties affirmed that there had been an agreement, a public church wedding was arranged, though the bride did not wear the usual wedding crown and the pair were instructed not to hold a wedding feast (instructions to which they often paid no attention.) They were both generally subject to punishment as well, which might include fines, public shaming rituals, and imprisonment. If the man disputed the woman's claim to an agreement, she or her father could take him to court to force him to marry her, though her chances of winning the case were slim in many jurisdictions.

Cases of fornication might also lead to rape charges, although these were quite rare. To secure a conviction on a rape charge the woman had to prove that she had screamed and made attempts to fight off the attacker, come to the authorities quickly after the incident, and be of spotless reputation. In the minds of some judges, pregnancy disproved rape, as one early modern theory of how conception occurred posited that women also released "seed" upon orgasm; pregnancy indicated the woman had enjoyed the intercourse and thus it was not rape. This notion was not accepted everywhere, however, and a more serious hindrance to bringing a rape charge was the severity of sentence if it was proved. Rape was in theory a capital crime, though this was viewed by many communities as too harsh a sentence; men were instead charged with lesser crimes and punished with fines or brief imprisonments.

Many instances of fornication did not involve either rape or a promise of marriage, and for these the treatment and punishment varied widely. Though in theory men and women were to be treated equally, in fact single men found guilty of fornication were let go with a light fine or simply an oath not to engage in such behavior again. Single women were imprisoned, punished corporally, and sometimes banished, even when no pregnancy resulted, although some reformers advocated milder treatment. (Fornication cases in which no pregnancy was involved were only a small share of the cases, for they had to rely on eye-witnesses and the confessions of the accused to be prosecuted; of the 1,951 fornication cases recorded in the Scottish county of Stirling for the period between 1637 and 1747, for example, only 26 women were not pregnant.)

When pregnancy was involved the matter was much more serious. An unmarried woman suspected of being pregnant out of wedlock was watched, questioned, and sometimes physically examined; those who worked in the same household were questioned about whether she had been menstruating. During the birth, midwives or officials were sent to force her to reveal the identity of the father; in England, midwives were instructed to refuse to assist her until she named the father. In the Swiss city of Neuchâtel, officials warned women about lying, which "would be an unforgivable sin instead of simply fornication"; women's words on these occasions were generally trusted, for the only way a man could deny a paternity charge was for both him and the woman to undergo torture, a procedure which did happen occasionally.[16] In other areas as well, most unmarried men confessed when accused of fathering children out of wedlock, even though this might make them liable for child support. Sometimes, however, the woman refused to name a father, or admitted to having sexual relations with several men, or was known to be promiscuous; in these cases, and in those where the father had left the area, the woman was the only one charged with fornication. (The sexual history of the putative father was never mentioned in court, though that of the mother always was.) By the eighteenth century the balance in fornication accusations in many jurisdictions was between four and ten women for every one man, making fornication a female crime.

The consequences of having an illegitimate child varied widely across Protestant Europe, and were often related more to economic structures and changes than to religious ideology. Areas in which there was a labor shortage were relatively tolerant, including countries such as Scotland and Prussia where one might have expected harsh punishment; unmarried mothers had to do a humiliating public penance, but then they were regarded as purged of their sin and could gain employment. In rural Norway, mothers frequently married men other than the father of their child shortly after the birth.

For many women, however, the economic and personal consequences of a pregnancy out of wedlock were severe. This was particularly the case in pregancies in which the father was the woman's married employer or was related by blood or marriage to her, for this was adultery or incest rather than simple fornication and could bring great shame on the household. Women in such situations were urged to lie about the father's identity or were simply fired; they received no support from the wife of the father, whose honor and reputation were tightly bound to her husband's. Even when the man was accused of rape, his wife would stoutly defend him, asserting, as one village woman did that "he always acted honorably during the 23 years that they have been married, so this person [the pregnant maid] must have seduced him into doing this."[17] A pregnant woman fired by her employer was often in a desperate situation, as many authorities prohibited people from hiring or taking in unmarried pregnant women, and charged them with aiding in a sexual offense if they did.

In situations such as these, women attempted to deny the pregnancy as long as possible and occasionally attempted abortion. They tied their waists very tightly, carried heavy objects, slammed their stomach into walls, or took herbal mixtures which they made themselves or bought from someone with a reputation for knowledge about such things. Recipes for what we would term abortificients were readily available in popular medical guides, cookbooks, and herbals, generally labeled as medicine which would bring on a late menstrual flow, or "provoke the monthlies." Both doctors and everyone else regarded regular menstruation as essential to maintaining a woman's health, so anything that stopped her periods was dangerous. Pregnancy was only one possible reason, and a woman could not be absolutely sure she was pregnant until she quickened, that is, felt the child move within her. As we saw in the last chapter, this was the point at which the child was regarded as gaining a soul to become fully alive; a woman taking medicine to start her period before quickening was generally not regarded as attempting an abortion.

Penalties for attempting or performing an abortion after the child had quickened grew increasingly harsh during the early modern period in both Protestant and Catholic areas. The *Carolina* made aborting a "living" child a capital offense in 1532, prescribing death by decapitation for men and by drowning for women (the methods of execution specified for adulterers in Geneva.) Midwives were ordered that, "when they come upon a young girl or someone else who is pregnant outside of marriage, they should speak to them of their own accord and warn them with threats of punishment not to harm the fetus in any way or take any bad advice, as such foolish people are very likely to do."[18] Abortion was very difficult to detect, however, and most accusations of abortion emerged in trials for infanticide, in which a mother's attempts to end her pregnancy before the birth became evidence of her intent. Contraception was even harder to detect, and though all Protestants opposed it, there were almost no cases in which it was an issue; it was also never a major theme in Protestant attacks on extra-marital sexuality.

Infanticide had always been the method of last resort for desperate women, but during the Middle Ages courts heard very few cases of infanticide as they recognized it was very difficult to tell if a child had been born dead, had died of natural causes, or had been killed. Though there were no improvements in medical procedures or understanding, this reticence about infanticide changed during the sixteenth century, and more women were executed for infanticide in early modern Europe than for any other crime except witch-craft. In some areas it was much more dangerous to be accused of infanticide than of witchcraft; in Geneva, for example, 25 women out of 31 charged with infanticide during the period 1595–1712 were executed, as compared with 19 out of 122 for witchcraft.

With justifications which spoke of a rising tide of infanticide, early modern governments, both Protestant and Catholic, began to require all unmarried women who discovered they were pregnant to make an official declaration of their pregnancy; if they did not and the baby subsequently died before baptism, they could be charged with infanticide even if there was no evidence that they actually did anything to cause the death. This was made law in France in 1556, in England in 1624, in Scotland in 1690, and in various German states throughout the seventeenth century. In some jurisdictions, midwives were ordered to help enforce these laws by checking the breasts of women who denied giving birth to see if they had milk, and at times even checking the breasts of all unmarried women in a parish for signs of child-birth; male heads of household were required to report any unmarried female employee they thought might be pregnant.

Such examinations of the bodies of unmarried women indicate how far early modern governments were willing to go in their attempts not only to stop infanticide, but also to control the sexual activities of those who did not gain the rights to sexual activities through marriage. Sometimes this surveillance, or at least suggestions for surveillance, bordered on the porno-graphic; an eighteenth-century German physician suggested, for example, that all unmarried women between the ages of 14 and 48 should be viewed monthly at a public bath to see if their bodies showed any signs of preg-nancy. Suspicion of unmarried women more often took the form of laws forbidding them to live in inns or on their own, and sometimes even to live with their own mothers if their fathers were not alive. In the words of the Strasbourg city council in 1665, allowing unmarried women to live outside of a male-headed household "causes nothing but shame, immodesty, wanton-ness and immorality."[19] The city council of Wismar in Germany ordered all unmarried women who were not domestic servants to leave town in 1572, noting that these women "pretended to sew in order to have a free life," but really "carried out great lewdness," and in the eighteenth century the city of Neuchâtel banished women for walking around the streets at night.[20] Even domestic servants were not free from such suspicions, for increasing numbers of moralists and pamphleteers in the sixteenth and seventeenth centuries described maids as whores who were out to seduce the head of household or one of his sons, though court records reveal that the reverse was much more often the case.

Unmarried men were also the targets of preachers and moralists, but this was more often for wearing flamboyant clothing, drinking, and rowdy behavior than for sexual activities. Though this might be seen as evidence of a continuation of the traditional double standard, it may also have been the result of men policing their own behavior. Craft guilds often expelled journeymen found guilty of fornication, a punishment the journeymen themselves supported. Indeed, independent journeymen's guilds sometimes became more moralistic than craft guilds or clerical officials. While in the fifteenth century they had organized gang rapes of prostitutes and put great emphasis on sexual prowess, by the second half of the sixteenth they barred members known to frequent prostitutes or associate with women of questionable reputation. Any contact with women, whether in the streets, the shop, or even a marital bed, was disparaged, with journeymen refusing to work next to either a woman or a married colleague. These trends were reinforced by misogynist ideas which rivaled those of medieval monks, but journeymen's hostility to all contact with women is somewhat surprising given the importance of sexual activity in most definitions of masculinity. Their rejection of sex may have resulted partly from journeymen's attempts to distinguish themselves from the guild masters who employed them; for masters, a true man was a sexually active head of household with a wife and children. Thus by not associating with women, journeymen asserted their independence from their elders, though this also may have contributed to their propensity for drinking and fighting.

Church and state authorities were not willing to let guilds be the only guarantors of male sexual behavior, however. (Nor were most unmarried men members of journeymen's guilds.) Along with punishing those found guilty of fornication, they also attempted to restrict occasions which they increasingly viewed as sources of sexual temptation, such as parish festivals, spinning bees (where young women gathered in the evenings, attracting young men for flirting and joking), and dances. Pastors harangued against male clothing styles in which the penis was contained in a separate codpiece, often brightly colored, stuffed to make it more prominent, and worn with a shortened doublet so that everyone could see it; municipal sumptuary laws which regulated the clothing of urban residents sometimes specifically prohibited codpieces. Dancing was attacked in great detail in laws and sermons, such as that of the Protestant preacher Melchior Ambach:

> To the music of sweet strings and unchaste songs people practise easygoing, whorish gestures, touch married women and virgins with unchaste hands, kiss one another with whorish embraces; and the bodily parts, which nature has hidden and covered in

> shame, are uncovered by lechery; and under the cloak of diversion and entertainment, shame and vice are covered.[21]

The most thoroughgoing attempts at restriction of activities judged immoral were in Calvinist cities such as Geneva and Nîmes, where along with dancing the consistories condemned low-cut necklines, cosmetics, certain hairstyles, codpieces, comic plays, games of cards and dice, masquerades, and carnival (Mardi Gras) parties. In Nîmes, dancing proved the hardest to eradicate, with over 1,000 people (out of a population of about 20,000) hauled before the consistory in about 50 years for participating in what one elder called "the devil's pimp."[22]

Prostitution

Along with metaphorical pimps such as dancing, Protestant authorities also combated real pimps and prostitutes. During the period from 1520 to 1590, almost all cities in Germany, first Protestant and then Catholic, closed their municipal brothels, sometimes quietly and sometimes with great fanfare and proclamations against "whoredom" *(Hurerei)* and "procuring" *(Kuppelei)*. In England, the Bankside brothels outside of London, the only legal and protected brothels in the country, were closed by royal statute in 1546. Until very recently, scholars linked this wave of closures to fears about syphilis, which first entered Europe in 1493. Intensive study of city records has shown, however, that leaders very rarely mentioned syphilis as a cause; no one discussed brothel closures at all until several decades after the 1490s, although people realized very quickly that syphilis was spread most easily by sexual contact and associated syphilis with sin.

The harsh language of many reformers about prostitutes and the general trend toward prohibition of all extra-marital sexual activity was clearly more influential than worries about disease in changing the resigned acceptance of prostitution into active opposition to it. Religious and civic leaders increasingly regarded prostitutes as worse than other criminals, for they seduced other citizens from the life of moral order that authorities regarded as essential to a godly city. The closing of municipal brothels did not, of course, end prostitution, and authorities continued to investigate all women suspected of making their living by selling sex. Because many women combined occasional prostitution with other types of wage labor such as laundering or selling at the public market, this concern with "whores" contributed to the suspicion of all unmarried women noted above. The boundaries between prostitution and fornication were not sharp, in the minds of authorities, who charged people with pimping if they arranged any sexual encounter outside of marriage, even if no money was explicitly involved. The figure of the female pimp – the procuress – was portrayed extremely negatively in sermons, popular plays, and ballads, and the word "whore" used metaphorically to describe one's religious opponents; Luther, for example, regularly called Rome a "whore" and English anti-Catholic writers in the 1680s were even more vituperative, terming the Catholic Church "a foul, filthy, old withered harlot . . . the great Strumpet of all Strumpets, the Mother of Whoredom."[23]

Women charged with prostitution were most often so poor that punishment by fine was impossible, so they were imprisoned, punished corporally, and then banished; by the seventeenth century in England this banishment occasionally included deportation to the colonies. Repeat offenders were sometimes executed, especially if they were also involved in other sorts of crime or had previously been banished and had broken their oath not to return to an area. The increasingly harsh criminal penalties did not keep women from prostitution, however, and the religious wars brought about by the Reformation may have actually led to an increase in the number of women – and occasionally men – who made their living at least in part by selling sex.

Sodomy

It was not simply the occasional male prostitute that linked sodomy and prostitution in the minds of Protestant authorities, but also the tendency to lump together all sexuality outside of marriage. Sodomy became a capital crime in both England and the Holy Roman Empire during the 1530s, although the two areas defined it slightly differently; in the empire it included relations between two men, two women, or any person and an animal, while in England relations between two women were not mentioned. Theoretical definitions did not always matter in reality, however, for both church and state authorities sometimes acted without any specific statutes. The Scots Parliament, for example, refused a request from the leaders of the Scottish church to outlaw the vices described in the book of Leviticus in the Old Testament, but courts executed people for sodomy and bestiality anyway, with an eighteenth-century Scottish jurist noting that the authority of Leviticus was sufficient. (Along with adultery in Geneva, this is a good example of law following practice rather than shaping it.) Because it was viewed as breaking one of God's central commandments, sodomy was linked with heresy in the minds of many jurists; one German jurist commented that "such a monster (Unmensch) is called a heretic, and generally punished as a heretic, by fire."[24]

Despite such attitudes, however, the number of actual sodomy cases in the sixteenth and seventeenth centuries was very small, with many jurisdictions never seeing a single case in either ecclesiastical or secular courts. Calvinist areas were more likely than Lutheran or Anglican ones to prosecute individuals for homosexual activity, although the level of prosecution varied widely. In Geneva there were 62 prosecutions for sodomy and 30 executions during the period between 1555 and 1678, while in the Calvinist city of Emden in Germany homosexual cases made up less than 1 percent of all of the cases of sexual misconduct which came before the consistory during the period 1558–1745. The Puritans who ruled England during the period 1640–1660 were much more worried about blasphemy and illegitimacy than sodomy, and there were very few cases, most of which also involved other crimes such as heresy or assault.

This lack of concern about sodomy in comparison with other types of sexual misconduct resulted in part because homosexual relations did not lead to a child who might require public support, and in part because most male homosexual relations seem to have occurred between a superior and inferior, such as an older man and a younger, or a master and servant. The dominant individual was generally married and heterosexually active, with his homosexual activities not viewed as upsetting the social order. This began to change in the late seventeenth century, when homosexual subcultures started to develop in many European cities with special styles of dress, behavior, slang terms, and meeting places; these networks brought together men of different social classes and backgrounds, and did not necessarily involve a dominant and a subordinate partner. In many places homosexual men began to dress and act effeminately, at least in private, with wigs and fancier clothing, and to meet in special houses – termed "molly houses" in England – for sexual relations and socializing.

Authorities occasionally responded brutally when they discovered homosexual networks and subcultures, though the timing of these crackdowns has not been fully explained. During the 1730s, upon (in the words of a Dutch newspaper), "the most extraordinary and accidental discovery of a tangle of ungodliness," authorities in the Dutch Republic carried out a campaign against male homosexuals which involved interrogations with torture and secret denunciations.[25] Perhaps as many as 100 boys and men were executed, and others punished by long imprisonment; waves of persecutions continued throughout the eighteenth century, though the number of executions declined. In London the Society for the Reformation of Manners, founded in 1690 as a private group with a paid staff that would bring complaints regarding drunkenness, swearing, prostitution, and other moral offenses to the attention of authorities, organized raids on molly houses, some of which led to trials and executions. Gradually the link between sodomy and heresy grew weaker in the minds of many authorities, however, and by the middle of the eighteenth century punishments were much more likely to consist of imprisonment or banishment than burning or hanging. Trials or even accusations in rural areas were very rare throughout this whole period, in part because people were unwilling to believe that anyone they knew engaged in behavior portrayed as so monstrous it could not be described. (Sodomy was often termed "the unmentionable vice" and pastors warned that any more concrete description than that might give people ideas.)

Women were not immune from sodomy accusations and trials on the continent, although there were only a handful in all of Europe during the early modern period. In part this was because, in the minds of male authorities, sex always involved penetration, so that female homosexuality was seen as a kind of masturbation. (And though Protestants opposed masturbation, they worried very little about it during this period; the great concern with masturbation began in the late eighteenth century.) The cases which did come to trial generally involved women who wore men's clothing, used a dildo or other device to effect penetration, or married other women. The horror with which they were regarded sprang more from the fact that they had usurped a man's social role than that they had been attracted to another woman. In all of these cases, the woman who had remained in women's clothing received a milder punishment, and in none of them is there any discussion of a lesbian subculture.

Trials for homosexual acts and the development of male homosexual subcultures were urban phenomena in early modern Europe; in rural areas accusations of sodomy were much more likely to involve animals than persons of the same sex. In Sweden, for example, during the period between 1635 and 1754, 1,500 people (1,486 males and 14 females) were charged with bestiality and only eight (all males) with homosexuality. Of those accused of bestiality, at least 500 people were executed, together with the animals involved; bestiality accounted for about one-third of all capital punishment in Sweden, far more than witchcraft. These figures are extremely high compared to the rest of Europe, where bestiality trials usually numbered less than one per decade in most jurisdictions, and the reasons for the Swedish situation are complex. There was clearly no popular condoning of the practice, for most cases were brought to court by watchful neighbors, who later willingly turned in any animals that had been implicated rather than "feel abomination to have such an animal in her house." Both learned and popular opinion linked bestiality with the Devil; as one maid who caught a herdsboy behind a cow stated, "God help you, you have let the devil betray you."[26]

Witchcraft

Other than in Sweden, the Devil in Protestant Europe led far more people to witchcraft than to bestiality. Though exact numbers are impossible to obtain and hotly debated, most scholars agree that during the sixteenth and seventeenth centuries somewhere between 100,000 and 200,000 people were officially tried, and between 50,000 and 100,000 executed for witchcraft. Of these, about 80–85 percent were women, though this percentage varied throughout Europe. Both Protestant and Catholic authorities tried and executed witches, and secular courts were far more deadly than religious ones; the Inquisition, as we will see in the next chapter, was remarkably mild in comparison to central European courts.

The early modern upsurge in witch trials – often called the "Witch Craze" or the "Great Witch Hunt" – is an extremely complex phenomenon which has been the subject of a huge number of studies over the past 30 years. These studies have explored the economic, social, political, legal, theological, and intellectual aspects of beliefs in witches and actual witch trials, and a few have focused specifically on the issue of why most witches were women. They have discovered that in the late fifteenth century the popular stereotype of witches as people who did evil deeds by magical means (such deeds are termed *maleficia*) became linked to a learned stereotype which viewed witches as people who worshipped the devil and did his bidding. Officials and judges in many parts of Europe accepted this learned demonology, which claimed that witches were organized in an international conspiracy bent on overthrowing Christianity, whose adherents flew through the night to meetings called sabbats which parodied the mass, stole communion wafers and unbaptized babies to use in their rituals, and engaged in wild sexual orgies with the devil. Trials often began with neighbors or acquaintances accusing someone of *maleficia;* the accused was then questioned and sometimes tortured to extract a confession and learn the names of accomplices; during this process she (or, more rarely, he) was also accused of diabolical practices, and at this point the investigation could grow much larger; once the primary charges became *being* a devil-worshipping witch rather than *doing* specific evil deeds, many people could be implicated and in some cases hundreds were tried and executed. These trials were conducted using the type of inquisitorial procedure developed in the thirteeenth century, in which all proceedings were in secret and the judge had wide discretionary powers. In areas where diabolism never became an important part of the witch stereotype, such as Scandinavia, the northern Netherlands, or England, mass trials were very rare and the rate of execution was much lower than in places where demonic connections were emphasized.

Learned demonology was created by Catholic thinkers in the fifteenth century, and was brought together in the *Malleus Maleficarum (The Hammer of Female Witches),* written by two German Dominicans, Heinrich Krämer and Jacob Springer, and published in 1486. The *Malleus* not only describes witchcraft, but also guides witchhunters in recognizing and questioning witches; it went through many editions over the next several centuries, was translated into German, French, Italian, and English, and was frequently quoted by later demonologists, both Protestant and Catholic. Though it was not popular everywhere, it was particularly influential in Germany and eastern France, the parts of Europe which saw the most intense outbreaks of the witchcraze. The authors of the *Malleus* are obsessed with sex (even some of their fellow investigators and demonologists thought that they overdid it), viewing this, and not evil deeds, as the key issue in witchcraft. Sex was the reason women were witches, as they tirelessly state: "All witchcraft comes from carnal lust, which in women is insatiable . . . Wherefore for the sake of fulfilling their lusts they [women] consort even with devils."[27]

Demonologists and witchhunters gradually worked out the details of satanic sex, and then based their questioning on the notions they had developed. The devil and his demons were impotent, so they changed first into female demons (*succubi*) and drew as much semen as possible out of men, either by seducing them with a voluptuous appearance or by extracting the semen when the men were asleep or drunk. (Homosexual relations with the Devil appear to have been impossible for even demonologists to imagine.) The demons then changed into male demons (*incubi*) and had sex with female witches, who were attracted to them out of lust; widows and unmarried older women were particularly likely candidates, because women's sexual drive was thought to increase with age. Sex with the Devil was not satisfying, however, for his penis was cold and hard, and so witches also had sex with other demons, with their animal familiars, and with each other. These orgiastic sexual relations left their mark on a witch's body, which was either an extra nipple for the animal familiar to suckle or a place that did not feel pain. Thus many trial processes included a search for extra nipples (which often involved shaving off all body hair) or "witch-pricking" with needles to find insensitive parts. These investigations were generally carried out by a group of male officials – judges, notaries who recorded the witch's answers, the executioner who did the actual pricking or other types of torture – with the witch at least partially naked, so that it is difficult not to view them as at least partly motivated by sexual sadism.

Though learned demonology – with its *incubi* and *succubi*, sabbats, night-flying, and animal familiars – gradually infiltrated popular notions of witchcraft (including our own with its black cats and broomsticks), most trials still began with an accusation of *maleficia*. Many of these also had a sexual component, however, for witches were sometimes accused of causing impotence in men, drying up a woman's milk or menstrual flow, or lessening fertility in women or animals; the witches themselves were described as barren, hard, and dry, unable to menstruate, weep, lactate, or feel either emotional or physical pain. They were also often charged with actions that were the inversion of the nurturing expected of a good wife and mother – poisoning children with food instead of sustaining them, talking back to men instead of obeying them, souring cream rather than turning it into butter. Very often it was women who brought these charges against other women, for they arose in situations which were largely confined to women – food preparation and preservation, pregnancy and childbirth, the care of young children. As one English witch confessed, "she touch[ed] the said John Patchett's wife in her bed and the child in the grace-wife's [midwife's] arms. And then she sent her said spirits to bewitch them to death, which they did."[28]

The timing of the most extreme phase of the witchcraze – from 1560 to 1660 – suggests some link with the Reformation, and historians have pointed out that extirpating witches was regarded by all sides in the religious controversy as proof of their religious zeal. A godly society that could not include fornicators, adulterers, or sodomites could certainly not include witches. Religious differences do not explain very much about witchcraft patterns, however: Calvinist Geneva had an extremely low execution rate (21 percent) while the nearby Calvinist area of Vaud had the highest in Europe (90 percent); the Catholic prince-bishops of Germany sometimes oversaw the executions of hundreds of people in less than a decade, while there is no clear evidence that the Roman Inquisition ever executed any witches. The Protestant ideal of the nurturing wife and mother certainly provided a standard against which deviant female behavior could be judged and found wanting, as women charged with either infanticide or witchcraft (or both) discovered to their peril. That ideal, however, and the corresponding ideal for masculine behavior of the responsible household head who has sex only with his wife and never with maids, boys, or demons, was one that – as we shall see in the next chapter – came to be accepted by Catholics as well.

Witchcraft cases provide the most extreme – and deadly – example of the coming together of popular traditions, learned ideas, and new mechanisms for control; but in many ways all regulation of sexuality in Protestant Europe was dependent on these three factors operating together. The Protestant message about the centrality of marriage to the social order fitted with urban and village values that preceded the Reformation, and Protestant authorities depended on the cooperation of city residents and villagers to report infractions. (Indeed, in an era before professional police forces, there was no other way.) Practices which reformers opposed but which did not upset marriage – such as sexual relations between engaged persons – continued despite all efforts to eradicate them. Protestant authorities did intervene in people's sexual lives more than their pre-Reformation counterparts had, but this inter-vention was largely accepted and supported by most people, for whom appropriate marriages and stable families were a central economic, as well as ideological issue.

This chapter has often referred to "church and state authorities" in one breath because, despite frequent disputes over jurisdiction, the treatment of sexual issues did not differ markedly between secular and ecclesiastical courts. Though some sexual activities merited only religious sanctions such as temporary or per-manent exclusion from communion, in general territorial and national ordi-nances adopted stringent church prohibitions into secular law during the sixteenth and seventeenth centuries. This process has been termed the "crimi-nalization of sin," and in some cases church courts were actually more lenient than secular ones. In the eighteenth century – in England as early as 1660 – eccle-siastical courts lost their jurisdiction over some sexual matters to secular courts, which increasingly concentrated on sexual conduct that had economic conse-quences, such as the bearing of illegitimate children. As this happened, some sins began to be decriminalized; in parts of Prussia, for example, pregnancy out of wedlock was decriminalized in 1765 with the argument that this might lessen infanticide. Such changes were not simply the result of changes in jurisdiction, however, for by this point church courts had already begun to stop prosecution of fornication, though the laws against it had not changed.

This cooperation and agreement between church and state authorities in Protestant Europe may come as no surprise because the Protestant churches throughout Europe were to a large degree state churches, with their officials regarded as state employees and often responsible for political actions such as announcing new laws from the pulpit. (Calvinist churches in some parts of Europe and radical groups such as Mennonites and Quakers were the excep-tions.) The next chapter will allow us to see whether this was also the case where church and state were at least in theory independent from one another.

Notes

1 The motto of the consistory at Nîmes, translated and quoted in Raymond A. Mentzer, "*Disciplina nervus ecclesiae*: The Calvinist Reform of Morals at Nîmes," *Sixteenth Century Journal* 18 (1987): 89.

2 *Luther's Works,* ed. Walter Brandt, vol. 45: *The Estate of Marriage* (Philadelphia: Muhlenberg Press, 1955), 36.

3 *Luther's Works,* ed. Jaroslav Pelikan, vol. 7: *Lectures on Genesis* (St. Louis: Concordia, 1965), 76.

4 The quotation from Calvin is from the *Institutes* 2.8.44, ed. John T. McNeill, trans. Ford Lewis Battles, 2 vols., Library of Christian Classics, vols. 20–21 (Philadelphia: Westminster Press, 1960), 1: 408.

5 Robert Cleaver, *A Godley Form of Household Government* (1603), quoted in Daniel Doriani, "The Puritans, Sex, and Pleasure," in Elizabeth Stuart and Adrian Thatcher, eds, *Christian Perspectives on Sexuality and Gender* (Leominster: Gracewing, 1996), 42.

6 Quoted in James Strayer, "Vielweiberei als 'innerweltliche Askese': Neue Eheauffasungen in der Reformationszeit," *Mennonitische Geschichtsblätter* 37 (1980): 34. Strayer's translation.

7 Lawrence Clarkson quoted in Christopher Hill, *The World Turned Upside Down: Radical Ideas during the English Revolution* (London: Penguin, 1972), 215.

8 Translated and quoted in Richard Greaves, "Church Courts," in *Oxford Encyclopedia of the Reformation*, ed. Hans Hillerbrand (New York: Oxford University Press, 1996), 1: 437.

9 Quoted in Richard L. Greaves, *God's Other Children: Protestant Nonconformists and the Emergence of Denominational Churches in Ireland, 1660–1700* (Stanford: Stanford University Press, 1997), 293.

10 Ordinance of 1533 of a girls' school in Wittenberg, translated and quoted in Gerald Strass, *Luther's House of Learning: Indoctrination of the Young in Luther's Germany* (Baltimore and London: The Johns Hopkins University Press, 1978), 197.

11 *Eheordnung* of 1562 and *Ehegerichtsordnung* of 1563, quoted and translated in Joel F. Harrington, *Reordering Marriage and Society in Reformation Germany* (Cambridge: Cambridge University Press, 1995), 188, 189.

12 Records of the Strasbourg XXI, translated and quoted in Merry E. Wiesner, *Working Women in Renaissance Germany* (New Brunswick: Rutgers University Press, 1986), 20.

13 London Consistory Court Deposition Books, quoted in Laura Gowing, *Domestic Dangers: Women, Words and Sex in Early Modern London* (Oxford: Clarendon Press, 1996), 221–222. Spelling and orthography modernized.

14 Marriage court records of Zurich, quoted and translated in C. Arnold Snyder and Linda A. Heubert Hecht, eds, *Profiles of Anabaptist Women: Sixteenth-century Reforming Pioneers* (Waterloo, Ontario: Wilfrid Laurier University Press, 1996), 41.

15 Quoted in Roderick Phillips, *Putting Asunder: A History of Divorce in Western Society* (Cambridge: Cambridge University Press, 1988), 290.

16 Notary's record from Neuchâtel, quoted and translated in Jeffrey R. Watt, *The Making of Modern Marriage: Matrimonial Control and the Rise of Sentiment in Neuchâtel, 1550–1800* (Ithaca: Cornell University Press, 1992), 103.

17 Prussian court record of 1746, quoted in Ulrike Gleixner, *"Das Mensch" und "der Kerl": Die Konstruktion von Geschlecht in Unzuchtsverfahren der Frühen Neuzeit* (Frankfurt: Campus, 1994), 158. My translation.

18 Memmingen ordinance of 1578, quoted in Wiesner, *Working Women,* 62.

19 Statute of the city of Strasbourg, translated and quoted in Merry E. Wiesner, "Having Their Own Smoke: Employment and Independence for Singlewomen in Germany, 1400–1750," in Amy Froide and Judith M. Bennett, eds *Singlewomen in the European Past, 1300–1800* (Philadelphia: University of Pennsylvania Press, 1999), 197.

20 Quotation from Beate Schuster, *Die freien Frauen: Dirnen und Frauenhäuser im 15. und 16. Jahrhundert* (Frankfurt: Campus, 1995), 399; my translation.

21 Melchior Ambach, *Von Tantzen . . .* , Frankfurt, 1564, fo. B iv–v, quoted and translated in Lyndal Roper, *Oedipus and the Devil: Witchcraft, Sexuality and Religion in Early Modern Europe* (London: Routledge, 1994), 155.

22 A. Rulman, *Harangues,* quoted and translated in Philippe Chareyre, "'The Great Difficulties One Must Bear to Follow Jesus Christ': Morality at Sixteenth-century Nîmes," in Raymond A. Mentzer, ed., *Sin and the Calvinists: Morals Control and the Consistory in the Reformed Tradition,* Sixteenth Century Essays and Studies, vol. 32 (Kirksville, Mo.: Sixteenth Century Journal Publishers, 1994), 88.

23 Quoted in Patricia Crawford, *Women and Religion in England, 1500–1720* (London: Routledge, 1993), 16.

24 Quoted and translated in E. William Monter, *Ritual, Myth and Magic in Early Modern Europe* (Athens: Ohio University Press, 1983), 118.

25 Quoted and translated in Theo van der Meer, "Sodomy and the Pursuit of a Third Sex in the Early Modern Period," in Gilbert Herdt, ed., *Third Sex, Third Gender: Beyond Sexual Dimorphism in Culture and History* (New York: Zone Books, 1994), 141.

26 Swedish court records, translated and quoted in Jonas Liliequist, "Peasants Against Nature: Crossing the Boundaries between Man and Animal in Seventeenth- and Eighteenth-century Sweden," *Journal of the History of Sexuality* 1: 3 (1991): 407, 401.

27 *Malleus Maleficarum,* translated and quoted in Alan C. Kors and Edward Peters, eds, *Witchcraft in Europe 1100–1700: Documentary History* (Philadelphia: University of Pennsylvania Press, 1972), 127.

28 *The wonderful discoverie of the witchcrafts of Margaret and Philippa Flower,* 1619, printed in Barbara Rosen, *Witchcraft in England 1558–1618* (Amherst: University of Massachusetts Press, 1991), 379.

Selected further reading

The reformers' ideas about sexuality are usually presented in the context of their ideas about women and the family or human nature and sin. See, for example, Merry E. Wiesner, "Luther and Women: The Death of Two Marys," (123–137) and Daphne Hampson, "Luther on the Self: A Feminist Critique," (215–224) both in Ann Loades, ed., *Feminist Theology: A Reader* (London: SPCK, 1990); Stephen B. Boyd, "Masculinity and Male Dominance: Martin Luther on the Punishment of Adam," in Stephen B. Boyd, W. Merle Longwood, and Mark W. Muesse, eds, *Redeeming Men: Religion and Masculinities* (Louisville: Westminster John Knox, 1996), 19–32. Susan Karant-Nunn, "*Kinder, Küche, Kirche:* Social Ideology in the Sermons of Johannes Mathesius" in Susan Karant-Nunn and Andrew Fix, eds, *Germania Illustrata: Essays Presented to Gerald Strauss* (Kirksville, Mo.: Sixteenth Century Journal Publishers, 1991), 121–140 discusses the ideas of a typical early Lutheran pastor. Steven Ozment, *When Fathers Ruled: Family Life in Reformation Europe* (Cambridge, Mass.: Harvard University Press, 1983) discusses the ideas of a number of Protestant thinkers, as does Scott Hendrix, "Masculinity and Patriarchy in Reformation Germany," *Journal of the History of Ideas* 56 (1995): 177–193. There is no book-length study of Luther's ideas about women, gender, or sexuality available in English.

For studies in English of the actual process of social disciplining in German-speaking areas, see: Lorna Jane Abray, *The People's Reformation: Magistrates, Clergy, and Commons in Strasbourg, 1500–1598* (Ithaca: Cornell University Press, 1985); James Martin Estes, *Christian Magistrates and State Church: The Reforming Career of Johannes Brenz* (Toronto: University of Toronto Press, 1982); Thomas Robisheaux, *Rural Society and the Search for Order in Early Modern Germany* (Cambridge: Cambridge University Press, 1989); Scott Dixon, *The Reformation and Rural Society: The Parishes of Brandenburg-Ansbach-Kulmbach, 1528–1603* (Cambridge: Cambridge University Press, 1996); several of the essays in R.W. Scribner, *Popular Culture and Popular Movements in Reformation Germany* (London: The Hambledon Press, 1987); R. Po-Chia Hsia, ed., *The German People and the Reformation* (Ithaca: Cornell University Press, 1988); Karin Maag, ed., *The Reformation in Eastern and Central Europe* (New York: Scholars' Press, 1997).

The ideas of John Calvin about women have been the focus of a number of good studies, including Jane Dempsey Douglass, *Women, Freedom and Calvin* (Philadelphia: Westminster, 1985) and John Lee Thompson, *John Calvin and the Daughters of Sarah: Women in Regular and Exceptional Roles in the Exegesis of Calvin, His Predecessors and His Contemporaries* (Geneva: Droz, 1992). As yet there is no similar study of Calvin's ideas about sexuality. The actual impact of Calvin's ideas about marriage and morals has been investigated in: Robert M. Kingdon, "The Control of Morals in Calvin's Geneva," in Lawrence P. Buck and Jonathan W. Zophy, eds, *The Social History of the Reformation* (Columbus: Ohio State University Press, 1972), 3–16 and *Adultery and Divorce in Calvin's Geneva* (Cambridge, Mass.: Harvard University Press, 1995). Kingdon and a team of scholars are preparing a transcription of the handwritten registers of the Geneva consistory for the period 1541–1562. See also Jeffrey R. Watt, "Women and the Consistory in Calvin's Geneva," *Sixteenth Century Journal* 24 (1993): 429–439. For the impact of Calvinist thought elsewhere in Europe, see Michael F. Graham, *The Uses of Reform: "Godly Discipline" and Popular Behavior in Scotland and Beyond 1560–1610* (Leiden: Brill, 1996); Ben Kaplan, *Calvinists and Libertines: Confession and Community in Utrecht, 1578–1620* (Oxford: Oxford University Press, 1995); Greaves, *God's Other Children* (note 9); Mentzer, *Sin and the Calvinists* (note 22).

For an analysis of the thought of other reformers, see: Amy Nelson Burnett, "Church Discipline and Moral Reformation in the Thought of Martin Bucer," *Sixteenth Century Journal* 22 (1991): 439–456; H.J. Selderhuis, *Marriage and Divorce in the Thought of Martin Bucer*, trans. John Vriend and Lyle D. Bierma (Kirksville, Mo.: Sixteenth Century Journal Publishers, 1998).

For the ideas of English reformers, see Kathleen M. Davies, "The Sacred Condition of Equality – How Original were Puritan Doctrines of Marriage?" *Social History*, 2 (1977): 563–580; John K. Yost, "Changing Attitudes towards Married Life in Civic and Christian Humanists," *American Society for Reformation Research, Occasional Papers*, 1 (1977), 151–166; Edmund Leites, *The Puritan*

Conscience and Modern Sexuality (New Haven: Yale University Press, 1986); Margo Todd, *Christian Humanism and the Puritan Social Order* (Cambridge: Cambridge University Press, 1987). For an analysis of social disciplining in England, see Marjorie Keniston McIntosh, *Controlling Misbehavior in England 1370–1600* (Cambridge: Cambridge University Press, 1998).

For the ideas of the radicals, see Joyce Irwin, ed., *Womanhood in Radical Protestantism* (New York: E. Mellen, 1979); Wes Harrison, "The Role of Women in Anabaptist Thought and Practice: The Hutterite Experience of the Sixteeenth and Seventeenth Centuries," *Sixteenth Century Journal* 23 (1992): 49–70; Craig D. Atwood, "Sleeping in the Arms of Christ: Sanctifying Sexuality in the Eighteenth-century Moravian Church," *Journal of the History of Sexuality* 8 (1997): 25–47; Snyder and Hecht, *Profiles of Anabaptist Women* (note 14); Lyndal Roper, "Sexual Utopianism in the German Reformation," in her *Oedipus and the Devil* (note 21).

Changes in legal codes have been discussed in two books by R.H. Helmholz, *Roman Law in Reformation England* (Cambridge: Cambridge University Press, 1990) and *Canon Law in Protestant Lands* (Berlin: Duncker and Humboldt, 1992). For the actual operation of Protestant church courts, see Ralph Houlbrooke, *Church Courts and the People During the English Reformation, 1520–1570* (Oxford: Oxford University Press, 1979); John Addy, *Sin and Society in the Seventeenth Century* (London: Routledge, 1989); G.R. Quaife, *Wanton Wenches and Wayward Wives: Peasants and Illicit Sex in Early Seventeenth Century England* (New Brunswick: Rutgers University Press, 1979); Ronald A. Marchant, *The Church Under the Law: Justice, Administration and Discipline in the Diocese of York, 1560–1640* (Cambridge: Cambridge University Press, 1969). Paul Hair, ed., *Before the Bawdy Court: Selections from Church Court and Other Records Relating to the Correction of Moral Offences in England, Scotland, and New England, 1300–1800* (London: Elek, 1972) provides extracts from court documents, and Ian McCormick, ed, *Secret Sexualities: A Sourcebook of 17th and 18th Century Writing* (London: Routledge, 1997) includes pamphlets about trials, though not actual trial documents themselves.

Three books which explore a slightly later period and directly address issues of sexuality and the state are: Rosalind Mitchison and Leah Leneman, *Sexuality and Social Control: Scotland 1660–1780* (Oxford: Basil Blackwell, 1989), Isabel V. Hull, *Sexuality, State, and Civil Society in Germany, 1700–1815* (Ithaca: Cornell University Press, 1996), and Tim Hitchcock, *English Sexualities, 1700–1800* (New York: St Martin's, 1997).

There are several studies which focus specifically on the regulation of marriage, using court cases and a variety of other documents: Thomas Max Safley, *Let No Man Put Asunder: The Control of Marriage in the German Southwest* (Kirksville, Mo.: Sixteenth Century Publishers, 1984); Martin Ingram, *Church Courts, Sex and Marriage in England 1570–1640* (Cambridge: Cambridge University Press, 1987); Eric Josef Carlson, *Marriage and the English Reformation* (Oxford: Blackwell, 1994); Richard Adair, *Courtship, Illegitimacy and Marriage in Early Modern England* (Manchester: Manchester University Press, 1996); Watt, *Making of Modern Marriage* (note 16); Harrington, *Reordering Marriage* (note 11).

In addition to these studies which explore the control of marriage, there are also many which focus on marriage and the family more broadly, for the early modern family has been a very contentious issue over the past several decades. For an overview of the issues and an extensive bibliography, see my "Family, Household, and Community," in Thomas A. Brady, Jr., Heiko A. Oberman, James D. Tracy, eds, *Handbook of European History 1400–1600* (Leiden: E.J. Brill, 1994), 51–78.

Changes in engagement and wedding ceremonies have been explored most fully in: Susan C. Karant-Nunn, *The Reformation of Ritual: An Interpretation of Early Modern Germany* (London: Routledge, 1997) and David Cressy, *Birth, Marriage and Death: Ritual, Religion, and the Life-cycle in Tudor and Stuart England* (Oxford: Oxford University Press, 1987); see also Lyndal Roper, "Going to Church and Street: Weddings in Reformation Augsburg," *Past and Present* 106 (1985): 62–101 and several of the essays in Robert Forster and Orest Ranum, eds, *Ritual, Religion and the Sacred: Selections from the Annales* (Baltimore: Johns Hopkins University Press, 1982).

The books noted above on marriage all discuss divorce, and there are also several works which focus on divorce specifically: Phillips, *Putting Asunder* (note 15) and Lawrence Stone, *Road to Divorce: England 1530–1987* (Oxford: Oxford University Press, 1990) are both broad overviews. Stone has also written two books of case studies, *Uncertain Unions: Marriage in England 1660–1753* (New York: Oxford, 1992) and *Broken Lives: Separation and Divorce in England 1660–1857* (New York: Oxford, 1993).

Along with being viewed through the lens of marriage, the regulation of sexuality has also been explored as part of the history of crime. Richard van Dülmen, *Theatre of Horror: Crime and Punishment in Early Modern Germany,* trans. Elisabeth Neu (New York: Polity Press, 1990) provides good statistics, while the essays in Jenny Kermode and Garthine Walker, eds, *Women, Crime and the Courts in Early Modern London* (Chapel Hill: University of North Carolina Press, 1994) explore a number of issues, as do those in V.A.C. Gatrell, Bruce Lenman, and Geoffrey Parker, eds, *Crime and the Law: The Social History of Crime in Western Europe since 1500* (London: Europa Publications, 1980). Peter C. Hoffer and N.E.H. Hull, *Murdering Mothers: Infanticide in England and New England 1558–1803* (New York: New York University Press, 1981) and Mark Jackson, *New-born Child Murder: Women, Illegitimacy and the Courts in Eighteenth-century England* (Manchester: Manchester University Press, 1996) examine legal, economic, and social factors affecting women charged with killing their infants or small children, while Ulinka Rublack focuses on the role of the community in "The Public Body: Policing Abortion in Early Modern Germany," in Lynn Abrams and Elizabeth Harvey, *Gender Relations in German History: Power, Agency and Experience from the Sixteenth to the Twentieth Century* (Durham: Duke University Press, 1997), 57–79.

Several studies have paid particular attention to the way women and men portray themselves or are portrayed in cases involving sex and gender relations: Lynda E. Boose, "Scolding Brides and Bridling Scolds: Taming the Woman's Unruly Member," *Shakespeare Quarterly* 42 (1991): 179–213; Frances E. Dolan, *Dangerous Familiars: Representations of Domestic Crime in England 1550–1700* (Ithaca: Cornell University Press, 1994); Garthine Walker, "Rereading Rape and Sexual

Violence in Early Modern England," *Gender and History* 10 (1998): 1–25. Gowing, *Domestic Dangers* (note 13) is the best analysis of these issues from the point of view of a historian rather than a literary critic. Several recent essay collections bring together the work of historians, art historians, and scholars of literature: Robert Purks Maccubbin, ed., *'Tis Nature's Fault: Unauthorized Sexuality during the Enlightenment* (Cambridge: Cambridge University Press, 1987); James Grantham Turner, ed., *Sexuality and Gender in Early Modern Europe: Institutions, Texts, Images* (Cambridge: Cambridge University Press, 1993). Richard Burt and John Michael Archer, eds, *Enclosure Acts: Sexuality, Property, and Culture in Early Modern England* (Ithaca: Cornell University Press, 1994) looks at the setting and enforcement of territorial and sexual boundaries.

The fullest study of late medieval and early modern prostitution is that by Beate Schuster mentioned in note 20, which has, unfortunately, not been translated. See also: Lyndal Roper, "Discipline and Respectability: Prostitution and the Reformation in Augsburg," *History Workshop* 19 (Spring 1985): 3–28; Randolph Trumbach, "Sex, Gender, and Sexual Identity in Modern Culture: Male Sodomy and Female Prostitution in Enlightenment London," *Journal of the History of Sexuality* 2: 2 (1991): 186–203. Peter Spierenberg includes discussion of prostitutes in his *The Prison Experience: Disciplinary Institutions and their Inmates in Early Modern Europe* (New Brunswick, NJ: Rutgers University Press, 1991).

The first major study of homosexuality in the early modern period was Alan Bray, *Homosexuality in Renaissance England* (London: Gay Men's Press, 1982; revised edition New York: Columbia University Press, 1995), which still remains extremely useful, as does E. William Monter, "Sodomy and Heresy in Early Modern Switzerland," *Journal of Homosexuality* 6 (1980/81): 41–53. Since then there have been a number of important essay collections: Kent Gerard and Gert Hekma, eds, *The Pursuit of Sodomy: Male Homosexuality in Renaissance and Enlightenment Europe* (New York: Harrington Park Press, 1989); G. S. Rousseau, *Perilous Enlightenment: Pre- and Post-modern Discourses. Sexual, Historical* (Manchester: Manchester University Press, 1991); "Gay and Lesbian Studies Forum," *Eighteenth Century Studies,* 30 (1997): 289–318. Richard Davenport-Hines, *Sex, Death and Punishment: Attitudes to Sex and Sexuality in Britain since the Renaissance* (London: Collins, 1990) looks at both homosexuality and venereal disease. Randolph Trumbach, *Sex and the Gender Revolution,* Vol. 1: *Heterosexuality and the Third Gender in Enlightenment London* (Chicago: University of Chicago Press, 1998) explores the construction of sexual identities.

Most of the studies in the previous paragraph focus exclusively or primarily on men. Same-sex relations between women have been investigated in: Emma Donoghue, *Passions Between Women: British Lesbian Culture 1668–1801* (London: Scarlet Press, 1993); Randolph Trumbach, "London's Sapphists: From Three Sexes to Four Genders in the Making of Modern Culture," in Gilbert Herdt, ed., *Third Sex, Third Gender: Beyond Sexual Dimorphism in Culture and History* (New York: Zone Books, 1994), 111–136; Rudolf M. Dekker and Lotte C. van de Pol, *The Tradition of Female Transvestism in Early Modern Europe* (New York: St Martin's, 1989). General essay collections which include studies of both women and men in the early modern period are: Salvatore Licata and Robert Petersen, eds,

Historical Perspectives on Homosexuality (New York: Haworth, 1981); Martin Duberman, Martha Vicinus, and George Chauncey, Jr., eds, *Hidden From History: Reclaiming the Gay and Lesbian Past* (New York: Meridian, 1989). The best and most up-to-date bibliography on early modern homosexuality in Europe may be found on the website of my colleague Jeffrey Merrick: www.uwm.edu/jmerrick.

Studies of homosexual and homoerotic themes in early modern literature are appearing at a great rate. See, for example, Jonathan Goldberg, *Sodometries: Renaissance Texts, Modern Sexualities* (Stanford: Stanford Univeristy Press, 1992) and an essay collection edited by Goldberg, *Queering the Renaissance* (Durham: University of North Carolina Press, 1994).

Early modern witchcraft has a huge literature. For an overview of the issues, especially those relating to women, see the chapter on witchcraft in my *Women and Gender in Early Modern Europe* (Cambridge: Cambridge University Press, 1993); this also has a long bibliographic essay. Studies which address the issue of witchcraft and the Reformation include: Sigrid Brauner, *Fearless Wives and Frightened Shrews: The Construction of the Witch in Early Modern Germany* (Amherst: University of Massachusetts Press, 1994); Sigrid Brauner, "Martin Luther on Witchcraft: A True Reformer?" and Allison P. Coudert "The Myth of the Improved Status of Protestant Women: The Case of the Witchcraze," in Jean R. Brink, Allison P. Coudert, and Maryanne C. Horowitz, eds, *The Politics of Gender in Early Modern Europe* (Kirksville, Mo.: Sixteenth Century Journal Publishers, 1989). Two studies which address the issue of motherhood and witchcraft are Lyndal Roper, "Witchcraft and Fantasy in Early Modern Germany," in her *Oedipus and the Devil* (note 21) and Deborah Willis, *Malevolent Nurture: Witch-Hunting and Maternal Power in Early Modern England* (Ithaca: Cornell University Press, 1995). Two studies which link witchcraft with male control of female sexuality are Marianne Hester, *Lewd Women and Wicked Witches* (London: Routledge, 1992) and Anne Llewellyn Barstow, *Witchcraze: A New History of the European Witchhunts* (New York: Pandora, 1994). An excellent critique both of work which emphasizes male control and of that which avoids the issue of gender is Diane Purkiss, *The Witch in History: Early Modern and Twentieth-century Representations* (London: Routledge, 1996). Robin Briggs, *Witches and Neighbours: The Social and Cultural Context of European Witchcraft* (New York: HarperCollins, 1996) provides a thoughtful discussion of the complexities of the link between gender and witchcraft, and also discusses witchcraft within the context of sexual and family relationships. Brian Levack has edited a 12-volume collection, *Articles on Witchcraft, Magic and Demonology* (New York: Garland, 1992); Volume 4, *The Literature of Witchcraft,* includes articles on learned demonology, and Volume 10, *Women, Witchcraft and Society*, includes articles which touch on many of the issues discussed here.

The Glorification of the Virgin Saints, attributed to the Jesuit artist Giovan Battista Fiammeri, and hung in 1600 in San Vitale in Rome, the first permanent Jesuit novitiate for the Roman Province. San Vitale was endowed and founded by Isabella della Rovere, a wealthy Italian noblewoman, and the painting reflects her interest in the topic of virginity. Photo: ICCD, Rome 20262.

CATHOLICISM AND
ORTHODOXY IN EUROPE

CATHOLICISM AND ORTHODOXY IN EUROPE

T HE PROTESTANT REFORMATION divided western Christianity, and was responsible for significant changes in areas which remained Catholic as well. Many historians see the developments within the Catholic Church after the Protestant Reformation as two inter-related movements, one a drive for internal reform linked to earlier reform efforts, and the other a Counter-Reformation which opposed Protestants intellectually, politically, militarily, and institutionally. Reform measures which had been suggested since the late Middle Ages – such as doing away with the buying and selling of church offices (termed simony), requiring bishops to live in their dioceses, forbidding clergy to hold multiple offices (termed pluralism), ending worldliness and immorality at the papal court, improving clerical education, changing the church's tax collection and legal procedures – were gradually adopted during the sixteenth century. Beginning with Pope Paul III (pontificate 1534–1549), the papal court became the center of the reform movement rather than its chief oppo-nent. Paul III and his successors supported the establishment of new religious orders which preached to the common people, the opening of seminaries for the training of priests, the end of simony, and stricter control of clerical life.

Reforming popes also supported measures designed to combat the spread of Protestant teaching. Paul III reorganized the Inquisition or Holy Office, put its direction in the hands of a committee of cardinals in Rome, and gave it the power to investigate those suspected of holding heretical opinions or committing acts deemed theologically unacceptable. One of his successors, Paul IV (pontificate 1555–1559) promulgated an Index of Prohibited Books, which forbade the printing, distribution, and reading of books and authors judged heretical. (The Index was formally abolished in 1966.) Both of these popes served as patrons to what would become the most important of the new religious orders, the Society of Jesus or Jesuits founded by St Ignatius Loyola. Jesuits were soon active establishing schools and colleges throughout Europe and converting areas which had become Protestant back to Catholicism; they also ministered to Catholics in areas under Protestant rule such as England and Ireland, and travelled far beyond Europe as missionaries in Asia and the Americas. In 1545, Paul III convened the Council of Trent, an ecumenical council which met with several breaks over the next 18 years to define Catholic dogma and reform abuses. In terms of dogma, Trent reasserted traditional Catholic beliefs in response to Protestant challenges: good works as well as faith were necessary for salvation; tradition along with Scripture contained essential Christian teachings; seven sacraments were effi-cacious and could usually be administered only by a priest; the Virgin Mary and the saints were to be venerated. The Council of Trent also issued a large number of disciplinary decrees, though these were not accepted in all Catholic areas of Europe as Tridentine dogmatic decrees were. (Regulations from the Council of Trent, held at Trento in northern Italy, are termed "Tridentine" from the Latin name for the city, Tridentum.)

Popes were not the only officials intent both on reforming the Catholic Church and on countering Protestantism. In many parts of Europe, other church officials such as bishops, abbots, or abbesses carried out reform drives to raise standards of education and conduct in the institutions under their juris-diction, and individuals such as St Teresa of Avila (1515–1582) founded new institutions which followed stricter standards. As they had in the Middle Ages, secular rulers also saw themselves as religious reformers and defenders of the faith, supporting seminaries, promoting higher standards of clerical morality, suppressing heretical opinions, and fighting Protestants. The most dramatic example of secular rulers taking the lead was in Spain, where in 1478 the rulers Ferdinand and Isabella established an independent Spanish Inquisition under their control rather than the papacy's, initially designed to investigate the sincerity of Jewish conversions to Christianity. The Spanish Inquisition later investigated a huge range of individuals and activities (including Teresa of Avila for suspected heretical opinions), always answering to the rulers of Spain. In the 1520s Charles V established an Inquisition in the Netherlands, and in the 1530s the rulers of Portugal received papal approval to establish a separate Inquisition there as well. Though the kings of France never established an Inquisition, they, and not the papacy, determined the level of toleration accorded Protestants within their territory; in 1598 Henry IV (ruled 1589–1610) gave French Protestants (termed Huguenots) political and religious rights in a decree termed the Edict of Nantes, and in 1685 Louis XIV (ruled 1643–1715) revoked the Edict of Nantes and declared France a Catholic country.

In some parts of eastern Europe as well, secular rulers also controlled many aspects of church life. With the Turkish overthrow of Constantinople in 1453, many Orthodox Christians lived under Muslim rule, so that the patriarch had greater control over their religous and civil lives than he had had when the Christian emperors were still in power. The limits of Christian independence were set by the Turkish rulers, however, and in other parts of eastern Europe secular rulers had even more authority. The Russian patriarchate was moved from Kiev to Moscow, and in 1589 came under the direct control of the tsar. This level of control was not enough for Tsar Peter the Great, who in 1721 abolished the patriarchate and established a synod which he controlled as the ultimate voice of authority in the the Russian Orthodox Church. Eastern Orthodoxy did not see a dramatic split in the sixteenth century as the Western Church did, but it was affected by movements of moral reform.

Whether the impetus came from the papacy or from other church and secular officials, regulating the sexual lives of both clergy and lay people was a key part of Catholic (and to a lesser degree, Orthodox) reform moves which began in the sixteenth century. Both clergy and laity had to be taught correct doctrine on matters of sexual and marital conduct, so that sexual issues became a central part of Catholic as well as Protestant confessionalization. Education and training alone were not sufficient to encourage godly behavior, however, and Catholics along with Protestants used church and secular courts and other institutions in a process of social disciplining. As noted in the previous chapter, reformers of all religious denominations aimed to create a moral and pious society, with patterns in the regulation of sexuality differing less across Europe than one might have expected. Nevertheless, Roman Catholic and Orthodox ideas, institutions, and procedures did differ from those of Protestants, as well as from each other. This chapter will explore the regulation of sexuality in Roman Catholic Europe – Spain, Portugal, Italy, France, Poland, parts of Ireland, Germany, and Austria – and in Orthodox eastern Europe. The boundaries of Roman Catholic, Protestant, and Orthodox Europe were not stable during the early modern period, as Catholics and Protestants in western Europe fought wars of religion for over a century and Christians in eastern Europe fought the Turks. There was wide variety within Roman Catholicism and Orthodoxy as well, with the situation, for example, in Spain differing greatly from that in small Catholic principalities in Germany. This fluidity and diversity make generalizations difficult and also made religious authorities uneasy; they responded by attempting to enforce greater uniformity in the handling of sexual issues as well as in matters concerning doctrine and ritual.

Catholic ideas

In the same way that the Catholic Reformation as a whole was both a continuation of earlier reform moves and a battle against Protestantism, Catholic ideas about sexuality both linked with pre-Reformation notions and developed in certain ways because of Protestant ideas. As we saw in the previous chapter, Luther and most other Protestant thinkers affirmed Augustine's link between original sin and sexual desire, and regarded sexual desire as so powerful that only a very few individuals could ever live a truly chaste life. They thus recommended marriage for almost everyone, clergy and laity alike, writing voluminously in praise of appropriate marriages and in condemnation of all other forms of sexual activity.

This Protestant championing of marriage and family life was not completely new, however. As noted in Chapter 1, civic leaders and guilds in the late Middle Ages favored stable family units and supported the suppression of any sexual activity which disrupted public order. At the same time, Christian humanists went beyond a critique of the practice of clerical celibacy to question the entire thoery behind it; the most prominent of these, Desiderius Erasmus (1464–1536), praised marital life in his treatise *The Institution of Christian Matrimony*. Two theologians at the University of Paris, Martin Le Maistre (1432–1481) and John Major (1470–1550), suggested that marital sex for pleasure was no more sinful than, in Major's words, "to eat a handsome apple for the pleasure of it."[1]

Catholic doubts about the value of celibacy continued right through the Council of Trent. Many representatives to the council reported that most priests in their areas had concubines, and that Protestant accusations of hypocrisy on the issue of clerical chastity were certainly warranted. The delegate representing Duke Albrecht of Bavaria called for an end to mandatory clerical celibacy, commenting that:

> Many other men who are aware of the current state of affairs in Germany . . . believe that chaste marriage would be preferable to sullied celibacy. They further warn that most able and knowledgeable men in the population would rather have wives without ecclesiastical benefices than benefices without wives.[2]

By this point, however, a rejection of clerical celibacy was clearly identified with Protestantism, and though the issue was hotly debated, the Council eventually affirmed the policy of mandatory clerical celibacy, to be enforced through stricter supervision and earlier weeding out of unsuitable priests. It further countered Protestant ideas by stressing the spiritual superiority of celibacy over marriage.

The Bavarian representative spoke only about men and their wives, but women's celibacy and chastity was also a great concern of the Council of Trent, particularly because accounts of lustful nuns were a staple of Protestant criticism, both learned and popular. Trent's solution was a new emphasis on Pope Boniface VIII's policy of strict enclosure for all female religious houses, enforced by a threat of excommunication or secular punishment. Women were to be sharply cut off from the temptations of the world:

> The holy council commands all bishops, calling the divine justice
> to witness and under threat of eternal damnation, to ensure the
> enclosure of nuns in all monasteries subject to them . . . they
> should coerce any who are disobedient and refractory by eccle-
> siastical censures and other penalties, setting aside any form of
> appeal, and calling in the help of the secular arm if need be.[3]

This policy was bolstered by warnings about the power of female sexuality combined with extravagant praise of female virginity; especially in Italy, new chapels and churches were dedicated to the virgin martyrs of early Christianity and cults in their honor developed in many cities. Male religious authorities did not want the physical virginity of nuns to be a source of independence, however, and ordered that convents be closely supervised. They regarded strict oversight by a bishop or other authority as particularly important because by the sixteenth century many women had entered convents not because they had a religious vocation, but because their families wanted to preserve family wealth by minimizing the number of expensive dowries they had to pay out. Reforming bishops occasionally tried to limit convent entrance to those women who had a true vocation as a nun, but prominent families fought such measures and the bishops resigned themselves to emphasizing spiritual direction and physical control. Convent residents also included wives whose husbands were maneuvering to get their marriages annulled and daughters whose parents regarded them as difficult to control. Such women in convents against their will were mixed in with those who had chosen a religious life, and all ordered to think of themselves as "brides of Christ," the visible signs of the union of Christ and the church.

Though there was no change on the issue of clerical celibacy, the Council of Trent did agree to changes in other areas of marital doctrine. Discussion of marriage went on over 15 years, and reforms were finally codified in the decree *Tametsi,* issued in 1563. *Tametsi* affirmed that the basis of marriage was still the free exchange of vows by spouses, but stipulated that to be valid this exchange had to take place before witnesses, including the priests of the parish where the parties had originally agreed to wed; priests were ordered to keep records of all marriages in their parishes. Secret marriages were not binding, and though parental consent was not explicitly required, it became much more difficult for individuals to contract a marriage without the knowledge of their families. *Tametsi* contained a number of other provisions, including ones which banned concubinage for both clergy and laity and which adjusted the rules regarding consanguinity and affinity in the choice of marital partners. The Council debated many options in terms of divorce, but finally decreed that adultery did not create grounds for divorce and that separation from bed and board with no right of remarriage was the only option for spouses who no longer wished to live together. Annulment was still a possibility, but only in a very few cases such as total impotence or barrenness.

Geminianus Monacensis, a popular seventeenth-century preacher in Munich, brought together Catholic doctrine succinctly in his sermon on marriage. In describing the paintings of a cherub surrounded by lilies and two palm trees which decorated Solomon's temple in Jerusalem, he commented:

> Enlightened by God, Solomon wanted to prefigure with his temple's adornments in what way the Holy Christian Catholic Church was going to be adorned with three kinds of estates: the first being the ecclesiastical epitomized through the Angel Cherub . . . The lilies [next] are an image of the virginal [estate] and the chaste estate of the widow . . . The third adornment of God's church is the holy estate of matrimony represented by the palm trees; it appears as if God created this plant for this very end as to be a mirror for the spouses . . . these plants have such love for one another they cannot bear fruit without each other . . . as soon as they get close to one another . . . their roots . . . intertwine to such a degree that no human being can dissolve them . . . In between these images of marriage Solomon places the Cherub in order to explain: Who is it that must unite these two loving plants? The Angel, that is the Priest: after this kind of union has taken place the two plants can never be divorced again.[4]

Thus at the top of the hierarchy is a celibate priesthood, which solemnizes marriage and makes it a sacrament; in the middle are women who have eschewed a sexual life, either virgins or widows; at the bottom are married persons who "can never be divorced" living in a "holy estate."

Catholicism was fortunate in having a single figure who could be venerated both for virginity and matrimony, the Virgin Mary, who was increasingly important in both learned and popular Catholicism in the sixteenth century.

Many of the most prominent reformers were especially devoted to the Virgin, and new shrines were established marking places where she had performed miracles. Marian devotion had been strong at various points in the Middle Ages, but after the Reformation verbal and visual portrayals of Mary changed to fit with the new emphasis on marriage. Mary became more girlish, and Joseph changed from a weak old man hovering at the edge of the story to a strong man in the prime of life on whom Mary depended. The events of Mary and Joseph's marital life, particularly their betrothal and the dream in which Joseph learned the facts of her pregnancy, became very popular as subjects of paintings, plays, and sermons; in Spain three special feast days were set in honor of the betrothal, and the Inquisition regulated how this event was to be depicted and described. It attempted without success to suppress a very popular story about how Joseph in the company of other young men first met Mary; all the young men were carrying staffs, but only Joseph's staff burst into white flowers when he saw her. The sexual imagery of this story (reinforced by Joseph's being shown with a flowering staff even in non-betrothal scenes) and Joseph's growing role as the patron saint of marriage − prayed to by couples who were having difficulty conceiving or who were being reconciled after an adulterous relationship − captures Catholic ambiguity about male sexuality. Joseph carried a flowering staff and offered Mary husbandly protection, but official opinion declared that their marriage was unconsummated; the patron saint of marriage was thus a man who remained a virgin all his life.

Though some parts of Catholic Europe were slow in adopting them, once they were adopted the decree *Tametsi* and other Tridentine decrees regarding marriage and sexuality formed the basis for Catholic marriage law to a great degree until today. They were codified in the Roman Catechism of 1566, designed to present Tridentine theology in simple language to the faithful, and inspired commentaries and elaborations; the most influential of these was *The Holy Sacrament of Matrimony,* by the Spanish Jesuit, Tomás Sánchez (1550–1610). In this work, Sánchez treats marital sexuality in great detail, taking a position in agreement with Le Maistre and Major (and Luther) that sexual enjoyment in marriage was at most only a minor sin. He clinically discusses the levels of sin involved in fondling, fantasies, fellatio, and foreplay, and ultimately judges them to be minor sins or perhaps even sinless as long as they were a prelude to "natural" intercourse, with the man on top and no barriers to conception. Masturbation was still a mortal sin, according to Sánchez, and even spontaneous orgasm should be discouraged if possible through prayers and pious thoughts, but between spouses almost anything that could "show and foster mutual love" was acceptable.[5] Along with several other Catholic theologians such as the Dominicans Peter de Ledesma (d. 1616) and Domingo de Soto (1495–1560), Sánchez asserted that either spouse could refuse intercourse if he or she thought the family was too poor to sustain, or the educational opportunities for existing children might be harmed by, the birth of another. Even more startlingly, Sánchez proposed that in a sexual relationship outside of marriage (already a mortal sin, of course), coitus interruptus might be preferable to completed intercourse because having an illegitimate child only made the situation worse.

This move away from viewing procreation as the chief justification for marriage and the only justification for sexual intercourse was opposed by more rigorist theologians, including Pope Sixtus V (pontificate 1585–1590). Sixtus was an extremely severe moralist who made adultery a capital crime in Rome and declared in the papal bull *Effraenatam* of 1588 that all abortion and contraception were homicide. Those found guilty of administering or taking contraceptives or abortificants were to be excommunicated, an excommunication that could be lifted only by the pope himself. Sixtus's stance was too extreme even for most of the rigorists, however, and his successor Gregory XIV ordered a return to earlier policy, in which excommunication was the punishment only for abortion after the fetus had been "ensouled," a point set at 40 days after conception for males and 80 for females. (In 1869 the papacy reverted to Sixtus's opinion and determined that ensoulment occurred at conception, which remains official Catholic teaching.) Sixtus V also forbade all men without testicles or the ability to produce semen to marry (a policy that remained in force until 1977), which had particular effect on the castrated male singers who were becoming increasingly popular in Italy during this time. (Castrati often sang female parts in secular and sacred performances in Spain and Italy from the sixteenth through the nineteenth centuries, a practice encouraged by bans on women singing in church and on public stages.)

While some of Pope Sixtus's measures were very short lived, a more rigorist position gradually gained greater acceptance, with theologians such as Sánchez and Soto accused of "laxism" and their works placed on the Papal Index. In the seventeenth century the attack on "laxism" became associated in France and some parts of the Low Countries and Germany with a movement called Jansenism, named after a Dutch Catholic theologian, Cornelius Jansen (1585–1683). Jansenism called for personal holiness and moral reform and was attractive to many lay people and nuns as well as male clergy. Jansenists took a harsh, neo-Augustinian view of all sexuality, including marital; the Jansenist theologian Louis Habert (d. 1718), for example, declared that the flood of the Old Testament was brought about by lust in the marriage bed.

Jansenists were particularly concerned that "lax" ideas about sexual relationships were not simply discussed in learned theological treatises, but were communicated to ordinary Christians in confession. The Council of Trent had reiterated the requirement that all believers confess their sins at least once a year after minutely examining their own conscience and actions. Thus the onus of recognizing sexual sins shifted from the priest to the penitent, and priests were even advised *not* to ask excessively detailed questions about sexual acts but to rely on penitents' self-reflection. Jesuit confessors in particular developed a new style of moral theology often termed "casuistry" or "moral probablism," in which the intentions and desires of the individual were weighed in any assessment of the level of guilt. As the moral theologian Jean Benedicti (1573–1662) wrote regarding masturbation: "If a person commits this sin while fantasizing about a married woman, as well as masturbation he is guilty of adultery; if he desires a virgin, indecent assault; if he fantasizes about a relative, incest; a nun, it is sacrilege; if he fantasizes about another male, then it is sodomy."[6]

This concentration on subjective feelings in confession was part of what many scholars see as a gradual transformation of European culture from one in which shame acted as the most effective control of people's actions to one in which guilt was the more important motivator. To the Jansenists, however, most confessors were not making people feel guilty enough, but were instead excusing their actions and thoughts by noting the mitigating factors and moral complexity of many situations. Because such casuistry was particularly associated with Jesuit confessors, the battle in France is often described as one between Jansenists and Jesuits. Many Jansenists in France also opposed the power of the papacy, and Jansenism was condemned several times in the seventeenth century and officially suppressed by papal bulls in the early eighteenth century. Despite these measures, its influence continued among many Catholic clergy.

Among the bulk of the clergy, however, attitudes toward sexual issues moderated in the eighteenth century, or at least did so in terms of calls for the investigation and punishment of sexual sins. The most influential Catholic writer on moral issues from this period, St Alphonsus Liguori (1697–1787), clearly advised confessors not to treat too harshly those who were unaware that their practices were sinful and not to concentrate too much on sins they had little hope of eradicating, such as lustful thoughts or fornication. In his opinion, explaining the sinfulness of acts that people would not give up simply transformed unwitting sins into mortal ones.

Institutions

Had Liguori lived two centuries earlier, such statements would have led to a trial rather than a canonization process, because in the sixteenth century simply to express the view that fornication was not a mortal sin could lead to indictment before a variety of church courts. The system of church courts that had been set up in the Middle Ages continued after the Reformation in Catholic areas, but the level of their activities increased right after Trent as they attempted to enforce the new decrees. One of the aims of the Council of Trent was to increase the power of bishops, and the ability of other types of church officials such as archdeacons or papal legates to hear cases was curtailed. Episcopal decisions could be appealed to Rome, however, and after Trent the papacy attempted to centralize and standardize procedure, requiring local court decisions to fit with those of the central papal courts such as the Rota. Judges in the Rota often published collections of Rotal decisions and their justifications, and these became standard reference works for church lawyers throughout Europe.

Though episcopal courts were more active after Trent than they had been before, they gradually concentrated more on doctrinal uniformity and less on matters of morality. In part this was because municipal and national secular courts were increasingly successful in their claims to jurisdiction over matters of marriage and morals; in France, for example, royal courts even heard cases involving priests if a "public scandal" was involved, this being increasingly defined as any sexual relationship. In part, however, this shift in emphasis was also a result of Tridentine directives which ordered bishops to pay more attention to extirpating heresy than policing morality. The visitations which bishops were to conduct every two years, sending officials around the diocese to investigate clergy and laity, were also to concentrate primarily on confessional issues. As in Protestant areas, these visitations were sometimes a joint venture of state and church, with both ecclesiastical and secular officials asking questions about religious beliefs and practices. The sanctions for heresy also showed church and state operating together; in many areas one could not only be excommunicated for unrepentant heresy, but banished and sometimes executed as well.

The most famous (or infamous) church court operating in the early modern period was the Inquisition in its various forms – Spanish, Roman, Netherlandish, Portuguese. Just as with bishops' courts, the primary focus of the Inquisition was investigating heresy, which in different parts of Europe meant different things. In Spain and Portugal the Inquisition initially focussed on converted Jews and Muslims, and later on those suspected of magical and superstitious practices. In Italy and the Netherlands it primarily investigated suspected Protestants and freethinkers, and after the 1580s – when religious heterodoxy had been almost completely eradicated – those accused of magical practices. In all of these places, however, certain actions involving sexuality also came under its jurisdiction, though its jurisdiction was sometimes contested by secular courts or bishops' courts, and in some places such as Naples it operated through the bishops' courts. In Spain, for example, of roughly 44,000 cases heard by the Inquisition during the period 1540 to 1700, 2,645 or 5.9 percent were for bigamy, 1,131 or 2.5 percent for solicitation of sexual favors by priests within the confessional, thousands more for carrying out love magic or making statements which differed with Church teachings on sexuality. In the kingdom of Aragon about 15 percent of the Inquisition's activity in this period involved sexual matters, with similar figures for the Roman Inquisition.

In sharp contrast to Liguori's position later, the Iberian Inquisitions regarded lack of familiarity with Church doctrines as something to be corrected rather than indulged. For example, to commit fornication was a sin, but to say that sexual relations between two unmarried people was not a sin was much worse, even if done in ignorance. Such persons were to be punished, "for in this way they will be relieved of their ignorance, and the punishment will have its terrifying effect on others."[7] Such ignorance was also to be combatted by an annual reading of the Edict of Faith from every pulpit, in which approved Catholic positions on a range of matters were explained in simple language, and people were encouraged to report to the Inquisition any neighbor or acquaintance whose statements or actions were in contrast to these. In addition to accusations which originated from private witnesses, the Inquisition also conducted regular visitations and established a system of commissioners and unpaid lay agents, called *familiares,* who were to report suspects and also assist in bringing them in for investigation; in some cities there came to be as many as one *familiar* for every 50 people, though there were far fewer in the rural areas.

According to many of its historians, the Inquisition thus created a climate of suspicion in some parts of its jurisdictions; the social stigma of being investigated had such a strong "terrifying effect" that severe punishments were not necessary. In contrast to its modern reputation, executions based on trials before the Inquisition were rare; of the 44,000 cases in the Spanish Inquisition noted above, only 826, or 1.8 percent resulted in an execution, though in an additional 1.7 percent a sentence of execution was set, but the accused had fled and so he or she was burned in effigy. Both the execution rate and the number of investigations as a whole also decreased beginning in the early eighteenth century, as the result of a clear decline in inquisitorial zeal and activities, and a possible decline in prohibited activities after decades of repression. (The records of the Roman Inquisition and Papal Index were opened to scholars in 1997, so that future research will be able to give a more detailed picture of their activities; existing studies based on local records of the Roman Inquisition have also found a moderation in punishment similar to that of the Spanish Inquisition.)

Like Protestantism, Catholicism did not rely solely on courts and visitations to communicate its ideas about proper sexual behavior and concepts. Though the sermon was not the center of the Catholic mass as it was of the the Protestant service, the Council of Trent emphasized the importance of preaching for both communication and control; the frequency of sermons increased in many areas, and by 1600 printed collections of Catholic sermons on moral as well as theological topics were widely available in Latin and the vernaculars. Trent authorized the preparation of the Roman Catechism of 1566, which explained basic doctrine on all issues. Its discussion of the purposes of marriage added nothing new, but it did give a slightly more positive interpretation than many medieval commentators had by ranking companionship and mutual help as more important than procreation and the avoidance of fornication. Catholic officials supported the publication of other devotional books and pictures and the presentation of plays which also communicated Catholic doctrine and stressed both heroic deeds of chastity and pious family life. While some materials were promoted, others were banned; the Index censored books which it judged "lascivious and obscene" as well as those it judged heretical, ordered books to be confiscated and offending passages to be blacked out, or prevented their publication altogether.

Many Catholic areas lagged behind Protestant ones in the establishment of primary and secondary schools, but they had other types of institutions for communicating moral values which were unavailable to Protestants. As noted above, confession was one avenue, and during the sixteenth and seventeenth centuries, new kinds of religious confraternities, congregations, and sodalities devoted to Mary or to other aspects of Catholic devotion such as the rosary developed in many parts of Europe. In these organizations, lay men and women – under the direction of clergy – devoted themselves to piety, prayer, and good works. Especially in northern Europe, these congregations and confraternities, which sometimes numbered hundreds of people, encouraged their members to uphold high standards of moral purity in their own lives, forbidding them, for example, to visit the house of their betrothed between engagement and marriage. The confraternities also combatted immorality in their surrounding communities. Just like Calvinists, confraternities opposed dances and carnival celebrations, and attacked prostitution. Unlike Protestants, Catholics proposed to solve the problem of prostitution not by banishment or marriage, but by establishing houses for former prostitutes or young women in danger of becoming prostitutes, which would "shelter the modesty of girls from the lewdness of men."[8] Along with such refuges for former prostitutes, legal brothels were also regarded as safeguarding morality; Catholic authorities in many areas continued to defend them as a way to maintain the virtue of "honorable" women.

While lay people learned pious moral values in confraternities, priests learned them in the new seminaries which were established after the Council of Trent. Trent ordered each bishop to establish a seminary in his diocese, and although this level was never attained, slowly a seminary education became more common for priests. Even those areas such as Ireland which did not have their own seminaries received priests from Irish colleges on the continent, such as those at Rome and Louvain, which still function. Seminaries promoted the virtues of celibacy to candidates for the priesthood, and turned away some who were clearly unable to maintain a celibate life. As Inquisition and other records make clear, seminary training did not end problems with clerical sexuality, but it eventually provided more parishes with priests who could perform basic pastoral duties such as preaching, administering the sacraments, and teaching catechism, thus enabling Catholic doctrine to reach a wider audience.

Effects of the Catholic Reformation

As in Protestant areas, generalizing about the effects of new or reinvigorated ideas and institutions in Catholic areas is difficult. Though we might expect more uniformity in Catholicism than in Protestantism, and expect that uniformity to increase during this period as conformity to approved practice was such an important issue for the Council of Trent, in actuality variations continued. Conflicts between "rigorists" and "laxists," bishops' courts and inquisitors, or church and secular authorities created national and local differences in the way sexuality was regulated. Tridentine regulations and other measures of social discipline were much easier to enforce in cities and towns than in more isolated rural areas, where older notions and practices continued and reform efforts often had little or no impact. Enforcement of regulations and discipline was particularly difficult in areas where Catholics lived under Protestant governments, such as Ireland or England, for such institutions as bishop's courts, and in some periods bishops themselves, were illegal.

Because of these variations, historians often focus on a single geographic area, studying in depth a city or region which offers rich sources about marital relations, sexual conduct, policing efforts, and other matters. Occasionally records such as trial documents or episcopal visitations are so extensive that patterns may best be discerned by computer-assisted indexing; cases for which trial summaries (termed *relaciones de causas)* survive for the Spanish Inquisition, for example, number about 100,000, and are currently being indexed by a team of scholars. (The numbers cited above about sexual cases come from their initial indexing of about 44,000 cases.) Thus both qualitative and quantitative research is contributing to our understanding of sexual practices and their control in post-Reformation European Catholicism.

Marriage among the laity

The new definition of marriage set out in the decree *Tametsi* was only slowly adopted in Catholic Europe. Local betrothal and wedding practices which stood in sharp contrast to the Council of Trent's call for publicity and piety were often maintained for decades or even centuries, sometimes in opposition to the wishes of local clergy and sometimes with their participation. In parts of Italy and France, for example, people were very worried that envious or malicious neighbors might try to cast a spell on the marriage, so did not want to celebrate their weddings publicly. Despite prohibitions, they went to neighboring villages for the blessing or began sexual relations immediately after the marriage contract was signed (before a priestly blessing) so that magical or demonic forces would not intervene and cause impotence or marital strife. Visitation reports from rural areas and letters written by various reformers indicate that well into the seventeenth century the signing of a marriage contract or verbal agreement between families was the point at which villagers expected sexual relations to begin; as one horrified reformer noted of the Basques, "They marry their wives on a trial basis . . . and do not receive any nuptial blessing until they have lived with them a long time, have probed their habits and have learnt by results about the fertility of their soil."[9]

Catholic reformers encouraged solemnity in the marriage ceremony, suggesting that the ritual blessing of the marriage bed, when it was continued at all, be the occasion of a solemn sermon about marital chastity rather than that of a noisy and ribald celebration of fertility. Wedding feasts and dances (which continued despite all efforts of reformers) were moved away from the church and churchyard, in an effort to free the sacrament of marriage from profanation by worldly concerns. Traditional marital rituals changed slightly to incorporate post-Tridentine emphases, such as that on Mary; in parts of Germany, for example, Mary's image was carried in a procession to the home of newlyweds, then placed on the marital bed before the priestly blessing.

Both church and state officials also attempted to restrict or prohibit popular rituals of social control such as the boisterous, noisy, and sometimes smelly *charivaris* we discussed in Chapter Two, held when villagers regarded a marriage as somehow socially unacceptable, *asouades* (forcing someone, usually a man, to ride a donkey or pole if he was viewed as hen-pecked or if there were frequent marital disputes), or the setting up of maypoles with phallic symbols outside the houses of marriageable girls. These rituals were generally carried out by the young men in a village, and prohibitions were largely ineffective, for the men in power in most villages had taken part in them when they were young and so tolerated them. They usually culminated in the victims' buying off the young men with drinks and food, but sometimes they escalated into more serious violence. Seminary-trained priests preached and spoke against such rituals, but they themselves then became the targets of a gang of youths, who "in response to my prayers and warnings . . . told me to address their behinds, and . . . accompanied their words with gestures of the hand." [10]

Along with popular traditions, secular governments sometimes stood in opposition to the reforms of Trent. Where Catholics lived under Protestant governments, as in Ireland or England, priests sometimes had to conduct marriages in secret. Once some level of toleration was accorded to Catholics, marrying parties still had to pay a fee to a minister of the Church of England or Church of Ireland before a priest could marry them, and it was difficult to observe Tridentine rules.

Secular opposition to Trent could also be found in Catholic countries. In France, the Royal Council refused to acknowledge the decisions of Trent as the laws of the kingdom, so royal and not church legislation became the basis of matrimonial law. To a large decree the edicts of the French kings agreed with *Tametsi,* but they made parental consent almost always obligatory, and provided severe penalties, including in theory capital punishment, for minors who married against their parents' wishes. (Minors were defined as men under 30 and women under 25.) Though in actuality they were not executed, young people who defied their parents were sometimes imprisoned by what were termed *lettres de cachet,* documents which families obtained from royal officials authorizing the imprisonment without trial of a family member who was seen as a source of dishonor. *Lettres de cachet* were also used against young people who refused to go into convents or monasteries when their families wished them to, or against individuals whose behavior was regarded as in some way scandalous, such as wives whose husbands suspected them of adultery or men from prominent families who engaged in homosexual activities; this practice was often abused, and individuals imprisoned for years if their families refused to agree to their release.

As noted in the previous chapter, mixed marriages between Protestants and Catholics were not unusual, especially in areas where denominations lived close to one another. Though religious authorities agreed to recognize the marriages of other religions, the possibility of divorce among Protestants created a problem for Catholic authorities. Should a person who had legitimately divorced while a Protestant but then converted be allowed to marry someone else in a Catholic ceremony? Generally this was decided on a case-by-case basis and depended on the situation and the status of the parties involved. Catholicism continued to prohibit divorce, although judicial separations were allowed by church and state in many areas. Such separations were usually sought by the wife, and were seen as a last resort for women in cases of violence and cruelty; they were rare, and found mostly among the well-to-do. In France, men occasionally used *lettres de cachet* as a means of solving marital disputes, convincing authorities that family honor demanded the imprisonment of their wives. In Italy and Spain, a "disobedient" wife could be sent to a convent or house of refuge for repentant prostitutes.

In southern Europe, "mixed" marriages or other types of sexual relationships involved non-Christians or converts as well as different types of Christians. The expulsion of practicing Muslims and Jews from Iberia was ordered in the late fifteenth century, so that open relationships, whether marriage or prostitution, between persons of different faiths were no longer officially possible. Marriages between Christians and converts were generally allowed, and at times even promoted; in 1548, for example, an edict of the Spanish crown ordered converted Muslims to marry Old Christians. (Old Christians were those whose ancestors were not known to have been Jewish or Muslim.) At the same time, however, laws which favored "purely" Old Christian families (generally termed "purity of the blood" laws) worked against intermarriage, and Christians, former Muslims, and former Jews all tended to marry people with whom they already had some lineage ties.

Marriage was also an issue in the earliest European colonies. In 1492, the Portuguese crown sent 2,000 newly baptized Jews to its African island colonies, hoping they would intermarry with Portuguese Christians who were already there and increase the islands' population. The effort was not very successful, so Portuguese authorities instead encouraged sexual relations between Portuguese men and African slave women, generally baptizing the women and thereby avoiding sanctions regarding sexual relations between Christians and Muslims. These relationships sometimes involved formal marriage, though such marriages were not necessarily recognized by either Portuguese or African authorities; more often the men involved also had a wife and children in Portugal, so the crown defined their African marriage as concubinage and their colonial children as illegitimate.

Though a marriage to an African could be discounted, a second marriage in Europe could not, and in areas in which there was a great deal of mobility, such as the port cities of Spain and Portugal or the border area between Spain and France, trials for bigamy became quite common. Most bigamists were young, male, and mobile, and were liable for punishment in secular courts, episcopal courts, and/or the courts of the Inquisition. (The Inquisition claimed jurisdiction over bigamy because it was an offense against the sacrament of marriage, although its jurisdiction was often disputed by other types of courts.) Though bigamists were rarely executed, male bigamists were generally sentenced to five years as oarsmen in the king's galleys, which was often the functional equivalent of a death sentence, while female bigamists were whipped and exiled.

Clerical sexuality

Assessing the success of reform efforts to promote chastity and sexual propriety among the clergy depends to some degree on where one looks and how long a time frame one takes. In some areas the reforms were quite successful. In the diocese of Würzburg in Germany, for example, 45 percent of the rural clergy had, or were suspected of having, concubines at the time of the Council of Trent, but by 1616–1631, after a series of reforming bishops, only 4 percent of the clergy lived with concubines. This process came about much more slowly in other areas, in part because the establishment of seminaries which stressed celibacy to priestly candidates was slow – all of Spain had only 26 seminaries by 1700 and even Paris did not have a seminary until 1696 – and regular visitations by bishops were sporadic. As late as 1652, the bishop of Autun reported:

> Concubinage here is extremely common and priests have no fear of maintaining in their quarters immodest women and the children they have with them. They nourish and raise these children, train them to serve at the altar, marry them, dower them all as if they were legitimate. Parishioners are so accustomed to these practices that when interrogated about the morals and deportment of the clerics who keep these immodest women, they respond that these clerics live justly . . . and so they see no evil, being so used to seeing their priests live with women that they assume it is acceptable.[11]

This lay tolerance of clerical concubinage continued into the nineteenth century in some parts of Europe; complaints against clerical sex were made only when the priest was promiscuous or negligent in the support of his children, or the relationship was adulterous. In other areas lay people took the lead in forcing higher standards of behavior among the clergy. In Burgundy in the 1560s, for example, lay courts grew frustrated at the leniency of church courts and began to try sexually active clergy; in the early seventeenth century lay courts even sentenced some priests and their lovers to death. By the late seventeenth century they usually ordered banishment or galley service rather than execution, but still took seriously any priest whose behavior made him unworthy of being a mediator between God and his parishioners or who used his office to gain sexual favors. Such secular jurisdiction over the sexual lives of clergy was highly unusual, however, for in most parts of Europe only the women involved with priests came before secular courts, while the priests continued to appear before bishops' courts or the Inquisition; this generally resulted in a great disparity in their punishments, with the priest simply fined and the woman forced to endure public humiliation on the pillory and then exiled.

The most dramatic example of priests abusing the trust placed in them was seduction, solicitation, or rape which occurred during confession, a matter which became a staple first of Protestant and then of anticlerical polemic. Because confession was a sacrament and viewed as one of the key elements of post-Tridentine Catholic practice, the papacy regarded this as a serious issue and gave the various Inquisitions jurisdiction over solicitation during confession. People were ordered to report any solicitation and denied absolution if they did not, though the requirement of two independent witnesses often meant that cases were only reported years after they happened. The accused priest was imprisoned, given a defense attorney, questioned, and urged to confess; if the Inquisition decided there was enough evidence to convict, he was usually deprived of the right to hear confession, exiled from his parish, and often confined to a monastery. Opportunities for solicitation were many, as confession often occurred with priest and penitent simply sitting together somewhere in the church; the closed, divided confessional box was first introduced in the 1560s in Italy, but was not introduced in many parishes until the eighteenth century, and even then the screen divider was often torn or missing.

Solicitation by priests had certainly occurred in the pre-Reformation church, but some aspects of post-Tridentine Catholic practice encouraged it. People were urged to confess frequently, and there is some evidence that they did confess more often, particularly if they belonged to one of the new religious organizations such as the confraternities dedicated to the Virgin Mary. As noted above, confession was to entail a detailed examination of one's conscience and a minute accounting of sins; confessors sometimes defended themselves by saying they needed to use sexually suggestive language to get a penitent to understand her or his sins. Women who were religiously scrupulous, whether nuns or lay women, were especially likely to confess often, and to develop an intense emotional relationship with their confessor. By the seventeenth century, church authorities recognized that not all confessors could handle this, and sometimes excluded nuns and women under 40 from a priest's first license to hear confessions; only after a second examination and trial period could he hear confessions from all parishioners.

Church authorities were especially cautious about the relationships which developed between confessors and women who dedicated themselves to lives of religious devotion and piety without taking solemn vows as nuns did. As the Synod of Dublin ruled in 1614, "we decree that priests shall not have in their houses any women – even more those who have made a vow of virginity or chastity, or any others, since they might be a cause of scandal: and they are not to undertake the care of such women, even as a spiritual ministry, without further authorization." [12] The special situation of Ireland at that point, where the convents had been dissolved and solemn vows officially prohibited by English laws, caused authorities to relent somewhat and allow priests to shelter women who wished to live a religious life but not maintain cloister. The Council of Trent eliminated this option for women in Italy, but such women were also quite common in Spain. These women, termed *beatas,* were often religious visionaries and mystics, revered in their neighborhood and beyond for their piety and intense spiritual experiences; some lived communally with other women, but others simply lived with their families. Their visions and ecstatic trances sometimes led to their being investigated by the Inquisition, which was also concerned about their modesty and chastity. Diego Pérez de Valdivia, a professor at the University of Barcelona, complained that some beatas had "much freedom and little modesty" and were easily tempted by "the devil, the world, and their own flesh."[13] Valdivia advised that beatas put themselves under the close direction of their confessors, though other authors warned about the dangers of this and advised priests to "apply [themselves] more to the treatment of men, where there is less danger and greater advantage."[14] The best solution, in the minds of most authorities, would be for such women to enter convents; they might still develop an emotional or sexual relationship with their confessors, but other dangers to their chastity would be avoided.

While education and supervision were the main tools of the post-Tridentine church in its efforts to enforce chastity on male clerics, strict enclosure was its main tool for female religious, a policy that was also slow in gaining acceptance. In many areas, convents that had allowed women out to visit their families or permitted family members to visit resisted enclosure, and in others new groups were established – on the model of the Jesuits – by women who wanted to devote themselves to helping the sick and poor. As long as these groups retained their lay status, they sometimes won papal approval, but if they chose or were compelled to become actual religious orders they were ordered to cut off contact with the world. There is no way to measure how the policy of enclosure actually affected the sexual lives of nuns, for neither before nor after the Reformation were many nuns involved in permanent sexual relationships which could be counted as priests' concubines could. Women with little religious vocation continued to be placed in convents by their families if the family could not find an appropriate marriage partner or raise the dowry necessary for a good marriage, and their unhappiness comes out in court records, visitation reports, and occasionally in their own writings. Enclosure did affect the stories that were told about sex in convents by their opponents, both Protestant and Catholic. In the sixteenth century the most lurid of these told of babies born, killed, and buried in the convent after wild encounters when nuns met their lovers in the convent or outside of it, while in the eighteenth century they reflected the enclosed setting and instead told of lesbian sadism or exotic rituals of exorcism conducted over swooning nuns by lascivious confessors.

Fornication, blasphemy and insults

Although Trent attempted to draw a sharp line between the married and the not-married, ending clandestine marriages and prohibiting sexual relations until after the church ceremony, these new departures were as slow in being accepted in many parts of Catholic Europe as they were in Protestant areas. Visitations of rural parishes in the diocese of Salzburg, Austria, in the 1670s and 1680s, for example, found a 30 percent illegitimacy rate, clear indication that intercourse was expected to begin with betrothal. At the same time the situation in France was quite different, for the rural illegitimacy rate there in the seventeenth century was around 1 percent. How much this was the result of Catholic Reformation preaching and how much the result of existing traditions which discouraged post-betrothal intercourse is difficult to say, however. The sharp difference between Austria and France may also be partly the result of different types of sources; the Austrian figure comes from a visitation report about actual families, while the French figure uses baptismal registers, which may not have recorded the baptism of all children born out of wedlock. (A similar disjuncture occurs in many cities of the United States today between births recorded by birth certificates and those for which there is a birth announcement in the newspaper, because some newspapers refuse to publish birth announcements for children born out of wedlock.)

In some parts of Catholic Europe, such as France, secular laws reinforced church sanctions against clandestine marriage, or were even stronger. France refused to accept the disciplinary decrees of the Council of Trent in part because the decrees regarded clandestine marriages as valid. French ordinances defined all marriages without parental consent as *rapt* (abduction), even if they had involved no violence (such cases were termed *rapt de seduction*). Such cases could thus be tried in secular courts, which increasingly levied monetary fines payable to the woman or her family as the standard punishment, though the ordinances themselves called for much harsher penalties. Secular courts also heard cases of women accused of not declaring their pregnancies, which generally came to light when the baby subsequently died; as noted in the previous chapter, France was the first country in Europe to declare that a woman "be held and reputed to have murdered her child and, in reparation, be punished by death and the last agony" if it died after birth and she had "hidden, covered and concealed both her pregnancy and her childbearing, without having declared one or the other."[15] Though Belgium did not have a similar law about reporting pregnancies, women found guilty of infanticide certainly received a "last agony." They were generally also accused of witchcraft – the reasoning being that only the Devil could lead a mother to kill her child – and executed in gruesome ways, such as being impaled on a stake and then buried alive, or having the offending hand cut off before being drowned.

Women who *did* declare their pregnancies often subsequently showed up in church courts in breach of promise cases, stating that the father of the child had promised marriage and requesting that the court enforce his promise, or at least order financial support for the child. Such breach of promise cases were also common in Catholic courts in areas where there was no law requiring a declaration of pregnancy, and courts regularly awarded the woman at least some money. They varied in how willing they were to force a marriage, as this directly violated the doctrine of consent. There is evidence from some parts of Catholic Europe that the amounts and frequency of monetary compensation declined in the sixteenth century, as did the total number of cases. Authorities at the time may have chosen to view this decline as a mark of the success of campaigns against extra-marital sex, though it may also have resulted from women's recognition that the court was not going to be very sympathetic to their plight, and so not bothering to take cases to court.

The high point of attempts by both church and state authorities to control fornication varied throughout Catholic Europe, depending on the local political situation and the enthusiasm of reforming leaders, both religious and lay. Zealous leaders sometimes went beyond setting punishments to attempting to restrict occasions for fornication, including dances and spinning bees; the 1680 Synod of Troyes in France ruled, "We prohibit men and boys on pain of excommunication . . . to meet with women and girls in the places where they gather at night to spin and work."[16] In Italy both city governments and the church tried another tactic, forbidding unwed mothers to raise their own children, and requiring them instead to leave them in foundling homes *(ospizi)*. If women could not afford the fees required, they were forced to give birth in jail and then work in a foundling home as a wetnurse for their own and other infants; despite attempts to feed and care for them, the vast majority of children in such homes died.

In Spain, the Inquisition shared jurisdiction over actual cases of fornication and births out of wedlock with other courts, but it had exclusive jurisdiction over people who *said* that fornication was not a sin or was only a venial sin, as this implied disrespect for the sacrament of marriage. The actual rate of prosecution for such statements varied widely and changed over time; in some areas they were ignored, while in others, such as Toledo, they made up as much as one-third of the Inquisition's cases during brief campaigns of repression. Most of the people charged were men, who regarded sex outside of marriage as acceptable, especially if the man paid the woman for it. The church's teachings about fornication became part of the Edict of Faith read regularly to parishioners, and slowly the idea was communicated to villagers, as the following deposition makes clear:

> The witness declared that he believed he had been summoned to testify about a certain statement that García Ruiz had made which seemed to him to run counter to what the parish priest had said in a sermon fifteen or twenty days ago. In effect, he had declared that their Honors the Inquisitors of Toledo had ordered all the parish priests in the district of Santa Olalla to admonish their parishioners in such a way that no one could pretend ignorance that having relations with a woman other than one's own legitimate wife was a mortal sin, and that to maintain the opposite view was heresy. Now on Friday the 14th of May, when García Ruiz and Diego Gómez were shearing their sheep at the witness's house, they spoke with his son, Juan Hernández Duque the younger. García Ruiz said, "Do you know that I had sex with a woman that I met on the road?" And then she said, "Sweetie, would you give me something to eat?" And García Ruiz promised her some eggs and fish and gave her a coin because he had made love with her. And he stated that, for a man, it was not a sin to make love to a woman even if she was a prostitute. Then his friends Diego Gómez and Sancho de Rojas the elder who were there, admonished him and told him to shut up because this was heresy. And the other continued to insist that if one paid it was not a sin. Everyone there stared at him and continued to reproach him, saying: "Shut up: it was a great sin, didn't you hear the priest?" Diego Gómez said: "May the devil take you. With the wife you have why are you looking for another woman?" And García Ruiz replied, saying, "Leave me in peace, I had a good time with her!" Then he said to this witness's son, "Don't look so sad, sell one of your father's sheep and find another like her."

At this time the said Juan Hernández Duque the younger replied: "Go to the Devil, you and your filth."[17]

Along with trying people for statements about fornication, the Iberian and Roman Inquisitions also tried people for "heretical blasphemy" which often had to do with sex. Sometimes this occurred when people found certain Christian doctrines hard to believe. Women, in particular, were charged with claiming marriage was more holy than celibacy, and María de Cardenas, a shepherd's daughter in central Spain, appeared before the Inquisition in 1568 because she asserted that "God did it to Our Lady like her father [did] it to her mother" and "persisted in believing that God had known Our Lady carnally."[18] Men's statements were generally more direct: "Christ the cuckolded faggot" or "Virgin Mary the whore." Even clergy were not immune from such comments, terming their fellow clerics "God's vaginas," or making sexual insults about other men's wives. Inquisition records from southern Italy and Sicily are especially full of such cases, with one priest charged with singing insults of a man's wife through a window, calling her a "pockmarked whore, public and practiced" who sold her "fig, fig" (a hand gesture symbolizing a woman's genitals) for "a penny a pound."[19] Punishments for insulting private persons were generally fines, but obscenities which mentioned religious figures or Inquisition officials might be punished with years of galley service.

Prostitution and women's prisons

Though we have no way of knowing whether the priest's insult was warranted in the case just cited, it does capture one facet of early modern prostitution – the lack of clear borders between an "honorable" woman, one whose sexual life was irregular by community standards, and a prostitute. Particularly in villages where there were no official brothels, women charged with "prostitution" might be occasional sellers of sex, but they might also be servants, widows, or women whose husbands had deserted them who were living in a non-marital arrangement with a man, a situation religious authorities would have defined as "concubinage." If the village accepted such a couple, the arrangement could go on for years, but if the villagers did not approve, they could use charges of prostitution to drive out unwanted single or deserted women.

Such fluid borders became increasingly unacceptable to Catholic authorities intent on drawing sharp lines between honor and dishonor. Though in some areas, they, like Protestants, closed all licensed brothels and attempted to eradicate prostitution by imprisonment and banishing, their more common response was to require prostitutes to register and live in particular houses or quarters of the city. Only those women who had not registered officially or lived elsewhere, that is, who attempted to straddle the boundary between honorable and dishonorable, were to be punished.

This more pragmatic approach to the sale of sexual services was upset from time to time in Catholic areas by reforming preachers or clergy who were occasionally successful at getting brothels closed, at least for short periods. Reformers had a more long-term impact through institutions they opened rather than closed, for during the sixteenth century asylums for repentant prostitutes and other "fallen women" whose honor was questionable were set up in many southern European cities. Such houses, often dedicated to Mary Magdalene, also began to admit women who were regarded as in danger of becoming prostitutes, generally poor women with no male relatives; the ordinances stated explicitly that the women admitted had to be pretty or at least acceptable looking, for ugly women did not have to worry about their honor. Many of these asylums were started by reforming bishops or leaders of religious orders, and some began to admit a variety of other types of women along with prostitutes, such as girls who had been raped, women whose husbands threatened them, attractive daughters of prostitutes, or poor young widows. They were an attractive charity for those interested in moral reform, and were sometimes also supported by taxes on registered prostitutes and courtesans.

In such asylums, the women did not take vows and could leave to marry, but otherwise they were much like convents, with the women following a daily regimen of work and prayer. Some of them stressed penitence and moral reform while others were more purely punitive, closer to prisons than convents. The latter were seen as particularly appropriate for women who refused to change their ways; who – in the words of the reforming nun Madre Magdalena de San Gerónimo, "insult the honesty and virtue of the good ones with their corruption and evil" and as "wild beasts who leave their caves to look for prey" spread "family dishonor and scandal among all the people." Madre Magdalena recommended to King Philip II of Spain in 1608 the establishment of a special women's prison, "where in particular the rebellious incorrigible ones will be punished."[20]

This mixture of punishment and penitence may be seen very clearly in the Parisian women's prison of the Salpêtrière. In 1658, Louis XIV ordered the imprisonment there of all women found guilty of prostitution, fornication, or adultery, with release coming only when the priests and sisters in charge determined the inmate was truly penitent and had changed her ways. Imprisoning women for sexual crimes marks the first time that prison was used as a punishment in Europe rather than simply as a place to hold people until their trial or before deportation. Such prisons later became the model for similar institutions for men and young people – often specifically called "reformatories" – in which the inmate's level of repentance determined to a great degree the term of incarceration. (This, of course, is still true for prisons and "reform schools" today.) Once men and boys as well as women and girls were locked up, however, sexual crimes were no longer the basis of the majority of incarcerations as they were in the earliest women's prisons.

Sodomy

In contrast to prostitution, imprisonment was rarely set as a punishment for sodomy in Catholic Europe until the mid-eighteenth century, though men accused of sodomy might spend months or years in prison awaiting trial. (And in Seville in Spain they were isolated from other prisoners in a special royal jail.) Like so many other sexual crimes, jurisdiction over sodomy was often shared or disputed. In the Iberian peninsula, the Inquisition had jurisdiction over all sodomy in Aragon after 1524 (though in some areas local authorities fought this) and over homosexual sodomy in Portugal; in Castile, secular courts heard all sodomy trials after 1509. Though Sicily was part of the kingdom of Aragon, the Inquisition was denied jurisdiction over sodomy there unless the case involved its own officials or *familiares.*

All of these areas had somewhat distinctive patterns of prosecution. The Portuguese Inquisition, for example, compiled two large books with over 4,400 names of all those accused of or confessing to homosexual sodomy during the period 1587 to 1794; of these about 400 were actually put on trial and about 30 appear to have been executed. Secular courts in Castile were less thorough in record-keeping, but more harsh in punishment. Sodomy was punished by burning adult offenders alive, with juvenile offenders – who were not liable for execution – quickly passed through the fire so that, as officials commented, they could get a foretaste of what was to come if they did not change their ways.

The Aragonese Inquisition held almost 1,000 trials for homosexual sodomy and bestiality during the period between 1570 and 1630, and about 150 men died (roughly as many as were executed for heresy during this period); of these slightly over half the trials were for homosexual sodomy, but well over half the executions were for bestiality. Many of those executed for homosexual sodomy were Italians or slaves from Africa and Asia, a situation exacerbated by the reputation both groups had among the Spanish for being particularly likely to engage in this "nefarious sin." Many of those executed were from all-male environments such as monasteries or the military, and almost all of the cases involved an older and younger man or a man and an adolescent. Those charged with homosexual sodomy were sometimes tortured to reveal other names, so that sodomy accusations often occurred in waves. The executions were generally carried out at public *autos da fé,* where bigamists and other individuals regarded as disturbing God's natural order were also either executed or displayed for public ridicule. Bestiality cases often involved young men from rural areas who occasionally denounced themselves when their consciences became too burdened; a disproportionate number of these were farm workers from France, a fact which both resulted from and supported Spanish stereotypes about French sexual habits. The severity of the Aragonese Inquisition in sodomy cases ended early; no one was executed in Aragon after 1633, about a century before executions for homosexuality ended in both Castile and northern Europe.

Along with charges of male homosexual sodomy and bestiality, the Inquisition in Aragon also heard a handful of cases of heterosexual and female homosexual sodomy. In the mid-sixteenth century the Inquisition ruled that sex between women was not sodomy unless they used an artificial phallus (a ruling later forgotten in one case), but that heterosexual anal intercourse, even between husband and wife, was. Cases were rare and usually emerged when a wife who was angry at her husband denounced him or a confessor urged a woman to bring the accusation; if the husband could prove malice on the wife's part, the case was dropped, though there are a few instances of executions or lesser punishments for heterosexual sodomy, including one in which the charge was brought by a group of neighbors. Courts elsewhere in Catholic Europe similarly heard very few cases of sodomy involving women, whatever the gender (or species) of their sexual partners; female sodomy was not unimaginable to most religious authorities, it was simply rare. (Trial records indicate that people in some areas *did* regard female sodomy as unimaginable, and even had difficulties understanding male sodomy; two young peasants in Hungary, for example, accused their employer of witchcraft when he stroked their penises, explaining that he must have wanted their sperm for magical purposes because why else would a man do this?)

In Aragon and elsewhere, the social standing of the accused could shape the punishment, even in sodomy trials. Though some clergy were executed and sent to the galleys, most were generally treated more leniently than lay men, and the wealthy more leniently than the poor. The toleration of male homosexuality at the highest levels has been studied most for the French court, because it included the royal family; King Henry III (ruled 1574–1589) wore women's clothing to balls and parties and surrounded himself with male favorites, his so-called *mignons,* while Philippe d'Orléans, the brother of Louis XIV, also regularly cross-dressed and had homosexual affairs. The goings-on at court were avidly reported in scurrilous pamphlets and broadsides, with religious reformers in France worried that this "aristocratic vice" would spread to other classes. By the early eighteenth century in Paris, police began to track "sodomites" using spies and informers, including clergy to spy on other clergy. Court records continued to use religious language in sodomy cases, and the police occasionally sent those they rounded up to confession, in the hopes that this would induce guilt and repentence. Men found guilty of sodomy were forced to sign a document repenting of their acts if they wished to avoid or get out of prison; one of these confessions in a police report from 1738 notes, "He [the accused] admitted the above facts, saying that he is a miserable sinner, whom God would not want to ruin, that he had permitted it [the arrest] to happen to him so that he would repent and do penance."[21] Such statements did not prevent a very high rate of recidivism, however, and French courts also used banishment or army service as punishment for sodomy.

Witchcraft and magic

The chronological pattern of prosecution for sodomy and other sexual crimes in Catholic Europe – an upsurge in the 1560s after Trent, and then a decline to the eighteenth century, punctuated by brief panics and group arrests – was very similar to the pattern of prosecution for witchcraft. The geographical pattern of witchtrials was very different, however, for only certain parts of Catholic Europe felt the full force of the witchcraze. These were the duchy of Lorraine in eastern France along with the Rhineland and territories ruled by prince-bishops in Germany, all of which saw mass panics and the execution of hundreds or thousands of people. By contrast, Ireland saw almost no witchtrials, and the only mass panic in Spain was in Navarre in 1610, when the area came briefly under the influence of the French demonologist Pierre de Lancre. Other than this, the Inquisition in Spain executed only a handful of witches, the Portuguese Inquisition only one, and the Roman Inquisition none, though in each of these areas there were hundreds of cases.

The development of diabolism and the links between witchcraft and sexuality traced in the previous chapter for Protestants were very similar to those of the parts of Catholic Europe that saw mass trials, and the most eminent demonologists of the late sixteenth century were Catholic, including the French jurist Jean Bodin and the Flemish Jesuit Martin Del Rio. Thus the aspect of Catholic treatment of witchcraft that was most distinctive was the leniency of the Inquisition. Inquisitors firmly believed in the power of the Devil and were no less misogynist than other judges, but they doubted very much whether the people accused of doing evil deeds (*maleficia*) had actually made a pact with the Devil which gave them special powers. They viewed them not as diabolical devil-worshippers, but as superstitious and ignorant peasants who should be educated rather than executed. Their main crime was not heresy, but rather undermining the church's monopoly on supernatural remedies by claiming they had special powers. Thus Inquisitors set witchcraft within the context of false magical and spiritual claims, rather than within the context of heresy and apostasy.

Other types of magical and spiritual claims investigated by the Inquisition often had a sexual component. Women who asserted that God had given them special powers – to survive though eating nothing but the Communion host, to see visions – occasionally described the angels who appeared to them as attractive young men. In their assessment that such women were "false saints," Inquisition officials agreed with this description, but noted that these were either "demons [who] appeared to her in the form of a handsome young man" or completely faked.[22] Throughout Catholic Europe, women who claimed to be possessed by demons often described this possession in sexual and bodily terms, and the exorcisms which were the Catholic Church's main weapons against possession might involve touching the woman or anointing her with oil as she lay on her bed with her hair and clothes in disarray.

Some claims to magical powers were sexual not only in origin, but also in purported effects. Included among the many cases of illicit magic which came before the Inquisition there were always a good share involving love charms, incantations, and concoctions. Many of these blended Christian and non-Christian rituals and objects: prayers to the Virgin were combined with magical incantations, knots thought to cause impotence were tied in strings at mass, holy water mixed with semen or menstrual blood was sprinkled or poured on doorsills and clothing, scraps of paper with charms written on them were placed under the altar cloth at mass. At times local priests were not unknowing parties in such magic, but actively involved. They said masses over magical objects, or baptized magnets with a person's name, complete with godparents and holy oil. (Magnets baptized with a name were thought to have the power to draw that person to the holder of the magnet.) They also conducted rituals designed specifically to lift love charms, for people who thought they had been the victims of such a charm often turned first to their priest to lift its spell; only after this did not work did they bring the matter to the attention of the court, a step they were loath to take as this required admitting they believed the love charm had worked.

Official Inquisitorial opinion about love charms was somewhat self-contradictory. Charms were outlawed both because the women who sold them cheated their customers by selling something that was ineffective, and because they subverted free will and coerced people to sin by being *too* effective. Despite the ambiguity in official reasoning, love magic was uniformly condemned, with punishments ranging from scoldings to whipping and exile.

The making of love charms was often a specialized practice of networks of women on the margins of society, who traveled around peddling their wares. Their continued success in finding hopeful customers, most of them women, demonstrates the importance most women in Catholic Europe attached to a permanent relationship with a man. If one's dowry and family connections could not win one a husband, then a charm which made the object of one's affections impotent with any other woman was an option, whatever the Inquisition or other religious authorities might say.

Orthodoxy

Many aspects of Roman Catholic teachings about sex and the treatment of sexual issues found parallels in eastern Europe, although few of these have received the extensive study that western Europe has been accorded during this period. The most important means of communicating church ideas about sexuality was confession, for, as in the post-Tridentine Catholic Church, confession was required and people appear to have followed this requirement. Penances were imposed for a range of acts related to sex, including those which were not under the control of the penitent, such as nocturnal emissions and miscarriages. Thus the strong emphasis on the intentions of the penitent found in post-Tridentine Catholicism was not a major part of Orthodox confession, which still concentrated primarily on correct sexual conduct rather than subjective motives and feelings, although confessors were advised to set mild penances for lustful thoughts. Penances and punishments ranged up to excommunication, which excluded one from church rituals and was reinforced by social ostracism from the community.

Because of the centrality of confession, priests sometimes gave short sermons as part of the ritual which often included discussion of moral issues. Metropolitan Daniil (in office 1522–1539), for example, warned about prostitutes and effeminate young men who paid too much attention to their appearance. He noted that marriage and the monastery were both appropriate paths to salvation, but that the monastery was harder; married life with all things in moderation was his recommendation for most people. Moderation was also the main theme of a popular handbook on behavior, *Domostroi*, written in the 1560s, which stressed the importance of sexual purity especially for women and obedience to the wishes of one's parents for both sexes.

Studies of illicit sexuality based on records of large numbers of actual cases such as those of the Inquisition in Aragon have not yet been undertaken for eastern Europe, but evidence from laws and prescriptive literature indicates that, as expected, fornication and prostitution were prohibited, though the penances and punishments set were dependent on the social status of the people involved. Sodomy was construed quite widely to include masturbation and heterosexual intercourse other than in the approved position, as well as bestiality and homosexual relations. As noted in Chapter 1, male homosexual relations were not regarded as that much worse than illicit heterosexual relations, particularly if they did not involve anal penetration. Actions which upset the proper gender order, such as a man shaving off his beard so that he looked more like a woman, were regarded as more serious violations of church law. This also applied to female homosexual relations, which were generally considered a form of masturbation unless one of the women sat on top of the other as a man was expected to. Occasionally, however, female homosexual activity was linked with pagan rituals which had survived the Christianization of Russia; women who engaged in homosexual activities were called "God-insulting grannies" and charged with praying to evil spirits.[23] Witchcraft was also linked with paganism, but was not particularly female-identified. There were no large-scale witch hunts in Russia and no strong demonic concept of witchcraft; most of the people prosecuted for this practice were men charged with sorcery or with harming people and animals through magic.

Beginning in the fifteenth century, the Ottoman Turks ruled a large part of south-eastern Europe and many Orthodox Christians lived under Muslim rule. As in Spain, open intermarriage was not acceptable, but in some areas, such as Cyprus, women who had been Orthodox converted to Islam in order to marry Muslim men. In a few cases Orthodox women who were already married divorced their husbands and married Muslim men, though to do this they had to swear in a Muslim court that they had converted of their own volition and that their husbands had refused conversion. Because no Christian courts were in operation, Orthodox and Latin Christians used the Muslim courts to settle other issues regarding marriage as well.

During the seventeenth century, a number of reformers emerged in the Russian Orthodox Church, who – like both the Protestants and Roman Catholics who were their inspiration – wanted to strengthen the role of the clergy in parish life and rid popular piety of its – to their eyes – non-Christian elements and immoral excesses. They complained, for example, of the carnivalesque Yuletide celebrations that undermined the solemnity of the religious holiday:

> From Christmas to Epiphany they have games in their houses and men and women assemble for the evil games . . . and they perform these games of the devil's imagining with evil images, blaspheming God's mercy and his Mother's holidays. They make wooden figures like horses and bulls and decorate them with linen cloth

and hang bells on the horse; and on themselves they put hairy animal masks and clothes to fit and in the back they put tails, looking like devils, and on their faces they carry the shameful members [penises] and bleat devilish things like goats and reveal their shameful members.[24]

Tsar Alexei (reigned 1645–1676) outlawed such rituals, although the prohibitions were largely ineffective, and his son, Peter the Great, himself sponsored them.

   The legal provisions for the formation and termination of marriages remained relatively stable in Russia in this period, although the reforming tendencies gradually left their mark. The minimum age for marriage remained at 15 for boys and 12 for girls (later raised to 15), although it was not rigorously observed. By the sixteenth and seventeenth centuries, even peasants included the obligatory church ceremony in their weddings, although it was viewed as less important than the secular agreement and the rituals that accompanied it. Parental consent continued to be required for first marriages, as it was throughout Orthodox Europe; as earlier Serbian law had put it, "If a maiden refuses to marry the young man to whom her parents promised her, she shall be considered shameless and dishonorable among her friends and before the people."[25] But at the end of the seventeenth century, revised versions of the church marriage ceremony introduced an innovation: the bride and groom themselves stated their consent to the marriage. Divorce was allowed, for incompatibility, drunkenness, and violence as well as adultery, though it was frowned on, as was remarriage. Russian law strongly protected the honor of women of all classes, ordering that men who dishonored them, either by actions or by insulting them verbally, be required to pay a fine, either to the woman or to her male relatives. In the sixteenth and seventeenth centuries it became customary in Russia to further protect the honor of elite women, especially marriageable daughters, by secluding them in the *terem,* separate women's quarters. Although women in the *terem* could engage in paid work and entertain guests, they rarely appeared in public.

   Alexis's reign also saw the most significant split within the Russian Orthodox Church in its long history, between those who followed the reforms in liturgy and prayers of the patriarch Nikon – designed to make Russian rituals more like those in the Greek and Ukrainian Orthodox churches – and those who wanted to stay with traditional practices, termed Old Believers. Old Believers were convinced that the reforms were the work of the Antichrist and that the Apocalypse was at hand. Consequently they saw little purpose in marriage and procreation, although they moderated this position when it became apparent that the end of the world was more distant than they had originally calculated. Because they cast the tsar and the government as the "spirit of the Antichrist" and rejected their authority, they were subjected to persecution, often severe. Some Old Believers chose the route of martyrdom, usually by self-immolation; others fled to the fringes of the vast Russian Empire or even abroad; still others found ways of accommodation, politically and ideologically, with the Russian state.

The modest adoption of western practices advocated by Patriarch Nikon paled in comparison with that demanded several decades later by Alexei's son, Peter I (ruled 1682–1725), who became known as Peter the Great. In his church reform of 1721, Peter abolished the office of patriarch (which had been vacant since 1700) and instead established a committee, the Holy Synod, as the church's ruling body, and effectively made it into a department of the secular government. Peter was intent on modernizing and westernizing Russia, in order to make it a larger and more powerful state. To this end he engaged in nearly constant warfare, and so favored anything that would increase the Russian population. Peter was convinced that unhappy marriages produced fewer children; in 1722 he added his voice to that of the Orthodox Church in forbidding forced marriages at all social levels. Landlords were not to compel their serfs to marry against their wishes – a common practice despite church opposition – for, in the words of the eighteenth-century scholar Mikhail Lomonosov, "where there is no love, there is no hope of fruitfulness either."[26] Peter required that elite women abandon the *terem,* and appear at public social gatherings, mingling with men. He required that men and women of the elite dress in western style, ordering men to shave their beards in defiance of Orthodox tradition, and women to don the corsetted gowns and adopt the bare-headed coiffures of the West.

In the new political and social milieu, young men and women found greater authorization to choose their own spouses, without being pressured to yield to parental will. The opportunities for romantic liaisons outside of marriage increased, and the stigma attached to them declined. To take care of the children from such liaisons, the state established foundling homes, and encouraged desperate mothers to bring their newborns there, instead of abandoning their babies or practicing infanticide, which was criminalized. Male homosexual activity was also criminalized, based on Western models.

Popular rituals which stressed female purity, such as showing the bride's blood-stained sheets or nightgown after the wedding night, were prohibited, and women who bore children out of wedlock were not to be forced to marry the father, though they were allowed to. (As in western Europe, children conceived or even born out of wedlock in rural areas generally brought little dishonor if their parents subsequently married.) Peter regarded marriages between social equals as preferable, and so required spouses to be of the same social class. Religious differences, on the other hand, were not an issue; against the objections of the church, he allowed marriages between spouses of different Christian denominations, demanding only that the children be baptized into the Orthodox faith. With the endorsement of the church hierarchy, Peter required parish priests to keep records of births, baptisms, marriages, and deaths. These records allowed the state to determine men's status for taxation and military service, and also allowed the church to try to prevent bigamous or incestuous marriages. Because Peter saw no purpose in wasting human resources on monastic life, he forbade physically capable men and women of childbearing years from taking vows.

Although the church and state of Peter's era issued many new regulations, it proved much more difficult to alter ingrained attitudes and behavior. Church leaders complained about peasants' ignorance of Christian teachings, but made little concrete effort to remedy it. Nobles successfully lobbied Peter's successors to repeal some of his laws concerning the financial provisions of marriage. Among peasants especially, young people could not exercise free choice of spouses. Rules concerning entrance into monasteries were relaxed, and displaced middle-aged women in particular sought this alternative. Western concepts of romantic love and western forms of socializing gradually gained predominance, however, despite the objections of conservatives, who bemoaned what they saw as a lack of morals.

The attitude toward sexuality which is often loosely termed "Puritan" was clearly shared by religious reformers of all creeds in early modern Europe. Catholic and Orthodox leaders were just as suspicious of sexual pleasure as many Protestants, and just as intent to reform or repress sexual activities which they viewed as improper in a godly community. The actual effects of their reform efforts came much more slowly than they had anticipated – just as they did for Protestants – and were accepted most readily when they fitted with local traditions or when the priests or other officials who implemented them responded to local ideas. Though the exact timing differed slightly, all of Europe saw increasing clerical and bureaucratic control of marriage and sexual discipline during the sixteenth and seventeenth centuries, accompanied by activities and institutions designed to help – or force – clergy and laity to internalize stricter moral standards. Church and state authorities throughout Europe despaired over people's inability or unwillingness to live up to the standards they wished to impose, however, and by the mid-eighteenth century, or even earlier, they decided that draconian punishments for most moral and sexual crimes were ineffective or inappropriate.

Church and state attempts at reform and repression did not end at the borders of Europe, for this period also saw, of course, the first wave of

European overseas exploration and colonization. Christian missionaries and institutions accompanied all of the colonial powers, and the control of the sexuality of both indigenous people and colonists was an essential part of colonial religious and political policy. The following three chapters will thus examine developments outside of Europe, where the local traditions and ideas were far more diverse than any reformer complaining about Basque trial marriages or Russian blasphemous costumes could have imagined.

Notes

1 John Major, *In quartum Sententiarum* (Paris, 1519) translated and quoted in John Noonan, *Contraception: A History of Its Treatment by the Catholic Theologians and Canonists* (New York: New American Library, 1965)), 374.

2 *Concilium Tridentinum* 8: 624, translated and quoted in James A. Brundage, *Law, Sex, and Christian Society in Medieval Europe* (Chicago: University of Chicago Press, 1987), 568.

3 Decrees of the Council of Trent session 25, Ch. 5, translated and quoted in Elizabeth Makowski, *Canon Law and Cloistered Women: Periculoso and Its Commentators 1298–1545* (Washington, DC: The Catholic University of America Press, 1997), 128.

4 Geminianus Monacensis, *Geistlicher Weeg-Weiser gen Himmel* (Munich 1679) translated and quoted in Ulrike Strasser, " '*Aut Maritus aut Murus*'? Women's Lives in Counter-Reformation Munich (1571–1651)," PhD Dissertation, University of Minnesota, 1997, 25–26.

5 Tomás Sánchez, *De sancto matrimonii sacramento,* translated and quoted in Noonan, *Contraception,* 391.

6 Jean Benedicti, *Somme des péchés* (Paris, 1601), translated and quoted in Pierre Hurteau, "Catholic Moral Discourse on Male Sodomy and Masturbation in the Seventeenth and Eighteenth Centuries," *Journal of the History of Sexuality* 4 (1993): 13.

7 Letter written in 1585 by the inquisitors of the provinces of Galicia and Asturias, translated and quoted in Jaime Contreras and Gustav Henningsen, "Forty-four Thousand Cases of the Spanish Inquisition (1540–1700): Analysis of a Historical Data Bank," in Gustav Henningsen and John Tedeschi, eds, *The Inquisition in Early Modern Europe: Studies on Sources and Methods* (Dekalb: Northern Illinois University Press, 1986), 120.

8 Archives of the Society of Jesus at Rome, 1593, translated and quoted in Louis Chatellier, *The Europe of the Devout: The Catholic Reformation and the Formation of a New Society* (Cambridge: Cambridge University Press, 1989), 45.

9 Letter from Jean d'Arrerac, translated and quoted in André Burguière and François Lebrun, "Priest, Prince and Family," in André Burguière, et al., eds, *A History of the Family: Volume Two – The Impact of Modernity* (Cambridge, Mass.: Harvard University Press, 1996), 128.

10 Village priest in France, 1774, translated and quoted in Nicole Castan, et. al., "Community, State and Family: Trajectories and Tensions," in Roger

Chartier, ed., *A History of Private Life: III: Passions of the Renaissance* (Cambridge: Harvard University Press, 1989), 567.

11 Visitation report of 1652, translated and quoted in Andrew Barnes, "The Social Transformation of the French Parish Clergy," in Barbara B. Diefendorf and Carla Hesse, *Culture and Identity in Early Modern Europe (1500–1800): Essays in Honor of Natalie Zemon Davis* (Ann Arbor: University of Michigan Press, 1993), 142.

12 Quoted in Phil Kilroy, "Women and the Reformation in Seventeenth-century Ireland," in Margaret MacCurtain and Mary O'Dowd, eds, *Women in Early Modern Ireland* (Edinburgh: Edinburgh University Press, 1991), 189.

13 Diego Pérez de Valdivia, *Aviso de gente recogida* (1585), translated and quoted in Stephen Haliczer, *Sexuality in the Confessional: A Sacrament Profaned* (New York: Oxford University Press, 1996), 111.

14 Baltasar Alvarez, *Escritos Espirituales,* translated and quoted in Jodi Bilinkoff, "Confessors, Penitents, and the Construction of Identities in Early Modern Avila," in Diefendorf and Hesse, *Culture,* 86.

15 Edict of Henry II, 1556, translated and quoted in Burguière and Lebrun, "Priest," 111.

16 Burguière and Lebrun, "Priest," 129.

17 Inquisition deposition of 1575, translated and quoted in Jean-Pierre DeDieu, "The Inquisition and Popular Culture in New Castile," in Stephen Haliczer, ed., *Inquisition and Society in Early Modern Europe* (Totowa, NJ: Barnes and Noble, 1987), 139–140.

18 Inquisition records in the diocesan archives of Cuenca, translated and quoted in Sara T. Nalle, *God in La Mancha: Religious Reform and the People of Cuenca, 1500–1650* (Baltimore: Johns Hopkins University Press, 1992), 61.

19 Legal proceedings in the Archivo della Curia Vescovile, Gallipoli, 1749, translated and quoted in David Gentilcore, *From Bishop to Witch: The System of the Sacred in Early Modern Terra d'Otranto* (Manchester: Manchester University Press, 1992), 58.

20 Madre Magdalena de San Gerónimo, *Razón, y forma . . .* (1608) translated and quoted in Mary Elizabeth Perry, "Magdalens and Jezebels in Counter-Reformation Spain," in Anne J. Cruz and Mary Elizabeth Perry, eds, *Culture and Control in Counter-Reformation Spain* (Minneapolis: University of Minnesota Press, 1992), 135–136.

21 Translated and quoted in Michael Rey, "Police and Sodomy in Eighteenth-century Paris: From Sin to Disorder," in Kent Gerard and Gert Hekma, eds, *The Pursuit of Sodomy: Male Homosexuality in Renaissance and Enlightenment Europe* (New York: Harrington Park Press, 1989), 141.

22 Inquisitorial examination of Magdalena de la Cruz, 1546, translated and quoted in Alison Weber, "Saint Teresa, Demonologist," in Cruz and Perry, *Culture and Control,* 173.

23 *Potrebnik* (1651), translated and quoted in Eve Levin, *Sex and Society among the Orthodox Slavs, 900–1700* (Ithaca: Cornell University Press, 1989), 204.

24 Translated and quoted in Paul Bushkovitch, *Religion and Society in Russia: The Sixteenth and Seventeenth Centuries* (New York: Oxford University Press, 1992), 55–56.

25 Translated and quoted in Levin, *Sex and Society*, 99.
26 Mikhail Lomonosov, *Sochineniia,* translated and quoted in Natalie Pushkareva, *Women in Russian History from the Twelfth to the Twentieth Century,* trans. Eve Levin (Armonk, NY: M.E. Sharpe, 1997), 158.

Selected further reading

Many of the works mentioned in the reading lists of previous chapters also include material which discusses post-Reformation Catholicism and Orthodoxy. For an overview of Catholicism in this period, see R. Po-Chia Hsia, *The World of Catholic Renewal, 1540–1770* (Cambridge: Cambridge University Press, 1998).

There are many good collections of articles which include discussions of the issues mentioned in this chapter. For France see: Philippe Aries and André Bejin, eds, *Western Sexuality: Practice and Precept in Past and Present Times* (Oxford: Blackwell, 1985) and Jean-Louis Flandrin, *Sex in the Western World: The Development of Attitudes and Behavior*, trans. Sue Collins (Chur, Switzerland: Harwood, 1991). For Italy see: Edward Muir and Guido Ruggiero, eds, *Sex and Gender in Historical Perspective: Selections from* Quaderni Storici (Baltimore: Johns Hopkins University Press, 1990); Marilyn Migiel and Juliana Schiesari, eds, *Refiguring Women: Perspectives on Gender and the Italian Renaissance* (Ithaca: Cornell University Press, 1991); Samuel K. Cohn, Jr., ed., *Women in the Streets: Essays on Sex and Power in Renaissance Italy* (Baltimore: Johns Hopkins University Press, 1996); Trevor Dean and K.J.P. Lowe, *Crime, Society, and the Law in Renaissance Italy* (Cambridge: Cambridge University Press, 1994). For Spain see: Magdalena S. Sanchez and Alain Saint-Saëns, eds, *Spanish Women in the Golden Age: Images and Realities* (Westport, Conn.: Greenwood Press, 1996); Alain Saint-Saëns, ed., *Religion, Body, and Gender in Early Modern Spain* (San Francisco: Edwin Mellen Press, 1991) and *Sex and Love in Golden Age Spain* (New Orleans: University Press of the South, 1996); Cruz and Perry, *Culture and Control* (note 20). For Ireland, see: MacCurtain and O'Dowd, *Women* (note 12). Single articles include: P.J. Corish, "Catholic Marriage under the Penal Code," in Art Cosgrove, ed., *Marriage in Ireland* (Dublin: College Press, 1985), 56–74; István György Tóth, "Peasant Sexuality in Eighteenth-century Hungary," *Continuity and Change* 6 (1991): 43–58; Guido Ruggiero, "Marriage, Love, Sex, and Renaissance Civic Morality," in James Grantham Turner, *Sexuality and Gender in Early Modern Europe: Institutions, Texts, Images* (Cambridge: Cambridge University Press, 1993), 10–30; James R. Farr, "The Pure and Disciplined Body: Hierarchy, Morality, and Symbolism in France During the Catholic Reformation," *Journal of Interdisciplinary History* 21 (1991): 391–414.

For the opinions of the most influential Christian humanist on marriage and women, see Erika Rummel, ed., *Erasmus on Women* (Toronto: University of Toronto Press, 1996). Ute Ranke-Heinemann, *Eunuchs for the Kingdom of Heaven: Women, Sexuality and the Catholic Church,* trans. Peer Heinegg (New York: Doubleday, 1990) provides an extremely critical analysis of Catholic opinion. For a fine overview of the veneration of Mary, see Marina Warner, *Alone of All Her Sex: The Myth and Cult of the Virgin Mary* (London: Weidenfeld and Nicolson, 1976).

Assessments of the impact of the Council of Trent are provided in: W. David Myers, *"Poor, Sinning Folk": Confession and Conscience in Counter-Reformation Germany* (Ithaca: Cornell University Press, 1996); Marc Forster, *The Counter-Reformation in the Villages: Religion and Reform in the Bishopric of Speyer, 1560–1720* (Ithaca: Cornell, 1992); Louis Châtellier, *The Religion of the Poor: The Rural Missions in Europe and the Formation of Modern Catholicism, c. 1500–1800*, trans. Brian Pearce (Cambridge: Cambridge University Press, 1997); Nalle, *God in La Mancha* (note 18); Gentilcore, *From Bishop to Witch* (note 19).

The way in which confraternities and other new religious groups shaped post-Tridentine piety has been examined in: Maureen Flynn, *Sacred Charity: Confraternities and Social Welfare in Spain, 1400–1700* (Ithaca: Cornell University Press, 1989); Elizabeth Rapley, *The Dévotes: Women and Church in Seventeenth-century France* (Montreal: McGill/Queen's University Press, 1990); Nicolas Terpstra, *Lay Confraternities and Civic Religion in Renaissance Bologna* (Cambridge: Cambridge University Press, 1995); Chatellier, *Europe of the Devout* (note 8). Rapley, *The Devotés,* and Ruth P. Liebowitz "Virgins in the Service of Christ: The Dispute over an Active Apostolate for Women during the Counter-Reformation," in *Women of Spirit: Female Leadership in the Jewish and Christian Traditions* (New York: Simon and Schuster, 1979), 131–152 discuss post-Tridentine efforts to assure the enclosure of female monasteries.

The Inquisition's role in the regulation of sexuality has been studied in many works by William Monter, such as: "Women and the Italian Inquisitions," in Mary Beth Rose, ed., *Women in the Middle Ages and the Renaissance: Literary and Historical Perspectives* (Syracuse, NY: Syracuse University Press, 1986), 73–89; *Ritual, Myth, and Magic in Early Modern Europe* (Athens, Ohio: Ohio University Press, 1983); *Frontiers of Heresy: The Spanish Inquisition from the Basque Lands to Sicily* (Cambridge: Cambridge University Press, 1990). Other relevant studies of the Inquisition include: Henry Kamen, *Inquisition and Society in Spain in the Sixteenth and Seventeenth Centuries* (London: Weidenfeld and Nicolson, 1985); Stephen Haliczer, *Inquisition and Society in the Kingdom of Valencia, 1478–1834* (Berkeley: University of California Press, 1990); André Fernandez, "The Repression of Sexual Behavior by the Aragonese Inquisition between 1560 and 1700," *Journal of the History of Sexuality* 7 (1997): 469–501; Haliczer, ed., *Inquisition and Society* (note 17); Henningsen and Tedeschi, *Inquisition* (note 7).

Relationships between confessor and penitents have been explored in: Rudolph M. Bell, "Telling Her Sins: Male Confessors and Female Penitents in Catholic Reformation Italy," in Lynda L. Coon, et. al., eds, *That Gentle Strength: Historical Perspectives on Women in Christianity* (Charlottesville: University of Virginia Press, 1990), 118–133; Stephen Haliczer, *Sexuality in the Confessional: A Sacrament Profaned* (New York: Oxford University Press, 1996); Bilinkoff, "Confessors" (note 14). Fulvio Tomizza, *Heavenly Supper: The Story of Maria Janis*, trans. Anne Jacobsen Schutte (Chicago: University of Chicago Press, 1993), Richard Kagan, *Lucrecia's Dreams: Politics and Prophecy in Sixteenth Century Spain* (Berkeley: University of California Press, 1990), and Luisa Ciammitti, "One Saint Less: The Story of Angela Mellini, a Bolognese Seamstress (1667- 17[?])" in Muir and Ruggiero, *Sex and Gender,* 141–176, provide case studies of women accused of being false saints.

Popular rituals and their control have been examined in: Edward Muir, *Ritual in Early Modern Europe* (Cambridge: Cambridge University Press, 1998); Natalie Zemon Davis, "The Reasons of Misrule," in her *Society and Culture in Early Modern France* (Stanford: Stanford University Press, 1975), 97–123; Christiane Klapisch-Zuber, "The 'Mattinata' in Medieval Italy," in her *Women, Family, and Ritual in Renaissance Italy*, trans. Lydia Cochrane (Chicago: University of Chicago Press, 1982), 261–282; Peter Burke, *Popular Culture in Early Modern Europe* (London: T. Smith, 1978). Robert Forster and Orest Ranum, eds, *Ritual, Religion and the Sacred: Sections from the Annales* (Baltimore: Johns Hopkins University Press, 1982) contains several articles on wedding rituals in Catholic areas.

The Iberian peninsula offered several situations not found elsewhere in Catholic Europe. Mark D. Meyerson, *The Muslims of Valencia in the Age of Ferdinand and Isabel: Between Coexistence and Crusade* (Berkeley: University of California Press, 1991) discusses Christian–Muslim sexual relations, while Mary Elizabeth Perry, *Gender and Disorder in Early Modern Seville* (Princeton: Princeton University Press, 1990) analyzes the situation in one important Spanish city.

The especially strong alliance in France between families and state authorities in the control of marriage and other aspects of behavior has been investigated in James R. Farr, *Authority and Sexuality in Early Modern Burgundy* (New York: Oxford University Press, 1995) and Sarah Hanley, "Engendering the State: Family Formation and State Building in Early Modern France," *French Historical Studies* 16 (1989): 4–27.

Questions relating to illegitimacy, infanticide, and abandonment are discussed in: Peter Laslett, Karla Oosterveen, and Richard M. Smith, eds, *Bastardy and its Comparative History* (Cambridge: Harvard University Press, 1980); René Leboutte, "Offense against Family Order: Infanticide in Belgium from the Fifteenth through the Early Twentieth Centuries," *Journal of the History of Sexuality* 2 (1991): 159–185; David I. Kertzer, *Sacrificed for Honor: Italian Infant Abandonment and the Politics of Reproductive Control* (Boston: Beacon, 1993).

Houses for prostitutes and disorderly women have been studied in: Philip F. Riley, "Michel Foucault, Lust, Women, and Sin in Louis XIV's Paris," *Church History* 59 (1990): 35–50; Sherrill Cohen, *The Evolution of Women's Asylums Since 1500: From Refuges for Ex-Prostitutes to Shelters for Battered Women* (Oxford: Oxford University Press, 1992); Lucia Ferrante, "Honor Regained: Women in the Casa del Soccorso di San Paolo in Sixteenth-century Bologna," in Muir and Ruggiero, *Sex and Gender,* 46–72; John Henderson and Richard Wall, eds, *Poor Women and Children in the European Past* (London: Routledge, 1994). Elizabeth Cohen, "No Longer Virgins: Self-Representation by Young Women in Late Renaissance Rome," in Marilyn Migiel and Juliana Schiesari, eds, *Gender and the Italian Renaissance* (Ithaca, NY: Cornell University Press, 1991), 169–191 analyzes ways in which young women's views of their own sexuality differed from official views.

For love magic, see: María Helena Sánchez Ortega, "Sorcery and Eroticism as Love Magic," in Mary Elizabeth Perry and Anne J. Cruz, eds, *Cultural Encounters: The Impact of the Inquisition in Spain and the New World* (Berkeley: University of California Press, 1991), 58–92; Guido Ruggiero, *Binding Passions: Tales of Magic,*

Marriage, and Power at the End of the Renaissance (New York: Oxford University Press, 1993); Mary O'Neil, "Magical Healing, Love Magic, and the Inquisition in Late Sixteenth Century Modena," in Haliczer, *Inquisition and Society,* (note 17), 88–114. A good local study of witchcraft in a Catholic area is Ruth Martin, *Witchcraft in Venice, 1550–1650* (Oxford: Blackwell, 1989).

Many of the works on homosexuality listed in the 'Further reading' to Chapter 2 also discuss Catholic Europe; see also Judith C. Brown, *Immodest Acts: The Life of a Lesbian Nun in Renaissance Italy* (Oxford: Oxford University Press, 1986); Jeffrey Merrick, "Sodomitical Scandals and Subcultures in the 1720s," *Men and Masculinities* 1: 4 (1999); Hurteau, "Catholic Moral Discourse," (note 6).

For Orthodoxy, in addition to the studies mentioned in the notes and in the reading list following Chapter 1 see: Nancy Shields Kollman, "Women's Honor in Early Modern Russia," in Barbara Evans Clements, et. al., eds, *Russia's Women: Accommodation, Resistance, Transformation* (Berkeley: University of California Press, 1991), 60–73 and "The Seclusion of Muscovite Women," *Russian History* 10 (1983): 170–187; Russell Zguta, "Witchcraft Trials in Seventeenth-century Russia," *American Historical Review* 82 (1977): 1187–1207; Georg Michels, "Muscovite Elite Women and Old Belief," *Harvard Ukrainian Studies* 19 (1995): 428–450. For the situation in Cyprus, see Ronald C. Jennings, *Christians and Muslims in Ottoman Cyprus and the Mediterranean World, 1571–1640* (New York: New York University Press, 1993).

Illustration from *El Primer Nueva Coronica y Buen Gobierno* (1615), a history of the Spanish conquest of the Andes written by Felipe Guaman Poma de Ayala, an Andean convert to Christianity. The text reads, "The *corregidor*, the priest, the lieutenant go wandering about and looking at the shameful parts of women." By permission of Siglo Veintiuno Editores.

LATIN AMERICA

LATIN AMERICA

A T PRECISELY THE time when Catholics and Protestants in western Europe were in combat with one another from the pulpit, on paper, and on the battlefield, and Christian religious authorities of all denominations were attempting to impose stricter moral standards on those under their authority, some European countries were engaging in overseas explorations and colonization. The first European colonies outside of Europe were those of the Portuguese in the Atlantic islands, Brazil, West Africa, and Asia, and the Spanish in Central and South America and the Philippines. In all of these areas, colonial forces included Catholic missionaries and religious authorities who worked both to convert indigenous people and to establish church structures for immigrants. Catholic missionaries, primarily members of religious orders such as the Franciscans, the Dominicans, and later the Jesuits, also travelled to areas outside of European control such as China and Japan in conversion efforts. Beginning in the seventeenth century, Protestant clergy accompanied Dutch and English merchants and settlers as they established trading centers and colonies in Asia, southern Africa, and North America, although the main Protestant missionary effort did not begin until the early nineteenth century.

Along with explaining the theological and spiritual concepts central to Christianity, missionaries also attempted to persuade – or force – possible converts to adopt Christian sexual morality; in many areas, once one was baptized, following Christian patterns in terms of one's marriage rituals and sexual demeanor became a more important mark of conversion than understanding the Trinity or transubstantiation. As they did in Europe, Catholic religious authorities began to oversee marriages, hear cases of fornication, adultery, bigamy, and love magic in church courts, and attempt to shape sexual life through confession. They worked with colonial political authorities in areas under European control, and in some areas, such as the missions of South and Central America, they actually *were* the political authorities.

Catholic clergy largely shared the dominant ideas about proper sexual morality we traced in the last chapter – that sexual intercourse was to be limited to monogamous marriage, that marriage was indissoluble, that virginity and celibacy were superior to marriage and required of the clergy, that masturbation, sodomy, contraception, and abortion were mortal sins, that all sexual sins were to be confessed to a priest. Though some of these ideas were already present in the cultures they encountered, many of them were perhaps even more strange than Christian theological concepts. In addition, indigenous peoples quickly noted that Christian conquerors and colonists – sometimes including the clergy themselves – did not practice what they preached, but raped local women, entered into bigamous marriages, or engaged in numerous sexual relationships. Thus even those who converted often selectively adopted certain aspects of Christian sexual morality and rejected others, in the same way that they selectively adopted and adapted Christian spiritual notions. In some places, missionaries and other clergy also adapted their teachings to fit better with existing sexual mores or with those developing in the colonial context. Thus in order to examine the Christian regulation of sexuality outside of Europe in the early modern period, it is important to know something about sexual mores and marital patterns before contact with Europeans.

Learning about sexuality in some cultures, such as China and Japan, is relatively easy, as there are extensive written records about both norms and practices. For many other cultures, however, this is much more difficult, for there are no written records until European contact, so that all information comes from archeological evidence, writings by Europeans or other outsiders, or oral traditions recorded much more recently. Some cultures, such as those of the Andes or central Mexico, fall in between – there are some records in indigenous writing systems or some sources by indigenous people from the early modern period in their own languages or a European language, as well as reports by Europeans and the oral and archeological record. Most of these indigenous authors had learned to read and write from European clergy, however, so there is great debate among historians about how "authentic" their voices are, how much they were seeing and recording their original cultures through eyes that were already acculturated to Christian and European ways. At least in part, indigenous authors adopted views of Indian sexuality held by Europeans, which usually emphasized either innocence or lasciviousness. Thus both they and European authors tend to fit what they observed into a preconceived model.

Because the record is often so thin and involves layers of interpretation, historians disagree about a great many aspects of sexual life before European colonialism, but they generally agree that sexual patterns which developed in colonial societies were a combination of indigenous and Christian. Like all other aspects of life in the colonial world, they represented an encounter and blending of several cultures, rather than a one-sided conquest. Thus this chapter and the two chapters which follow are organized geographically rather than by colonial power, and each begins with a brief examination of indigenous sexual ideas and norms before going on to discuss changes which accompanied the introduction and institutionalization of Christianity. It is important to keep in mind that the areas under examination are vast and have widely varying patterns, and that the cultures within them about which we know the most are those which had systems of keeping records or which quite quickly developed writing using the Western alphabet. We also tend to know more about cultures, such as the Aztecs in central Mexico or the Incas in the Andes, that were politically dominant at the point of first European contact. Because encounters with these cultures shaped the way the colonial church developed and responded to groups with which it later came into contact, however, their ideas were the most influential.

Ideas and patterns before the arrival of the Europeans

Historical and archeological research makes clear that there was wide variety in indigenous sexual mores in Central and South America and the Caribbean. Some scholars suggest that the more highly organized and stratified societies, such as the Aztecs and Incas, were more strict than those which did not have strong centralized political control. Information about jungle and tribal societies in the early modern period is very limited, and in some cases is largely based on anthropological research conducted within the past century. How much one can project these findings back to earlier centuries is hotly contested, with some scholars arguing that existing patterns continued completely or largely unchanged for centuries, and others contending that assuming this overlooks how changeable and dynamic "tradition" can actually be.

Generalizing is thus fraught with perils, but there do appear to be a few traditions which most cultures shared: They had some sort of marriage ceremony, with marital partners generally chosen by the family or community rather than the individuals themselves. The marriage was sometimes preceded by a period of trial marriage in which the potential husband lived and worked in his father-in-law's house; sexual relations might begin during this period. If a marriage did not work out, the partners were often free to leave the marriage and marry elsewhere. Certain close relatives appear to have been prohibited as marital partners, with harsh punishments for incest, although in some cultures a man was expected to marry his brother's widow, a practice similar to the Jewish tradition of levirate marriage. Marriage was often monogamous, although more powerful men in some groups had more than one wife and rulers sometimes had a great many wives. Marriage among the powerful might be used as a means of cementing alliances, with women given to men to gain their favor or their allegiance, and outsiders incorporated into a kin group through marriage or other sexual ceremonies.

For women, pre-marital sexual relations were regarded as much less serious than extra-marital ones, which could be punished very severely; for men, sexual relations before or outside of marriage were generally not punished unless they upset community norms or family alliances. Some cultures linked control of the body with order and control in society and the cosmos, and excessive sexual energy or activity in both women and men was viewed as harmful; in a few cultures, all sexual activity was seen as disruptive so that sexual intercourse occurred outside houses or other buildings. Both women and men appear to have had positions as religious leaders, although women were generally not the primary religious leaders, and women who were still of child-bearing age were specifically excluded from some religious ceremonies. In some places kinship groups were linked to specific holy places, gods, or religious figures.

More specific information may be gained about certain cultures, particularly those of central Mexico and the Andes. About a century before the Spanish conquest, central Mexico was conquered by the Mexica, who formed the Aztec state; the Mexica were one of the Nahua peoples, who shared a language – Nahuatl – and many cultural traits with other groups in central Mexico. Many of the earliest missionaries in the New World learned Nahuatl in order to be more effective at conversion (the New World's first book was, in fact, a Nahuatl catechism from 1539) and were interested in Nahua traditions. They thus recorded conversations with Nahua elders and described Nahua laws and practices, and were particularly excited when they found what appeared to be parallels between Nahua values and Christian ones. For example, Nahua devotional practices included periods of sexual abstinence, sexual transgressions led people to participate in rituals of confession, and infants were given a ritual bathing to free them from pollution associated with the parents' sexual activity. Adultery (defined as sex with a married woman), abortion, and incest were at least in theory harshly punished, as was homosexual activity (though there is some debate about this among contemporary historians). Marriages were marked by a ceremony tying the cloaks of a man and a woman together, and a distinction was made in terms of inheritance between children born in and out of wedlock. Couples living together without being married could be harshly punished. Young women were advised to be modest in their demeanor and wives to obey their husbands; in the words of a *huehuetlatolli* (a discourse by Nahua elders), "when he [your husband] asks you something [or] entrusts something to you [or] when he tells you to do something, you are to obey him properly."[1] The missionaries' desires to find similarities between Christianity and Nahua beliefs and their lack of familiarity with Nahua culture caused them to misinterpret certain things, however. Nahua culture saw the basic conflict in the cosmos as order versus disorder rather than good versus evil, but regarded the proper life as a balance between these two rather than a life of order alone. Thus the Nahua sexual ideal was moderation, not abstinence. There was no notion of consequences in an afterlife or a soul distinct from the body, so nothing which directly equated with Christian ideas of guilt or sin; sex made one physically, not morally, impure. Some Aztec religious rituals also linked human sexuality and fertility with agricultural fertility in ways that the missionaries found shocking, including (most famously) human sacrifice and ritual cannibalism, and young male priests processing with erect penises or dressed in the flayed skin of a woman. Most Nahua peoples and other residents of Mexico such as the Maya did not carry out ceremonies of large-scale human sacrifice, which were part of the Aztec state cult of the sun; many of the Aztecs' sacrificial victims actually came from such groups, who because of this allied themselves with the Spanish against the Aztecs. Mayas did share some basic notions of sexuality with the Nahuas, such as a concern for balance and moderation and a condemnation of sexual excess.

The political situation in the Andes was similar to that of central Mexico, in that the Inca Empire – whose ruler was also called the Inca – conquered a large territory shortly before the Spanish came. Though human sacrifice was very rare, the Incas also had a cult of the sun, and a large number of other gods and revered ancestors. Certain young women were chosen as *aclla* (women dedicated to the sun), and either remained virgin-priestesses in special buildings or married the Inca or one of his favorites. The Incas demanded such women from all the peoples they conquered, and sent a special official, the *ochacamayo* ("he who chastizes") to order any man killed who had sexual relations with women chosen to be *aclla*. Like Aztec cosmology, that of the Incas was based on a notion of equilibrium and balance, including balance between masculine and feminine, though things associated with men – order, height, structure, light – were also viewed as superior to those associated with women, and defeated warriors were paraded through the streets of Cuzco in women's dress; this plus the tribute of *aclla* linked the Incas with masculinity and all other groups with femininity. In addition to the Inca state cults, individuals, families, and groups also venerated *huacas,* devotional objects or sacred places often regarded as having previously been ancestors or gods. Some devotional practices involving *huacas* had sexual aspects; girls occasionally married a *huaca*, and married men and women abstained from sexual relations during certain ceremonies. According to Catholic authorities, married persons were more likely to have *huacas* or other sacred objects than unmarried persons were, perhaps indicating that people received them as part of Andean marriage ceremonies.

In Inca society everyone except the *aclla* was expected to marry, and marriages, except for those of the Inca and his favorites, were monogamous. Fertility and procreation were viewed as extremely important, with a girl's first menstruation marked by a special ceremony giving her her adult name and clothing. The coming-of-age ceremony for a boy also included his being given his adult name and a loincloth, and having his ears pierced for large ear spools, so that he shed blood the way a girl did at menstruation. The emphasis on procreation and on the complementarity of men and women may have been part of the reason why Incas appear to have ordered death for homosexual activity, though some historians argue that this may be a later addition by Christian authors. In contrast to central Mexico, missionaries in the Andes did not learn Quechua, the native language, and works describing Inca practices by both Europeans and indigenous peoples are all in Latin or Spanish; Incas did keep records on *quipus,* groups of knotted strings, but deciphering these was the work of trained officials and knowledge of how to do this has been lost.

Smaller and less centralized Indian groups have left much less information, so that what we know comes from generally hostile Spanish reports or much later records. These indicate wide varieties in sexual and religious patterns. The Caribs of the Caribbean and northern South America, for example, appear to have gained most of their marital partners through raiding other tribes, a practice that was also found elsewhere. In contrast to the state religions of the Incas and Aztecs, indigenous groups elsewhere, including Florida and what later became the American Southwest, had largely animistic religions in which natural objects such as animals and plants were viewed as guardian spirits, and there was no organized priesthood.

Colonial institutions

The arrival of Europeans and Africans in the Caribbean and Central and South America brought dramatic change. Hispano-Indian contact began between 1492 and 1519 in the Caribbean; in 1519, Hernando Cortez led an expeditionary force to Mexico, and two years later defeated the Aztec Empire; in 1532, Francisco Pizarro led a force which took over the Inca Empire. From these bases, Spanish officials and colonists established various types of economic and administrative units which sought to extract the natural and agricultural wealth of the New World and provide resources for Spanish power. They thus attempted to organize the indigenous population into tribute-paying units or groups for labor, which worked in some areas, but failed in many others because of resistance combined with dramatic depopulation brought on by disease. The Spanish, and slightly later the Portuguese in Brazil and other European powers in the Caribbean, began to bring slaves from Africa to work on plantations and in mines, so that the population in many areas was a mixture of Indians, Africans, and Europeans.

These three population groups did not stay separate, for the vast majority of Europeans and Africans who came to Central and South America and the Caribbean were men, who immediately began sexual relations with indigenous women. It was thus clear from the beginning to Spanish – and to a lesser extent Portuguese – authorities that the regulation of sexuality would be a key part of colonization, and within less than a decade after Columbus's initial voyage, church and state were already setting policies regarding intermarriage and other aspects of sexual life, and establishing institutions which would enforce these policies. The papacy granted special privileges – the *Patronato* – to the Spanish and Portuguese crowns to control almost all aspects of religious life in the colonies, and only established a special group to supervise missionaries world wide – the *Congregatio de Propaganda Fidei* – in 1622. As in Europe, however, church and state generally worked together to control marriage and sex; the crown set policies and appointed church officials, who then exercised control of marriage and sexual life largely free of royal interference. To the 1760s or 1770s the church had complete legal control over marital issues in all parts of Latin America. Within the framework set by royal decree, institutions like those which operated in Europe – church courts, the Inquisition, confession – shaped sexual life, as did new institutions, such as the mission, which were created specifically for the colonial situation. In addition to enforcing Christian sexual norms as they did in Europe, many of these institutions were also working to convert Native Americans, Africans, and persons of mixed race (termed *mestizos* or *castas*) to Christianity. A rejection of Christian teachings (often termed "idolatry" by clergy) was closely linked with sexual practices which deviated from Christian norms, in the same way as heresy and "deviant" sexuality had been linked in medieval Europe. In the Latin American setting, however, these issues were also linked with race and with the acculturation of indigenous people and Africans to European Christianity.

Crown policies

Essentially the Spanish and Portuguese crowns wanted families to follow an Iberian model, but as the colonial situation changed, the ways in which they attempted to do this also changed. There were also competing schools of thought in Iberia and among Iberian officials in the New World about how to handle relations, sexual and otherwise, between population groups, and policy never followed a clear line. Because of hostility toward Jews and Muslims in Spain, sexual intercourse between Christians and non-Christians was officially prohibited, which meant that the earliest conquistadores often claimed they baptized Indian women before they had sexual relations with them. The secretary on Fernando De Soto's expedition across Florida, for example, commented that soldiers who wanted women "to make use of them and for their lewdness and lust . . . baptized them more for their carnal intercourse than to instruct them in the faith."[2] The earliest royal instructions (in 1501, 1503, and 1514) encouraged marriage between European men and Indian women in the Caribbean, and records indicate that in some areas a significant number of Spanish men had native wives, although the more common pattern was one of concubinage or casual relationships. The Spanish Crown officially prohibited the enslavement of Indians (unless they were judged to be cannibals), although it is clear that enslavement continued, sometimes specifically for sexual purposes.

Policies on marriage had to address the issue of Africans as well as Europeans and Indians, for there were Africans on the expeditions of both Cortez and Pizarro, and slaves began to be imported from Africa in substantial numbers in the early sixteenth century. Africans worked in mines and plantations as these were established, but also in towns as artisans and servants, and in some cities by the end of the sixteenth century people of African descent outnumbered those from any other single racial group. The crown officially promoted marriage of slaves with other slaves, and prohibited masters from selling spouses too far apart so that conjugal relations could be maintained; because of such restrictions owners prevented or did not encourage slave marriage.

In Mexico, the Spanish crown initially hoped to keep the Indian, European, and African populations apart, but the shortage of Spanish and African women made this impossible, and some policies of the crown actually promoted intermarriage; men granted *encomiendas,* the rights to collect tribute and labor from the natives, were ordered to marry or forfeit their grant, and in the early decades after conquest the racial origins of the wife did not matter. By the mid-sixteenth century things had changed. There was more immigration of Spanish women – perhaps as much as 30 percent by the 1570s – and racial origins became a consideration in inheritance and the ability to attend school or enter a convent. There were no explicit laws against intermarriage, but racial prejudice worked just as effectively, especially in the upper reaches of society. Eventually crown policies followed elite opinion, and maintaining social distinctions – including those of class as well as race – was declared more important than maintaining women's honor in many cases of seduction:

> If the maiden seduced under promise of marriage is inferior in status, so that she would cause greater dishonor to his lineage if he married her than the one that would fall on her by remaining seduced, he must not marry her . . . for the latter is an offense of an individual and does no harm to the Republic [i.e., New Spain], while the former is an offense of such gravity that it will denigrate an entire family, dishonor a person of pre-eminence, defame and stain an entire noble lineage, and destroy a thing which gives splendor and honor to the Republic.[3]

The crown actively promoted the immigration of married European women, ordering all men who had been married when they arrived to send for their wives or it would send them back to Spain. In Mexico, the bishop was in charge of enforcing these policies, and he sometimes ordered searches for single men, and then arrested and deported them; only those who were too old or were physically impaired (a condition determined by the bishop) were exempt from the marital requirement. In general, however, these laws were very difficult to enforce, and the wife could also certify in writing that the husband's presence in the New World was necessary to support her, so there were ways to get around them. Such laws did eventually lead to more immigration by women, especially as married women often brought their unmarried daughters, nieces, and servants. The Spanish Crown officially opposed unmarried women going to the Indies by themselves, however, and there was never any organized movement of immigration by unmarried women as there would be later in Quebec and Virginia.

Though the Portuguese crown did at times limit government positions to white men married to white women, and sponsored the immigration of white married couples, it never passed laws requiring husbands to cohabit with their wives, and there appear to have been an even smaller proportion of European women in Brazil than in the Spanish New World. Most relationships between European men and Indian women in Brazil did not result in formal marriages, although both the crown and the church recognized forms of common-law marriages as legally binding. In the eighteenth century policy changed rapidly: In 1726 the crown decreed that only white women were acceptable marriage partners for white men; in 1755, under the influence of the reforming Prime Minister the Marques de Pombal, it ordered that those men who married Indians be preferred for government offices and positions; after Pombal fell from power in 1777, it reversed its decision again.

Whatever the crown policies of the moment were, in reality most sexual relations between races were outside marriage, and by the late sixteenth century about half of the mixed-race and free black population in urban areas of Latin America was born out of wedlock; royal policies toward these children vacillated as much as those regarding mixed marriages did. In 1591, for example, the Spanish crown authorized the Viceroy of Mexico to legit-imate mixed-blood children born out of wedlock, then in 1625 it reversed the decision and barred the legitimation of such children. Children born of unions between slave men and free Indian women remained legally free, however, which is one reason such relationships were attractive to male slaves and often opposed by their owners.

Church courts

The Spanish military conquest of what became Latin America was remark-ably swift, and the church was nearly as swift in establishing ecclesiastical structures modeled on those of Europe. The first bishopric west of the Atlantic was set up in 1511 (Santo Domingo in the Caribbean), and by the mid-sixteenth century there were bishops throughout the Caribbean and Mexico and in Venezuela, Peru, Argentina, and Brazil. Along with overseeing missionary work, the establishment of parishes, and the construction of churches, bishops were officially appointed as inquisitors; they ran church courts and appointed various officials to hear cases, including those of sexual misconduct. Initially these courts had jurisdiction over natives as well as Europeans and Africans, and the first case involving an Indian was in 1522 for concubinage.

The level of activity by church courts varied with the personality of the bishop. During the mid-sixteenth century, there were several vigorous campaigns to wipe out native beliefs along with indigenous sexual practices such as concubinage and bigamy, including a campaign by the first bishop of Mexico, Juan de Zumárraga, who had been active fighting witches in the Basque country before coming to the New World. Zumárraga concentrated primarily on prominent individuals who had been converted and then relapsed rather than on ordinary people, but the harshness of his judgments toward these people led to his being removed from the office of inquisitor, though he remained bishop. Subsequent campaigns against indigenous beliefs and practices, such as those carried out against the Mixtecs (in 1544–1547 by

Francisco Tello de Sandoval) and the Yucatan Maya (in 1559–1562 by Fray Diego de Landa), were broader and even more stringent. Similar attacks on "idolatry" were undertaken in the Andes in the seventeenth century, again under the leadership of crusading bishops such as Pedro de Villagómez. In all of these episcopal investigations and visitations, people were asked to speak out about their own or others' "sinful" activities, with charges of idolatry and immorality closely linked.

Jurisdiction over serious matters of faith was taken from the bishops in 1571, when independent branches of the Spanish Inquisition were established by King Philip II in Mexico City and Lima; Mexico's first auto-da-fe was held in 1574, attended by a huge crowd, with many sentences read out. (The Portuguese crown never established an independent Inquisition in Brazil, although visiting officials from the Portuguese Inquisition did carry out investigations.) These branches were given more restricted powers over sexual matters than those in parts of Spain, for they were to hear only bigamy cases and those involving clergy; all other sexual irregularities were to be tried by episcopal church courts, and the Mexican Inquisition was specifically warned by Rome in 1580 that it was not allowed to try cases of incest or sodomy.

A more substantial restriction of powers was Phillip II's removal of Indians from the authority of the Holy Office in 1571, with the justification that their conversion was too recent so that they were not "gente de razón" (reasonable people) and could not be held fully responsible for any deviations from the faith. However, another institution, called by various names – the Indian Inquisition, the Office of the Provisor of Natives, the Tribunal of the Faith of the Indians – did have jursidicion over them. Staffed by ecclesiastical judges under the authority of the bishops, it lasted until 1820. It held autos-da-fe for bigamy and concubinage, as well as idolatry, superstition, and sorcery; its most common punishments were whipping and public humiliation. Though in theory the Indian Inquisition was separate from the Inquisition proper, in practice the same individuals often acted as judges in both, so that differences in jurisdiction were not clear.

By the eighteenth century, church courts were no longer linking immorality to idolatry, but to activities similar to those in Europe, such as dancing, drinking, and festivals. Mexican priests sound much like their Calvinist counterparts, warning about the dangers of dance: "You women, dancers of the devil, scandalous persons, you are the damnation of so many souls. Oh! What horror! . . . You provocative women, dancers of the devil, scandal, nets of the devil, basilisks of the streets and windows, you kill with your stirrings . . ."[4] As in Protestant Neuchâtel, public dances were prohibited in parts of Mexico for a brief time.

Clergy and their assistants

Along with church courts, both regular clergy (members of religious orders such as the Dominicans and the Franciscans) and secular clergy (parish priests) were important agents of church control of sexuality. The most distinctive type of religious unit in Latin America was the mission, in which the Indians were settled by members of religious orders into compact villages (termed *reducciónes* or *congregaciónes)* for conversion, taxpaying, assimilation, and in some areas, protection from slave-raiding. Converts to Christianity in missions were wards of the Spanish crown, and missionaries had great control over all aspects of their lives, including hearing both civil and criminal cases. They also acted as agents of punishment, whipping and jailing mission residents, or forcing them to be confined in stocks. The first Spanish missions were in the sixteenth century in Mexico and Florida, and by the seventeenth century missions existed from what is now northern California to Argentina, in some areas serving as the only real evidence of Spanish power. In some places mission priests vigorously enforced royal aims, but in others they conflicted with secular political authorities such as governors and military commanders. The most famous example of this was the Jesuit mission with the Guaraní Indians in Paraguay, where the missionaries fought Spanish demands for tribute. Mission priests, who were regular clergy, also came into conflict with secular clergy over the treatment of Indians under their jurisdiction or over issues involving Indian–white relations.

Both regular and secular clergy tended to be concentrated in certain areas; for example, by 1560, there were 800 regular clergy in Mexico, but many fewer in other parts of New Spain, such as Honduras. The shortage of clergy could have been solved by ordaining Indian or mestizo converts, but the earliest Latin American church councils (in 1555 and 1565) declared all Indian men and those of mixed blood unfit for the priesthood, and in some areas mission priests refused even to teach their converts Spanish. Lack of interest in virginity was one of the reasons given for excluding Indians from the priesthood; Bishop Zumárraga of Mexico commented in 1540 that elite Indian young men were highly skilled in learning Latin, but "the best students among the Indians are more inclined to marriage than to continence."[5] These absolute prohibitions were relaxed somewhat for mestizos later in the century, and a mestizo could be granted a dispensation to enter the priesthood or a religious order if his father was prominent enough, but in actuality there were very few mestizo or Indian priests until late in the eighteenth century. The first convent for Indian nuns, Corpus Christi in Mexico City, also opened only in 1728, overcoming Jesuit objections that Indian women would never be able to fulfill a vow of chastity; the women admitted had to be full blooded, and have their virtue attested by the nuns or chaplains of convents in which they had previously worked as lay sisters or servants.

Prejudice against mestizo or Indian clergy did not apply to assistants, however, and from the earliest decades after conquest, European clergy were assisted by lay Indian or mestizo *fiscales* who did much of the parish work. The *fiscales* (who sometimes had a different title) kept church records, supervised building projects and Sunday services, punished those found guilty of moral lapses, taught catechism classes, examined candidates for marriage and communion, buried, and baptized; though most of these officials were male, in some places female officials made sure women went to church and administered disciplinary whippings to married women, whose honor would have been violated by being whipped by a priest. (Priests did administer whippings to women themselves from time to time, occasioning complaints to their superiors from mission residents.) In places where the number of European clergy was particularly small or where they were not involved with their Indian parishioners, Indian officials even conducted their own masses and confessions, bringing in elements of traditional forms of worship. The *fiscales* were central to church control of sexuality, as they often brought cases of alleged adultery, consanguinity, and bigamy to the attention of the local priest, who rarely began an investigation on his own, and carried out the questioning of those who wished to marry. In addition, the Indian "governors" of towns and villages often acted with church authorities, so that courts in cities sent Indians found guilty of sexual crimes back to their home villages for punishment, especially if the crime was something like adultery which was also regarded as illicit in indigenous society.

Church officials and other clergy generally paid more attention to converting indigenous people than Africans. Though royal decrees ordered slave owners to let their slaves hear mass and provide religious services for them, these were only sporadically enforced. Parish priests made few systematic efforts to convert slaves, and masters often thought Christianization lowered slaves' value as it made them more rebellious. In some parts of Latin America, members of religious orders did work to convert Africans, promoting confession in the "language of Angola" and using music and incense to attract converts.

European, Indian, and African Christians also formed (almost always racially separate) confraternities for men and women, which had different purposes. Some sponsored religious festivities, others provided charity for the poor, others arranged funerals for their members. Members of these confraternities were ejected for immoral or "scandalous" behavior, so they served as an additional policing agent. Confraternities also shaped marital arrangements, as they frequently gave dowries to poor girls and women who wished to marry, if they judged them "honorable" and the potential husband acceptable. The activities and aims of confraternities were shaped by the cultural values of their members along with Christian teachings, so that African, European, and Indian confraternities played somewhat different social and religious roles.

Indoctrination methods

External agents such as courts could only go so far in keeping people's behavior in line with Christian teachings; most missionaries and church authorities regarded the development of internal agents, such as notions of guilt and sin, to be much more effective in the long run. Thus, as in Europe, they used a variety of means to communicate Church teachings about marriage and morality. In central Mexico, missionaries preached sermons in Nahuatl, and sponsored plays with songs and dances loosely translated from Spanish plays by Nahua scholars. In Florida, catechisms and confessional manuals were translated into Indian languages. The cults of both the Virgin Mary and St Joseph were promoted throughout Latin America through sermons, feast day celebrations, and artwork, in the case of Mary to spread ideas about virginity and humility and of Joseph to communicate Christian notions of marriage and family life. Joseph became the patron saint of the Viceroyalty of Peru, and the cult of Mary grew so intense that groups such as university students, confraternities, and even artisans' guilds often took special vows to defend the doctrine of the Immaculate Conception. (This is the teaching that Mary was conceived and born without original sin, that is, that the act of sexual intercourse between her parents that produced her was the only one since Adam and Eve that did not pass down their sin; it was made official Roman Catholic dogma in 1854 though it was widely held before that.) Informal teaching, especially about Christian norms of marriage, took place at the screening process before marriage (*diligencia matrimonial),* when every couple had to come before a priest and say that they were free to marry and that they consented to the marriage; often this occurred before witnesses, who would both verify the couple's statements and hear the priest's message. Couples were instructed about the proper hierarchy in marriage, with the word for the woman's expected submission to her husband, *reducción,* the same as that describing native subordination in the missions.

Formal teaching was more limited than early colonial church authorities had hoped; though Bishop Zumárraga urged that Indian girls be taught the virtues of monogamous marriage as well as housekeeping, very few schools for Indians were actually established, and the few that were were almost all for elite boys. Mission priests often singled out a small group of boys for more intensive teaching, took them from their kin group, and gave them a new name. Such boys often later became clerical assistants and were more vigorous than the European friars in their condemnation of indigenous religious and cultural practices. Most Indian or mixed-race children did not receive this kind of indoctrination, however, and their training in church doctrine was limited to occasional catechism classes.

The sacrament of confession and penance provided a more common opportunity for teaching Christian ideas than schools. Penitential guides for priests prepared by missionaries took special interest in sex, with specific questions in Latin, Spanish, and Indian languages about sodomy, anal intercourse, bestiality, abortion, contraception, adultery, fornication, and incest. The 1631 penitential of Juan de Pérez Bocanegra, a bilingual priest working in the Andes, for example, listed 236 questions to be asked in regard to sex, many of which were designed to teach converts that traditional practices such as marriage of relatives or trial marriage were now to be considered sinful. Confessors also asked about thoughts, "the filthy pleasure within your heart," a concept new to many Indian groups for whom fault could only arise from something one had actually done and not simply fantasized about or contemplated.[6] This interest in both sexual practices and desires continued throughout the colonial period, for a confessional guide from the eighteenth century in Chumash for the Indians of the Santa Barbara area by Fray Juan Cortés instructs priests to ask parishioners whether they had wished to do or had done "bad things for pleasure with a woman, with women, with a man, with men."[7] Many historians regard confession and penance as ultimately more successful than the Indian Inquisition in shaping the conduct of Christian converts, for the Inquisition concentrated only on spectacular cases while confession was expected of all converts. After the Council of Trent, annual confession was also expected of European, African, and mestizo Christians, and though such frequency was rarely achieved, confession was sometimes powerful enough to convince adulterers or bigamists to denounce themselves.

Effects

If generalization is difficult for Catholicism in Europe, it is even more so in Latin America. Some areas were totally untouched by church authority throughout the early modern period, and indigenous groups continued their original practices. In other areas there were a few isolated missions where converts were taught Christian notions, surrounded by vast territories whose inhabitants were hostile to Christianity and to colonial political power, which they correctly viewed as linked. In these missions and among the Indian and mestizo population elsewhere, the understanding of Christianity which developed was often one which blended indigenous ideas and Christian teachings, a process of cultural negotiation that is currently being examined by a number of historians. In the same way as Christian parishes and other ecclesiastical units (termed *doctrinas)* were based on existing indigenous governmental units, and Christian devotional practices such as the Day of the Dead grew in importance if they paralleled existing ceremonies, Christian sexual mores were more readily accepted if they fitted with indigenous notions. This blending and the colonial setting itself also affected the handling of sexual issues among non-Indians; though authorities tried to recreate Iberian society, many patterns were distinct to Latin America.

Heterosexual relations among the laity

Iberian authorities, both clerical and secular, claimed to be imposing a Christian model of marriage and Iberian notions of sexual honor on their colonial holdings. In reality, not only did the sexual relationships which developed never live up to the ideal, but authorities themselves aided in making distinctions – such as those between married and unmarried, legitimate and illegitimate, honorable and dishonorable – much less clear than they were in the abstract. Thus it is not as easy as it is in Europe to divide heterosexual relations between lay persons into licit and illicit; marriage, concubinage, fornication, and even prostitution must be considered together, as a spectrum of possibilities, not as mutually exclusive categories.

The earliest Spanish conquests occurred decades before the Council of Trent defined Catholic marriage doctrine explicitly, but during the first decades clergy sought to introduce the central aspects of Christian marriage customs, viewing this as a key part of Christianizing the indigenous population. As we have seen, many of these were not very different from existing customs, and Catholic wedding rituals were often simply added to existing rituals. On certain issues there was more divergence, and thus more avoidance and resistance. Indian nobles were unwilling to give up the privilege of polygamy, and either simply refused to alter their household, or chose their favorite as their wife and kept their additional wives on as servants. Because of the Catholic prohibition of divorce, people often had a Catholic service for their first marriage and then traditional ceremonies for any subsequent ones. Thus monogamy remained an ideal, but serial and occasionally simultaneous polygamy continued in practice. Catholic rules on consanguinity in marriage partners were often avoided or bent by not revealing family relationships, or were overcome by obtaining a priestly dispensation. Rules about consent were also bent as families and clans continued to exert influence on spousal choices. Because procreation was viewed as vital to marriage, "trial marriages" continued for centuries after conquest in some areas and actual marriage was delayed until the woman became pregnant. This disturbed some clergy, such as the Jesuit José de Acosta, who misunderstood the practice and used it to disparage Indian morals in general: "However great and almost divine is the honor which all other peoples pay to virginity, these beasts consider it to be all the more despicable and ignominious."[8]

There was occasional overt resistance to Catholic marriage doctrine; mission residents abandoned missions when priests tried to enforce policies about the marriage of cousins, and some native priests and healers supported a continuation of concubinage and bigamy as symbols of resistance. In the late 1520s to 1530s, some Nahua leaders argued that the religion of the friars opposed all earthly happiness, and the marriage and moral standards they preached were only meant for Indians, because the Spanish did not follow the ideals they preached. In 1680, the Pueblo Indians revolted against Spanish Franciscan missionaries, with the missionaries' attempts to enforce monogamous marriage one of the grounds for the revolt.

Not every avoidance of Christian marriage can be seen as a sign of resistance, however, as this may often have been done more out of a desire to avoid clerical marriage fees or simple negligence; in widely dispersed communities clergy were simply unable to enforce Christian marriage practices, and traditional practices, including polygamy, continued for decades. Many missionaries clearly regarded success on this issue as extremely important, however, and occasionally reported miracles which assisted their efforts, such as that in the memorial of Fray Alonso de Benavides, a Franciscan missionary in New Mexico:

> These Indians were well taught in church doctrine. And in the year just past of 1627, Our Lord confirmed His Holy Word with a miracle among them. As it happened, it was difficult for them to stop having so many women, as it was their custom before they were baptized. Each day, the friar preached to them the holy sacrament of matrimony, and the person who contradicted him most strongly was an old Indian sorceress. Under the pretext of going to the countryside for firewood, she took along four good Christian women, and married at that, all conforming to the good order of Our Holy Mother Church. And coming and going in their wood gathering, she was trying to persuade them not to continue with the kind of marriage our padre was teaching, saying how much better off a person was practicing her old heathenism.
>
> These good Christians resisted this kind of talk. They were getting close to the pueblo again, and the sorceress was carrying on with her sermon. The sky was clear and serene, but a bolt

from the blue struck that infernal instrument of the devil right in the middle of those good Christian women who had been resisting her evil creed. They were spared from the bolt, and quite confirmed in the truth of the holy sacrament of matrimony. The entire pueblo ran to the spot. Seeing the results of the thunderclap from heaven, everyone who had been secretly living in sin got married and began to believe mightily in everything the padre taught them. He, of course, made this episode the subject of a sermon.[9]

Emphasis on monogamous marriage in the missions was accompanied by an emphasis on the nuclear family, which upset existing kinship patterns and hierarchies of gender and age, although priests were sometimes unaware that they were substituting a conjugal family for a consanguinal corporate one. Christian doctrine on the centrality of a hierarchical spousal relationship as the core of the family was reinforced by colonial legal practice which affirmed the authority of husbands over wives and fathers over children, and kept all records according to nuclear families rather than according to existing indigenous household structures. Indigenous paternal authority had a limit in the missions, however, for everyone – including adult men – was under the authority of the friars, who often carried out ceremonies designed to humiliate adult men at the same time as they took away their traditional powers in hunting and choosing the clan's marital partners.

Clerical control could never be as strong outside the missions as it was within them, and Nahua leaders were correct in pointing out that the Spanish did not live up to the ideals preached by Catholic clergy. Actual marital practices varied widely and changed throughout the early modern period. At the very beginning, the Spanish tried to work through native elites (termed *caciques); intermarriage between Spanish men and the daughters of *caciques* was both encouraged and practiced. The acceptance of intermarriage changed during the middle decades of the sixteenth century, when racial origins became a consideration in inheritance and the ability to attend school or enter a convent, and when more Spanish women had immigrated. Sexual relations between European men and native or mestizo women continued, but these were more likely to be concubinage or prostitution, either instead of or along with marriage to a European wife. Like the households of wealthier Indians, those of wealthier Spaniards and men of Spanish background born in Latin America (termed "creoles") tended to include a hierarchy of women and children; one official wife and her children, who were regarded as legitimate, and several other women, slave and free, whose children were not regarded as legitimate and so were legally disadvantaged. In some frontier areas where the number of Spanish women was very small, Spanish men had essentially polygamous households with five or six Indian concubines; they would then choose the most intelligent male offspring to legitimize, and make his mother the official wife. In the larger cities of New Spain, women often significantly outnumbered men, a further impetus to the development of irregular unions of all types.

African slaves and free blacks were added to this mixture almost from the very beginning of the colonial period. (There were also some licenses for "white slaves" (*esclavos blancos)* given to Mexican residents in the 1530s and 1540s; these were probably Moors, Berbers, or Jews from Morocco, and were most likely women imported for household service or prostitution. At least one Morisca woman accompanied Pizarro's army on its initial conquest of the Incas, and by the seventeenth century there were a few Asian women in Latin America, also household servants or prostitutes.) Both the Spanish and Portuguese crowns wanted slaves to marry, hoping this would make them less likely to run away, and pushed for their marrying other blacks. In Brazil and the Caribbean, slaves did marry other slaves in Catholic ceremonies, yet the sex ratio among slaves (three men for every one woman) meant that this was not an option for most people, and it required the owner's permission in any case. Thus the more normal arrangements for both male and female slaves were informal unions, either with other slaves or across racial categories, for men with Indian women and for women with whites or mixed-race men. Crown policies discouraged marriages between whites and Africans, though they took no notice of non-marital unions involving women who were not white. Almost all European men in the Caribbean had sexual relations with slaves or free mixed-race women, and half of all slave children in Brazil were baptized with an unknown father, often a white or mixed-race man. Children born to a slave mother were also slaves, though they might later be freed by their fathers; those with slave fathers born to Indian women were generally free. Individual clerics sometimes objected to the sexual activities of white men, but such protestations did not affect church policy. Slaves were occasionally successful in gaining annulments of forced marriages in church courts, but usually only if these were especially scandalous.

Whatever crown or church policies were, the realities of colonial life thus involved sexual relationships across many lines. The children who resulted from these relationships challenged existing categories, but the response by colonial society was simply to devise more categories and attempt to make the boundaries between them fixed. One's legal status and social rank came to be based on a complex system of socio-racial categories termed *castas,* that was in theory based on place of birth, assumed race, and status of one's mother, but was very difficult to enforce. In practice, except for individuals who had clear connections to Spain or Portugal or who lived in isolated native villages, *casta* was to a large extent determined by appearance, with lighter-skinned mixed-race persons accorded a higher rank than darker people, even if they were siblings. Thus many historians have termed the social structure which developed in colonial Latin America a "pigmentocracy," a system based on skin color, though contemporaries always claimed that color was linked to honor and virtue so that one's social status – termed *calidad* – involved a moral as well as physical judgment. By forbidding Indian, African, and mixed-race men to become priests, the church bolstered the system; by occasionally granting licenses which made mixed-race men "white" and allowing them to attend seminaries, it also affirmed how subjective the system was.

This concern about *casta*, color, and bloodlines combined with increasing dowry size and families' desires to hold on to property and privileges, to create a pattern of intermarriage within the extended family among the white elites. Because of church prohibitions of consanguinity, distant cousins were the favored spouses, with older women in the family often in charge of keeping track of who could marry whom. For high-status white women, the group of suitable spouses was often very small, and many were sent into convents instead of making what the family regarded as a disadvantageous marriage. This trend was most dramatic in Portuguese colonies such as Bahia, where in the seventeenth century only 14 percent of the daughters of leading families married, while 77 percent went into convents. By the eighteenth century the pattern of cousin-intermarriage had spread to mestizo elites as well, as had the practice of giving a significant dowry upon marriage.

Thus for Indian and white families, marriage remained a family matter, which at times conflicted with the Catholic doctrine of the centrality of spousal consent. At times the church enforced its requirement of consent, prohibiting, for example, the custom whereby Indians married only with the permission of their native leaders, and occasionally annulling a marriage if one of the spouses could prove he or she had been tricked or forced into it. At other times it turned a blind eye to forced marriages, especially if these involved the servants, slaves, or sometimes daughters of prominent men. Both Indian and white families generally used tactics other than force to convince children to marry in the family's best interests, instead using persuasion and coercion (which was allowed by the church), making marital arrangements when children were young, or (for whites) secluding girls so that they met no other men. Girls whose parents had died were thought to be especially at risk of seduction or making bad marital choices, and they were often secluded in convents or other houses of refuge.

Individuals occasionally used church courts to try to enforce marriages as well as break them up. As in Europe, one common scenario was a woman (usually pregnant) who claimed that a man had made a promise of marriage (termed a *palabra de casamiento)* before they began sexual relations, but was now refusing to marry her. At least in Mexico, to about 1690, church and state authorities generally cooperated in enforcing the marriage, giving the man the choice of marriage or deportation to the Philippines to work on building royal fortresses there. After that point, punishment for seduction declined to a three-year prison sentence or financial compensation for the woman, and by the eighteenth century the church decided such suits were no longer its business at all, but a private legal matter between the woman and her seducer. Suits in which couples alleged their families were trying to block a marriage were also less likely to be heard by the eighteenth century; in earlier centuries, church courts had even broken their own rules in regard to marriage and performed secret marriages to get around family pressure, justifying this as the best way to preserve the woman's honor and prevent the sins of fornication or concubinage.

For slaves, many persons of mixed race, and poor people of all types, family and property considerations did not enter into marital considerations, and in most cases people simply did not get married at all. The number of births out of wedlock in Latin America remained startlingly high by comparison with most of Europe (although Spain did have the highest rate of out-of-wedlock births in Europe). During the period 1640–1700 in Central Mexico, 33 percent of the births to Spanish or creole women were out of wedlock, along with 66 percent of those of mixed-race individuals. These relationships were not always short-term, however, for a very large number of what the church termed "irregular unions" or "concubinage" involved planning and commitment and lasted for years; such unions were recognized and sanctioned by the community, and those involved were expected to uphold standards of fidelity. Though the church decried extra-marital sexuality, it also occasionally sponsored group weddings to regularize a number of informal unions at one time, complete with legitimation of the existing children.

Both Spanish and Portuguese law also made distinctions among varieties of illegitimacy. In Spanish America, the degree of illegitimacy depended on the relationship between one's parents – children born of long-term irregular unions ("natural" children) ranked the highest, those of prostitutes in the middle, and those of adulterous unions or unions with clergy ("illegitimate" or "sacrilegious" children) on the bottom. Portuguese law in Brazil also made a distinction between natural children (those born to people who could have been married but were not) and spurious children (those born to people who could not have married, such as priest's children or those born in adulterous relationships). Natural children were equal to legitimate children in matters of inheritance except among the nobility, while spurious children could not inherit. Pregnant women of high social standing could also give birth privately, with their family then adopting the child as an "orphan"; the church colluded in this by not giving the mother's name on the birth certificate, in the same way as it agreed to decree mixed-race men white so that they could be priests. A subsequent marriage – even on the deathbed – usually also legitimated the children, so that the boundaries of sexual honor were not as sharp in reality as they were in theory.

Irregular unions were favored by many people for a number of reasons. In a society intensely concerned with racial and class status, they allowed relationships between people for whom marriage was socially unacceptable. (Though in the mid-eighteenth century the Marquis of Pombal had tried to promote intermarriage, at least in Brazil, this reform was short-lived. By the late eighteenth century, marriages between "persons of different quality" were legally prohibited by secular law as well as social custom, though the church officially continued to favor the marriage of non-equals over concubinage.) Women from lower *castas*, including slaves, realized there could be benefits to themselves and their families from sexual relationships with whites or mixed-race men, and sometimes sought them out, a situation which horrified church officials. The bishops gathered at the Second Council of Lima in 1567 commented: "Many women had abandoned their own husbands and joined themselves to others. In order to live licentiously and shamelessly they had chosen themselves a man, whom they call either a spouse, or a brother, or blood relative, but never lover or male concubine."[10] Judging by the frequency with which attacks on sexual misconduct were repeated, the bishops' criticism had little effect; two centuries later the Bishop of Peru, Mariano Martí, continued to blame women, charging that their dancing, drinking, riding horses with men, and wearing capes in a provocative manner seduced men into sin.

As well as allowing relationships across *castas*, concubinage was socially useful for a number of other reasons. Spouses were often separated for long periods of time, and women in particular might spend years not knowing if their husband was alive or dead. To avoid charges of bigamy, they thus chose an irregular union.

For some people, the possibility or actuality of bigamy was preferable to concubinage. As in Spain, the Inquisition had jurisdiction over bigamy in Latin America because it violated the sanctity of a sacrament; records from bishops' courts and the Inquisition reveal a great deal about bigamous unions involving white, black, or mixed-race individuals. Bigamists had clearly internalized Christian notions of the importance of marriage, sometimes stating this explicitly; a Spanish woman named Inés Hernández stated to Mexican inquisitors in 1525 (after she had married again without knowing if her first spouse was dead), that it was "better to live [as a bigamist] in one sin than as a single woman in many."[11] Though men sometimes entered bigamous marriages in order to snatch more than one dowry, in more cases bigamy was caused by people accepting the ideal of married life taught them by their priests. They thus left marriages that did not live up to this ideal, that were instead a *mala vida* (bad life), which for women usually involved abuse, overwork, and lack of financial support, and for men wifely insubordination and fighting.

As in Spain, the punishments for bigamy could be harsh: for women, whipping, public abjuration, and three to five years' confinement, and for men, 100–200 lashes, being paraded through the streets with a crier shouting their crime, and five to seven years' galley service. Both women and men were held in cells while the investigation was carried out, which could take months. Though no bigamists were executed, many died during their period of punishment, and if they returned it was back to the original spouse. In contrast to Indian caciques, no Spanish bigamists defended bigamy in theory, though they did try to justify their actions by pointing to the evils of their first marriage. As with concubinage, it is clear that, despite church doctrines, bigamy was often socially accepted as a way to get around marital difficulties; many known bigamists lived peacefully for years and were only investigated when a local dispute led their neighbors to denounce them.

If desertion (and perhaps subsequent bigamy) was not an option, there were other ways to get out of an unacceptable marriage. Though official church doctrine did not allow divorce, colonial church officials in many areas were willing to grant annulments (which were usually termed divorces) at a rate that worried some church officials. The Second Council of Lima blamed the same group it had blamed for concubinage, women:

> Many persons, especially women, for extremely shallow reasons and with the intention of regaining their freedom, fulfilling their lust, and avoiding the burdens of marriage, are too quick to initiate divorce proceedings . . . We order that from now on nobody, but the bishop himself, may be allowed to hear divorce cases. The bishop may do so only for absolutely certain, rational, and manifest causes.[12]

Later reports indicate that rulings such as these were ineffective in limiting the number of annulments, especially for the wealthy, which were granted for lack of consent, consanguinity, previous agreements to marry someone else, total or "partial" impotence (defined as the inability to have sexual relations with one's spouse, though one could with others), or the lack of proper procedure during the wedding. Annulments were also granted if one could prove one's spouse had been deceptive or in error about his or her social or racial status.

If one could not gain an annulment for any of these reasons, church courts were sometimes willing to grant a separation from bed and board (also often termed a divorce) though these did not allow remarriage. Petitions for separation were almost always brought by women, and generally involved abuse or desertion. While the case was being investigated – which might take months – the woman was locked up in the home of a respected man or a convent in a process termed *depositio,* being deposited. The damage to one's honor resulting from such treatment no doubt gave women pause about proceeding with separation cases, and the difficulties of getting out of an unhappy marriage may have made concubinage a more attractive option.

Both church and state authorities despaired that the lines separating honorable and dishonorable sexual conduct, especially among women, were not as sharp as they should be, and attempted to rigidify them. One way of doing this was to separate prostitutes clearly from other women, in the same way as European cities had. This began very early in the Spanish colonies; in 1527, for example, the crown issued licenses to one man in Puerto Rico and another in Santo Domingo to open "a house for public women . . . in a suitable place, because there is a need for it in order to avoid (worse) harm."[13] Many of the residents in such houses were women of mixed race, as were those who were brought along largely for their sexual services on expeditions of conquest, euphemistically labeled "ladies of games" or "women of love" in the records. Some of these women came of their own accord and, at least in the early period before social categories hardened, later married men from the Spanish force. The crown occasionally worried about the type of Spanish women who were immigrating when it received reports that they were running brothels as well as working in them, and attempted – with little success – to examine their backgrounds. In the 1530s, because of such worries, the crown outlawed immigration by single women on their own, but illegal immigration continued.

Church authorities largely followed the crown (and St Augustine) and accepted prostitution as a necessary evil; it was generally not criminalized in Latin America until the nineteenth century. As in Catholic Europe, however, authorities also attempted to encourage women to change their ways by opening asylums for repentant prostitutes and other – in the words of the Count of Lemos, the Viceroy of Peru who established such a house – "women accustomed to living licentiously [who] have decided to reform and act in a modest and penitent manner."[14] These houses – termed *recogimientos* – subsequently came to be used as places where men sent their wives when they traveled or if they suspected them of adultery, preferring informal seclusion to the scandal of a public accusation. In larger cities such as Lima or Mexico City, they might also take in orphan girls, women seeking separation from their husbands, or women who simply wanted a secluded life without the vows of a convent. The number of willing penitents or other inmates was often not equal to the capacity of such houses, however, so by the late seventeenth century they were also used as prisons where women accused of scandalous behavior were held against their will, or as places for women waiting to hear church court decisions about their petititions for separation. The various types of inmates were supposed to be housed separately, but being sent to such a place marked one as a woman whose honor was in question, whatever one's ostensible reason for going, and they thus served to blur the very border between honor and dishonor they were established to enforce.

In most of Latin America such asylums did not exist, and women found guilty of serious moral offenses were deposited in the households of prominent white males or priests, ordered to obey them and work as their servants. (Men found guilty of moral offenses might be banished, but were generally only required to confess and promise to change their ways; they were never deposited as servants in this way.) Although in theory being held *en depositio* was supposed to be a safeguard and corrective, giving a woman a "Christian education" so that "her eyes might be opened to her blind passion," it might actually put the woman in greater danger; in several cases from Mexico, priests who were housing women were charged with rape.[15]

Clerical sexuality

Raping women to whom they were supposed to be giving moral lessons was clearly unacceptable sexual behavior on the part of clergy, but in many instances the tolerance of theoretically illicit sexual behavior accorded to lay people was extended to them, and they lived quietly with women for years, provoking little comment. Complaints emerged only if the cleric's behavior was publicly scandalous, or if there were other objections to him as well. Often these emerged as the final straw in a long list of complaints, and may have been used by communities who wanted to get rid of a priest as they knew these would be effective with the Holy Office. For example, in 1631 eleven Maya women complained that their friar was violent and forced them to spin for his profit; they urged authorities, "do not let the maidens be instructed at the church anymore, because nothing good comes from it, for he [the friar] fornicates with them."[16] The most common sexual complaints against priests were solicitation in the confessional, having children with their housekeepers, and public lewdness, though none of these was especially frequent. Of the 1,474 cases in records of the Lima Inquisition during the period 1569 to 1820, for example, only 109 were for clerical solicitation. Punishments for this offense ranged up to ten years' exile and loss of the license to hear confessions, but such sentences were given only for notorious repeat offenders, despite the fact that the Supreme Council of the Inquisition in Madrid gave specific instructions to the Inquisition in Mexico to punish priests found guilty of sexual crimes more severely. Women were often hesitant to bring charges, knowing the reluctance of the church to punish priests and the general skepticism about women's testimony, and, as in Europe, came to church courts only when ordered to do so by a subsequent confessor.

Along with being tried for sexual conduct, clergy were occasionally tried for unorthodox sexual ideas, mostly for saying that concubinage was acceptable or that fornication was not a sin. The most spectacular of these cases was that of the Dominican Francisco de la Cruz, who was burned by the Inquisition in Lima in 1578. De la Cruz had adopted ideas found among the Andean people, combining these with visions to predict the establishment of a millenarian kingdom somewhere in America where the clergy would marry and laymen live in polygamy.

Charges of sexual misconduct involving nuns or other female religious were rare, despite the fact that in some areas large numbers of women lived in convents; one in five of the female population of Lima in the seventeenth century, for example, lived in convents, though most of these were servants, slaves, and lay sisters, not professed nuns. The Tridentine rules on enclosure made little impact in Peru, and bishops constantly complained about the number of servants employed by nuns and the number of visitors in convents at all hours. These complaints were often expressed in language about the unseemliness of convent life, but the main problem appeared to be luxury rather than lust. This – to male eyes surprising – lack of sexual misconduct also included Indian women who lived in convents or convent-like situations. Antonio Pérez, a priest commenting on the foundation of Corpus Christi convent for Indian women in Mexico City, noted that Indian women were already living like nuns without actual vows, and that this "increases my confusion . . . seeing young girls who have no obligation to fulfill the greatest perfection, living with such total perfection."[17]

As in Europe, there were a few *beatas* in Latin America, mystical women who lived outside of convents. The most famous of these was Rose of Lima, who gathered around her a group of spiritually devout women, some of them unmarried and some married women who gave up sexual relations with their husbands. At her early death in 1617 Rose was viewed by many as a living saint, but eight years later religious authorities cracked down on her followers, calling them deluded and demonic. In similar cases in Europe such charges often included imputations of aberrant sexual behavior, but these did not emerge in the attack on Rose's followers. Criticism of her followers did not dent Rose's great public following, however, and in 1671 she was made a saint.

Sodomy

The issue of sodomy, particularly male homosexual sodomy, in pre-colonial Latin America, is complicated, and currently quite contentious. Many European travellers, clergy, and officials accused certain Indian groups of sodomy, but these charges were very often part of a standard list of practices, also including cannibalism, incest, anal intercourse, and polygamy, designed to show the inferiority or barbarity of that group. (Cannibalism was an essential part of this stereotype, as the Spanish crown had banned the enslavement of Indians except for those who were cannibals.) This complex of charges was often used to separate "good" Indians – those who were less resistant to Spanish domination – from "bad" Indians – those who resisted colonial moves – and also to separate "advanced" Indians, such as the Aztec and Inca Empires, from "backward" ones; bad and backward Indians always engaged in cannibalism and sodomy. These charges were also used by Indians themselves to describe other tribes who were their enemies, either because they knew it would be effective with the Spanish or because they also viewed sodomy and cannibalism as signs of inferiority. At least among groups such as the Aztecs and the Incas, defeated enemies were regarded as feminized and forced to wear women's clothing, with ceremonies of defeat which may have included being penetrated by their conquerors. This link between sexual domination and military prowess or political leadership may have provided one context in which homosexual relations among men were acceptable, as long as one took the active "male" role and not the passive "female" one. It also led to the conquest being understood in sexualized terms, for the Incas conceived of Spanish swords as penises and saw themselves as having suffered symbolic sexual violation.

How much – or whether – this symbolic sexual violation extended to actual practice, or whether Indians engaged in homosexual relations in other contexts, has been hotly debated since the sixteenth century. In his multivolume *General History of the Indies,* the Spanish historian Gonzalo Fernández de Oviedo charged natives with a range of aberrant sexual practices, including male homosexual sodomy and cross-dressing; his work was widely read, and (not surprisingly) similar charges emerge from many other authors. His charges were vigorously refuted by the Dominican bishop Bartolomé de las

Casas, who denied that any Indians practiced homosexuality, and went on to write extensive – and also very influential – defenses of Indian culture and attacks on Spanish actions. He pointed out that the Aztecs and the Incas both punished male sodomy severely and saw this as one of many indications of their advanced level of culture.

As with most issues regarding sexuality, all sources which mention sodomy are the work of Europeans or indigenous authors who were at least partly acculturated and Christianized, so that it is impossible to escape the influence of Christian attitudes. This has led a few historians to argue that all reports of laws against sodomy among the Incas and Aztecs were the post-conquest inventions of European or Indian writers, designed to make these more advanced empires look more like Christians, and that sodomitical relations were acceptable in certain contexts. They note that among many Indian groups there were – and are – individuals who combine the tasks, behavior, and clothing of men and women. Most of these individuals are morphologically male, and the Europeans who first encountered them regarded them as homosexuals and called them "berdaches," from an Arabic word for male prostitute. Now most scholars choose to use the term "two-spirit people," and note that they were found among the Aztecs and Incas at the time of conquest. Such two-spirit people may have taken the female role (i.e. passive and penetrated) in sexual relations at least in ceremonial contexts and perhaps in everyday life. Other historians dispute this interpretation, pointing out that two-spirit people are distinguished from other men more by their work or religious roles than their sexual activities, and that sexual relations between a two-spirit person and a man may have not been understood as "same-sex" in any case, because two-spirit people are actually thought of as a third gender rather than effeminate males. They note that such individuals are not found in every Indian culture and are always rare, and they discount reports of widespread sodomy as colonial inventions.

Whatever the prevalence or acceptability of homosexual relations before European conquest, there is no disagreement about the opinions of church and state authorities during and after conquest. During his march across Panama in 1513, the conquistador Vasco de Balboa was reported to have massacred the brother and 40 followers of the *cacique* Quarega who were dressed like women. Missionaries throughout Latin America preached that God had sent the Spanish to conquer the Indians because they had engaged in sodomitical behavior, and, as noted above, confessionals advised priests to ask their parishioners about sodomitical behavior, both homosexual and heterosexual. Pérez Bocanegra's extensive penitential includes questions for men asking whether they had touched or been touched by male friends, and for women asking whether they had "sinned with another woman, like yourself?" Bocanegra apparently could not imagine that such behavior in women could be motivated by homosexual desire, because he then instructs priests to ask the women who they had been thinking about: "When you were engaged in this abominable sin, were you thinking about married men? unmarried men? the priest? the friars? your male kinfolk? those kin of your husband?"[18] Special prayers for the delivery from sodomy were printed in Mexico City in the early eighteenth century.

The effects of prohibition and confession on the actual practice of sodomy is much more difficult to trace in Latin America than in Iberia, because the Inquisition did not have jurisdiction over it and records are scattered among different church courts; none of these maintained the type of records the Aragonese Inquisition did, and none kept a list of sodomy accusations like that of the Portuguese Inquisition. There were occasional mass trials, such as one in 1658 in which 123 men were accused, apparently including some members of the clergy. Sodomy was punishable by death to the mid-eighteenth century, though, as in Spain, actual executions ended during the seventeenth century. It is clear from scattered reports that prosecutions were much rarer than the practice; for example, anal intercourse, both heterosexual and homosexual, was the sin most commonly confessed to visiting Portuguese Inquisitors at Pernambuco in Brazil during their visitation of 1594–1595, but this did not lead to any upsurge in trials. Such confessions may be used as evidence for both sides of the debate about homosexuality before the conquest: those who argue that it was widespread note the continued frequency, those who argue that it was unacceptable before Christianization note that it was easy to make people view it as a sin. What is clear from these records – and sometimes stated explicitly by confessants – is that even in cases of sodomy, people distinguished between a "vida práctica" which people actually lived and religious and legal standards set so high that people could not follow them.

Magic and witchcraft

The distinction between theoretical standards and actual practice was also clear in matters involving witchcraft and magic. European demonologists such as Pierre de Lancre linked witchcraft in the Old and New Worlds by asserting that the reason for the rise in witchcraft in Europe was the coming of Christian missionaries to the New World, which had forced Satan and his demons to return to Europe. They regarded New World and Old World witches as both guided by Satan in the same way, an idea that slowly spread to missionaries active in the New World, who began to define pre-conquest religious practices as demonic. Thus it was important to destroy all religious objects, or anything that might have a link to idolatry, such as texts in native languages.

Fr Diego de Landa's campaign against idolatry among the Maya is generally regarded as having destroyed 90 per cent of the existing Maya texts; intentional and unintentional destruction left only three pre-conquest Maya texts intact. Campaigns against witchcraft and idolatry continued the longest in Peru, which was more resistant to Christianization than Mexico, with practitioners of indigenous religions, female and male, accused of both magic (hechicería) and the more serious demonic witchcraft (brujería). These campaigns picked up in the seventeenth century, as some Andean residents combatted Spanish policies by returning to native beliefs and practices.

As in Europe, accusations of witchcraft frequently had sexual overtones throughout Latin America, such as a Jesuit report that women's ritual dances were "demonically inspired lascivious and drunken spectacles" designed to promote "indolence, incest, and idolatry."[19] In another instance, a group of Indians in Mexico was charged with worshipping the devil as God, and being "taken up into the air by a devil while copulating carnally"; their leader was accused of having a picture showing her and other Indians "coupled with each other." [20] In the Andes, witchcraft charges might result from too little sex as well as too much; women who chose to abstain from sexual relations in order to serve as leaders in resurgent native belief systems were often charged with witchcraft along with paganism and idolatry.

Despite campaigns against idolatry, however, Spaniards often approached Indians for the very magical (and perhaps demonic) powers the church judged so dangerous. Indians, Africans, and persons of mixed race, especially women, were widely regarded as having special skills in finding lost objects, healing illnesses, and performing love magic designed to attract, repel, or hold a lover or spouse. Love magic was used by clients – usually women – of all social classes. For example, of five African women tried for magic during Zumárraga's campaign, two were slaves, accused of buying aphrodisiacs to better please their masters sexually so that they would get better treatment. At the other end of the social scale was an upper-class Spanish woman in Colombia, accused in 1551 of paying a mixed-race woman named Juana Garcia for magical assistance in aborting a child conceived out of wedlock. The bishop and the governor decided to hush up the case by exiling Garcia rather than opening an official church investigation, probably to hide the identity of her client, whose name is not mentioned in the records. As in this instance, love magic often brought women of different social groups and ethnicities together as they shared remedies. Many spells and cures mixed elements from many cultures; a woman who wished to keep her spouse loyal might be given a love bundle made of a hummingbird to sew into her clothing (an Indian remedy) and also advised to feed him soup made from water in which she had washed her body mixed with the dust from an altar (a European remedy) or to seek a spirit medium (an African remedy). The most dramatic example of syncretic magic in the New World was Haitian *vodu* (or voodoo), which mixed religious practices from Dahomey and Togo in West Africa with Christian rituals; though *vodu* was used for purposes of love magic, it was (and is) a complete religious system, although in the colonial period its adherents – most of them slaves – were baptized and buried in Catholic ceremonies.

Most of those involved in cases of love magic that made it into the records tell quite desperate stories, of husbands who beat or abandoned them, of poverty from which marriage was the only hope of escape, of rape or seduction that left them pregnant. Because most of those involved were women and many of them were socially marginal, church courts and the Inquisition generally did not take such actions terribly seriously, but trivialized them and denied that the women accused of practicing magic had any powers. If making a demonic pact was part of their love magic, they were taken more seriously during the sixteenth and seventeenth centuries, but by the eighteenth even parish priests discounted these as well, no longer sending such cases on to the Inquisition but simply scolding the women for deluding themselves. Cases sometimes emerged when men came to church authorities charging that women were performing love magic on them, but more often when the women themselves confessed or voluntarily came to the Inquisition, thus turning to the church to resolve their ambivalent feelings about love magic. A few men also show up in church records voluntarily confessing their use of love magic, though their feelings of guilt at doing so may have been influenced by the fact that their efforts were unsuccessful; offering their soul while "inflamed with desire for a woman" had not allowed them to "lull women to [their] carnal desires."[21]

The process of Christianization in Latin America used to be described as a "spiritual conquest," in which indigenous beliefs and practices were largely wiped out through a combination of force and persuasion, transforming most of the countries of Latin America into Catholic countries on a European model. The spread of Catholic Christianity is now viewed very differently, not simply as conquest and resistance, but as a process of cultural negotiation, during which Christian ideas and practices were accepted but also transformed. This transformation did not simply involve indigenous people, however, but also Europeans, Africans, and people of mixed race; Latin American Christianity became part of a new shared culture, though a culture with many local differences. The church's regulation of sexual practices was part both of that shared culture and of local distinctions, as theories about proper marital relationships and sexual deportment were played out in different colonial contexts. Interwoven with this – again part of the shared culture but with local differences – was the multi-racial nature of colonial societies, for only through the control of sexual activities could racial distinctions be defined and maintained. The Catholic Church in Latin America was an important player in this link between sexuality and race, as it was in other parts of the world where European traders and colonists journeyed. Here it was joined by Protestant churches as well, and it is in Africa and Asia that we can find an even more complex and varied situation developing.

Notes

1 Translated and quoted in Arthur J. O. Anderson, "Aztec Wives," in Susan Schroeder, Stephanie Wood, and Robert Haskett, eds, *Indian Women of Early Mexico* (Norman: University of Oklahoma Press, 1997), 60.

2 Lawrence A. Clayton, Vernon James Knight, Jr., and Edward C. Moore, eds *The De Soto Chronicles: The Expedition of Hernando De Soto to North America in 1539–1543*, 2 vols. (Tuscaloosa: University of Alabama Press, 1993), 1: 289.

3 Royal order of 1752, translated and quoted in Ramón A. Gutiérrez, *When Jesus Came, the Corn Mothers Went Away: Marriage, Sexuality, and Power in New Mexico 1500–1846* (Stanford: Stanford University Press, 1991), 217.

4 Translated and quoted in Ramón Gutiérrez, "From Honor to Love: Transformations of the Meaning of Sexuality in Colonial New Mexico," in Raymond T. Smith, ed., *Kinship Ideology and Practice in Latin America* (Chapel Hill: University of North Carolina Press, 1984), 244.

5 Quoted in Stephen Neill, *A History of Christian Missions* (New York: Penguin, 1964), 171.

6 From Fr Juan de la Anunciacíon, *Doctrina christiana muy cumplida donde se contiene la exposición de todo necesario para doctrinar a los indios* (Mexico City, 1575), quoted and translated in Serge Gruzinski, "Individualization and Acculturation: Confession Among the Nahuas of Mexico from the Sixteenth to the Eighteenth Century," in Asuncion Lavrin, ed., *Sexuality and Marriage in Colonial Latin America* (Lincoln: University of Nebraska, 1989), 101.

7 Quoted and translated in Harry Kelsey, *The Doctrina and Confesionario of Juan Cortés* (Altadena, CA: Howling Coyote Press, 1979), 115.

8 Acosta, *Historia Natural y Moral de las Indias* (Seville, 1590), translated and quoted in C.R. Boxer, *Mary and Misogyny: Women in Iberian Expansion Overseas 1415–1815* (New York: Oxford University Press, 1975), 108.

9 *A Harvest of Reluctant Souls: The Memorial of Fray Alonso de Benavides, 1630*, translated and edited by Baker H. Morrow (Niwot: University Press of Colorado, 1996), 31–32.

10 Translated and quoted in Luis Martín, *Daughters of the Conquistadores: Women of the Viceroyalty of Peru* (Albuquerque: University of New Mexico Press, 1983), 152.

11 Translated and quoted in Richard E. Boyer, *Lives of the Bigamists: Marriage, Family, and Community in Colonial Mexico* (Albuquerque: University of New Mexico Press, 1995), 103.

12 Ibid., 128.

13 Quoted in Boxer, *Mary and Misogyny,* 51.

14 Letter of Count of Lemos to Queen Regent Mariana (1669) translated and quoted in Nancy E. van Deusen, "Defining the Sacred and the Worldly: *Beatas* and *Recogidas* in Late Seventeenth-century Lima", *Colonial Latin American Historical Review* 6 (1997): 464.

15 Archives of Chihauhau, translated and quoted in Cheryl English Martin, *Governance and Society in Colonial Mexico: Chihauhau in the Eighteenth Century* (Stanford: Stanford University Press, 1996), 174.

16 Translated and quoted in Robert Haskett, "Activist or Adulteress? The Life and Struggle of Doña Josefa María of Tepoztlan," in Schroeder, *Indian Women,* 149.

17 Translated and quoted in Elisa Sampson Vera Tudela, "Fashioning a *Cacique* Nun: From Saints' Lives to Indian Lives in the Spanish Americas," *Gender and History* 9 (1997): 187.

18 Juan de Pérez Bocanegra, *Ritual formulario . . .* (1631) translated and quoted in Regina Harrison, "The Theology of Concupiscence: Spanish–Quechua Confessional Manuals in the Andes," in Francisco Javier Cevallos-Candau, ed., *Coded Encounters: Writing, Gender, and Ethnicity in Colonial Latin America* (Amherst: University of Massachusetts Press, 1994), 146.

19 Jesuit report, quoted and translated in Susan Deeds, "Indian Women in Jesuit Missions," in Schroeder, et al., *Indian Women,* 261.

20 Mexican Inquisition records, translated and quoted in Fernando Cervantes, *The Devil in the New World: The Impact of Diabolism in New Spain* (New Haven: Yale University Press, 1994), 38–39.

21 Ibid., 87.

Selected further reading

A good place to start for many of the issues discussed in this chapter is one of the collections of articles on women edited by Asuncion Lavrin, *Latin American Women: Historical Perspectives* (Westport, Conn.: Greenwood, 1978) and *Sexuality and Marriage in Colonial Latin America* (Lincoln: University of Nebraska Press, 1989). Lavrin also has a more recent article, *"Lo femenino:* Women in Colonial Historical Sources," in Cevallos-Candau, *Coded Encounters,* (note 18). Ann Pescatello, *Power and Pawn: The Female in Iberian Families, Societies, and Cultures* (Westport, Conn.: Greenwood, 1976) also provides a good overview, and Della M. Flusche and Eugene H. Korth, *Forgotten Females: Women of African and Indian Descent in Colonial Chile, 1535–1800* (Detroit: Blaine Ethridge, 1983) investigates women often excluded from the story. The many books of Charles R. Boxer provide useful general information: *Race Relations in the Portuguese Colonial Empire 1415–1825* (Oxford: Clarendon Press, 1963; *The Church Militant and Iberian Expansion, 1440–1770* (Baltimore: Johns Hopkins University Press, 1978); *Mary and Misogyny* (note 8).

General works on the experience of Africans in Latin America which touch on issues of the regulation of sexuality include: Frederick P. Bowser, *The African*

Slave in Colonial Peru, 1524–1650 (Stanford: Stanford University Press, 1974); Colin A. Palmer, *Slaves of the White God: Blacks in Mexico, 1570–1650* (Cambridge, Mass.: Harvard University Press, 1976); Herbert S. Klein, *African Slavery in Latin America and the Caribbean* (New York: Oxford University Press, 1986); John Thornton, *Africa and Africans in the Making of the Atlantic World, 1400–1680* (Cambridge: Cambridge University Press, 1992). For a discussion of racial mixing, the indispensible work is still Magnus Mörner, *Race Mixture in the History of Latin America* (Boston: Little, Brown, 1967).

Gender relations in the Aztec Empire are hotly debated; for a review of the debate, see Louise M. Burkhart, "Mexica Women on the Home Front: Housework and Religion in Aztec Mexico," and Stephanie Wood and Robert Haskett, "Concluding Remarks" in Schroeder, et al., *Indian Women* (note 1), 25–54 and 313–330. (This book also has an extremely useful 30-page bibliography.) For another look at the issue, see Cecelia Klein, "Fighting with Femininity: Gender and War in Aztec Mexico," *Estudios de Cultura Náhuatl* 24 (1994): 219–253.

Most of the newer and some of the older studies of pre-Hispanic and early colonial cultures stress the ways in which post-conquest culture blended European and indigenous elements in many areas of life, among them marital patterns and other aspects of sexuality. For Mexico, see: Matthew Restall, *The Maya World: Yucatec Culture and Society, 1550–1850* (Stanford: Stanford University Press, 1997); Charles Gibson, *The Aztecs Under Spanish Rule: A History of the Indians of the Valley of Mexico 1519–1810* (Stanford: Stanford University Press, 1964); James Lockhart, *The Nahuas After the Conquest: A Social and Cultural History of the Indians of Central Mexico, Sixteenth through Eighteenth Centuries* (Stanford: Stanford University Press, 1992); S.L. Cline, *Colonial Culhuacan, 1580–1600: A Social History of an Aztec Town* (Albuquerque: University of New Mexico Press, 1986); Susan Kellogg, *Law and the Transformation of Aztec Culture 1500–1700* (Norman: University of Oklahoma Press, 1995); Nancy M. Farriss, *Maya Society Under Spanish Rule: The Collective Enterprise of Survival* (Princeton: Princeton University Press, 1984); Rebecca Horn, *Postconquest Coyoacan: Nahua–Spanish Relations in Central Mexico, 1519–1650* (Stanford: Stanford University Press, 1997); J. Jorge Klor de Alva, "Spiritual Conflict and Accommodation in New Spain: Toward a Typology of Aztec Responses to Christianity," in George A. Collier, Renato I. Rosaldo, and John D. Wirth, eds, *The Inca and Aztec States 1400–1800: Anthropology and History* (New York: Harcourt Brace, 1982), 345–366; Matthew Restall and Pete Sigal, "'May They Not Be Fornicators Equal to those Priests': Post-colonial Yucatec Maya Sexual Attitudes," and Kimberly Gauderman, "Father Fiction: The Construction of Gender in England, Spain, and the Andes," in Lisa Sousa, ed. *Indigenous Writing in the Spanish Indies, Special Issue of UCLA Historical Journal* 12 (1997): 91–121, 122–151; S.L. Cline, "The Spiritual Conquest Reexamined: Baptism and Christian Marriage in Early Sixteenth-century Mexico," *Hispanic American Historical Review* 73 (1993): 453–480; Sonya Lipsett-Rivera, "The Intersection of Rape and Marriage in Late-Colonial and Early-National Mexico," *Colonial Latin American Historical Review* 6 (1997): 559–590; Charlene Villaseñor Black, "Love and Marriage in the Spanish Empire: Depictions of Holy

Matrimony, Discourses of Gender and Ideologies of Marriage in the Seventeenth Century," *Sixteenth Century Journal,* forthcoming; Jerome Offner, *Law and Politics in Aztec Texcoco* (Cambridge: Cambridge University Press, 1983); Louise M. Burkhart, *The Slippery Earth: Nahua–Christian Moral Dialogue in Sixteenth-century Mexico* (Tucson: University of Arizona Press, 1989) and "Moral Deviance in Sixteenth-century Nahua and Christian Thought: The Rabbit and the Deer," *Journal of Latin American Lore* 12 (1986): 107–139; Inga Clendinnen, *Ambivalent Conquests: Maya and Spaniard in Yucatan* (Cambridge: Cambridge University Press, 1987), *Aztecs: An Interpretation* (Cambridge: Cambridge University Press, 1991) and "Ways to the Sacred: Reconstructing 'Religion' in Sixteenth-century Mexico," *History and Anthropology* 5 (1990): 105–141.

For the Andean regions, see: Regina Harrison, *"True" Confessions: Quechua and Spanish Cultural Encounters in the Viceroyalty of Peru,* Latin American Studies Series 5 (College Park, Md: University of Maryland Press, 1992); Steve J. Stern, *Peru's Indian Peoples and the Challenge of Spanish Conquest: Huamanga to 1640,* 2nd edn. (Madison: University of Wisconsin Press, 1993); Ward Stavig, "Living in Offense of Our Lord: Indigenous Sexual Values and Marital Life in the Colonial Crucible," *Hispanic American Historical Review* 75 (1995): 597–622; Constance Classen, *Inca Cosmology and the Human Body* (Salt Lake City: University of Utah Press, 1993); Sabine MacCormack, *Religion in the Andes: Vision and Imagination in Early Colonial Peru* (Princeton: Princeton University Press, 1991); Irene Silverblatt, *Moon, Sun and Witches: Gender Ideologies and Class in Inca and Colonial Peru* (Princeton: Princeton University Press, 1987), "Andean Witches and Virgins: Seventeenth-century Nativism and Subversive Gender Ideologies," in Margo Hendricks and Patricia Parker, eds, *Women, "Race," and Writing in the Early Modern Period* (London: Routledge, 1994), 259–286 and "Family Values in Seventeenth-century Peru," in Elizabeth Boone and Tom Cummins, eds, *Native Traditions in the Postconquest World* (Washington: Dumbarton Oaks, 1998), 63–89; Karen Spalding, *Huarochirí: An Andean Society under Inca and Spanish Rule* (Stanford: Stanford University Press, 1984); Verena Stolcke, "Invaded Women: Gender, Race, and Class in the Formation of Colonial Society," in Hendrichs and Parker, *Women, Race, and Writing,* 272–286.

For the experience in Spanish Florida and the American Southeast, see David Hurst Thomas, ed., *Columbian Consequences, Vol. 2: Archeological and History Perspectives on the Spanish Borderlands East* (Washington: Smithsonian Institution Press, 1990); Charles Hudson and Carmen Chaves Tesser, eds, *The Forgotten Centuries: Indians and Europeans in the American South, 1521–1704* (Athens: University of Georgia Press, 1994); Jerald T. Milanich, *Florida Indians and the Invasion from Europe* (Gainesville: University Press of Florida, 1995); James Axtell, *The Indians' New South: Cultural Change in the Colonial Southeast* (Baton Rouge: Louisiana State University Press, 1997). For the American Southwest, see Evelyn Hu-DeHart, *Missionaries, Miners, and Indians: Spanish Contact with the Yaqui Nation of Northwestern New Spain 1533–1820* (Tucson: University of Arizona Press, 1981) and Gutiérrez, *When Jesus Came* (note 3).

Some of the most influential descriptions of indigenous practices by accultur-ated Indians or European clergy who had learned native languages are available in translation: *The Incas: The Royal Commentaries of the Inca Garcilaso de la Vega 1539–1616* , trans. Maria Jolas (New York: Orion Press, 1961); Fr Bernardino de Sahagún, *Florentine Codex; General History of the Things of New Spain,* 12 vols., ed. and trans. Arthur J.O. Anderson and Charles E. Dibble (Sante Fe and Salt Lake City: School of American Research and University of Utah Press, 1950–1982). Rebecca Overmyer-Velázquez, "Christian Morality Revealed in New Spain: The Inimical Nahua Woman in Book Ten of the *Florentine Codex,*" *Journal of Women's History* 10 (1998): 9–37 analyzes the representation of women in Sahagún's work.

There are many works which investigate various attempts to extirpate native religious practices, and include information on attempts to end polygamy and concubinage. The most recent of these include: J. Jorge Klor de Alva, "Colonizing Souls: The Failure of the Indian Inquisition and the Rise of Penitential Discipline," and Roberto Moreno de los Arcos, "New Spain's Inquisition for Indians from the Sixteenth to the Nineteenth Century," both in Anne J. Cruz and Mary Elizabeth Perry, *Colonial Encounters: The Impact of the Inquisition in Spain and the New World* (Berkeley: University of California Press, 1991), 3–22, 23–36; Amos Megged, *Exporting the Catholic Reformation: Local Religion in Early Colonial Mexico* (Leiden: Brill, 1996); Kenneth Mills, *Idolatry and Its Enemies: Colonial Andean Religion and Extirpation* (Princeton: Princeton University Press, 1997) and "The Limits of Religious Coercion in Mid-Colonial Peru," *Past and Present* 145 (1994): 84–121. Some of the works of those intent on ending native religion have been translated, and in these we can get a glimpse of at least what Christian writers understood native practices to be. These include: Pablo Joseph de Arriaga, *The Extirpation of Idolatry in Peru*, ed. and trans. L. Clark Keating (Lexington: University of Kentucky Press, 1968); Hernando Ruiz de Alarcón, *Treatise on the Heathen Superstitions That Today Live Among the Indians Native to This New Spain,* ed. and trans. J. Richard Andrews and Ross Hassig (Norman: University of Oklahoma Press, 1984).

Studies of the activities of church courts and the Inquisition in Latin America include: Richard Greenleaf, *Zumárraga and the Mexican Inquisition, 1536–1543* (Washington: Academy of American Franciscan History, 1961) and *The Mexican Inquisition of the Sixteenth Century* (Albuquerque: University of New Mexico Press, 1969); Nicholas Griffiths, *The Cross and the Serpent: Religious Repression and Resurgence in Colonial Peru* (Norman: University of Oklahoma Press, 1996).

The history of missions was for many years generally written by members of the religious order which had established the mission, and so is more hagiography than history. Studies which break from this pattern and also contain information on sexuality include: Christopher Vecsey, *On the Padres' Trail* (South Bend, Ind.: Notre Dame University Press, 1996); Erick Langer and Robert H. Jackson, eds, *The New Latin American Mission History* (Lincoln: University of Nebraska Press, 1995); David Bock, *Mission Culture on the Upper Amazon: Native Tradition, Jesuit Enterprise and Secular Policy in Moxos, 1660–1880* (Lincoln: University of Nebraska Press, 1994). William B. Taylor's monumental study, *Magistrates of the Sacred: Priests and Parishioners in Eighteenth Century Mexico* (Stanford: Stanford University Press, 1996), includes material on church regulation of sexual matters both on and off the missions.

Several articles look specifically at women's activities in response to colonialism and the spread of Christianity. See: Inga Clendinnen, "Yucatec Maya Women and the Spanish Conquest: Role and Ritual in Historical Reconstruction," *Journal of Social History* 15 (1982): 427–442; Frank Salomon, "Indian Women of Early Colonial Quito as Seen through their Testaments," *The Americas* 44:3 (January 1988): 325–341; Tudela, "Fashioning," (note 17); van Deusen, "Defining the Sacred" (note 14) and the special issue of *Ethnohistory*, "Women, Power, and Resistance in Colonial Mesoamerica," 42: 4 (1995), edited by Kevin Gosner and Deborah E. Kanter.

For works which focus primarily on people of European background, see Patricia Seed, *To Love, Honor and Obey in Colonial Mexico: Conflicts Over Marriage Choice, 1574–1821* (Stanford: Stanford University Press, 1988); Boyer, *Lives of the Bigamists* (note 11); Martín, *Daughters of the Conquistadores* (note 10). R. Douglas Cope, *The Limits of Racial Domination: Plebian Society in Colonial Mexico City, 1660–1720* (Madison: University of Wisconsin, 1994) and Martin, *Governance and Society* (note 15) include information on marital patterns for a range of urban groups.

In terms of sodomy, the most influential recent study has been Richard Trexler, *Sex and Conquest; Gendered Violence, Political Order, and the European Conquest of the Americas* (Ithaca: Cornell University Press, 1995), which links male homosexual practices to conquest by both Europeans and Amerindians, and discounts Aztec and Inca laws against homosexuality. Pete Sigal, "The Politicization of Pederasty among the Colonial Yucatecan Maya," *Journal of the History of Sexuality* 8 (1997): 1–24 also views at least literary discussions of certain types of homosexuality among the Maya as positive. Trexler's interpretations have been criticized by a number of reviewers, and older studies on Aztec law such as those listed above generally accept that prohibitions existed before European contact. Though it deals with a later period and so pays less attention to religion, Rudi Bleys, *The Geography of Perversion: Male-to-Male Sexual Behavior outside the West and the Ethnographic Imagination, 1750–1918* (New York: New York University Press, 1995) reviews reports about homosexuality among non-Westerners from a range of sources and includes translations as well as quotations in the original language. Francisco Guerra has also translated a large number of Spanish reports about Indian sodomy in *The Pre-Columbian Mind* (London: Seminar Press, 1971), though his interpretations of these have been seriously challenged.

Ruth Behar has written a number of articles on love magic in Mexico, including "Sex and Sin, Witchcraft and the Devil in Late Colonial Mexico," *American Ethnologist* 14 (Feb. 1987): 34–54, and "Sexual Witchcraft, Colonialism, and Women's Powers: Views from the Mexican Inquisition," in Lavrin, *Sexuality and Marriage*, pp. 178–208. Both Silverblatt (*Moon, Sun, and Witches* and "Andean Witches and Virgins") and Griffiths (*The Cross and the Serpent*) discuss the campaigns against magic in Peru, though they come to different conclusions; Silverblatt views these as serious campaigns directed primarily against women who were practitioners of native religion, while Griffiths asserts the Spanish did not single women out, and were attempting to trivialize all native religious practitioners by saying they simply claimed to practice magic to defraud people.

AFRICA AND ASIA

Painting depicting the Fifteen Mysteries of the Rosary, designed to be used as an aid to conversion and painted in the early seventeenth century by a Japanese convert to Catholicism trained by the Jesuits in Japan. By permission of Kyoto University General Museum.

AFRICA AND ASIA

THE DEVELOPMENT AND operation of Christian institutions for the regulation of sexuality in Africa and Asia parallels that of Latin America in many ways. In all of these areas, members of Catholic religious orders were the most numerous religious personnel, almost all of them coming from Europe. These religious orders often established missions or otherwise tried to centralize communities of converts, and they had secular as well as religious authority in these communities. Religious personnel of all types urged the establishment of schools, though the actual number of schools was much smaller than they hoped, and most religious instruction was oral and informal. Church courts were established to oversee doctrinal conformity and sexual morals, but their level of activity and enforcement was highly erratic.

However, there are significant contrasts between Latin America, on the one hand, and Africa and Asia, on the other. In Latin America, most pre-colonial religious traditions were localized and based largely on oral transmission; in Asia and Africa, Christians confronted both local religions and other text-based and widespread religions such as Hinduism, Buddhism, and Islam, with complex and highly developed structures for regulating sexuality. Islam in particular was winning converts at the same time as Christianity, and people often had to work hard to negotiate the hostilities between these two faiths. These hostilities could split families as some members joined one faith and others another, or force families and villages to switch religions quickly when the faith of government leaders or the overseeing authority changed.

In addition to other text-based religions, in a few places there were also indigenous variants of Christianity that long predated European voyages. When the Portuguese reached the southwest coast of India, for example, they met a well-organized Christian church that dated back at least to the fifth century, and regarded itself as having been founded even earlier by the apostle Thomas. (This group is generally termed the "St Thomas Christians," the "Malabar Christians," or the "Syrian Christians.") When European missionaries reached Ethiopia, they also discovered a Christian community with ancient roots and a long history of independent rule, although it was currently living within a Muslim state.

In Latin America, the establishment and operation of Christian institutions for the regulation of sexuality before 1750 was – with a few exceptions like the brief period of Dutch rule in Brazil or British, Dutch, and Danish colonies in the Caribbean on the north coast of South America – a completely Catholic undertaking, while in Asia and Africa Protestants and indigenous Christians were also involved. In some of these areas, Protestants moved in after Catholics had already begun conversions and established institutions, so that Protestants confronted Catholic ideas and practices, indigenous non-Christian traditions, indigenous Christian traditions, and mixtures of all of these. Thus the patterns of sexual regulation that developed were extremely varied.

In Latin America, the Spanish and the Portuguese were intent on establishing colonies based on agriculture or extractive industries, with a significant European population, at least in urban areas. In many parts of Africa and Asia, the colonial powers before 1750 were largely interested in the profits of maritime trade and had no intentions of setting up large land-based colonies or transplanting large numbers of Europeans. They were consequently much less interested in the conversion of the indigenous population than was the Spanish crown in Latin America, for conversion did nothing to further their national objectives. (As we will see, the Spanish colony in the Philippines was an exception to this, and intentionally followed the Latin American model.)

In Latin America, the establishment of Christian institutions and European-based political institutions occurred at roughly the same time. This was also true in some parts of Africa and Asia, but in many areas, such as China and Japan, Christian missions operated within political structures that were modified only slightly by European influence. In other areas, such as the Dutch colonies of South Africa and Batavia, the ruling political body was a private company – the United East India Company or Verenigde Oost-Indische Compagnie (generally abbreviated VOC) – rather than the Dutch state.

As these differences suggest, the influence of Christian ideas and institutions was much more geographically limited in Africa and Asia before 1750 than it was in Latin America. Except in places with indigenous Christian churches such as southwest India or Ethiopia, Christians were generally found in a few pockets surrounding European trading centers, with isolated missionaries operating in between. For the vast majority of the populations of Africa and Asia, Christianity – along with other aspects of European culture – made no difference at all. Until the second wave of European colonialism which began in the nineteenth century, most people had not heard of Christianity, and in large areas – Africa and Asia away from the coasts, most of Australia and the Pacific Islands – no one had seen a European. Nevertheless, just as Spanish contacts with the Aztec and Inca states shaped subsequent encounters with other Latin American groups, in Africa and Asia early encounters were extremely influential. Reports by early European missionaries, merchants, and explorers were avidly read by missionaries and colonial officials of the nineteenth century, and so influenced later religious, political, and social developments. Many historians are currently evaluating the complex relationships among race, gender, sexuality, and empire in the nineteenth century, yet the roots of these relationships go back to the first European voyages of exploration.

Ideas and patterns before the arrival of European Christianity

It is very difficult to summarize sexual ideas and practices across such a vast geographic area; over the last century anthropologists, historians, and religious scholars have taken great pains to point out how such matters as marital patterns, kinship structures, religious beliefs and practices, and sexual norms differ among groups that are often geographically quite close to one another and similar in terms of political or technological development, to say nothing of the populations of regions as disparate as were those of Africa and Asia before 1450. The following will thus be a necessarily general overview.

Most cultures of Africa south of the Sahara accepted polygyny, with families living in house-compounds in which each wife had her own house, cattle, fields, and property. Marriage was an agreement between families, and in areas where there were larger states, rulers used marriage to cement political and military alliances; as a result they might have a very large number of wives and concubines. Even in stateless areas, men demonstrated their wealth and power by the size of their households. Most women married young and lived in polygynous households, while men married late and some had no opportunity to marry at all. Some scholars have viewed this competition for wives as one reason for the intense generational tension and harsh male initiation rituals in many African cultures, as young men competed with their fathers and each other for the right eventually to marry. Because much of Africa had too little population for the land available, fertility was a constant concern in religious and magical rituals, and barrenness or impotence was ascribed, as it was in Europe, to witchcraft, with barren women particularly suspect. Both men and women acted as leaders and priests in indigenous religions, which generally honored male and female gods and spirits through complex rituals designed to assure the health and prosperity of the family and community. The spirit world often included one's ancestors, who were represented by masks and statues and honored through rituals and sacrifices. In Ethiopian Christianity, only men were priests, although, as in Orthodoxy, married men could be accepted into the priesthood. Priests could not marry after ordination, however, and monks were expected to be celibate and ascetic; it was these monks, rather than priests, who provided the intellectual and political leadership in the Ethiopian church.

In northern Africa, the Near East, and parts of Asia, sexual norms and patterns were shaped primarily by Islam, though with some adaptations to local practices. Intermarriage played an important role in the growth of Islam; Arabic traders often married local women to gain access to economic and political power through kin connections; such households then blended Islamic and indigenous marital practices, religious rituals, and norms of behavior for men and women. These blends were also shaped by social class, with elite households generally following Islamic norms more closely than those of more ordinary people.

Women seem to have been quite active in the spread of Islam during Muhammed's lifetime (570–632), but shortly thereafter the seclusion and veiling of women became part of official Muslim law – the shari'a – which is regarded as having divine authority. Marriage in the shari'a was viewed as a reciprocal relationship in which the husband provides support in return for the wife's obedience. Seclusion and veiling were marks of class status as well as religious or cultural norms, and appear to have begun among the upper classes, although gradually adopted even by quite poor families whenever possible. The seclusion of women was possible in large part because of the expansion of slavery, for slave women – who came from outside Islam and were unveiled – could carry out many basic female tasks such as shopping or fetching water. Slave women also served as concubines – the Qur'anic limitation of four wives at any one time did not apply to concubines – and their children were regarded as fully legitimate and free. Marriages were often arranged by family members or marriage brokers, and in some parts of the Islamic world marriages within the extended family were favored in order to promote the consolidation of family property.

The Qur'an recommends marriage for everyone, and women generally married at quite a young age; men often married later when they had established themselves. Because Islam regarded sexuality within marriage or other approved relationships as a positive good, contraception was acceptable and, judging by discussions in medical and legal texts, a fairly common practice. In contrast to Christianity, sexual relations in Islam did not have to be justified by reproduction, though having children, and particularly having sons, was seen as essential to a good life. This lesser emphasis on procreation may have played a role in Islam's toleration of homosexual relations between men; though officially forbidden by Muslim law, they were not punished with any great severity, and in the period of the Abbasid caliphate (750–1258) homoerotic literature praising beautiful young men was a popular genre among some urban circles. Heterosexual relations outside of marriage, especially adultery with a married woman or concubinage, were punished much more severely for men than homosexual relations. Homosexual relations between women in the Muslim world have left few literary or legal records, and so are very difficult to study.

In India, Hinduism treated family life and procreation as religious duties, and so all men and women were expected to marry; anything which interfered with procreation, including exclusively homosexual attachments, was viewed negatively. Hindu families often attempted to marry their daughters off at a very young age – the recommended age by the year 1000 was between eight and ten – to insure that they were already married before they began menstruating. During the tenth century, Islam began to spread into parts of India, and Islamic ideas mixed with those of Hinduism to encourage the veiling and seclusion of women – termed purdah – although the strictness and exact rules of this practice varied according to social status and region. In southwest India, the St Thomas Christians combined Christian with Hindu practices, following many of the same birth, puberty, marriage, and death rituals as their Hindu neighbors. Though they had a loose affiliation with patriarchs in Iraq or Turkey, each church was largely independent, led by married hereditary archdeacons rather than celibate priests.

Hinduism celebrated male sexuality; one of the most important male gods, Siva, was often worshipped in the form of a symbolic phallus, the *lingam.* Female sexuality was regarded more ambiguously, as both creative and destructive; this duality can be seen in the nature of Hindu goddesses, who range from beneficent life-givers such as Devi or Ganga to faithful spouses such as Parvati or Radha to fierce destroyers including Kali and Durga. Hinduism also had many variants, some of which, such as Tantric Hinduism, emphasized the sexual androgyny of the Supreme Being and incorporated sexual activities as part of their rituals. In northern India, this divine androgyny was replicated in the human world by religious ascetics termed *hijra,* impotent or castrated men who nonetheless are believed to have the power to grant fertility.

Though Buddhism began in India, by 1500 it was no longer a major religion there, but it was the predominant religion in Sri Lanka and in parts of East and South-east Asia. In Buddhism, the spiritually superior life required the renunciation of all earthly desires, including sexual ones, and nuns and monks were warned about both homosexual and heterosexual relationships. Buddhism was never completely comfortable with women who gave up family life, however, and the ideal woman in Buddhism – both historically and in sacred texts – was more often a married woman with children who supported a community of monks or who assisted men in their spiritual progress rather than a nun. In theory, the Buddhist path to enlightenment (*nirvana* or *nibbana*) is open to all regardless of sex or caste, though some Buddhist texts also deemed women to be incapable of achieving enlightenment unless they first became men.

In the thirteenth century, Islam began to spread into some parts of South-east Asia, bringing with it greater expectations for female seclusion. Other parts of South-east Asia, Australia, and the Pacific Islands did not experience the introduction of any text-based religion, however, but remained animist, with local cults of various spirits and deities. Women often served as the religious personnel or spirit mediums in these local religions. Both women and men also took part in rituals of ancestor worship, generally at home altars rather than at specialized temples; deceased ancestors assisted and watched over everyone, in particular warning against possible dangers. These rituals brought together all members of the extended family and were ways to demonstrate one's loyalty to the family and a sense of debt and obligation for having been given life. This sense of moral debt to one's parents and family, termed *òn* in Vietnamese and *hiya* in Tagalog, the language of part of the Philippines, was as powerful as the notion of original sin in Christianity, but it was not linked to sexuality other than obliquely through having been born.

The concepts of debt and obligation were important not only in family life in South-east Asia, but also in the larger political and economic realm. People were often enmeshed in a complex system of dependency, sometimes placing themselves or family members into slavery to another in return for support – what is often termed "debt-slavery" – or otherwise promising loyalty or service. One also gave gifts in order to have others in one's debt; gift-giving was an important way to make alliances, pacify possible enemies, and create links and networks of obligations among strangers. Often these gifts included women, for exchanging women was considered the best way to transform strangers into relatives. These unions were often accompanied by a marriage ceremony and the expectation of spousal fidelity, but they were also understood to be temporary. If the spouses disagreed with one another or the man returned to his home country, the marriage ended, just as marriages between local spouses ended if there was conflict or one spouse disappeared for a year or more. Both sides gained from such temporary marriages; the woman and her family acted as local liaisons for the foreigner, and thereby gained prestige through their contact with an outsider. Concepts of debt also structured marriage patterns in other ways, as in some South-east Asian cultures where a prospective groom worked for his father-in-law for a period of time to pay off his debt for his bride. European travellers and officials, used to a system in which women brought a dowry, were often startled at this pattern of bride-service. They were more startled at men who inserted pins or balls into their penis, reportedly to increase women's sexual pleasure, which was rarely a concern of European men.

As in India, some South-east Asian cultures had ritualized religious roles which were permanently or temporarily androgynous. In the Philippines, religious leaders termed *baylans* or *catalonans* were generally married older women, regarded as to some degree androgynous because they were no longer able to have children. They were thought to be able to communicate with both male and female spirits, and this, in addition to their lack of fertility, gave them greater freedom of movement than younger women had. When men performed rituals as *baylans* or *catalonans*, they wore women's clothing or a mixture of men's and women's clothes. In South Sulawesi (part of Indonesia), individuals termed *bissu* carried out special rituals thought to enhance and preserve the power and fertility of the rulers, which was conceptualized as "white blood," a supernatural fluid that flowed in royal bodies. The *bissu* were linked to the androgynous creator deity; they could be women, but were more often men dressed in women's clothing and performing women's tasks, like the two-spirit people of the Americas.

In China, the dominant philosophical–religious system, known as Confucianism, taught that the order and harmony of the universe began with order and harmony in the smallest human unit; if human affairs were disrupted in families, they would necessarily be disrupted in the larger political realms. The universe was structured in a balanced but hierarchical relationship between Heaven – the superior, creative element – and earth – the inferior receptive one. Proper human relationships, especially familial ones, were those which were based on the model of Heaven and earth, hierarchical and orderly. Loyalty and honor were to be extended not only to one's living family, but also to one's ancestors, and sons were needed to carry out the rituals honoring family ancestors properly. As a result, various ways were devised to provide sons for a man whose wife did not have one: taking second or third wives or concubines, legitimizing a son born of a woman who was not a wife or concubine, or adopting a nephew, an unrelated boy or young man. A woman whose husband had died before she gave birth to a son might be expected to marry his brother, so as to produce a son who was legally regarded as the child of her deceased husband. (This practice is called a levirate marriage.) Even if their wives had sons, most upper-class men had one or more concubines, often poor girls whose parents had sold them to marriage brokers. (To be a wife instead of a concubine, a woman had to bring a dowry, something beyond the reach of poor families.) Until the beginning of the Qing dynasty in 1644, Chinese culture appears to have been tolerant of male homosexuality, for male homosexual subcultures developed among imperial officials, intellectuals, and actors.

Though in Confucianism the roles of both women and men were essential to the cosmic order, men were regarded as superior and women expected to be subordinate and deferential. This emphasis on hierarchy was accompanied by a stronger emphasis on the disruptive power of sexuality during the Neo-Confucian movement of the Sung dynasty (960–1279). Sexual attraction was regarded as so powerful that individuals alone could not control it; walls, laws, and strong social sanctions were needed to keep men and women apart. In many parts of China, women of the middle and upper classes were increasingly secluded, and even peasant houses were walled; boys and girls were cheap to hire as servants for tasks that needed to be done outside the walls. Female seclusion was also accomplished through footbinding, a practice which began in the Sung period among elite women and was gradually adopted by the vast majority of the female population in central and northern China. The origins of footbinding are obscure and debated, for contemporary official documents rarely discuss it. It does appear frequently in pornography, however, where the pointed shape that bound feet assumed was compared to lotus blossoms – an erotically charged image – and where the hobbled walk of women with bound feet was described as increasing their sexual prowess by lubricating their genitals.

Though Confucian notions of hierarchy and order found strong resonance in Japan, Japanese culture never adopted footbinding, and many ideas about sexuality found in other Asian cultures were simply absent from Japan: virginity in brides was not a preoccupation and marriage was not regulated by either church or state. François Caron, who worked for 20 years for the Dutch East-India Company in Japan and had five children with a Japanese woman, pointed out what appeared most distinctive to Europeans about Japanese marriage customs:

> These people neither make love nor woo, all their marriages being concluded by their Parents, or for want of such near relations, by the next of kin. One Man hath but one Wife, though as many

Concubines as he can keep; and if that Wife do not please him, he may put her away, provided he dismiss her in a civil and honorable way. Any man may lie with a Whore, or common Woman, although he be married, with impunitie, but his Wife may not so much as speak in private with another Man, as is already said, without hazarding her life. What is said of divorce, relates only to the Citizen, Merchant, and common Souldier; a Gentleman or Lord may not put away his Wife, although she should not please him, and that out of respect to her quality and his own Person; he must maintain her according to her condition and necessities; but may freely divert himself with his Concubines and Women.[1]

Japan was religiously pluralistic, with traditional Japanese religion (termed Shinto) mixing with Buddhism and other imported religious beliefs. Many of these belief systems held ambivalent ideas about sexuality: women carried out important religious rituals, yet were also regarded as sources of pollution through menstruation and childbirth; Buddhist monks were encouraged to abstain from all sex, yet homosexual relationships between monks and acolytes were common and sometimes celebrated in Buddhist monasteries. As in China, male homosexuality in both Japan and Korea was largely tolerated among certain groups, such as officials and intellectuals.

From this brief survey, it is evident that norms and patterns of sexuality in Africa and Asia fitted with those of European Christianity in some regards, but differed markedly in others. The emphasis on procreation, and particularly the birth of sons, was largely shared, as was the notion that marriage was an important matter and fundamental to social order. The very centrality of marriage and procreation also generated differences, however, for in most of the world's cultures, marriages were arranged by families and could be dissolved or additional wives secured if the first marriage failed to produce children. The consent of the spouses – especially that of the wife or wives – was not a major concern. Many cultures also allowed a range of sexual relationships rather than a strict dichotomy between married and unmarried, with the children of these unions often able to inherit, but generally disadvantaged in some way compared with the children of the primary wife or wives. In cultures with text-based religions, sexual desire was generally regarded as powerful and dangerous if it was socially disruptive, but not in itself evil. Thus there was no censure of any type of sexual activity between spouses, and little censure of men's sexual relationships, whether heterosexual or homosexual, unless they interfered with marriage. Women's sexuality was often feared or regarded ambiguously; women were accused of seducing men from their true religious and political duties – a point of agreement with Christianity – but the actual treatment of sexually active unmarried women varied tremendously by class, location, and specific situation. The treatment of married women who had sex with men not their husbands was uniformly harsh, though; except in Muslim areas, such cases were handled by the family or political authorities, not religious courts.

Christian institutions

As noted in the previous chapter, European exploration and the establishment of trading outposts in Africa and Asia began in the mid-fifteenth century, with Portuguese ventures on the Atlantic Islands such as the Cape Verde Islands and São Tomé, and on the west coast of Africa. In 1505 the Portuguese established a colony in Sri Lanka, and in 1510, another at Goa on the west coast of India. Over the next decades they set up other colonies at Melaka (Malacca), Cochin, Macao and a number of other ports. In 1565, travelling from Mexico, the Spanish established a permanent colony on the island of Cebu in the Philippines, and in 1571 on the island of Luzon. During the seventeenth century, the Dutch East India Company (VOC) began both to take over Portuguese centers and to establish their own, founding a colony in Sri Lanka and at Batavia on the island of Java in the early seventeenth century, and in many other parts of Asia and South Africa in the mid-seventeenth century. In all of these colonies and trading centers, religious personnel were part of the European presence. In addition, first Catholic and then (a few) Protestant missionaries travelled to countries not under European control such as China, Japan, and Vietnam in order to gain converts. Adding to this complex picture were indigenous Christian groups in southwest India and Ethiopia. In each of these situations, the institutions established and operated by religious authorities for the control of sexuality were quite different.

Portuguese colonies

The Cape Verde Islands and São Tomé were uninhabited before Portuguese colonization, so that Catholicism was the only official religion, with the church under the control of the Portuguese crown. Both of these areas became independent dioceses in the 1530s, and the crown hoped to use them as a springboard for further missionary work on the African continent. Their populations quickly became a mixture of Portuguese and African, and some Africans or men of mixed race travelled to Portugal for clerical training. A seminary was opened on São Tomé in 1571, but it operated only fitfully, and the total number of Africans or Eurafricans who were ordained to the priesthood there was small. Some of these men were active in missionary work on the African continent. The Atlantic islands themselves were one of the few places where institutions such as episcopal courts and the Inquisition were not staffed totally by Europeans. Both clergy and lay people spoke *Crioulo,* a mixture of Portuguese and African languages, and ceremonies and beliefs also blended European and African elements.

The Portuguese came to the kingdom of the Kongo in West Africa in 1485, though they gained few converts until the Jesuits and later the Capuchins began intensive missionary work. Very few missionaries spoke KiKongo, so they heard confessions through an interpreter. (A few did learn local languages, however; the first book printed in a Bantu language was a bilingual catechism in KiKongo and Portuguese, written in 1556 and printed in 1624.) Because missionaries often concentrated on converting rulers, conversion was influenced by political factors; ruling families saw Christianity as another means to increase their power. Thus they and their followers welcomed baptism and occasionally married in Christian ceremonies, which were viewed as favorable for procreation. Yet most converts did not have a Christian wedding, for this would have required identifying only one woman as "wife," and thereby upsetting the political alliances sealed by polygamous marriages. In other Portuguese colonies in Africa as well, Christian rituals were at most added to existing ones for their magical powers without altering existing marital or sexual patterns. Local patterns also continued in Ethiopia, where, except for a brief period, European missionaries had almost no success in converting Ethiopian Christians or Muslims to Catholicism; the Jesuits were, in fact, expelled from the kingdom in 1634.

In India, conversion was a slow process for the first several decades, and the Portuguese clergy were often quite lax, living with local women just as the soldiers and merchants did. With the arrival of clergy inspired by the Catholic Reformation in the 1540s, more rigorous standards were demanded of the clergy, and more intense efforts against existing religious practices began. Hindu temples were destroyed, and Hindu ceremonies, including marriage, were prohibited. Existing marriages between converts were blessed by a priest if they were found acceptable according to Christian rules about consanguinity and other matters. In many cases dispensations were needed and there was some question about whether authorities in India had been given adequate authority to grant them or whether such cases needed to be referred back to Portugal, a slow and arduous process.

Given the difficulties with relying on the Portuguese church for decisions, independent higher institutions were established locally. Goa became a bishopric in 1534, and an archbishopric in 1558; there were additional bishoprics at Cochin and Melaka. The first church council held in Asia was at Goa in 1567; among its many decrees, polygamy was forbidden, and men were ordered to live only with their first wife or to take one of their concubines as a wife. These institutions were, of course, under the authority of the pope, and Portuguese religious officials became increasingly unhappy with the fact that the St Thomas Christians were not. In 1599, Aleixo da Menezes, the Archbishop of Goa, arranged for a meeting with representatives of the St Thomas Church, and maneuvered them into agreeing to unite with the Catholic Church, swear allegiance to Rome, and affirm the decrees of the Council of Trent. They were allowed to conduct their services in Syriac instead of Latin, but otherwise were ordered to follow Roman practices; archdeacons were expected to be celibate, although some continued to pass on their titles, but to nephews instead of sons. (In 1652 some Syrian Christians renounced their ties to Rome, creating two separate Christian communities.)

Once bishoprics were established, the Inquisition began to operate in Portuguese colonies; it was set up in Goa in 1560 and held its first auto-da-fe there in 1563. Anyone who had converted and been baptized fell under the jurisdiction of the Inquisition, and it frequently investigated and tried those who had lapsed. This group often included what were termed "New Christians" – Portuguese whose families had been Jewish or Muslim but had converted – as well as former Hindus and animists. In some areas, such as the Canary Islands, indigenous men became officials in the Inquisition along with the Portuguese, but they had a somewhat lesser status because they were barred from taking part in cases that involved Jews, Moors, or members of the clergy.

In the earliest decades of Portuguese colonialism, there was an expectation that an indigenous clergy would develop, and there were occasional attempts to provide for the training of local priests. A seminary was opened in Portuguese Goa in 1541; it was soon taken over by the Jesuits, who also brought the first printing press there in 1556. Though most seminarians were members of high caste groups – Brahmins or Kshatrigas – or had European fathers, Portuguese authorities wanted them kept in subordinate positions, and they even refused to recognize the pope's appointment of Matthaeus de Castro, a Brahmin from Goa, as a bishop and vicar-apostolate. Despite this hostility, the number of native clergy in India continued to grow, although it was never sufficient to meet the needs of the widely scattered converts, and non-Europeans were never accepted as full members of religious orders in any Portuguese colony.

As in Latin America, various groups were formed in Asia to address the shortage of clergy. In seventeenth-century Vietnam, the Jesuit missionary Alexandre de Rhodes (1591–1660) set up communities of celibate men and women as catechists (they were termed "Amantes de la Croix"), who took vows of poverty, chastity, and obedience. They were not technically members of a religious order nor were the men ordained to the priesthood, but they did receive medical as well as religious training, and so their presence was widely tolerated. In other areas, lay religious confraternities of men and women were established, such as that of the Rosary in Melaka and on the south-east coast of India. These groups helped preserve Catholicism when the Portuguese colonies were taken over by the Dutch, who initially destroyed Catholic churches and prohibited Catholic clergy. The groups also carried out charity work among the poor and sick, cared for their own members, and encouraged their members to give up non-Christian religious and cultural practices. When the Dutch became military allies of the Portuguese in the eighteenth century they grew more tolerant in matters of religion; Catholic churches were rebuilt and Catholic clergy were allowed to return.

The Philippines

The Spanish program in the Philippines was directly influenced by the Spanish experience in Mexico, and members of religious orders were again in the forefront of both missionary work and political control. Because there were a large number of native languages in the islands, each order was assigned a specific area, so that its members would only have to learn a few of the native languages. Tagalog, the language spoken in the area around the Spanish settlement at Manila, was the most common language learned by Europeans, and the most commonly used for printed religious materials. The first book printed in the Philippines was a statement of faith from 1593, printed in Tagalog in both the Latin and traditional Filipino alphabet. (That alphabet did not survive long after the Spanish conquest; Tagalog is now written in Latin letters.) In order to hold their small groups of converts together, missionaries sought to establish compact settlements, intentionally modeling these on the *reducciones* of Latin America, but they met great resistance; most converts stayed near the missionary and church only on holidays, and otherwise lived in scattered villages.

Though King Philip II sought a bloodless conquest of the Philippines, there was to be no toleration of native religion, and missionaries cut down sacred groves of trees, destroyed religious objects, and Christianized childbirth and funeral rituals, offering pictures of the saints to assist people through difficult times. They also decided, when preparing catechisms and statements of faith, to leave certain key religious concepts in Latin or Spanish, to emphasize the break with the pagan past. The problem with this strategy, of course, is that such concepts were often interpreted and understood in very different ways from those the missionaries intended. Baptism, for example, was widely regarded as curing physical ailments, and confession was seen as a gift to God and the religious authorities that established a relationship of indebtedness, but did not involve an internalization of guilt or shame for one's actions. Such divergent understandings probably could have been lessened by the ordination of more Filipino clergy, and the crown in fact urged this agenda as early as 1677. The members of religious orders in the Philippines, most of whom were from Spain, refused to do this, however, and by 1750 there were still only a few Filipino clergy, most in subordinate positions. As in Latin America, the arguments against training indigenous clergy in the Philippines emphasized Filipinos' supposed inability to maintain a celibate life, or as Archbishop Filipe Pardo put it in 1680, because of "their evil customs, their vices, and their preconceived ideas . . . the sloth produced by the climate, effeminacy, and levity of disposition. Even the sons of Spainards, born in the islands, [are] unsuitable for priests, since they were reared by Indian or slave women."[2] There were many active lay confraternities for charitable and pious purposes, some intentionally established to counteract the powers *baylans* were thought to have over the sick and dying, but these groups were more effective at blending Christian rituals and folk customs than they were at transmitting Christian ideas as the missionaries understood them. Nevertheless, by 1750 a large proportion of the Filipino population identified themselves as Christians, were married in Christian ceremonies, and at least occasionally relied on a priest for advice on moral and sexual matters. There were several convents for women, including one founded in 1721 especially for indigenous women, although most of the Filipino women who lived in convents were servants or lay sisters rather than professed nuns.

Confessional manuals in Tagalog indicate that sexual sins were an important concern of clergy; desires as well as actions were to be described and confessed. One manual suggests these questions for a priest to ask: "I also suspect that every time you saw her or thought of her, you also lusted after her. Isn't this the case? And because of your lust, did you do anything to your body, any kind of lewdness? And did your body emit something dirty?"[3] A commentary on the Ten Commandments written in Tagalog by a Spanish cleric similarly railed against both acts and desires: "Everyone is burning with sexual passion and is evil in his heart towards the Lord God. Impurity has become man's favorite activity, and is engaged in without shame or fear . . . You would really be punished by the Lord God if you looked at a woman with desire, or the same would happen if a woman did a similar thing to a man, for they want to commit adultery in their hearts."[4]

Missionaries often saw sexual control as a near-miraculous sign of conversion in both men and women, relating many stories like the following:

> A certain woman, to whom God our Lord had communicated lofty
> purpose and sentiments of chastity and purity, was for a long time

beset with gifts and importunities from wicked men. Her refuge
was to confess and devoutly to receive communion, arming herself
with these holy sacraments. One day, after she had received communion in our house, one of these men lay in wait to seize her
when alone; and, with a bare dagger at her breast, was about to
slay her if she would not consent to his evil purpose. But she, for-
tified with the bread of the strong and with the wine springing forth
virgins, told him she was ready to die on the spot, rather than
offend God. He abused her with words, and even handled her
roughly, but left her, astonished and overcome by her chastity.[5]

Another [man], giving up all thought of God and of his own
salvation, had spent many years in dreadful sin, and especially in
a disgraceful lust, which was so deeply rooted and fixed in his
innermost heart that he regarded our priest, who strove to lead
him away from this vile manner of life, as only less than a fool.
So completely had he plunged himself into the filth of these pollu-
tions of his soul, that, like a sow in a wallow, he seemed to take
pleasure in nothing else. Yet at last this obstinate man yielded to
argument and persuasion, and not only gave up visiting his harlot,
but tore all lust from his heart by the roots as completely as if
he had no knowledge of it; for by a general confession of the
lapses of his past life he so corrected his morals that all those who
knew him were amazed at the sudden change in his life.[6]

Dutch VOC colonies

As we saw in Chapter 2, the Reformed Church in the Netherlands was
Calvinist in its theology and presbyterian in its organization; social discipline
was carried out by consistories, rather than by episcopal courts or the
Inquisition, and was to some extent independent of state interference. This
situation changed to some degree in the Dutch colonies, where the "state" was
a private company, the VOC. The directors of the VOC thought it important
to provide religious personnel for their own employees and to combat
Catholicism in formerly Portuguese areas, but kept these clergy strictly under
VOC control. In the Dutch colonies, clergy of the Dutch Reformed church
were under the authority of VOC officials and were paid directly by the VOC,
as were schoolmasters. The few who did not agree with VOC policies suffered; George Candidius, for example, was too vocal in his opposition to VOC
toleration of informal marriages, and lost his post in the Moluccas in 1627.

Not surprisingly, the VOC had difficulty finding and retaining suitable
men, and in some places augmented these positions with "Comforters of the

Sick" – lower-class men from the Netherlands charged with visiting the sick and holding prayer meetings – and "Proponents" – mixed-race or native laymen who were given a little theological training and expected to give religious instruction in local languages, including Portuguese Creole. Seminaries were also established at various times in Sri Lanka, but these were not particularly successful, and very few native clergy from anywhere in Asia were ordained. Consistories modeled on those in the Netherlands attempted to regulate sexual and moral conduct by imposing religious sanctions such as excommunication, and they could be very active. In Batavia, for example, during the period 1677–1693 over 800 people were censured by the consistory, about half of them for sexual or marital matters.[7] Not surprisingly, women predominated among those charged with sexual offenses, while men were more often charged with drunkenness, fighting, or not going to church.

Patterns of conversion varied widely in VOC colonies. In the Cape Colony of South Africa, the VOC was completely uninterested in converting either indigenous people or the slaves it imported, and very few non-Europeans became Christians. In many Asian VOC trading posts, conversion to Reformed Christianity was almost entirely the result of intermarriage, though in a few places, such as Sri Lanka, Amboina, and Taiwan, more widespread conversion occurred, generally among those who stood to gain financially or politically from conversion. In these cases whole villages sometimes converted cn masse after a Proponent or other native Christian convinced them of the spiritual and practical benefits of Christianity; baptism and church services were held in native languages whenever possible, with the sermon, rather than confession, the main method through which Christian doctrine was communicated to adults. The first translation of the New Testament into a South-east Asian language was into high Malay by a Dutch missionary in 1688, but as literacy levels were low, conversion remained largely an oral process. In some areas, such as Sri Lanka, the VOC supported the opening of primary schools for local children as well as those of Dutch fathers, because it viewed children as better candidates for conversion than adults; the actual establishment of such schools was more sporadic than company officials hoped, however. Opportunities to learn about Christian doctrine were so limited that church officials debated whether baptism should be separated from participation in communion, for the reformed church held that only those who had some basic knowledge of Christian teachings and whose lives at least loosely followed Christian patterns should take communion. (Women who had children out of wedlock, for example, were denied communion.) In some colonies, such as Amboina, the separation of sacraments became the norm and facilitated conversions on a larger scale. In others, such as Batavia, this policy was rejected on moral as well as theological grounds; opponents argued that it would discourage marriage, or as one put it, "Whoremongers already openly rejoice in the separation of the sacraments, as they can easily get their concubines baptized."[8] Indigenous women in Batavia who married Dutch men had to attend confirmation classes and be examined; though it is impossible to tell how they understood Christian doctrine, expectations about behavior were apparently being communicated, as the percentage of women among individuals denied admission to communion on moral grounds decreased steadily throughout the seventeenth century.

Japan and China

In the situations described so far in this chapter, the development of Christian institutions occurred within the context of European colonialism; in Japan and China, Jesuits and other missionaries also accompanied European traders, but they operated within the spheres allowed them by the existing government. In Japan, political disunity in the mid-sixteenth century, combined with the desire on the part of some Japanese nobles for European military technology, gave Jesuit missionaries beginning with Francis Xavier (1506–1552) the opportunity for large-scale conversions, including some members of the ruling class. Particularly under the leadership of Alessandro Valignano (1539–1606), Jesuits accommodated themselves to Japanese customs, learned the language, produced a number of catechisms and devotional books in various Japanese scripts, set up confraternities, trained indigenous assistants (termed *dōjuku* and *kambō*), and began to train an indigenous clergy. Valignano recognized that Christian opposition to divorce kept many Japanese from converting (especially prominent men, whose conversions would have brought political benefits) and tried unsuccessfully to obtain at least a temporary relaxation of the Tridentine legislation on marriage.

Later in the sixteenth century the political situation changed, and leaders attempting to unify Japan became convinced – in part through the arguments of Europeans opposed to Portuguese or Jesuit influence – that Christians were intent on military conquest and overthrowing the government. Christian sexual morals provided additional grounds for suspicion; Fabian Fucan, a Japanese convert who subsequently renounced Christianity, commented, "Jesus was born from a couple who had sworn chastity. What kind of a virtuous ideal is that? . . . The universal norm is that every man and every woman should marry. To go against that natural law is evil."[9] Edicts were passed in 1587 and 1614 expelling all missionaries and first restricting and then prohibiting Christianity; the 1614 edict was enforced by executions and gruesome torture designed to force Christians to recant. Despite an extensive system of surveillance with monetary rewards offered for the exposure of Christians, Christianity survived as an underground religion in remote farming and fishing villages of northern Kyushu and some smaller islands. These "hidden Christians" had no clergy, but lay leaders secretly taught, kept records, and baptized; they maintained their community by marrying within the group.

Christian conversion was slower in China than in Japan, though ultimately longer-lasting. Portuguese ships were on the Chinese coast by 1513, and a Portuguese trade mission went to Beijing in 1520, accompanied by missionaries. Most Chinese viewed the earliest missionaries as representing a variant sect of Buddhism rather than a new religion (this happened in Japan as well), and later the literary and philosophical activities of the Jesuit Matteo Ricci (1552–1610) led them to view missionaries as Confucian scholars from the West. Many of the ethical teachings of Christianity fit well with Confucian ideas, and even clerical celibacy could be understood as promoting a long life, which was a goal in many Chinese belief systems. Christian sexual ideas regarding lay people were harder to accept, however, and the chief obstacle to baptism among many of the intellectuals and political leaders otherwise attracted to Christianity was the requirement that they first give up their concubines and secondary wives. The raising of children – especially sons – was central to Chinese values, and missionaries were criticized for encouraging "some girls [to] renounce marriage for ever."[10] As we will see in more detail below, some Chinese converts urged accommodation on such issues, though others collaborated with European Jesuits to produce moral tracts which criticized certain aspects of traditional Chinese sexual morality, including the acceptance of concubinage and homosexual relationships. In the later seventeenth century missionaries travelled to many parts of China beyond Beijing, so that in many cities there were large Christian communities, for which hundreds of catechisms and devotional books were published.

In contrast to other parts of Asia and Africa, the admission of Chinese men as members of the Jesuit order and even as priests was quite rapid. For the purposes of ordination, they were (sometimes explictly) considered honorary whites; most (though not all) European missionaries saw them as members of highly developed cultures and thus better prepared for leadership positions than darker-skinned Christians found elsewhere in Asia or Africa. The first Chinese priest, Luo Wenzao (baptized Gregorio Lopez) was ordained in 1654, and later was named as a bishop, although his appointment was fought by many in the church hierarchy. The number of Chinese priests was never very large, however, and the operation of the Catholic church in China continued to rely on European clergy who were often divided by loyalties to their various religious orders and countries of origin. This situation, combined with changing politics at court, produced alternating periods of acceptance and repression, and though there was never a persecution campaign as severe as that in Japan, by 1750 Christianity in China had far less influence than it did 50 or 100 years earlier.

Other mission situations

During the early eighteenth century, a few Protestant missionaries went to other European colonies besides those run by the VOC. Most of them were pietists, part of a movement within European Protestantism which focussed on personal holiness and spiritual commitment. The German Lutheran pastor Bartholomew Ziegenbalg, for example, went to the tiny Danish colony of Tranquebar on the southeast coast of India and translated the New Testament into Tamil in 1714; he also advocated the training of indigenous catechists and the ordination of indigenous clergy, a process that proceeded slowly. Several other German missionaries were active in the territories held by the British East India Company in southern India, although in general the East India Company was hostile to missionaries because it thought their activities disrupted trade. The East India Company did provide chaplains for its own employees, who were, at least in theory, under the jurisdiction of the Anglican Church and its marital and sexual regulations. In practice, company employees in the seventeenth and early eighteenth centuries rarely brought their wives with them, but developed various informal relationships with local women; chaplains rarely commented on sexual matters and even more rarely brought them to the Company's attention.

Elsewhere in Asia and the Pacific, there was little development of Christian institutions before 1750, and none that has been studied in great detail. There were women on the Spanish expeditions to the Solomon and Marquesas Islands in the 1590s. In fact, the wife of one of the expedition leaders declared herself "queen" of the South Pacific when her husband died, a claim that was never ratified by the Spanish crown. Yet we know very little about such women or about the development and impact of Christian institutions there. There were no women on the European exploration and trading ventures along the Australian coast, a fact which occasioned comment from the aboriginal inhabitants, particularly as these men all had their bodies covered; in aboriginal eyes, such a covered-up, single-sex group must be either hostile or sacred, and there are reports that the Europeans were asked to remove their clothes and prove that they were, indeed, all men. Permanent European settlement in Australia did not begin until 1788.

Effects of Christian regulation

As one would expect, the actual impact of Christian efforts to regulate sexuality varied widely and is often very difficult to trace. Some issues cut across geographic and denominational lines, however, for Christian authorities were faced with certain issues in nearly every colonial context. The two most important issues were accommodation to existing marital and sexual practices, and the treatment of inter-racial sexual relationships, including marriage. Both issues were linked to wider concerns shared by religious and secular authorities and had implications for colonial social and economic policy, as well as Christian doctrine.

Accommodation to existing practices

In areas where the religious tradition was local, oral, and animist, accommodation was largely viewed as a practical and tactical matter. Some missionaries were hard-line about certain sexual practices, for example refusing to baptize men until they gave up all but one of their wives or married one of their concubines. The requirement of marital monogamy was difficult for men who were otherwise intellectually and spiritually prepared to convert; the Chinese intellectual Yang T'ing-yün, for example, delayed his own baptism for years, commenting: "The western fathers are really strange . . . Can they not allow me to have just one concubine?"[11] To give up polygamy was especially difficult for powerful men whose marriages cemented political alliances; in India, the family of one displaced wife killed the missionary who had inspired this action. Some missionaries recognized the function of polygamy and were more moderate. They justified their leniency by arguing that people needed to grow into Christian understanding and that Christian practice would eventually follow from baptism and teaching. Many of these arguments, particularly those justifying mass baptisms, are both racist and paternalistic, because they assume that the people concerned are too simple to understand the complexities of Christianity but nonetheless may be baptized because they have agreed to believe whatever the missionaries tell them.

A similar situation faced missionaries in Japan, where Chinese merchants often lived in temporary marriages with Japanese women, and then returned to China, leaving the women and their children behind. If the Japanese woman was a Christian, there may have been a Christian wedding, a ceremony that may have been unimportant to the Chinese merchant, but was of great importance in the eyes of the church. Valignano recognized this problem, and, in addition to asking Rome to relax rules about divorce in general, tried to gain some flexibility in this area. This was not forthcoming, and the abandoned women thus were not allowed to remarry in a Christian ceremony. Traditional marital patterns ultimately asserted themselves among Japan's "hidden Christians," who freely divorced and remarried. (This, plus their intermarriage within a small circle, would pose problems in the nineteenth century when European missionaries returned and attempted to convince them to rejoin Catholicism.)

Missionaries operating within cultures with a strong textual tradition, such as Confucianism, Buddhism, or Hinduism, viewed accommodation as an intellectual as well as practical issue, and they debated the degree to which certain practices were not merely tolerable, but spiritually and philosophically compatible with Christianity. The debate over accommodation emerged first in China, where it came to be known as the "Chinese rites controversy." The dispute centered on ancestor worship, funeral customs, and the words used for God. Those missionaries who regarded ancestor worship as compatible with Christianity – generally Jesuit followers of Matteo Ricci – argued that these were civic rituals designed to promote family cohesion, essentially veneration rather than worship and hence similar to the veneration of the saints. Those who opposed ancestor worship – generally Spanish Dominicans who had come to China from the Philippines – argued that it constituted paganism, and they opposed any adaptation to Chinese customs. A similar dispute – often termed the "Malabar rites controversy" – erupted in India; it centered on the policy of adaptation to Hindu customs begun in the early seventeenth century by the Italian Jesuit Roberto de Nobili. Nobili dressed and ate like a Hindu holy man, demonstrating his purity by refusing to look at a woman or talk with a European. He argued that accepting the caste system was the only way to attract upper-caste Hindus to Christianity, and that many Hindu practices were more cultural than religious.

Though most of the scholarship on the Chinese rites controversy and similar debates elsewhere in Asia has focussed on the intellectual issues involved, it is clear that sexual norms were also a key area of disagreement. For instance, Catholic baptism at the time involved more than the use of water; the priest also touched the converts' bare skin with salt, oil, and the priest's saliva, and breathed into their nostrils. Such close physical contact between an unrelated man and woman was unacceptable in many Asian cultures, as an anti-Christian book written in the early seventeenth century by the Chinese scholar Hsü Ta-shou makes clear:

> But in their [the Christian missionaries'] residences they themselves invite ignorant women at night to come in front of (instead of staying behind) the scarlet curtains (the teacher's seat). They

close the doors and mark the women with holy oil, give them holy water and even commit the crime of secretly lusting after them by placing their hands on five places of their bodies. What more can they add to the disorder between men and women?[12]

Hsü Ta-shou also objected to male and female converts mixing at services: "As for the wives and daughters of their followers, however, they let them mingle with the crowd in order to receive the secret teachings of the barbarians . . . all this in the dark night and [men and women] intermingling."[13]

Because of such sentiments, those who advocated accommodation modified their baptism rituals, as well as procedures at confession and other church services and rituals. Confession was held in a large room, with a mat suspended between the priest and his female confessant; a prominent male convert stood at the other end of the room, so that he could observe, but not hear. (This was certainly as private as most European confessions at the time; they often took place in the open in a crowded church, for the confessional box did not become widely used until the eighteenth century.) In India, Nobili allowed a woman who converted to wear the *tali* around her neck instead of a wedding ring as a sign of her marital status, and to receive gifts on the day of her first menstrual period after her marriage.

The Protestants also adapted to local practices. In Dutch Amboina, men and women did not eat together, and women were unwilling to attend church if it meant they would have to take communion alongside men. The Reformed Church in this case allowed them to wear a veil, though it would not allow separate communions. Similar considerations of sexual propriety shaped Lutheran practice in Tranquebar, where men and women (as well as persons of different castes) were allowed to sit separately at church.

Yet there were certain aspects of existing sexual practice which missionaries and church authorities refused to accommodate. The most prominent of these was male homosexuality. On seeing male prostitutes in Beijing, the generally tolerant Matteo Ricci severely regretted how "these miserable men are initiated in to this terrible vice."[14] A Jesuit moral tract published in 1604 in China by Diego de Pantoja (with the assistance of Yang T'ing-yün, the convert-to-be who could not give up his concubine), invokes both Christian and traditional Chinese arguments against homosexuality:

The sin of lust has many manifestations, but male homosexuality is the greatest. In my Western country, all sins have a name. Only this is the sin that dares not speak its name. As for this sin, those who commit it pollute their hearts, and those who speak of it pollute their mouths . . . The male is *ch'ien* and the female is *k'un*. This is the principle of generation. [And thus linked to cosmic generation, which was seen as binary.] A man and a woman, this is the way of humankind.[15]

As in Europe, certain groups in Asia and Africa were viewed as particularly likely to be sodomites – Moors in North Africa, Turks in the Near East, Chinese in the Philippines – as male homosexuality was linked to developing notions of racial and ethnic difference.

Opposition to homosexuality translated into repression. In Portuguese Goa, the Inquisition investigated a number of sodomy cases, and secular authorities publicly burned men found guilty of sodomy, including both native converts and Europeans. In 1599, royal authorities in the Philippines ordered that all who "commit or practice the said abomination against nature, or try to commit it. . . shall incur the penalty of being burned alive by fire, beside having all his goods confiscated to the treasury of his Majesty."[16] They particularly singled out Chinese merchants and posted notices in Chinese parts of Manila warning of the consequences of homosexual acts. These merchants countered that they were not converts and that such activities were acceptable in their own country, but Spanish authorities charged them with spreading the "abominable sin against nature" to native "Moro and Indian boys of these islands, by which God, our Lord, is greatly disserved," and punished those found guilty by flogging, galley service, and even execution.[17] (Flogging was also the standard punishment for any man in the Philippines found wearing a penis pin, as Spanish authorities attempted to end this practice.) In Japan, Jesuits referred to homosexual practices in Buddhist monasteries in arguments against Buddhism, and Valignano's catechism for Japanese converts specifically warns against homosexual behavior.

During the seventeeth century, on issues other than homosexuality, adaptation was widely accepted among both Catholics and Protestants, but in the first half of the eighteenth century this policy was reversed, especially among Catholics. Already in the seventeenth century Dominicans had complained to the papacy, and charged the Jesuits with illegitimate practices. The papal legate Charles Maillard de Tournon condemned any distinctive Malabar or Chinese rites in 1704 and 1707, and ordered all missionaries to follow Roman practice; this decision was reinforced by a papal bull in 1744. Not surprisingly, the pace of conversion slowed, and some converts gave up their allegiance to Christianity.

Despite all attempts at enforcing uniformity and official condemnation of "accommodationism," however, in actual practice African and Asian Christians retained many distinctive marital and sexual practices. Christian girls in India continued to marry at a very young age (though in one celebrated case this led to a very young girl's being forcibly taken from her older husband) and Christian widows in India, even very young ones, did not remarry. Caste still determined marital choice, as well as which confraternity one joined. Converts in Dutch Amboina continued to perform rituals which celebrated sexual maturity, such as circumcision or incision of the foreskin for boys and ritual cleaning after the first menstruation for girls. Christians in Mozambique celebrated a girl's first menstruation by invoking the "Most Holy Name of Jesus," despite the Inquisition's denunciation of such "rites, ceremonies, and superstitious abuses."[18] Filipino Catholics continued to begin sexual relations once the initial stages of marital agreements had been concluded and to petition for annulments with great frequency; European clergy working among them viewed such practices as a demonstration that sexual desire continued to be their "prince and master vice" and "so general that . . . it kept these regions aflame with an infernal and inextinguishable vice."[19] This assessment of the power of sexual desire among "tropical" peoples was communicated to the missionaries who began coming to Africa and Asia in much greater numbers after 1800, and it led them also to categorize indigenous marital and sexual practices as "vice" rather than social and cultural tradition.

Interracial sexual relationships

European authorities, both secular and clerical, brought with them a categorization of heterosexual relationships that was largely dichotomous: there was monogamous marriage, and there was everything else. As we have seen, they encountered societies with more complicated categories, and they were also confronted with additional complexities because of the colonial situation. Given the fact that almost all Europeans were men, interracial sexual relationships developed immediately, and colonial authorities were required to balance a variety of, at times, contradictory aims and norms. All of them wanted stable and peaceful colonies and realized that controlling sexuality was a key part of this, but they differed widely in their ideas about the nature of that regulation. Policy and its implementation were often determined by the personal opinions of governors, church leaders, and company officials, and so swung wildly. Church support of monogamous marriage often collided with secular political and economic aims, and with existing or newly developing racial and ethnic hierarchies.

Some authorities hoped to avoid the problems of interracial relationships, and favored the importation of more women from Europe. Beginning in the mid-sixteenth century, the Portuguese crown sent white orphan girls to Goa and West Africa, providing them with dowries in the form of an office or a piece of land for their future husbands, and ordering them to marry. In 1586,

Spanish residents in the Philippines petitioned the royal council for transport and dowry funds so that "ten, fifteen, or twenty women [be] brought from Spain, to be married to the common people of these islands, such as soldiers and others, that this country may secure an increase of population – which it has not at present, for lack of women and marriages."[20] In the early seventeenth century, VOC officials arranged for orphan girls, whom they termed "Company daughters," to be brought from the Netherlands to the East Indies, giving them clothing and a dowry. The numbers of such girls were never very great, and in general, the unmarried girls and women who were willing to leave Europe were not the sort that authorities favored. Peter Both, the first Dutch Governor-General of the East Indies, suggested that the VOC ban further female immigration, since the "light [meaning frivolous, not light-skinned] women" who had come were a "great shame to our nation," and in 1632 the VOC stopped sponsoring women as immigrants to any Dutch settlement east of Africa.[21]

Other authorities were realistic about the number of European women who could be encouraged to immigrate, and viewed interracial marriage as the best way to create stable colonies. The Duke of Albuquerque – the leader of the Portuguese forces which conquered Goa – hoped that his men would marry the widows of the Muslim defenders of Goa and never return to Portugal. He allowed soldiers who married to retire from the army, and gave them subsidies to set up a household. A similar policy was adopted by the directors of the VOC, who gave soldiers, sailors, and minor officials bonuses if they agreed to marry local women and stay in the VOC colonies as "free-burghers." This policy was opposed by some Dutch missionaries, but accepted by others such as George Candidius, who hoped marriage with local women would not only win converts but give missionaries access to female religious rituals. The petition by Filipino citizens asking for woman from Spain quoted above also requested dowries for native women to enable them to marry soldiers and sailors of lower ranks. The Directors of the British East India company gave additional encouragement in 1687, decreeing:

> The marriage of our soldiers to the native women of Fort St
> George is a matter of such consequence to posterity that we shall
> be content to encourage it with some expense, and are thinking
> for the future to appoint a Pagoda [4 rupees of Indian currency]
> to be paid to the mother of any child that shall hereafter be born
> of any such future marriage upon the day the child is Christened.[22]

There were limits to this acceptance of intermarriage, however, often explicitly along racial lines. Albuquerque encouraged marriage to higher-caste

Indian women who were "white and beautiful," but discouraged unions with the darker-skinned "black women" of the Malabar coast.[23] Rijkloff von Goens, one of the VOC governors of Sri Lanka, supported mixed marriages, but then wanted the daughters of those marriages married to Dutchmen "so that our race may degenerate as little as possible."[24] In the Dutch colony of the Cape of Good Hope (South Africa), though the races were not segregated and there was much sexual contact between European men and African women, this color hierarchy was so strong that it largely prevented inter-racial marriage. Until 1823, slaves in Cape Colony could not marry in a Christian ceremony; a man wanting to marry a slave had to baptize and free her first. Slaves marrying among themselves often devised their own cere-monies, or married in Muslim ceremonies even though Islam was not a recognized religion. In the Portuguese colonies of West Africa, marriages between Portuguese men and African women were not recognized as such by the crown, which periodically ordered the men to return to Portugal without their families.

Hesitation about intermarriage came not only from the European side, however. Asian families of high social standing were generally not eager to marry their daughters to the type of European men usually found in the colonies, especially as wives and children were required to adopt their husband's religion. This reluctance was clear to European colonists. In the 1640s, for example, the Goa municipal council wrote to the king, suggesting he pass a decree ordering all upper-class Indian families to marry their daugh-ters to Portuguese men born in Portugal and to give all their property to these daughters. They argued that this policy would create more Christians, soldiers, and wealth for Portugal, which it no doubt would have; it would also have led to revolt, a fact which the Portuguese crown recognized and so paid no attention to the request. Those women who were willing to marry Europeans were either lower-class or already separated from their families and place of origin. Thus in Goa, in contrast to Albuquerque's hopes, a visitor noted in 1524 that "all or the great majority [of Portuguese men] are married to Negresses, whom they take to Church on horseback."[25] (By "Negresses" the commentator means lower-caste Indians with dark skins, not women from Africa.) Some of these were slaves, and by the second and third generations many of them were women of mixed race. In Dutch and English areas, some of these women were Catholic, the children of marriages between Portuguese men and local women; Protestant church authorities worried about the women retaining their loyalty to Catholicism, raising their childern as Catholics and perhaps even converting their husbands. Thus although they often tolerated Catholicism in general, they required marriages between a Protestant and a Catholic to be celebrated in a Protestant church and demanded a promise from the spouses that the children would be raised as Protestants.

Intermarriage was accepted as a way to build up stable colonies, and various policies were adopted to make sure that families remained where they were. In VOC colonies in Asia, men were not allowed to take their Asian wives or children back to Europe with them, nor to return to Europe without them, a Catch-22 policy to which very few exceptions were made. European widows were obliged to stay in the colonies and find a new spouse there, and the daughters of European families to stay at least five years after they married, virtually assuring that they would marry someone willing to remain in the colonies.

Marriage was, of course, only one type of interracial sexual relationship, and perhaps the least common in most European colonies. At times government policy explicitly encouraged relations outside of marriage, especially in the earliest years of any colony. On São Tomé, the Portuguese crown apparently provided each European man with either a deportee from Europe or a slave from Africa explicitly to increase the population, and did not require a marriage ceremony. Though some clergy there and elsewhere in the Portuguese empire objected to such toleration of extra-marital sex, their views were moderated if the woman was baptized, and they could at least pretend a marriage might eventually result. Carmelites who visited São Tomé in the 1580s, for example, commented that both the European and African men there had "a wife or two as concubines" who had "a baby each year"; they approved of the formation of families, though weakly recommended that it would be better if Christian marriage ceremonies could be celebrated.[26] Most Portuguese men paid little attention to clerical opinion in any case, and many had households that had not only one or two, but a number of women. Nicolas Lancilotto, a Jesuit writing to Ignatius Loyola from Malaka in 1550, astutely linked this with the easy availability of slaves, commenting, "There are innumerable Portuguese who buy droves of girls and sleep with all of them, and subsequently sell them. There are innumerable married settlers who have four, eight, or ten female slaves and sleep with all of them, and this is known publicly."[27] In port cities, both Portuguese and indigenous pimps often bought and sold girls for sexual purposes, with the money going to the girl's family or the pimp; a small portion might go to the girl herself, through which she accumulated a dowry for her eventual marriage.

There were sporadic attempts to control extra-marital sex, particularly once a colony was established. By 1559 the Portuguese crown declared itself shocked at the situation in São Tomé where "many women give themselves publicly for money. They live irregularly in the town alongside married householders and other people who lead regular lives, from which arise many

scandals and bad examples and things which are a disservice to Our Lord."
Such women were ordered to move outside the towns and serve only local
customers; married men and clergy who maintained mistresses were also
ordered to give them up or pay a fine, with a penalty of deportation for the
third offense. The local bishop was to implement these measures, but he was
less than enthusiastic; he reported to the crown that the penalties set were
far too harsh, and that punishments should take into account "the quality of
the person concerned and the scandal of the offense. I am very merciful with
those who confess their fault and promise amendment."[28] VOC governors
periodically tried to ban the maintenance of female slaves and concubines
and to order all Christians living together to marry. Such prohibitions were
generally ineffective, for even high-ranking VOC officials and Protestant
schoolmasters maintained concubines or lived together with women without
an official church ceremony.

The fate of children from extra-marital, interracial unions varied enor-
mously. Some of them were legitimated by their fathers through adoption
or the purchase of certificates of legitimacy, and could assume prominent
positions in colonial society. For example, two of the sons of François Caron,
whose views of Japanese customs are quoted above, later became well-known
ministers in the Dutch church. On the Portuguese Atlantic Islands and in
Mozambique, mixed-race children from the first generations came to form
a local aristocracy, dominating both land ownership and the slave trade. On
the other hand, many children of lower-class European men did not get much
support from their fathers, and in some colonies survived by begging and
petty crime. This situation led to the opening of orphanages in many colonies,
which in theory were to take in only legitimate children, but in practice did
not look too closely at family background. In Goa, for example, an orphanage
called "Our Lady of the Mountain" was opened ostensibly for the legitimate,
white, "good-looking" daughters of soldiers who had died fighting, but in
actuality most of the residents were mixed-race, and some were born out
of wedlock. (The records do not reveal if requirements about appearance
were similarly ignored.) The VOC Council in Batavia tried to solve the issue
of mixed-race children born out of wedlock by banning their fathers from
returning to Europe, a policy which was counter-productive as it simply
discouraged European men from recognizing or supporting their children.

Like state and company policies, church policies regarding marriage and
morality were often counter-productive. In VOC colonies, for example,
marriages could only be solemnized when a pastor visited, which in remote
areas might be only every several years. This did not keep people from
marrying, however, but instead encouraged them to maintain traditional
patterns of marriage, in which cohabitation and sexual relations began with

the exchange of gifts, rather than a church wedding. Protestant missionaries advocated frequent church attendance, viewing sermons as a key way to communicate Protestant doctrine; the Asian wives of European men took this very much to heart and attended church so frequently and in such great style that sumptuary laws were soon passed restricting extravagant clothing and expenditures for church ceremonies. In Lutheran Tranquebar, children of European men and local women born out of wedlock were denied baptism, but they were simply taken down the road and baptized in Portuguese Catholic churches, clearly not the intent of the Danish authorities.

Other issues

Along with issues peculiar to the colonial situation, such as the level of accommodation and the regulation of interracial relationships, the Christian churches also faced many of the same problems they did in Europe, and their solutions were largely similar. Individual clergy were charged with concubinage, soliciting sex during confession, and otherwise not living up to the moral standards which church officials expected of them; the most frequent charges against priests handled by the Inquisition in the Philippines were for sexual lapses. Consequences could range from none to removal from office to imprisonment; members of religious orders such as the Jesuits were generally dismissed from their positions and sometimes from the order itself. In some of these cases the church may have been more upset than the local population, for whom clerical chastity was not a long tradition and who saw advantages in allying themselves with clergy through sexual relationships involving their daughters.

Asylums for repentant prostitutes and other women charged with sexual crimes were opened in some European colonies, including Goa, Batavia, and Manila. These sometimes housed orphans or other poor girls thought to be in danger of becoming prostitutes and also women who had been abandoned or mistreated by their husbands. Though according to the ordinances establishing these houses, the different groups of women who lived in them were to be separated, in practice the houses were often very small, and all the women lived together. As it was in France, Italy, and Spain, life in these asylums was a mixture of punishment and penitence, with work and strict discipline intended to "reclaim . . . such debauched women . . . from their ill course of life."[29]

Examples of love magic similar to those in Spain and Latin America emerge occasionally in the colonial secular and church courts. One such case in 1639 in Batavia concerned Catrina Casembroot who, "by various impermissible and ghastly means of witchcraft, charms, and administered potions has constrained and tried to force persons to her uncouth desires." Casembroot bought her poisons from indigenous women, and all of them were sentenced to be executed, "for their godless demeanor, fornication, thieving, devilish practices, and empoisonments."[30] As this example indicates, love magic was often termed "witchcraft" or "devilish practices," terms also applied to the rituals of indigenous religious practitioners, especially if they were women. This demonization of local religious practitioners did not lead to large-scale witchhunts, however, but to their being marginalized and trivialized, a process that also occurred in areas where other text-based religions such as Buddhism or Islam were spreading.

Examining the history of any aspect of Christianity in Asia and Africa before 1750 is in many ways examining a prehistory, for the major mass missionary efforts did not begin until after this date. The mid-eighteenth century did mark a significant break, however. In 1759 the Jesuits were expelled from Portugal and its colonies, in 1767 from Spanish areas, and in 1773 they were disbanded as an order. The Iberian colonies thus lost their most energetic missionaries, and both conversion and regulation efforts slowed; when the Jesuits were re-established in 1814, the colonial political scene was very different. At the same time, the British East India Company was becoming more important than the Dutch VOC in Asian trade and colonization, and, outside of Dutch and German colonies, subsequent Protestant missionary efforts would be largely British. Those missionary efforts would come to involve people with European backgrounds from what in 1750 were still colonies, that is, from the former British and French colonies of North America, later the United States and Canada. It was North America in the centuries before 1750 that gave European Christians their best opportunities to create moral and sexual utopias, whether among native converts or immigrants. It was in North America that the various experiments in how best to do this were most extreme.

Notes

1 François Caron, *A True Description of the Mighty Kingdoms of Japan and Siam*, reprinted in Michael Cooper, ed., *They Came to Japan: An Anthology of European Reports on Japan, 1543–1640* (Berkeley: University of California Press, 1965), 61–62.

2 Archbishop Filipe Pardo, in Emma Blair and James Robertson, *The Philippine Islands 1493–1898* (Cleveland: Arthur C. Clark, 1902–), 45: 182.

3 P. Sebastien Totanes, *Manual tagalog (1745)*, quoted and translated in Vicente L. Rafael, *Contracting Colonialism: Translation and Christian Conversion in Tagalog Society under Early Spanish Rule* (Ithaca: Cornell University Press, 1988), 105.

4 Antonio Ma-Rosales, O.F.M., *A Study of a 16th-century Tagalog Manuscript on the Ten Commandments: Its Significance and Implications* (Quzon City: University of Philippines Press, 1984), 53, 55, 57.

5 Relation of Pedro Chirino (1604) in Blair and Robertson, *Philippine Islands*, 13: 127.

6 Letter from Fr Francisco Vaez to Rev. Fr Claudio Aquaviva, general of the Jesuits, June 10, 1601, in Blair and Robertson, *Philippine Islands*, 11: 199.

7 Statistics in H.E. Niemeijer, *Calvinisme en koloniale Stadscultuur Batavia 1619–1725* (Dissertation, Free University of Amsterdam, 1996), 222–223.

8 Quoted in Leonard Blussé, *Strange Company: Chinese Settlers, Mestizo Women and the Dutch in VOC Batavia* (Dordrecht: Foris, 1986), 170.

9 Translated and quoted in George Elison, *Deus Destroyed: The Image of Christianity in Early Modern Japan* (Cambridge, Mass.: Harvard University Press, 1973), 279.

10 Cited in Jacques Gernet, *China and the Christian Impact: A Conflict of Cultures* (Cambridge: Cambridge University Press, 1985), 191.

11 Quoted and translated in N. Standaert, *Yang Tingyun, Confucian and Christian in Late Ming China: His Life and Thought* (Leiden: Brill, 1988), 54.

12 Quoted and translated in Adrian Dudink, "*The Sheng-Ch'ao Tso-P'i* (1623) of Hsü Tu-Shou," in Leonard Blussé and Harriet Zurndorfer, eds, *Conflict and Accommodation in Early Modern East Asia: Essays in Honour of Erik Zürcher* (Leiden: Brill, 1993), 115–116.

13 Ibid., 114–115.

14 Jonathan D. Spence, *The Memory Palace of Matteo Ricci* (New York: Viking Penguin, 1984), 220.

15 Diego de Patoja, Seven Victories, quoted and translated in Ann Waltner, "Demerits and Deadly Sins: Jesuit Moral Tracts in Late Ming China," in Stuart Schwartz, ed., *Implicit Understandings: Observing, Reporting, and Reflecting on the Encounters Between Europeans and Other Peoples in the Early Modern Era* (Cambridge: Cambridge University Press, 1994), 434–435.

16 Ordinances enacted by the Audience of Manila, 1598–1599, in Blair and Robertson, *Philippine Islands*, 11: 57.

17 Ibid., 56.

18 1771 Edict of the Inquisition at Goa, quoted and translated in C.R. Boxer, *Race Relations in the Portuguese Colonial Empire 1415–1825* (Oxford: Clarendon Press, 1963), 46, 45.

19 Pedro Murillo Velarde, Historia de Philipinas, 1749, in Blair and Robertson, *Philippine Islands*, 44: 93–94.

20 Memorial to the Council by the citizens of the Philippines, July 26, 1586 in Blair and Robertson, *Philippine Islands*, 6: 172.

21 C. R. Boxer, *The Dutch Seaborne Empire, 1600–1800* (New York: Knopf, 1965), 216.

22 Quoted in Stephen Neill, *A History of Christianity in India, The Beginnings to AD 1707* (Cambridge: Cambridge University Press, 1984), 372.

23 Quoted in Boxer, *Race Relations*, 64.

24 Quoted in Boxer, *Dutch Seaborne Empire*, 221.

25 Quoted in Neill, *Christianity in India*, 95.

26 Translated and quoted in John Thornton, *Africa and Africans in the Making of the Atlantic World, 1400–1680* (Cambridge: Cambridge University Press, 1992), 170.

27 Quoted in Boxer, *Race Relations*, 61.

28 Quoted and translated in C.R. Boxer, *Mary and Misogyny: Women in Iberian Expansion Overseas, 1415–1815* (New York: Oxford University Press, 1975), 20–21.

29 Johan Nieuhof, *Voyages and Travels to the East Indies, 1653–1670*, quoted in Barbara Watson Andaya, "From Temporary Wife to Prostitute: Sexuality and Economic Change in Early Modern Southeast Asia," *Journal of Women's History* 9: 4 (1998): 24.

30 Resolution of Batavian Council, 1639, translated and quoted in Blussé, *Strange Company*, 166, 167.

Selected further reading

Though the vast majority of scholarship on sexuality in Africa and Asia focusses on the nineteenth and twentieth centuries, there are increasing numbers of studies of earlier periods. A good overview of many issues, along with extensive bibliographies, may be found in: *Restoring Women to History: Teaching Packets for Integrating Women's History into Courses on Africa, Asia, Latin America and the Caribbean, and the Middle East* (Bloomington, Ind.: Organization of American Historians, 1990). André Burguière, et al., eds *A History of the Family: Volume One: Distant Worlds, Ancient Worlds* and *Volume Two, The Impact of Modernity* (Cambridge, Mass.: Harvard University Press, 1996) contains essays on the family in China, Japan, India, Africa, and the Arab world. Arvind Sharma's two books, *Women in World Religions* and *Religion and Women* (Albany: SUNY Press, 1987 and 1994) cover women's role and attitudes toward sexuality in many of the world's religions.

Of all of the areas covered in this chapter, China has received the most attention. For works which discuss traditional Chinese norms and structures, see: David Buxbaum, *Chinese Family Law and Social Change: In Historical and Comparative Perspective* (Seattle: University of Washington Press, 1978); Rubie S. Watson and Patricia Buckley Ebrey, *Marriage and Inequality in Chinese Society* (Berkeley: University of California Press, 1991); Robert H. van Gulik, *Sexual Life in Ancient China* (Leiden: E.J. Brill, 1961); Patricia Buckley Ebrey, *The Inner Quarters: Marriage and the Lives of Chinese Women in the Sung Period* (Berkeley: University of California Press, 1993). For works which discuss gender relations in other parts of Asia, see: Wakita Haruko, "Marriage and Property in Premodern Japan from the Perspective of Women's History," *Journal of Japanese Studies* 10:1 (1984): 73–99; Susan Bayly, *Saints, Goddesses and Kings: Muslims and Christians in South Indian Society* (Cambridge: Cambridge University Press, 1989); Neil Jamieson, "The Traditional Family in Vietnam," *Vietnam Forum* 8 (Summer–Fall 1986): 91–150; Anthony Reid, *Southeast Asia in the Age of Commerce 1450–1680, Volume One, The Lands Below the Winds* (New Haven: Yale University Press, 1988), especially 146–172 and *Volume Two: Expansion and Crisis* (New Haven: Yale University

Press, 1993), esp. 132–173; José Ignacio Cabezón, ed., *Buddhism, Sexuality and Gender* (Albany: SUNY Press, 1992).

Historical material on both gender relations and religion in Africa is generally discussed in broader studies of political and social developments. See, for example: Iris Berger, *Religion and Resistance: East African Kingdoms in the Pre-colonial Period* (Tervueren, Belgium: Musée royal de l'Afrique central, 1981); Wyatt MacGaffey, *Religion and Society in Central Africa: The BaKonga of Lower Zaire* (Chicago: University of Chicago Press, 1986); Anne Hilton, *The Kingdom of Kongo* (Oxford: Clarendon Press, 1985); Tamrat Taddesse, *Church and State in Ethiopia, 1270–1527* (Oxford: Clarendon Press, 1977). One of the few books which focusses specifically on gender in the pre-colonial period is: Onaiwa W. Ogbomo, *When Men and Women Mattered: A History of Gender Relations among the Owan of Nigeria* (Rochester: University of Rochester Press, 1997). By contrast, there are a number of studies which focus specifically on women or sexuality in Islam. See: Leila Ahmed, *Women and Gender in Islam: Historical Roots of a Modern Debate* (New Haven: Yale, 1992); Judith Tucker, *Gender in Islamic History* (Washington: American Historical Association, 1990) and *In the House of the Law: Gender and Islamic Law in Ottoman Syria and Palestine* (Berkeley: University of California Press, 1998); Basim Musallam, *Sex and Society in Islamic Civilization* (Cambridge: Cambridge University Press, 1983); Nikki R. Keddie and Beth Baron, eds, *Women in Middle Eastern History: Shifting Boundaries in Sex and Gender* (New Haven: Yale University Press, 1991).

Many general studies of the spread of Christianity in Africa and Asia, particularly older studies written from a clearly confessional viewpoint, make no mention of sex and very little mention even of marriage. Some which do, and which are useful in presenting the broader story, include: Elizabeth Isichei, *A History of Christianity in Africa: From Antiquity to the Present* (Grand Rapids, Mich.: William Eerdmans, 1995); John K. Thornton, "The Development of an African Catholic Church in the Kingdom of Kongo, 1491–1750," *Journal of African History* 25 (1984): 147–167; S.D. Franciscus, *Faith of Our Fathers: History of the Dutch Reformed Church in Sri Lanka* (Colombo (Sri Lanka): Pragna Publishers, 1983); Dauril Alden, *The Making of an Enterprise: The Society of Jesus in Portugal, Its Empire, and Beyond 1540–1750* (Stanford: Stanford University Press, 1996); George H. Dunne, S.J., *Generation of Giants: The Story of the Jesuits in China in the Last Decades of the Ming Dynasty* (South Bend, Ind.: Notre Dame University Press, 1962); Horacio de la Costa, *The Jesuits in the Philippines* (Madison: University of Wisconsin Press, 1961); Rafael, *Contracting Colonialism,* (note 3); Gernet, *China and the Christian Impact,* (note 10); Neill, *Christianity in India,* (note 22).

Christianity in Japan has been particularly well studied. See: C.R. Boxer, *The Christian Century in Japan, 1549–1650* (Berkeley: University of California Press, 1967); Richard H. Drummond, *A History of Christianity in Japan* (Grand Rapids, Mich.: William Eerdmans, 1971); Ann M. Harrington, *Japan's Hidden Christians* (Chicago: Loyola University Press, 1993).

Most of the scholarship on the VOC colonies is, not surprisingly, in Dutch, though there are several works in English which address some of the issues discussed in this chapter, including: Jean Gelman Taylor, *The Social World of Batavia:*

European and Eurasian in Dutch Asia (Madison: University of Wisconsin Press, 1983); J. van Goor, *Jan Kompenie as Schoolmaster: Dutch Education in Ceylon 1690–1795* (Groningen: Wolters-Noordhoff, 1978); Robert C.-H. Shell, *Children of Bondage: A Social History of the Slave Society at the Cape of Good Hope, 1652–1838* (Hanover: Wesleyan University Press, 1994); Leonard Blussé, "Retribution and Remorse: The Interaction between the Administration and the Protestant Mission in Early Colonial Formosa," in Gyan Prakash, ed., *After Colonialism: Imperial Histories and Postcolonial Displacements* (Princeton: Princeton University Press, 1995), 153–182 and *Strange Company* (note 8); Boxer, *Dutch Seaborne Empire* (note 21).

The issues discussed in this chapter are often framed in terms of Iberian colonialism as well as the spread of Christianity. For works which take this approach, see: C. R. Boxer, *The Church Militant and Iberian Expansion, 1440–1770* (Baltimore: Johns Hopkins University Press, 1978); Ann Pescatello, *Power and Pawn: The Female in Iberian Families, Societies and Cultures* (Westport, Conn.: Greenwood, 1976); John Leddy Phelan, *The Hispanization of the Philippines: Spanish Aims and Filipino Responses 1565–1700* (Madison: University of Wisconsin Press, 1967); M.V. Pearson, *The Portuguese in India*, New Cambridge History of India, 1 (Cambridge: Cambridge University Press, 1987); Albert Chan, "Chinese–Philippine Relations in the Late Sixteenth Century and to 1603," *Philippine Studies* 26 (1978): 63–86; Boxer, *Race Relations* (note 18).

Studies which focus specifically on gender and religion in the early modern period are still quite rare. These include: Barbara Watson Andaya, "The Changing Religious Role of Women in Pre-modern South East Asia," *Southeast Asian Research* 2, 2 (1994): 99–116; Mary John Mananzan, "The Filipino Woman: Before and After the Spanish Conquest of the Philippines," *Essays on Women* (Manila: Institute of Women's Studies, St Scholastica's College, 1989), 1–17; Carolyn Brewer, "From 'Baylan' to 'Bruha': Hispanic Impact on the Animist Priestess in the Philippines," *Journal of South Asia Women Studies: 1995–1997* (Milan: Asiatica Association, 1997), 99–117; Ivana Elbl, "Sexual Arrangements in the Portuguese Expansion in West Africa," in Jacqueline Murray and Konrad Eisenbichler, eds, *Desire and Discipline: Sex and Sexuality in the Pre-modern West* (Toronto: University of Toronto Press, 1996), 60–86. Several of the essays in Schwartz, *Implicit Understandings* (note 15) focus specifically on questions of gender, sexuality, and/or religion.

Studies of homosexuality and gender reversals in Africa and Asia are beginning to appear, though most of these are anthropological rather than historical. The works which do include historical materials all focus on Asia, including: Bret Hinsch, *Passions of the Cut Sleeve: The Male Homosexual Tradition in China* (Berkeley: University of California Press, 1990); Gary Leupp, *Male Colors: The Construction of Homosexuality in Tokugawa Japan* (Berkeley: University of California Press, 1995); Serena Nanda, *Neither Man nor Woman: The Hijras of India* (Belmont, Calif.: Wadsworth Publishing Co., 1990); Stephen O. Murray, ed., *Oceanic Homosexualities* (New York: Garland Publishing, 1992).

NORTH AMERICA

Caughnawaga women taking the vows of perpetual virginity in front of a statue of the Virgin Mary. From the *Narration annuelle* (1667–86) of Father Claude Chauchetière, a priest at the mission of Sault-Saint-Louis in Canada. Courtesy of the Archives départementales de la Gironde, Bordeaux.

NORTH AMERICA

THE INTRODUCTION OF Christianity into North America began in the Spanish-held areas of the southwest and Florida in the early sixteenth century. There was regular trade between Spanish areas and the rest of North America, which came to include goods such as rosaries or objects decorated with Christian symbols but not Christian ideas or institutions. These were thus not established until the seventeenth century brought permanent colonists from northern Europe.

Colonial development in America north of the Spanish- and Portuguese-held territories is generally seen as falling into three major patterns. In the far north beginning in the early seventeenth century, French explorers and fur traders established small colonies and traded with the indigenous population. The total French population remained very small throughout the seventeenth century, and the vast majority of French immigrants were men. By the early eighteenth century this had changed somewhat in the eastern areas of what would become Canada; in Acadia (present-day Nova Scotia, New Brunswick, and Prince Edward Island) and Quebec French farmers and fishermen settled in families. Western Canada remained a frontier area in which most Europeans were male fur-traders, for European women were banned from most fur-trading areas until the 1820s. The fur-trade companies were virtual rulers in many parts of Canada in the seventeenth and eighteenth centuries, and missionaries worked under their shadow in a relationship marked by both conflict and cooperation. Intermarriage between French traders and Indian women was far more common than in the English colonies, and marriage often tied traders to Indian communities.

Britain also claimed parts of what would become Canada, and the seventeenth and early eighteenth century saw intermittent conflicts between French and British, with each side allying itself with different Indian groups and territories switching from one power to the other. These wars were part of French–British conflicts taking place in Europe and resulted in part of Canada going to Britain in 1713, and the rest in 1763, after what Americans call the French and Indian War.

Despite eventual British dominance in Canada, in religious terms French Catholicism was far more important than English Protestantism. French Catholic missionaries, primarily Jesuits, began work among the indigenous residents of eastern Canada in the early seventeenth century, and they accompanied the fur traders further west and south shortly afterward. Many Jesuit missionaries were killed during periods of inter-tribal war, providing the Canadian church with its first martyrs and saints. In some places, missionaries established separate communities for Indian converts, loosely based on the Latin American mission model. The first of these was at Sillery outside Quebec in 1637, where the male missionaries were joined by several Augustinian nursing nuns two years later. In the same year, Marie de l'Incarnation and several others established an Ursuline house in Quebec, which soon took in both native women and European immigrants. In 1674 a French bishop, François Xavier de Laval (1623–1708), was installed at Quebec; he vigorously promoted missionary work, sometimes in opposition to the wishes of the French royal governor.

By contrast, English Protestant missionaries were far fewer in number than French Catholics, for Protestant clergy concerned themselves primarily with European immigrants. There was no institution for women in Protestantism corresponding to Catholic convents, and no Anglican bishoprics were established anywhere in North America in the colonial period. Thus Christian influence on sexuality in Canada in the colonial period is primarily the story of French missionaries' attempts to introduce European patterns of marriage and sexual relations among indigenous peoples, and to maintain some semblance of sexual "morality" among the largely male European population whose own conduct was far from ideal.

A second pattern of immigration and colonialism developed in New England. Here, beginning with the Pilgrims at Plymouth in 1620 and the Puritans in the Boston area in 1630, family groups of religiously inspired English Protestants were interested in permanent settlement rather than simply the extraction of natural resources such as furs. Immigration continued throughout the rest of the seventeeth century, and this, combined with a high birth rate and early marriage, meant a rapidly expanding European population. The early New England colonies were regarded by their founders as religious communities bound to God by a special contract or "covenant." Political participation was limited to men who had undergone a personal conversion experience and were church members. Women became church members independently through their own conversion experiences, and were regarded as part of the religious covenant, though this did not give them political rights. The Puritans had left England seeking a place to practice their religious faith without encumbrance, but this did not make their leadership willing to give others the same freedom. Religious dissenters were whipped, expelled, or even executed; though each church gradually became more independent – an organizational pattern called congregationalism – in the earliest years clergy in prominent churches were able to assert their control over doctrine and discipline.

In the first decades after settlement, adults had to make a confession to the whole congregation describing their personal conversion experience in order to be full church members. Children were regarded as sharing in their parents' covenant, however, and by the 1660s most congregations decided that people whose family background was within the church, but who had not personally confessed should also be admitted to church membership in what came to be termed the "Half-Way Covenant." Many historians regard this as an indication that the spiritual vigor in many congregations had begun to wane, and track this through changes in conduct as well as membership rules.

Because the European population of New England grew so quickly, the main story of native–immigrant relations is one of European appropriation of Indian land for new settlements, made easier by the dramatic drop in Indian populations from introduced diseases. This expansion was accompanied, in the seventeenth century, by a number of wars with various Indian tribes; these led to the eventual expulsion of Indians from many parts of New England. Even while this was going on, there was some missionary activity among the Indians. Separate settlements for Indian Christians, "praying towns" in which converts were expected to follow European Christian marital and sexual practices, were established, but the number of such towns was never very great in comparison with white settlements. In contrast to French Catholic missionaries, the main focus of most Puritan clergy was on European immigrants and their descendents, not on Indian converts. Tracing Christian regulation of sexuality in New England thus involves a primary focus on Puritan attempts to make their ideals a reality among white immigrants and a secondary focus on Indian–European encounters.

Many cultural historians view the experience of Puritan New England as central in the shaping of American culture, particularly in terms of American attitudes toward morality, the body, and sexuality. Suspicion of sexual pleasure or attempts to avoid discussion of sexuality are often termed "puritanical," with common ideas about the Puritans summed up by the author and critic H. L. Mencken, who defined Puritanism as "the haunting fear that someone, somewhere, may be happy." Defenders of the Puritans have argued that this is only part of the picture, for it overlooks Puritan ideals of companionate marriage and stable family life, but the debate goes on.

No one contends that the immigrants to the Chesapeake area of Virginia and Maryland, the third pattern of settlement in North America, were in any way puritanical. English settlers began to arrive there in the early seventeenth century, though, as in Canada, most of these were men, and many were indentured servants. The first Africans came in 1619 in a ship named the *Jesus*, and though in the early decades some Africans were indentured servants, most of them became permanent slaves. By 1720, 30 percent of the Virginia and 70 percent of the South Carolina population was black; by 1776, 20 percent of total United States population was black, of which 96 percent were slaves. Native Americans were also enslaved in many parts of the south, but their numbers were soon dwarfed by those of Africans.

A year after the first Africans came to Virginia, the Virginia Company began to import women from England as brides for men to purchase, hoping to encourage the growth of families and population. This development came about very slowly, however, and throughout the seventeenth century the gender balance among both whites and blacks in Virginia and Maryland was very skewed in favor of men. Many of the white women who did come were indentured servants rather than wives or daughters, and, like male indentured servants, were prohibited from marrying during the term of their service. Some masters also prohibited their slaves from marrying, although the usual respose was simply the denial of legal recognition for slave marriages rather than their explicit prohibition.

In theory the early settlers in Virginia and the Carolinas were part of the Anglican Church, with the clergy under the control of a bishop in England. However, clergy were financially supported by the local laity, and because the population was widely scattered on plantations rather than in compact settlements as in New England, pastors often travelled rather than having a permanent parish church. There was very little missionary activity among Indians in the south and very few churches for immigrants. As in Puritan New England, men who were not members of the official church were politically disadvantaged, but despite this, levels of church membership were very low.

As slavery rather than indentured servitude became the more common condition for people of African descent, slaveowners often chose not to baptize their slaves, for they feared this might mean they would have to free them. Some slaves had heard about Christianity in Africa through the Portuguese or even become converts there, but their religious allegiance was generally unrecognized. In 1667, the Virginia House of Burgesses passed a law stating that baptism did not change one's condition of servitude, but many owners still refused to allow their slaves to be baptized. This was also the case in the British-held islands of the Caribbean such as Jamaica, Barbados, and the Leeward Islands, where vast numbers of African slaves were imported to work on sugar plantations. Catholic slave owners in the French and Spanish Caribbean islands were more likely to baptize their slaves than British Protestants. Catholicism also appears to have been more appealing to slaves than Protestantism in the Caribbean, as it involved oral and visual elements similar to those of traditional African religions.

These three patterns of settlement and three types of religious structures – Catholic, Puritan, Anglican – were joined somewhat later in the seventeenth century by a fourth. Puritan intolerance led Roger Williams, Anne Hutchinson, and others to found communities in what became Rhode Island which offered religious freedom and toleration; in 1681 William Penn, a Quaker, founded a colony in what became Pennsylvania which also had no single official church. Catholics founded Maryland in 1634, with the understanding that this colony would also offer religious freedom. The diversity of settlers in the other colonies, some of which had originally been held by the Dutch, Swedish, or Danish – New York, New Jersey, Delaware and later Georgia – meant that these areas also never established a single strong state church as the southern or New England colonies did and it is difficult to make generalizations about them.

By the later seventeenth century, religious diversity was joined by disinterest in many parts of North America. People chose to be part of Baptist, Quaker, Presbyterian, Anglican, Catholic, Congregationalist, or other communities, or – more likely – chose to join no denomination at all. In contrast to the popular view of church-going Americans, most historians estimate that by 1700 the majority of colonial residents were not church members and rarely attended a service. Disinterest in religion changed somewhat in the 1730s and 1740s with the religious revival movement known as the Great Awakening. This was a movement of personal religious conversion which spread throughout the colonies, especially in frontier areas away from the coast where state churches were the weakest. It emphasized emotion, the spoken word, personal experience, and leadership based on a sense of calling, and attracted Indians and Africans as well as Europeans. People were encouraged to discipline their own conduct, but there was less focus on sexual sins than on those of pride, anger, and a lack of trust in God.

Ideas and patterns before the arrival of the Europeans

My cautionary words at the beginning of the chapter on Latin America about the difficulties in learning about or understanding indigenous patterns noted apply even more to the North American situation. In contrast to the peoples of central America, no North American group had a written language, so the words of Indians from the colonial period come largely through a European filter. In addition, the archeological record is sparser than it is for groups such as the Aztecs or Inca, and there are few stone structures or monuments which might reveal information about religious or social structures. Added to this is the fact that disease and war completely eradicated many of the peoples of eastern North America; diseases such as smallpox often preceded actual contact with Europeans in the interior of the continent, so that the first European traders and explorers encountered villages and settlements whose population levels were already much lower than they had been before 1600. For many groups, oral tradition, a central means of conveying Indian history, has been lost, disrupted, or diminished.

Difficulties with sources have led to debate among historians and anthropologists about many aspects of North American society in the seventeenth century, but there are some points on which most scholars agree. The peoples of the eastern woodlands were divided into a number of groups (what Europeans would term "tribes"), which can themselves be loosely divided into large linguistic groups, primarily the Algonkian (which includes the Delaware, Penobscot, Montagnais-Naskapi, Micmac, Ojibwa, Algonquin, and most of the other tribes in the eastern woodlands), Iroquoian (which includes the Huron, Mohawk, Seneca, and Iroquois), Siouan (which includes the Catawba and Winnebago), and Muskogean (which includes Choctaw, Chicasaw, Creek, and Seminole). They combined agriculture, gathering, and hunting activities in different degrees, and developed various types of political systems.

Despite linguistic differences and frequent warfare, certain characteristics were shared among tribes. They were often organized matrilineally into family and clan groups, with marriage generally occurring outside of the clan; what we think of as "tribes" were loose leagues of villages and clans linked by intermarriage. Marriage was a way to assimilate outsiders and bring them into the group; this would become very important in French-speaking areas where traders were encouraged to marry local women to facilitate peaceful relations. Adoption was another way to assimilate outsiders, and the women of a tribe often decided the fate of prisoners, who could either be executed or adopted to make up for lost relatives.

Marriages in some tribes were suggested or arranged by older women, including the mothers of the couple, although in other groups the parents had little say in the matter and the consent of the couple was all that mattered. Women apparently had more control over whom they married than was common among Europeans; a Protestant missionary among Mohawks in 1716 commented that "the Women court the men when they design Marriage."[1] Weddings generally involved a feast and an exchange of goods between the spouses to signify their complementary roles; she gave him corn bread, for example, while he gave her venison. Among some groups, there appears to have been a sort of "trial marriage", which could be easily broken if there were no children or the spouses proved incompatible. Most couples were monogamous, although, as in many other parts of the world, tribal leaders sometimes had more than one wife, occasionally marrying sisters in what is termed "sororal polygyny." Such polygyny may have resulted in part from a shortage of men, for there was no institutional role for women (or men, for that matter) who did not marry. Individuals abstained from sexual relations at different times for ritual purposes, but life-long chastity was regarded as bizarre and most people married at some point in their lives. Jesuit priests in Canada noted they were frequently teased about their lack of wives or offered women to marry, and one of the first sisters at the Quebec hospital reported that Hurons and Algonquins who met them were astonished "when they were told that we had no men at all and that we were virgins."[2] Attitudes towards pre-marital sexuality varied, with some groups regarding it as a normal precursor to marriage and others less accepting. Punishment for adultery also varied; some tribes set it at death or mutilation, while others did not punish it at all.

Many groups were matrilocal, which meant that husbands came to live with their wives' clans and related women lived together. Relations with one's mother's kin were thus more important than those with one's father's kin or even one's spouse. Among some groups divorce was frowned upon after children had been born, but among many, it was quite easy for either spouse to initiate. A man who wished to divorce simply left his wife's house, while a woman put her husband's belongings outside her family's house, indicating that she wished him to leave; the children in both cases stayed with the mother and her family. The ease with which this happened was noted by early missionaries, such as the Jesuit superior Father Barthelemy Vimont, who commented in 1639 that Indians had "a complete brutal liberty, changing wives when they pleased – taking only one or several, according to their inclination."[3]

As in Latin America, there were two-spirit people among some Indian groups in North America, who were usually morphologically male but combined what were regarded as masculine and feminine clothing, tasks, and behavior. Two-spirit people in the eastern half of North America were found primarily in Florida and the western Great Lakes, where French traders and missionaries encountered them later in the seventeenth century. Most tribes honored and accepted such individuals, although among some they were ridiculed; the reasons for this diversity of treatment are not yet clear. Two-spirit people often had special religious and ceremonial roles because they were regarded as having both a male and female spirit rather than the one spirit which most people had; they could thus mediate between the male and female world and the divine and human world.

Most individuals with religious and ceremonial authority among Native Americans were not two-spirit people, but men or women who gained their power through connections either with the spiritual realm in general or with a single special spirit. Such individuals, often termed shamans, had personal supernatural power achieved through dreams and visions rather than power that came through their positions in an institution as that of Christian clergy did. Connections with the spirit world were reinforced through ceremonies and rituals in which the entire tribe participated. They emphasized both success in hunting and agricultural fertility, viewed respectively as part of the male and female realms; many of these ceremonies involved specific rituals designed to promote individual and group health and vitality. Religious practices also included sexual taboos: women who were menstruating or giving birth were often separated from the rest of the tribe, viewed as both powerful and vulnerable; men preparing to hunt or engage in warfare remained sexually continent. Some aspects of native spiritual life, such as prayer, visions, and guardian spirits, appeared familiar to European observers, while others seemed very alien. The lack of understanding worked both ways, however, for just as Europeans regarded Indians as irreligious because they lacked churches and clergy (and Christ), Indians regarded Europeans as irreligious because they did not have rituals or taboos regarding the central events of life, such as birth, hunting, or warfare.

Although many aspects of native beliefs and traditions were shared across large areas and appear to have been maintained for a long time, significant changes occurred in the sixteenth and seventeenth centuries that were only tangentially related to the coming of the Europeans. During the seventeenth century, the Hurons, Montagnais-Naskapi, and Algonquins of British North America were repeatedly attacked by Iroquois coming from the south, who by mid-century were armed with firearms provided by the Dutch. In Virginia, the Algonquian-speaking chief Powhatan began building a military and economic alliance with other groups before the English arrived, cemented these alliances by collecting tribute and marrying women from dominated villages, and then sent them back once they had borne him a child. Such chiefdom-building tactics were a sharp break from earlier traditions, but they influenced the way in which Europeans assessed indigenous practices and mores.

Christian institutions

The pace of change in Native American culture speeded up dramatically with the coming of Europeans. Even those groups not directly in contact with Europeans were affected by their diseases, trading intentions, and political and religious structures, though the institutions established to spread and maintain Christianity, and to regulate sexuality, were quite different in each of the patterns of colonization noted above.

French Canada

The first systematic missionary work was begun among the Micmacs, an Algonkian-speaking people, in Nova Scotia in 1610, and during the following decade both Recollects and Jesuits began to proselytize among other tribes in various parts of eastern Canada, initially preferring the settled groups such as the Hurons over the more nomadic Algonquins and Innu (Montagnais). As in the Spanish colonies, many of these missionaries were sponsored by the monarchy, because the French kings viewed missionary work as an exercise of their royal power. Missionary work was seen by government authorities as spreading both Christianity and French culture, although the relationship between these two objectives was debated among the missionaries themselves. Did converts, as some missionaries maintained, first have to become French, by living in nuclear families in settled agricultural villages with men doing the majority of agricultural work, wearing French-style clothing, and speaking French? Or could they, as others argued, retain most of their native culture, and simply accept the essential beliefs of Christianity as explained to them in their own language and following the most important Christian norms of behavior? If the latter, which beliefs and norms of behavior *were* most important?

As we have seen, similar debates engaged missionaries in China at exactly the same time – the "Chinese rites" controversy – and in both places sexual conduct and marriage practices were important parts of the debate. The most contested issues in China were the practices of ancestor-worship and concubinage, while in Canada the key issues appear to have been trade goods and divorce. Father Vimont wrote in 1642, "The stability of marriage is one of the most perplexing questions in the conversion and settlement of the Savages; we have much difficulty in obtaining and in maintaining it," and in 1644, "Of all the laws which we propound to them, there is not one that seems so hard to them as that which forbids polygamy, and does not allow them to break the bonds of lawful marriage."[4]

Initially, most missionaries wanted to make converts settled and French, but with experience the Jesuits changed their tactics; they learned local languages and lived with potential converts, traveling with the more nomadic tribes. They used every occasion to preach and catechize, including funerals, councils, and visits to the sick, and employed imagery that fit with local traditions, often acting like shamans by curing illnesses and interpreting dreams. The conversion process was not simply an oral one, for missionaries also used pictures, chants, plays, music, bells, and holy objects such as amulets, crucifixes, and altar vessels. Jesuits tended to have a more positive view of indigenous culture, or at least of indigenous capacity for true conversion, than members of other orders did, although less positive than that of Jesuit missionaries in China. Though native converts became "prayer-captains" (dogiques) and a few Indian women became nuns, no Indian man became a priest, and most Indian women in convents were lay sisters rather than professed nuns.

The number of converts in Canada grew slowly during the seventeenth century, as conversion generally cut one off from the family and kin networks that were essential to survival; many of the early converts were war-captives, already separated from their native tribe. Adults often waited until they were near death to be baptized, and missionaries recognized it would be important to organize mission communities for those who converted earlier. Such communities, beginning with Sillery near Quebec, were closely supervised by a priest, with residents subject to strict discipline, administered by the priest himself or by the native dogiques. Such discipline included punishment for sexual and moral offenses, and for having contacts with non-Christians among one's own tribe, or with Europeans other than those approved by the priest. In these communities, churches were built with elaborate decorations, schools were opened, and confraternities were established. Indians often came to missions for protection during times of warfare or for recuperation after epidemics, for the priests offered material aid along with spiritual advice to those who converted. In some places, such as Kahnawake near Montreal, Indians formed Christian communities on their own as refuges from war and the alcohol-induced violence that was destroying many native communities.

Along with churches, schools, and religious institutions for Indians in French Canada, there were also churches and institutions for European residents, and, somewhat later, for people of mixed blood, termed metis. (There were very few black slaves in Canada, as there were no staple crops suitable to slave labor; most slaves were household servants in wealthy urban households.) Churches were found predominantly in the towns and cities of eastern

Canada, and were much fewer in number than those in the British colonies of New England, for the European population of French Canada grew very slowly in the colonial period. (Historians estimate that at the time Britain took over Canada in 1763, there were only 75,000 French people in the entire area, compared with perhaps two million in the British colonies.) The first confraternities were founded for men and women in New France in 1652, and the first schools, run by members of religious orders, at about the same time. The original women's houses of Ursulines and Augustinians grew to seven, which meant there were more religious orders for women, both European and Indian, than for men. By 1725, one out of every hundred residents in New France was a nun.

The French monarchy worried about the gender imbalance and low population levels in its colonies, and between 1646 and 1715, it sent a few young women, called the *filles du roi* (king's girls) to be wives. They were matched to prospective husbands by the heads of one of Quebec's religious communities for women, but their numbers were never great enough to have a significant effect on the population. Upper-class families in French Canada did attempt to follow French marriage norms as much as possible, requiring parental and familial consent for marriage and intermarriage. The majority of men in New France sought wives wherever they could; intermarriage with native women was accepted in many areas – even promoted by some of New France's early leaders as a means of transforming natives into French – and *metis* culture developed somewhat distinctly from both European and Indian.

After 1700 the number and vigor of missions declined in eastern Canada, as Jesuits focussed more on Europeans and *metis*. There were also increasing conflicts between Protestants and Catholics, because Protestant missionaries from the British colonies began working among Indians in French or disputed areas. Religion came to be seen as a way of holding Indians and Europeans to French or British loyalty, with each side prizing conversions, both from the "wrong" type of Christianity and from native belief systems.

New England

The norms of conduct in New England were derived originally from English Puritanism, and continually promulgated in sermons and printed tracts by New England clergy. They generally held that sexual relations within marriage were a positive good, as long as they were not excessive. John Robinson, the pastor of the Pilgrim settlers in Plymouth, warned:

> Marriage is a medicine against uncleanness . . . [but] As a man
> may surfeit at his own table or be drunken with his own drink;

so may he play the adulterer with his own wife, both by inordinate affection and action. For howsoever the marriage bed cover much inordinateness this way: yet must modesty be observed by the married, lest the bed which is honourable and undefiled (Hebrews 13:4) in its right use, become by abuse hateful, and filthy in God's sight.[5]

All sexual relations outside of marriage were unacceptable; the Puritan pastor Samuel Danforth argued that, "Uncleanness pollutes the body, and turns the temple of the Holy Ghost into a hog-sty and a dog's kennel."[6] Certain types of sexual acts were worse than others. Those between men and women – defined as "natural" – were deemed less polluting than those between persons of the same sex or persons and animals. These were described repeatedly as "unnatural" or, in the Puritan preacher Cotton Mather's words, "vile . . . unutterable abominations and confusions."[7]

Sexual deviancy and relgous heresy were often linked in the minds of religious leaders; in the trials of Anne Hutchinson and several Quaker women for heresy and sedition, Puritan clergy accused them of adultery, lascivious conduct, and breaking up families. Clerics referred to England as "Sodom," a society meriting punishment for its sexual sins, and worried that New England was also becoming lax. Such harsh opinions about sexual activities were not limited to clergy; a New Haven magistrate warned a couple suspected of fornication that this was:

a sin which shutts [them] out of the kingdome of heaven, without repentance, and a sinn which layes them open to shame and punishment in this court. It is that which the Holy Ghost brands with the name of folly, it is that wherein men show their brutishness, therfore as the whip is for the horse and asse so a rod is for the fooles back.[8]

A range of institutions were charged with enforcing standards of sexual behavior. The earliest law codes of New England, based on the Old Testament and English statutes, provided capital punishment for a number of sexual offenses. Included in these were adultery, defined as intercourse with a married or engaged woman, and rape, defined as forced sexual relations with a married or engaged woman, or with a single woman under the age of ten. Forced intercourse with an unmarried woman over age ten was excluded from definitions of rape in some colonies, as was any intercourse that resulted in pregnancy. Along with their European counterparts, colonial authorities accepted the notion that conception required female orgasm and would not occur if the woman truly objected to the intercourse; as a 1655 manual for justices of the peace stated, if the woman was pregnant, "consent must be inferred."[9] Bestiality was also a capital crime, as was sodomy, though its definition varied; in most colonies it included only male–male relations, though in New Haven it also covered female–female relations, heterosexual anal intercourse (described as "carnall knowledge of another vessel then God in nature hath appointed to become one flesh"), and male masturbation "in the sight of others . . . by example, or counsel, or both, corrupting and tempting others to doe the like."[10]

Law codes set lesser punishments for other types of sexual offenses, including fornication, "lewd and lascivious carriage" (overly flirtatious behavior), spouse abuse, "wanton dalliance" (appearing to give one's attention to several suitors), living apart from one's spouse, and courting a woman without first obtaining approval from her parents or the local magistrate. Punishments included fines, whipping, branding, loss of voting rights, and various shaming rituals. Massachusetts' leaders, for example, ruled later in the seventeenth century that instead of being executed, some adulterers could be given a milder punishment; they were to be whipped, stand with a rope around their necks on the gallows for one hour, and then "for ever after wear a capital A of two inches long, and proportional bigness, cut out of cloth of a contrary color to their clothes, and sewed upon their upper garments, on the outside of their arm, or on their back."[11] Authorities sometimes deferred to the wishes or rights of spouses in cases of adultery, but not always, for adultery was viewed as harmful to the community as well as the marriage.

Marriage was considered a civil contract, and all marriages were to be conducted by a secular magistrate, not a pastor. Because of its civil nature, and also because Puritans regarded harmony between spouses as essential in a marriage, most New England colonies allowed divorce for a variety of reasons, including desertion, impotence, adultery, cruelty, and bigamy. In some areas the remarriage of divorced spouses was limited, but in others, especially in New Haven, innocent spouses were given the blanket right to remarry. This relative ease of divorce stood in sharp contrast to practice in Britain, where after 1660, divorce was only possible by act of Parliament. In establishing such laws the colonies were, in fact, disobeying English laws and colonial mandates.

Laws regarding sexual acts were enforced by secular courts, which heard all of the types of cases that in Britain were handled by ecclesiastical courts. County courts heard the less serious cases, such as fornication, and circuit courts the more serious, such as divorce, adultery, rape, and infanticide. Courts ordered midwives to examine women accused of fornication, pregnancy out of wedlock, or infanticide, and charged neighbors to keep an eye on their neighbors, lest they be accused of being accessories in sexual crimes.

Courts were not the preferred avenue of enforcement, however, for Puritan communities favored informal mechanisms of control whenever possible. Clergy and concerned neighbors privately admonished families to control their unruly members, viewing the male head of household as the first line of defense. For this reason, unmarried adults in New England were officially required to live with a married or widowed head of household, preferably male. Living alone made one, in the words of an Essex County, Massachusetts, court, "subject to much sin and iniquity, which ordinarily are the consequences of a solitary life"; the convicted man in this instance, was ordered to "settle in some orderly family in the town, and be subject to the orderly rules of family government."[12] Though in this instance it was a man who was ordered to submit to "family government," women were the more common recipients of such admonitions. Wives were ordered to obey their husbands and authorities were often slow to interfere in cases of wife-beating, particularly if the wife was viewed as provoking her husband.

If family and neighborhood pressure did not work, church discipline was the next step. Members were admonished to confront individuals they suspected of moral infractions, and ask them for repentance. If this appeal was unsuccessful, they were to report the actions to the pastor, who was to handle the matter privately. If this still did not have the desired effect, suspected offenders were investigated by a church committee, and if the suspicions appeared to be warranted, they were asked to appear before the congregation and make a public, oral confession. If they did, and the congregations judged them properly penitent, they were reintegrated into the community, for the congregation was more interested in reclaiming sinners than in punishing them. Such confessions might be very dramatic, such as that of a Massachusetts woman accused of fornication in 1681 who, "being put to it to speak by way of acknowledgment of the sin, she gave noe answer but weept whether for the shame or the sin that was not known."[13]

If the sinner did not or would not confess, however, sterner punishments were available. Church records contain many cases similar to this one from the First Church in Boston in 1638:

> Anne Walker, the wife of one Richard Walker and sometime [i.e., previously] the wife and widow of our brother Robert Houlton having before this day been often privately admonished of sundry scandals, as of drunkenish, intemperate, and unclean or wantonish behavior, and likewise of cruelty towards her children and also of manifold lies and still to this day persisting impenitently therein,

> was therefore now with joint consent of the Congregation cast out
> of the Church.[14]

Excommunication had to be voted on by a majority of the adult male church members and was the strongest punishment the church could impose; excommunicates could nevertheless be liable for secular punishments for the same acts, as there was no notion of double-jeopardy.

The early involvement of the entire congregation in discipline changed somewhat beginning in the 1660s, when ministers were given a stronger voice in church deliberations and women became more numerous than men as church members. First women and then men were allowed to write their confessions for the minister to read, thereby reducing their dramatic effect. Slightly later the audience at such confessions was limited to full church members, so the whole community no longer listened in. With the acceptance of the Half-Way Covenant in 1662, the number of people required to make confessions increased, however, for now everyone who had been baptized was open to church discipline.

The disciplinary institutions described so far primarily involved the European population of New England; its African population was small in the colonial period, and only a few blacks were accepted as full church members. Although the original English colonial charters listed the conversion of Indians as an aim, missionary work among the Indians began slowly. In the 1640s Thomas Mayhew, Jr. began to preach to the Wampanoags on Martha's Vineyard, and John Eliot began work among the Massachusetts near Boston. In 1649, the New England Company was founded to support Eliot's work. He and one of his converts, Job Nesuton, prepared a Bible in Massachusetts, the first Bible translation into a North American language; it was printed in 1661 with only Eliot's name on the title page.

Like some of the early French missionaries in Canada, Eliot thought it essential that Indians adopt European dress, housing styles, economic organization, and social structures – what he termed "visible civility" – along with Christianity. He thus established "praying towns" for converts beginning with Natick, where Indians were to learn European agriculture along with Scripture and to form covenanted congregations modeled on those of their Puritan neighbors. Schools for Indian boys were an essential part of these praying towns, and many native converts became schoolmasters. Fourteen praying towns were established before King Philip's War in 1675 – a conflict between Europeans and Indians over the European invasion of Indian lands – and Eliot estimated that he and others had 2,300 converts, 300–400 of them baptized. Many converts were killed by both sides in that war, or taken by European authorities from their towns and forced to live on an island in Boston Harbor;

afterwards only four praying towns survived. Recovery from this decimation occurred very slowly, although by 1700 there were at least thirty Indian congregations in Massachusetts, some but not all in praying towns. Indians from Natick served as missionaries to other groups, confronting shamans with medical treatments, preaching, prayer, and psalm singing, and also served as preachers and catechists within their own congregations.

There were fewer converts outside of Massachusetts in the seventeenth century, for the few English missionaries in frontier areas such as Maine or New York were less successful than the French Jesuits who were also working in these areas. This situation changed somewhat in the early eighteenth century as the Anglican church began more intensive missionary efforts; it formed the Anglican Society for the Propagation of the Gospel in 1701 and sponsored translations of Scripture and the Book of Common Prayer into Mohawk. These frontier converts, however, were not organized into missions or praying towns. Conversion among Indians in southern New England also increased during the Great Awakening, when, like the whites around them, many individuals saw visions or experienced a sense of "calling."

Southern colonies

Colonization in the south (north of the Spanish colonies in Florida) began in Virginia and the Chesapeake, where the original authorities, although insitutionally Anglican, were just as interested in establishing order as were the Puritan leaders in Massachusetts. In 1619, the Virginia Assembly ordered ministers and other religious officials to report all "ungodly disorders," including "suspicions of whoredomes, dishonest company keeping with weomen and suche like," to the county courts so that such actions could be punished.[15] As in New England, religious and secular authority were intertwined. Ministers were ordered to read all new laws and ordinances from the pulpit, and lay church officials, termed "vestrymen" or "church wardens," often served as sheriffs and justices of the peace. Conversely, punishments set by secular courts for sexual and moral offenses included rituals of penance, such as wearing a white sheet in the local parish church.

Yet there were also some significant institutional differences between the two areas. The Church of England (Anglicanism) was the official state religion in the south throughout the colonial period, and Anglican churches had no system which paralleled the Puritan congregation's public confession. Thus matters of sexual and moral conduct were handled either informally through the family, or formally through the secular courts, which explicitly enforced the laws of the Church of England. In 1690, James Blair, the commissary of the Bishop of London and one of the most powerful men in Virginia, attempted to introduce church courts to that colony, but his plan failed. Anglican clergy were generally less powerful and less outspoken than their Puritan counterparts in New England, with laymen taking the lead in disciplinary matters. Because marriage did not carry as much ideological weight in Anglicanism as it did in Puritanism, adultery was not regarded quite as seriously – it was not a capital crime in the south; on the other hand, divorce was prohibited, for bad marriages were to be tolerated, not dissolved.

The settlement pattern of the Chesapeake area resulted in steady business for secular courts. As noted above, early gender ratios were highly skewed in favor of men, and three-fourths of the women who immigrated to the Chesapeake area in the early decades were indentured servants, generally travelling without their families and forbidden to marry during their term of servitude. These factors led to an incidence of pregnancy out of wedlock that was far higher than elsewhere in the English-speaking world; one out of five female servants bore a child outside of marriage. The punishment was originally set at a fine and an extra year or two of service, until authorities discovered that masters were intentionally impregnating their female servants to gain this extra time, in the same way as Spanish Christian men forced sex on Muslim women under their jurisdiction in order to receive them as slaves. The law was revised, and a servant who became pregnant by her master, "shall, after her time by indenture or custom is expired be by the church-wardens of the parish where she lived when she was brought to bed of such bastard, sold for two years, and the tobacco [which served as money in Virginia] to be imployed by the vestry for the use of the parish."[16] Only the servant and not the master was to be punished, for her original period of service with him was not shortened. Servants were also prohibited from engaging in secret marriages or promising themselves to one another, though this was impossible to stop.

Clandestine or extra-legal marriages were not limited to servants in the colonial south; because people often lived great distances from a church, visits by pastors were infrequent, and marriage licenses cost money (or tobacco). Thus although English marriage customs were supposed to be followed, in actuality people often held informal ceremonies and began living together in what became known as "common-law" marriages, accepting, in the words of one Maryland man in 1665, that "his marriage was as good as possible it could be made by the Protestants he being one because before that time and ever since there has not been a Protestant minister in the province and that to matrimony it is only necessary the parties consent."[17]

The first American marriage laws in the south made no racial distinctions; laws to regulate interracial unions began in the 1660s. In 1662, the Virginia Assembly declared that:

Whereas some doubts have arrisen whether children got by any Englishman upon a negro woman should be slave or free, *Be it therefore enacted and declared by this present grand assembly,* that all children borne in this country shalbe held bond or free only according to the condition of the mother, *and* that if any christian shall committ fornication with a negro man or woman, hee or shee soe offending shall pay double the fines imposed by the former act.[18]

In its first clause, the law makes paternity irrelevant for the children of slave women, reversing normal English practice. In its second, it distinguishes between "christian" and "negro," thus equating Christian with the "Englishman" of the first clause and ignoring the fact that some Africans were Christians. These lines of distinction were drawn slightly differently in the 1667 law regarding baptism, which stated explicitly that baptism would not free "slaves by birth." Through this law, conversion as well as paternity became irrelevant for the children of slave women, and Africans became a separate type of Christian.

Several decades later, "Christian" completely disappeared as a way of categorizing individuals in marital and sexual relationships, and racial distinctions were extended to other groups. A 1691 law marked the first use of the word "white" in Virginia statutes, and held that: "Whatsoever English or other white man or woman being free shall intermarry with a negroe, mulatto, or Indian man or woman bond or free shall within three months after such marriage be banished and removed from this dominion forever."[19] Though the basic law is gender neutral, the preamble is gender specific, warning of the "abominable mixture and spurious issue which hereafter may encrease in this dominion, as well by negroes, mulattoes, and Indians intermarrying with English, or other white women."[20] Further clauses in the law set severe punishments, including imprisonment, fines, and banishment, for white women who gave birth to mixed race children even if they did not marry the father, reinforcing the message of the preamble. Between 1700 and 1750, all of the southern states, and also Pennsylvania and Massachusetts, passed laws prohibiting all interracial sexual relationships, with steep fines set for any minister who performed an interracial marriage. Most abhorrent in the eyes of authorities was the rape of a white woman by a non-white man; punishment for attempted rape was set at castration in Virginia, Pennsylvania, and New Jersey, and punishment for a completed rape brought death.

As the 1691 Virginia law makes clear, in contrast to the complex racial hierarchy that developed in Latin America, all persons of mixed race in the southern colonies were regarded as black, including those whose proportion of "white blood" vastly outweighed their proportion of "black blood." As this

biracial system developed, Indians were generally regarded as black, a desig-
nation justified in part in white eyes by intermarriage between the two groups.
This polarization was accompanied by a steady stream of rhetoric describing
non-whites as sexually dissipated, as both animalistic and barbaric in their
sexual practices.

Once it was stipulated that children of slave women would be slaves, sexual relations among slaves themselves were rarely the concern of authorities.
As a Maryland judge put it, "we do not consider them as the objects of such
laws as relate to the commerce between the sexes. A slave has never maintained an action against the violator of his bed. A slave is not admonished for
incontinence, or punished for fornication or adultery."[21] Only in New England
were marriages between slaves legally recognized, and the churches in the
southern colonies made little effort to obtain for slaves the right to marry.
There were some marriages on the larger plantations in the south, but because
the gender balance among slaves was highly skewed in favor of men before
1750, there was little possibility of marriage or permanent relationships for
many slaves, which provided further evidence, to white eyes, of their lack of
sexual restraint.

There were no southern counterparts to the New England praying towns
for Indian converts, and the few schools for Indians that were established
were short-lived and had little impact. Boys who attended them seldom acted
as missionaries when they returned to their tribes, and white missionaries
were rare in the southern colonies. After 1701 there were a few missionaries sponsored by the Society for the Propagation of the Gospel and later,
especially in Georgia, by the Moravians and the Methodists, but most of these
ministered only to Indians who lived near white settlements or who came
to them. The French Jesuit practice of living in Indian villages or with nomadic
groups was not emulated in the southern colonies, whose governors and
political leaders regarded the primary task of the limited number of clergy
to be ministering to white residents.

Effects

Given the widely varying levels of institutional development among the
various Christian denominations in North America, it is not surprising that
there was also wide variation in the actual effects of regulation.

French Canada

There is no debate about the devastating effects of European diseases on the
indigenous population of Canada, but historians do disagree about the effects

of Christian teachings on marital patterns, sexual norms, and other aspects of gender structures. Some historians see Catholic teachings as imposed largely by force, particularly on Indian women, and as very disruptive to native traditions. They find that women were often the strongest opponents of the Jesuits, noting instances in which women recognized conversion would bring a loss of status, refused to convert, or urged male converts to renounce their faith. According to Jesuit reports, male converts placed in positions of authority as *dogiques* attempted to force women to comply with Christian norms, commenting "it is you women . . . who are the cause of all our misfortunes – it is you who keep the demons among us . . . You are lazy about going to prayers; when you pass the cross, you never salute it; you wish to be independent. Now know that you will obey your husbands; and you young people, you will obey your parents and our Captains; and, if any fail to do so, we have concluded to give them nothing to eat."[22] *Dogiques* enforced Catholic rules about the permanence of marriage, ordering women who had left their husbands to return to them or face imprisonment, and punished those who were otherwise disobedient. They were successful to some degree, for divorce was rare in missions, polygamy became increasingly unusual, and many mission residents chose to marry (or remarry, if they had been married earlier in Indian ceremonies) in Christian ceremonies.

Other historians point out that some women accepted Catholic ideas willingly, particularly those about the value of virginity; some female converts (and a few men) vowed perpetual virginity or agreed to live in spiritual marriages, with a few disfiguring themselves by cutting their hair or carrying out brutal self-mortification. The first and most famous of these was Kateri Tekakwitha, whose mother was Algonquian and whose father was Mohawk. In 1679, she became the first Indian to make a Christian vow of virginity and perpetual spirituality. Like the biographers of early Christian heroic virgins, Tekakwitha's Jesuit biographer notes approvingly:

> The women were not behind their husbands in the ardor they showed for a life of penance. They even went to such extremes that when it came to our knowledge we were obliged to moderate their zeal . . . On learning that they [nuns in Montreal] were Christian virgins consecrated to God by a vow of pepetual chastity, she [Kateri] gave me no peace until I had granted her permission to make the same sacrifice herself, not by a simply resolution to guard her virginity, such as she had already made, but by an irrevocable pledge which would oblige her to belong to God beyond recall . . . During the winter while she was in the forest with her companions, she would follow them at a distance, taking off her

shoes and walking with her naked feet over the ice and snow . . .
At another time she strewed the poor mat on which she slept
with large thorns . . . she rolled herself for three nights in succ-
cession on these thorns, which caused her the most intense pain.[23]

Tekakwitha's asceticism contributed to her death several years later, but after
this large numbers of healing miracles were attributed to her, and in 1980
she was beatified by the Catholic Church, the only Native American to reach
this level to date. (Beatification is one step short of sainthood; pressure to
have Tekakwitha declared a saint continues.)

In some places women allied with Jesuits to fight marriages they did not
want. Aramepinchieue, for example, the daughter of Chief Rouensa of the
Kaskaskia, refused to marry the French trader her father wanted her to marry
because he was a known opponent of church aims. The Jesuit missionary
Jacques Gravier supported her refusal, noting that "God did not command
her not to marry, but also that she could not be forced into doing so; that
she alone was mistress to do the one or the other."[24] She was also supported
by a group of at least fifty women and girls, who barricaded themselves in
a church in defiance of the male leaders of the Kaskaskias. The situation was
resolved when Aramepinchieue agreed to the marriage providing both her
father and the French trader agreed to become Christian, and their child was
the first to be baptized in what later became Illinois (in 1695, at Peoria).
This marriage became the model for subsequent marriages between French
men and Indian women in the Illinois area, for, though Jesuits and other
missionaries initially opposed intermarriage, they gradually came to support
it if both partners were Catholic. Native women could also effect conversion by preaching; the Sisters of the Quebec Hospital reported that Cécile
Gannendaris, a Huron, "was so solidly instructed in our mysteries and so
eloquent in explaining them that she was sent new arrivals among the Savages
who were asking to embrace the faith. In a few days she had them ready
for baptism . . . "[25]

Clearly there are many examples of both resistance and conversion in
French Canada, and also instances in which there was a blending of indigenous and Christian beliefs similar to that which we have already traced in
Latin America. Many Christian practices had parallels among Indian groups
such as the Iroquois: a Requickening ceremony similar to baptism, wampum
beads used somewhat like rosaries, individuals with special spiritual powers
who bridged two worlds. The popularity of the cult of the Virgin among
converts may have had roots in the spiritual roles traditionally accorded
women. Because of such syncretism, historians debate the level of conversion during the colonial period; some argue that outward acceptance of

Christianity was simply a political tactic that did not really change indigenous beliefs or structures, while others claim that Christianity dramatically
altered Indian communities and practices. All sides in this debate generally
agree, however, that disease, war, and alcohol had a greater impact over the
long run than Christian teachings alone.

Many of the issues involving religion and sexuality which emerged in other
parts of the world were largely absent from French Canada. There was no
Inquisition, and there were very few trials for witchcraft. Only three dozen
witchcraft accusations made it into the records for the entire period 1645 to
1830, most of them in larger towns, and no one was ever executed for
witchcraft in French Canada. All of the witchcraft cases involved Europeans,
for, in contrast to South America, the magical activities of Indians or mixed-
blood people were ignored by the Canadian Catholic Church. Both church
and state authorities also appear to have ignored homosexual activities except
among Europeans. A few cases of "crimes against nature" emerge in the
records of secular courts, especially among soldiers, but apparently none of
these resulted in an execution.

New England

Puritan concerns about moral conduct were, by some measures, vigorously
enforced in the earliest decades of settlement. Though rates of illegitimate
birth and bridal pregnancy were far lower than in England or the southern
colonies, fornication was the most frequent category of crime heard by lower
courts throughout New England in the seventeenth century, and sexual crimes
constituted between 20 and 40 percent of serious crimes. This concentration
on sexual matters meant that women made up a larger share of those prosecuted for criminal offenses than was normally the case in early modern
societies. Men were also convicted in fornication cases in the seventeenth
century, for the woman's word about her child's father was often taken seriously and the putative father pressured into confession. (Women who would
not name the father in cases of children born out of wedlock suffered excommunication along with secular punishments such as whipping, so that most
women named a father.) Courts and churches extended their concerns even
to those judged not guilty, forbidding people suspected of fornication but
not found guilty to see each other alone. Sexual gossip and rumors, along
with other types of slander, were prosecuted frequently, with the slanderer
ordered to bring proof or retract the inflammatory words in both court
and church.

Court records indicate that many people had internalized Puritan values.
Couples who had resisted confessing to having sexual relations during

betrothal generally gave in and confessed when they wanted to have the child baptized. Elizabeth Dane, a married woman, replied to a seducer who told her that no one would see their actions, "but God sees if nobody [else] sees, for God sees in the dark."[26] Divorce statistics indicate that the Puritan stress on the importance of the family, combined with the economic significance of the family as a unit of production, worked to keep most couples together. One count of divorces finds 128 in all of New England for the period 1620–1699, and some of them were actually annulments. Most divorces were sought by women, and most of these for desertion; men seeking divorce generally charged adultery. There were no divorces for cruelty or abuse alone, though cases of verbal and physical abuse were handled in courts and churches, and there were more convictions for adultery than divorces for it, indicating that spouses (usually wives) were willing to put up with adulterous behavior.

On the other hand, court records also provide evidence that even in the initial decades, Puritan external and internal control of morals was less stringent than popular stereotypes would lead one to believe. New England governments and churches did interfere more in personal and household behavior than did those in the southern colonies, but only in extreme cases were family heads actually punished. Neighbors reported on their neighbors in church or when questioned in support of a legal case, but despite admonitions about "mutual surveillance," almost no sexual offenses were actually brought to courts by prying neighbors. Fines for fornication or premarital sex could be steep – the price of a steer – but convictions did not bring permanent loss of status, as long as one confessed, and there is evidence that many New Englanders accepted the practice of sexual relations between betrothed couples. There were harsh sermons preached at sex-related executions, but there were very few of these. There was only one execution for adultery in Massachusetts Bay Colony during the colonial period, for example, and only 38 indictments in total during the period 1673–1774; most adultery cases were hushed up, or the people involved charged with a lesser crime, such as "lascivious behavior." This reduction of a capital crime to one less serious also occurred in rape cases, for there were only five executions for rape in seventeenth-century New England, and the only cases of forcible sex actually tried as "rape" were those in which the victims were under ten.

This disjuncture between rhetoric and reality is evident in the treatment of sodomy, for despite harsh denunciations of sodomy, actual prosecutions were very rare. There were about twenty sodomy prosecutions in British North America, of which two ended in hanging, both in the seventeenth century; two cases involved women, but they were termed "lewd" behavior rather than sodomy. Because sodomy convictions required proof of penetration and testimony of two witnesses, they were extremely difficult to prove, and it appears that communities were willing to tolerate a surprising amount of homosexual behavior, even among those expected to maintain higher moral standards. In one case, a Baptist minister in Connecticut was charged several times over a period of thirty years with "unchaste behavior with his fellow men when in bed with them," but the ultimate penalty was simply a brief dismissal from his position that ended quickly by congregational vote after he confessed his sins.[27] There is no evidence of a homosexual subculture in North America, in part because there were few large cities, a situation which also resulted in very little organized prostitution before 1750.

However one chooses to judge New England's moral behavior in the seventeenth century, it is clear that after about 1700 — the timing differs slightly from community to community — people's conduct became more like that elsewhere in the English-speaking world. The proportion of brides who were pregnant increased, and slander and defamation suits declined. Fewer adulterers made church confessions, and instead simply remained excommunicate, while those accused of lesser morals crimes joined a less stringent denomination. In large part this "decline" — for that is how preachers interpreted it — resulted from the success of the New England colonies. Many historians estimate that the white population of New England doubled every twenty-five years throughout the colonial period, an expansion which brought greater diversity and lessened the ability of all institutions — family, church, and state — to enforce behavioral conformity.

Changes in the eighteenth century also arose from secular authorities' lessening interest in enforcing godliness. Though the churches still heard confessions of fornication, many secular courts no longer handled fornication cases unless a child was involved, and shaming rituals and whippings became less frequent, even for illegitimacy. Secular authorities became more concerned with the economic issues involved in out-of-wedlock births than with the moral ones, so more of their cases involved marginal people, especially poor women. Because of this, scepticism about relying on the woman's word alone in fornication and rape cases increased. Also, after 1700, men increasingly fought paternity charges, usually successfully, and women were punished for not resisting their rapists. In Connecticut, coercive father–daughter incest became the only sexual act for which white men were always punished. Thus secular scrutiny of moral behavior was increasingly limited to the poor, with propertied men and women excluded. Puritan preachers decried this trend as a sign of moral decline, but they could do little to stop it.

This change in attitudes about the enforcement of godliness emerged most dramatically in New England in handling the two crimes most clearly associated with female sexuality, infanticide and witchcraft. Though the New

England colonies did not officially adopt the Jacobean law making an unmarried woman's concealment of her infant's death presumptive evidence of murder until the 1690s, convictions and executions on such grounds began in the 1630s, and the rates of indictment for infanticide in New England far exceeded those of England. In pamphlets, lectures, and sermons preached at executions, Puritan leaders in New England emphasized the gravity of infanticide, and linked it with moral depravity, concealment of sin, demonic actions, and women's weakness in the face of temptation. Writing about the first execution for infanticide in Massachusetts, John Winthrop noted, "she was so possessed with Satan that he persuaded her (by his delusions, which she listened to as revelations from God) to break the neck of her own child, that she might free it from future misery."[28] In *Pillars of Salt, an History of some Criminals Executed in This Land for Capital Crimes* (1699), Cotton Mather focussed on the uncleanness, concealment, and disobedience involved in infanticide, and linked the fires of lust with the fires of hell. Mather's work was timely, as the 1690s were the high point of convictions for infanticide in New England. As with other types of crimes related to sexuality, however, conviction rates declined after that, and after 1740 no woman was executed in New England on the evidence of concealment alone. In 1784, punishment for concealment of the death of an illegitimate child in Massachusetts was reduced to one hundred dollars or a year's imprisonment, with references to God, sin, or morality gone from the law.

The timing and tone of infanticide convictions directly parallels those for witchcraft in New England. The death penalty was set for witchcraft in 1641 in Massachusetts and 1642 in Connecticut; both laws stressed the diabolical compact discussed in the chapter on Protestant Europe. As in most parts of Europe, the majority of people accused of witchcraft in New England (over 300 between 1620 and 1725) were women. Trials often included issues of interference with sexual relations or birth, mothering, or harm to children. The only mass trial in North America, the Salem outbreak of 1692, began with teenage girls who attempted to use magical means to find out whom they would marry, and subsequently accused several women of bewitching them. Social, political, religious, sexual, and economic tensions in the Salem community led what might have been a minor incident to explode until almost 200 people were accused, at least 50 people confessed, and 19 were executed (those who confessed were not executed). Puritan leaders argued that Satan had enticed women into undermining their godly commonwealth, and that only executions would cleanse the community. Their language in this directly parallels their words about infanticide, and their concerns about the godly community partially explain why 95 percent of the known witchcraft accusations and 90 percent of the executions for witchcraft in British

North America happened in New England. The Salem trial turned out to be an aberration rather than a model, however, for a few years later many Puritan leaders, including those who had been judges at the trial, felt guilty about their actions, and in 1711 the Massachusetts General Court passed a bill reversing the convictions of 22 people.

One of the women initially accused in the Salem case was Tituba, a slave from Barbados who confessed to having helped the girls search out witches, though not to bewitching them. (She was not executed.) Her position as an outsider in a largely white society certainly made her more vulnerable, but in this, as in so much else, the Salem case was unusual, for Native Americans – Tituba was part African and part West Indian – were generally not charged with witchcraft. Those who had converted in New England were occasionally charged with sexual crimes – the first Indian was tried for adultery in Massachusetts in 1668 – and the praying towns had strict rules of conduct, forbidding idleness and drunkenness along with a range of sexual activities. Some of these rules, such as those prohibiting adultery and polygamy, were not great departures from Indian tradition; others, such as restrictions on sexual relations between persons intending to marry or on the practice of menstrual taboos, did break with existing practices. Enforcement of these rules was the responsibility of Indian as well as white leaders, and punishments such as fines and whippings were imposed. Many of the praying towns were so short-lived that it is difficult to assess the actual effects of regulations, and in areas away from central Massachusetts, such as Martha's Vineyard or the Maine and New York frontiers, Indian converts blended sexual and marital traditions just as they did other aspects of Christianity and indigenous beliefs.

Southern colonies

In some ways the actual pattern of sexual regulation in the south parallels that of New England. Serious sexual crimes such as sodomy, bestiality, rape, or incest, were very rare, while lesser moral offenses such as fornication, sexual slander, sexual relations during betrothal, or having children out of wedlock, made up a significant share of the business before the county courts. Some actions which were officially illegal – common law marriage or sex during betrothal, for example – were accepted by many people. Estimates of the Chesapeake area during the seventeenth century find that common law marriages actually outnumbered church marriages and that about one-third of brides were pregnant at marriage, a rate two to three times that of England during the same period. The frequency of bridal pregnancy led to some people actually being punished for this infraction to object. Thomas and Eady Tooker, for example, found guilty of premarital sex by a Virginia County Court in 1641, were ordered to do penance at their parish church, "standing in the middle ally of said church upon a stool in a white sheet, and a white wand in their hands, all the time of the divine service and shall say after the minister such words as he shall deliver unto them before the congregation." Instead Eady, "like a most obstinate and graceless person, did cut out and mangle the sheet wherein she did penance" and was sentenced to twenty lashes and to repeat the penance "according to the tenor of the said spiritual laws and form of the Church of England in that case provided."[29]

Adultery was generally punished with whipping and penance, and could be the basis of a legal separation, though not, as in New England, a divorce with right of remarriage. Legal separations were expensive and very rare, with desertion a more common solution to marital breakdown. Although in theory children were required to obtain the consent of their parents to any marriage, in practice the lack of marriage registration and the frequency of common-law marriage meant that no law about consent could be enforced. Marriages without parental consent were punishable by a fine, but the marriage itself was not voided, which gave parents (and the extended family) far less control over the marriages of their children than in areas under French or Spanish law, including French Canada and Latin America.

The declining moral fervor noted in New England also affected the south. During the seventeenth century, sex between unmarried persons, sex between engaged persons, and bearing an illegitimate child were all tried as fornication in the secular courts and punished by fines, whipping, and shaming rituals. Court records suggest that some people internalized feelings of shame, or at least said they did to authorities; Ann Gray, a married woman, voluntarily confessed to adultery in 1667, and the records note: "Her owne guilty conscience and desire to ask her husband's forgiveness did occasion this her confession of Adultery."[30] After confession and punishment, however, most of those involved, including women who had borne a child out of wedlock, were reintegrated into their communities.

By the eighteenth century the primary concern of the courts was the financial support of children born out of wedlock; charges of fornication were added to those of illegitimacy only when the mother was white and the child mixed-race. The courts concentrated on finding and securing money from the father, not on shaming him. He rarely appeared in court along with the mother, and the women who did appear were more often poor or marginal. These women appear to have had greater difficulty in subsequently finding a husband than was the case in the seventeenth century, in part because attitudes toward them had changed, and in part because the sex ratio was becoming increasingly balanced making it easier for men to find wives. As in New

England, southern courts were reluctant to punish men of property for sexual crimes; rape accusations by female servants were generally dismissed, and in one case the court ordered a seven-year-old rape victim to be "corrected by her mother for that her fault and for that there appeareth in her a signe of more grace and greife [grief] for her offence."[31]

All bastardy and rape records before 1750 focus on white women, for, with no legal recognition of slave marriage and little enforcement of miscegenation laws if white men were involved, the vast majority of black women were categorically excluded from the crimes of fornication or illegitimacy. (This was also true in the English colonies of the Caribbean.) Despite the lack of legal recognition for slave families, however, black residents of the south often celebrated marriages and developed strong family connections, frequently transplanting certain characteristics of African families, such as vigorous extended kin networks. Marriages were celebrated in Catholic or Anglican ceremonies, or with rituals devised by slaves themselves which might or might not incorporate Christian elements. Black membership in Christian churches grew with the Great Awakening; by the latter half of the eighteenth century some black churches were disciplining their own church members for moral issues such as adultery, fornication, or attempted rape, cases which, because they involved only blacks, would never appear before secular courts.

Other areas and groups

The discussion in this chapter has focussed primarily on three areas – French Canada, New England, and the southern colonies – and on three types of religious institutions – Catholicism, Puritanism, and Anglicanism – all of which operated in close cooperation with secular authorities. This is an incomplete picture of Christianity and sexuality in North America, however, for there were many other Christian groups which developed highly distinctive sexual and marital patterns. Some of these groups were localized and some found throughout the colonies; some operated in cooperation with or even became the secular authorities, while others were hostile to secular government; some of these groups began in Europe, and some, especially those which developed in the eighteenth century or later, started in North America.

Organized sexual variation – which opponents would term deviation – began in 1625 with Thomas Morton's settlement at Merry Mount near Plymouth, where both European settlers and Indians had sexual relations outside of marriage, including with each other. Morton was deported and later died after a harsh imprisonment, but the next group confronting the Puritan leadership was not so easily dismissed. In the 1630s Roger Williams,

Anne Hutchinson, and others were expelled for opposing Puritan leadership, but their followers grew in numbers in Rhode Island and other colonies. Many of them became Baptists and adopted rituals of adult baptism; each congregation made its own decision on most theological and disciplinary matters. Some congregations had elaborate disciplinary procedures with public confession and penance, with both women and men serving as petitioners, defendants, and witnesses.

English Quakers began to preach in Massachusetts and other colonies in the 1650s, and, despite harsh punishments including whipping, deportation, and execution, were not dissuaded from their mission. Quakers were more egalitarian than other Christian groups, with women as well as men serving independently as missionaries. This egalitarianism was also reflected in their structures of church governance. Quakers had no ordained clergy, but were guided by men's and women's meetings, which regulated morality along with doctrine. The first women's meetings were established in British North America in 1681, and generally oversaw marriage formation. To be allowed to marry "within the meeting" (Quakers used the words "meeting" and "meeting house" rather than "congregation" and "church") people had to produce a certificate stating that they were free to marry and that both parties were Quaker; marriage to non-Quakers was stringently opposed, with those who did so required either to repent or to face expulsion, and parents urged to cut "out-marrying" children off from inheritance.

Persecution of Quakers in Massachusetts led to the founding of Pennsylvania in 1681, where Quaker principles initially underlay the law codes and their enforcement. Quakers were pacifists and generally opposed killing, so that the only capital crime was willful homicide; sodomy, rape, and incest were to be punished by whipping and imprisonment. (Pennsylvania was forced in the early eighteenth century to reinstate the death penalty for sodomy, as Britain wanted to bring Pennsylvania laws in line with its own.) Divorce was allowed for adultery, bigamy, sodomy, or bestiality, and in the late eighteenth century, for cruelty, although, as in New England, the actual number of cases was very small.

Religious toleration in Pennsylvania led other groups to immigrate there in the eighteenth century, many of whom had very distinctive sexual ideas and patterns. Conrad Beissel (1690–1768) established Ephrata Cloister in 1732 in Lancaster County and preached the superiority of asceticism and celibacy for both women and men. Though there was some hostility from local men when their wives left them to join the Cloister, eventually a stable community of male and female celibates along with married couples developed, sustained by specialized trades such as printing for men and medicine preparation for women. In 1741, the Moravians founded a community at

Bethlehem, which quickly grew to several hundred residents and sent out scores of missionaries to both Indian and European communities. The members were organized into sex and age cohorts called "choirs", and were segregated by sex until marriage. Decisions on marriage partners were made by lot. A man seeking a wife came to the Elders' Conference, the group of all adult communicants, which proposed a possible spouse. Three colored ballots standing for "yes," "no," and "wait" were placed in a box, and one was drawn, which was regarded as "the Saviour's decision."[32] Prospective spouses and their families had to consent to the match, but the ultimate decision rested with the lot.

During the Great Awakening, small groups of people elsewhere in the British colonies developed unusual ideas about the relationship between Christianity and sex. In New England, small groups of "perfectionists" argued that religious conversion had made them free from sin, and "Immortalists" held that conversion had made them bodily incorruptible. Such ideas led a few people to "deny The Civil Authoritys Power in Marriage" and "hold that the union between two Persons when rightly married together is A Spiritual Union"; the spiritual nature of marriage led a handful to reject sex in marriage altogether.[33] Such actions horrified more traditional Puritan and Anglican clergy, who viewed them as proof of the continuing link between religious deviance and sexual disorder.

Experimentation with distinctive sexual patterns and family forms continued in North America after the American Revolution, with religious groups such as the Shakers and the Mormons, and in many ways continues today. All of these groups enforced their patterns primarily by expelling those members who objected or deviated, a procedure that, as we have seen, began with the earliest Puritan colonists. Because these later groups were not state churches, however, this expulsion was not reinforced by secular penalties; because expulsion occurred in areas where there were often many different denominations active, expelled members could usually find a different Christian group to join, or start their own. The same was true for Puritans in New England and Anglicans in the south by 1750, and slightly later for Catholics in Canada, as Moravians, Presbyterians, Baptists, Methodists and others all sent missionaries and established congregations.

In some ways North America offered early modern Christians the best opportunities to put their ideas about social discipline and the proper sexual order into action, either among Indians whom missionaries regarded as blank slates awaiting conversion or among colonists who intended to create model communities based on Christian principles. Unfortunately for the most eager souls, Indians were not the blank slates nor colonists the model citizens they had anticipated, and expectations about the ease with which sexuality and other aspects of human morality could be regulated were rather quickly dashed. The intersection between Indian and European – and in the southern colonies African – cultures, and the very early mixing of a range of Christian groups and ideas meant that diversity would outweigh conformity from almost the beginning of colonial history. By 1750, the drive to establish moral communities was no longer a politicial one enforced by secular courts, but largely a religious one enforced by religious bodies and binding only upon church members. Although challenging one's own tradition and leaving the denomination of one's family could be a wrenching experience, the religious landscape of North America offered so many choices in most areas that most people who did choose to break with their original faith community could find an acceptable alternative elsewhere.

Notes

1 From Society for the Propagation of the Gospel Records, cited in Daniel K. Richter, " 'Some of Them . . . Would Always Have a Minister with Them': Mohawk Protestantism, 1683–1719," *American Indian Quarterly*, 16 (1992): 478.

2 Jeanne-Françoise Juchereau de St Ignace and Marie Andrée Duplessis de Ste. Hélène, *Les Annales de l'Hôtel-Dieu de Québec, 1636–1716,* ed. Albert Jamet (Québec: Hôtel Dieu, 1939), 20, translated and quoted in Natalie Zemon Davis, "Iroquois Women, European Women," in Margo Hendricks and Patricia Parker, eds, *Women, "Race," and Writing in the Early Modern Period* (London: Routledge, 1994), 246.

3 Reuben Gold Thwaites, ed., *Jesuit Relations and Allied Documents* (Cleveland: Burrows Brothers, 1896–1901), Vol. 18: 125. (hereafter JR).

4 JR 24: 47; JR 25: 247.

5 John Robinson, *The Works of John Robinson, Pastor of the Pilgrim Fathers*, cited in Rosemary Radford Ruether and Rosemary Skinner Keller, eds, *Women and Religion in America. Volume 2: The Colonial and Revolutionary Periods* (San Francisco: Harper and Row, 1981), 161–162.

6 Samuel Danforth, *The Cry of Sodom Enquired Into* (Cambridge, Mass., 1674), cited in Richard Godbeer, " 'The Cry of Sodom': Discourse, Intercourse, and Desire in Colonial New England," *William and Mary Quarterly*, 3rd ser., 52 (1995): 263.

7 Cotton Mather, *An Holy Rebuke to the Unclean Spirit* (Boston, 1693) cited in Godbeer, "The Cry of Sodom," 264.

8 Quoted in Gail S. Marcus, "Criminal Procedure in New Haven," in David D. Hall, John M. Murrin, and Thad Tate, eds, *Saints and Revolutionaries* (New York: Norton, 1984), 132

9 Quoted in Else L. Hambleton, "The Regulation of Sex in Seventeenth-Century Massachusetts: The Quarterly Courts of Essex County vs. Priscilla Willson

and Mr. Samuel Appleton," in Merril D. Smith, ed., *Sex and Sexuality in Early America* (New York: New York University Press, 1998), 96.

10 Charles J. Hoadly, ed., *Records of the Colony or Jurisdiction of New Haven, 1653 to the Union* (Hartford, 1858) cited in Mary Beth Norton, *Founding Mothers and Fathers: Gendered Power and the Forming of American Society* (New York: Knopf, 1996), 349–350.

11 *The Charters and General Laws of the Colony and Province of Massachusetts Bay* (Boston, 1814) cited in Sylvia R. Frey and Marian J. Morton, eds, *New World, New Roles: A Documentary History of Women in Pre-Industrial America* (New York: Greenwood Press, 1986), 20–21.

12 *Records and Files of the Quarterly Courts of Essex County, Massachusetts* (Salem, Mass., 1911–1921) cited in Roderick Phillips, *Putting Asunder: A History of Divorce in Western Society* (Cambridge: Cambridge University Press, 1988), 146.

13 *Dorchester Church Records* cited in David H. Flaherty, *Privacy in Colonial New England* (Charlottesville: University Press of Virginia, 1967), 160.

14 Richard B. Pierce, ed., *Records of the First Church in Boston, 1630–1868* (Boston, 1961), cited in Frey and Morton, *New World,* 80–81.

15 Lyon Gardiner Tyler, ed., *Narratives of Early Virginia, 1606–1625* (New York, 1907), cited in Kathleen Brown, *Good Wives, Nasty Wenches and Anxious Patriarchs: Gender, Race, and Power in Colonial Virginia* (Chapel Hill: University of North Carolina Press, 1996), 91.

16 William Waller Hening, ed., *The Statutes at Large; Being a Collection of All the Laws of Virginia, from the First Session of the Legislature* (1823; facsimile reprint Charlottesville: University of Virginia Press, 1969), II: 166–167.

17 William Brown, et al., eds, *Archives of Maryland* (Baltimore, 1883–1912) cited in Frey and Morton, *New World,* 10.

18 Hening, *Statutes,* II: 170.

19 Hening, *Statutes,* III: 86.

20 Ibid.

21 Thomas Harris and John McHenry, eds, *Maryland Reports* (New York, 1809), cited in Winthrop Jordan, *White over Black: American Attitudes toward the Negro, 1550–1813* (Chapel Hill: University of North Carolina Press, 1968), 160.

22 JR 18, 105–107.

23 Father Cholenec, "Letter and Life of Katharine Tekakwitha, first to vow virginity among the Iroquois barbarians," (1715), cited in Ruether and Skinner, *Women and Religion,* 122–123.

24 JR 64: 195.

25 Juchereau de St Ignace and Duplessis de Ste. Hélène, *Les Annales de l'Hôtel-Dieu de Québec,* cited in Davis, "Iroquois Women," 255–256.

26 R.R. Wheeler, *Concord: Climate for Freedom* (Concord: Concord Antiquarian Society, 1967), 40.

27 Letter of the New London congregation to the General Meeting of Baptist Churches (1756) cited in Godbeer, "Cry of Sodom," 277.

28 John Winthrop, *Journal,* cited in Peter C. Hoffer and N.E.H. Hull, *Murdering Mothers: Infanticide in England and New England 1558–1803* (New York: New York University Press, 1981), 40.

29 Lower Norfolk County records, cited in James Horn, *Adapting to a New World: English Society in the Seventeenth-century Chesapeake* (Chapel Hill: University of North Carolina Press, 1994), 214.

30 Accomack County records, cited in Helena Wall, *Fierce Communion: Family and Community in Early America* (Cambridge: Harvard University Press, 1995), 60.

31 Cited in Brown, *Good Wives,* 194.

32 Adelaide L. Fries, et al., eds *Records of the Moravians of North Carolina,* cited in Ruether and Keller, *Women and Religion*, 304.

33 *The Diary of Isaac Backus* (1751), cited in Erik R. Seeman, "Sarah Prentice and the Immortalists: Sexuality, Piety, and the Body in Eighteenth-century New England," in Smith, *Sex and Sexuality,* 119.

Selected further reading

To date, there is one survey of sexuality in American history, John D'Emilio and Estelle B. Freedman, *Intimate Matters: A History of Sexuality in America* (New York: Harper and Row, 1988; 2nd edn 1997) and one collection of articles on sex in colonial America, Smith *Sex and Sexuality* (note 9).

The number of books which discuss the general history of the colonial United States and touch on Christianity and sexuality is, of course, far too enormous to even begin to list here. Many of the works which consider Indian and European history together rather than separately, such as those of James Axtell and Colin Calloway noted in the Introduction, pay special attention to the role of religion and/or sexuality in these encounters. See: Alfred Goldsworth Bailey, *The Conflict of European and Eastern Algonkian Cultures, 1504–1700,* 2nd edn (Toronto: University of Toronto Press, 1969); Neal Salisbury, *Manitou and Providence: Indians, Europeans, and the Making of New England 1500–1643* (New York: Oxford University Press, 1982); Margaret Connell Szasz, *Indian Education in the American Colonies, 1607–1783* (Albuquerque: University of New Mexico Press, 1988); Richard White, *The Middle Ground: Indians, Empires, and Republics in the Great Lakes Region, 1650–1815* (Cambridge: Cambridge University Press, 1991); Daniel K. Richter, *The Ordeal of the Longhouse: The Peoples of the Iroquois League in the Era of European Colonization* (Chapel Hill: University of North Carolina Press, 1992); Matthew Dennis, *Cultivating a Landscape of Peace: Iroquois–European Encounters in Seventeenth-century America* (Ithaca: Cornell University Press, 1992); Robert Grumet, *Historic Contact: Indian People and Colonists in Today's Northeast United States in the 16th-18th Centuries* (Norman: University of Oklahoma Press, 1995); Daniel R. Mandell, *Behind the Frontier: Indians in Eighteenth-century Eastern Massachusetts* (Lincoln: University of Nebraska Press, 1996); James Axtell, *The Indians' New South: Cultural Change in the Colonial Southeast* (Baton Rouge: Louisiana State University, 1997); Jean M. O'Brien, *Dispossession by Degrees: Indian Land and Identity in Natick, Massachusetts, 1650–1790* (Cambridge: Cambridge University Press, 1997). James Axtell, ed., *The Indian Peoples of Eastern America: A Documentary History of the Sexes* (New York: Oxford University Press, 1981) and Colin G. Calloway, ed., *Dawnland Encounters: Indians and Europeans in Northern*

New England (Hanover, NH: University Press of New England, 1991) and *The World Turned Upside Down: Indian Voices from Early America* (Boston: Bedford Books, 1994) all provide original sources.

Denise Lardner Carmody and John Tully Carmody, *Native American Religions: An Introduction* (New York: Paulist Press, 1993) is a good place to begin for a look at American religions before the coming of Christianity, and Nancy Shoemaker, ed., *Negotiators of Change: Historical Perspectives on Native American Women* (New York: Routledge, 1995) a good collection of recent work on women's roles. The classic study of two-spirit people is Walter L. Williams, *The Spirit and the Flesh: Sexual Diversity in American Indian Culture* (Boston: Beacon Press, 1986). A newer collection is Sue-Ellen Jacobs, Wesley Thomas, and Sabine Lang, eds, *Two-Spirit People: Native American Gender Identity, Sexuality, and Spirituality* (Urbana: University of Illinois Press, 1997).

General works on the history of Canada which provide useful background include: Bruce G. Trigger, *Natives and Newcomers: Canada's "Heroic Age" Reconsidered* (Kingston and Montreal: McGill-Queen's University Press, 1985); Olive Patricia Dickason, *The Myth of the Savage and the Beginnings of French Colonialism in the Americas* (Edmonton: University of Alberta Press, 1984); William Eccles, *The Canadian Frontier, 1534–1760*, rev. edn (Albuquerque: University of New Mexico Press, 1984); John Webster Grant, *Moon of Wintertime: Missionaries and the Indians of Canada in Encounter since 1534* (Toronto: University of Toronto Press, 1984); Alison Prentice et al., *Canadian Women: A History*, 2nd edn (Toronto: Harcourt Brace, 1986). The most important original source for the study of early Christianity in Canada is the 73-volume *Jesuit Relations and Allied Documents*, (note 3) which also includes material about French-speaking areas of what would become the United States; the documents in this collection are parallel translations, with both French (or occasionally Latin) and English. Nearly every volume has some comments about sexual issues, with volume 18 providing the most concentrated observations on this. Peter A. Goddard, "Augustine and the Amerindian in Seventeenth-century New France," *Church History* 67 (1998): 662–681 considers the ideas of several missionaries about original sin and other aspects of Augustinian thought.

Works which specifically address issues surrounding the conversion of Native American women include: Eleanor Leacock, "Montagnais Women and the Jesuit Program for Colonization," in Mona Etienne and Eleanor Leacock, eds, *Women and Colonization: Anthropological Perspectives* (New York: Praeger, 1980), 25–42; Carol Devens, *Countering Colonization: Native American Women and Great Lakes Missions, 1630–1900* (Berkeley: University of California Press, 1992); Karen Anderson, *Chain Her By One Foot: The Subjugation of Women in Seventeenth-century New France* (London: Routledge, 1991); Annemarie Shimony, "Iroquois Religion and Women in Historical Perspective," in Yvonne Yazbeck Haddad and Ellison Banks Findly, eds, *Women, Religion and Social Change* (New York: State University of New York Press, 1985), 397–418; Nancy Shoemaker, "Katerina Tekakwitha's Tortuous Path to Sainthood," in Shoemaker, *Negotiators of Change*, 49–71 and "The Rise or Fall of Iroquois Women," *Journal of Women's History* 2 (1990–1): 39–57; Davis, "Iroquois Women" (note 2).

The role of convents and women's orders in Canada has been discussed in: Leslie Choquette, "'Ces Amazones du Grand Dieu': Women and Mission in Seventeenth-century Canada," *French Historical Studies* 17 (1992): 626–655; Natalie Zemon Davis, *Women on the Margins: Three Seventeenth-century Lives* (Cambridge, Mass.: Harvard University Press, 1995).

There are several good overviews of women's experience in colonial America which include discussion of marriage and sexuality. These include: Lyle Koehler, *A Search for Power: The "Weaker Sex" in Seventeenth-century New England* (Urbana: University of Illinois Press, 1980); Mary Beth Norton, "The Evolution of White Women's Experience in Early America," *American Historical Review* 89 (1984): 593–619 and *Founding Mothers* (note 10); Carol Berkin, *First Generations: Women in Colonial America* (New York: Hill and Wang, 1996); Paula Treckel, *To Comfort the Heart: Women in Seventeenth-century America* (New York: Twayne, 1996); Larry D. Eldridge, *Women and Freedom in Early America* (New York: New York University Press, 1997). Many useful sources may be found in Frey and Morton, *New World* (note 11). Several essay collections about women and religion in America include colonial materials: Janet Wilson James, ed., *Women in American Religion* (Philadelphia: University of Pennsylvania Press, 1980); Ruether and Keller, *Women and Religion in America* (note 5).

The many works on the family also contain important information about attitudes toward sexuality and sexual practices. These began with several which focussed on the Puritan family, including Edmund S. Morgan, *The Puritan Family: Religion and Domestic Relations in Seventeenth-century New England* (New York: Harper and Row, 1966) and John Demos, *A Little Commonwealth: Family Life in Plymouth Colony* (New York: Oxford University Press, 1970). Works which look beyond the Puritans include: J. William Frost, *The Quaker Family in Colonial America* (New York: St Martins, 1973); Philip Greven, *The Protestant Temperament: Patterns of Child-rearing, Religious Experience and the Self in Early America* (New York: Knopf, 1977); Barry Levy, *Quakers and the American Family: British Settlement in the Delaware Valley* (New York: Oxford University Press, 1988); Carole Shammas, "Anglo-American Household Government in Comparative Perspective," *William and Mary Quarterly* 3rd ser., 52 (1995): 104–150; Wall (note 30). Puritan attitudes toward sex and their effects continue to be debated. For two largely opposing viewpoints, see Edmund S. Morgan, "The Puritans and Sex," *New England Quarterly* 15 (1942): 591–607 and Kathleen Verduin, "'Our Cursed Natures': Sexuality and the Puritan Conscience," *New England Quarterly* 56 (1983): 220–237; for a study which brings in other aspects of Puritan thought, see James T. Johnson, "The Covenant Idea and the Puritan View of Marriage," *Journal of the History of Ideas* 32 (1971): 107–118. For a study of the impact of Puritan attitudes, see R.W. Roetger, "The Transformation of Sexual Morality in 'Puritan' New England: Evidence from New Haven Court Records, 1639–1698," *Canadian Review of American Studies* 15 (1984): 243–257. For one example of decidedly non-puritan (with a lower case "p") sexual activities, see Michael Zuckerman, "Pilgrims in the Wilderness: Community, Modernity, and the Maypole at Merry Mount," *New England Quarterly* 50 (1977): 255–277.

Works which focus on women in New England include: Laurel Thatcher Ulrich, *Good Wives: Image and Reality in the Lives of Women in Northern New England*

1650–1750 (New York: Oxford University Press, 1980); N.E.H. Hull, *Female Felons: Women and Serious Crime in Colonial Massachusetts* (Urbana: University of Illinois Press, 1987); Susan Juster, *Disorderly Women: Sexual Politics and Evangelicalism in Revolutionary New England* (Ithaca: Cornell University Press, 1994); Cornelia Hughes Dayton, *Women Before the Bar: Gender, Law and Society in Connecticut, 1639–1789* (Chapel Hill: University of North Carolina Press, 1995); Elaine Forman Crane, *Ebb Tide in New England: Women, Seaports, and Social Change, 1630–1800* (Boston: Northeastern University Press, 1998); Hoffer and Hull, *Murdering Mothers* (note 28).

The Salem trial has been the best-studied witch case anywhere in the world; there are over twenty books, exploring it from every possible angle. Those which analyze sexual and gender elements include: Carol Karlsen, *The Devil in the Shape of a Woman: Witchcraft in Colonial New England* (New York: Random House, 1987); Elaine Breslaw, *Tituba, Reluctant Witch of Salem: Devilish Indians and Puritan Fantasies* (New York: New York University Press, 1995); Elizabeth Reis, *Damned Women: Sinners and Witches in Puritan New England* (Ithaca: Cornell University Press, 1997).

Along with studies of women, those which investigate the handling of moral offenses in New England also contain information about sexual practices. See, for example, Emil Oberholzer, Jr., *Delinquent Saints: Disciplinary Action in the Early Congregational Churches of Massachusetts* (New York: Columbia University Press, 1956); David H. Flaherty, "Crime and Social Control in Provincial Massachusetts," *The Historical Journal* 24 (1981): 339–360 and *Privacy* (note 13); David Thomas Konig, *Law and Society in Puritan Massachusetts: Essex County, 1629–1692* (Chapel Hill: University of North Carolina Press, 1979); Roger Thompsen, *Sex in Middlesex: Popular Mores in a Massachusetts County, 1649–1699* (Amherst: University of Massachusetts Press, 1986).

Newer studies of the Chesapeake include extensive discussions of sexual issues, as does Edmund S. Morgan, *American Slavery, American Freedom: The Ordeal of Colonial Virginia* (New York: Norton, 1975). Useful essays on marriage, demography and religious life in the Chesapeake may be found in: Aubrey C. Land, Lois Green Carr, and Edward C. Papenfuse, eds, *Law, Society, and Politics in Early Maryland* (Baltimore: Johns Hopkins University Press, 1977); Thad W. Tate and David L. Ammermann, eds, *The Chesapeake in the Seventeenth Century: Essays on Anglo-American Society* (Chapel Hill: University of North Carolina Press, 1979); Lois Green Carr, Philip D. Morgan, and Jean B. Russo, eds, *Colonial Chesapeake Society* (Chapel Hill: University of North Carolina Press, 1988). See also Mary Beth Norton, "Gender, Crime, and Community in Seventeenth-Century Maryland," in James Henretta, et al., eds, *The Transformation of Early American History* (New York: Knopf, 1991), 126–150 and Horn, *Adapting* (note 29).

The classic study of American attitudes toward Africans and their impact in the colonial period is Jordan, *White over Black* (note 21). Additional information about Africans in the New World may be found in: Morgan, *American Slavery, American Freedom*; John Thornton, *Africa and Africans in the Making of the Atlantic World, 1400–1680* (Cambridge: Cambridge University Press, 1992); Donald R. Wright, *African Americans in the Colonial Era: From African Origins Through the*

American Revolution (Arlington Heights, Illinois: Harlan Davidson, 1990); David Barry Gaspar and Darlene Clark Hine, *More than Chattel: Black Women and Slavery in the Americas* (Bloomington: Indiana University Press, 1996); Brown, *Good Wives* (note 15).

Studies which address specific issues include:

On divorce: Merril D. Smith, *Breaking the Bonds: Marital Discord in Pennsylvania, 1730–1830* (New York: New York University Press, 1991); Nancy F. Cott, "Divorce and the Changing Status of Women in Eighteenth-century Massachusetts," *William and Mary Quarterly*, 3rd ser., 33 (1976): 586–614; Sheldon S. Cohen, "What Man Hath Put Asunder: Divorce in New Hampshire, 1681–1784," *Historical New Hampshire* 41 (1986): 118–145; D. Kelly Weisberg, " 'Under Greet Temptations Heer': Women and Divorce in Puritan Massachusetts, " *Feminist Studies* 2 (1975): 183–193: Phillips, *Putting Asunder* (note 12).

On illegitimacy: Robert V. Wells, "Illegitimacy and Bridal Pregnancy in Colonial America," and Daniel Scott Smith, "The Long Cycle in American Illegitimacy and Prenuptial Pregnancy," in Peter Laslett et al., eds, *Bastardy and its Comparative History* (Cambridge, Mass.: Harvard University Press, 1980), 349–378.

On rape: Barbara Lindemann, "To Ravish and Carnally Know": Rape in Eighteenth-century Massachusetts," *Signs* 10 (1984): 63–82.

On homosexuality: Louis Crompton, "Homosexuals and the Death Penalty in Colonial America," *Journal of Homosexuality* 1 (1976): 277–293; Robert F. Oaks, " 'Things Fearful to Name': Sodomy and Buggery in Seventeenth-century New England," *Journal of Social History* 12 (1978): 268–281 and "Defining Sodomy in Seventeenth-century Massachusetts," in Salvatore J. Licata and Robert P. Peterson, eds, *Historical Perspectives on Homosexuality* (New York: Haworth Press, 1981), 79–83; Roger Thompson, "Attitudes Towards Homosexuality in the Seventeenth-century New England Colonies," *Journal of American Studies* 23 (1980): 27–40; Colin Talley, "Gender and Male Same-sex Erotic Behavior in British North America in the Seventeenth Century," *Journal of the History of Sexuality* 6 (1996): 385–408: Godbeer, "Cry of Sodom," (note 6).

On gender identity: Kathleen Brown, "Changed . . . into the fashion of man: The Politics of Sexual Difference in a Seventeenth-century Anglo-American Settlement," *Journal of the History of Sexuality* 6 (1995):171–193.

On defamation: Roger Thompson, " 'Holy Watchfulness' and Communal Conformism: The Functions of Defamation in Early New England Communities," *New England Quarterly* 56 (1983): 504–522; Mary Beth Norton, "Gender and Defamation in Seventeenth-century Maryland," *William and Mary Quarterly*, 3rd ser., 44 (1987): 3–39.

CONCLUSIONS

Homosexuals being burnt and hanged on the city square of Amsterdam during the Dutch persecution campaign of 1730–31, from "Temporal Punishments Depicted as a Warning to Godless and Damnable Sinners," a set of engravings published in Amsterdam by Gerrit Bos and Gerrit Bouman. From *The Gay Academic*, by permission of ETC Publications, Palm Springs, California.

CONCLUSIONS

THE HUNDREDS OF authors whose research has informed my study would no doubt have different answers to its central question: How did Christian ideas and institutions shape or attempt to shape sexual norms and conduct in the early modern world? The spectrum of scholarly opinions initially tempted me (invoking a vocabulary familiar to the discourses of Christianity and sexuality) to abstain from writing a conclusion, to bridle my desire to make grand sweeping statements in favor of the moderate chapter conclusions, and instead to allow readers to exercise their free will and rational capacities in making their own final judgements. I do not allow my students to avoid pulling material together, however, and further reflection convinced me that a final chapter was necessary. Though the preceding chapters have separated ideas, institutions, and effects – into what might be thought of as principle, policy, and practice – this one brings them back together in a final conversation.

Much of the current scholarship on sexuality and cross-cultural encounters has concentrated on questions of identity and difference, and such questions were also of great concern in early modern Christianity. "Christian" and its denominational subheadings – Catholic, Orthodox, Lutheran, Anglican, and so on – were primary identities, established not only by matters of belief, but also by outward behavior. The desired identity needed to be maintained through both external agents of control, such as courts and officials, and internalized agents of control, such as a sense of guilt or shame created through education, preaching, and confession. Together or in combination, these agents worked to minimize doctrinal deviance, a process which has been traced extensively in studies of the various Inquisitions, heresy trials, and religious wars of the early modern period. As we have seen, they also worked to curb moral and sexual deviance, by creating and maintaining boundaries between what was acceptable and unacceptable for Christian groups and individuals.

The notion of boundaries is a helpful way to think about many of the developments traced in this book. There are many different types of boundaries — between nations, languages, social classes, families, religions, ethnic groups — and they serve different functions. Some boundaries define spheres of influence, others set out permissible realms for action, others create or perpetuate ideological categories of difference. Some boundaries are sharp, while others are fuzzy and have liminal border areas; some are permeable, while others are impermeable; some are long-lasting, while others are constantly contested, modified, and revalued. Boundaries are defended through war, diplomacy, propaganda campaigns, or a variety of other means; these campaigns make up much of what we usually call "history." They are also maintained by regulating sexual activity. This may be done through laws prohibiting inter-group marriage or sexual contacts, but it is done more effectively through the establishment and fostering of traditions and other forms of internalized mechanisms of control. If children are taught very early who is unthinkable as a marriage partner, and unattractive as a sexual partner, the preservation of boundaries will not depend on laws or force alone.

The centrality of sex to the preservation of boundaries is something that nearly all human societies have recognized. They have developed laws and norms regarding marriage and other sexual contacts, both to keep their group distinct from others and to preserve hierarchies within the group. Societies sometimes allow elite men to marry or (more often) to have non-marital sexual relationships with non-elite women, and place various restrictions on the children of those unions. The reverse case is much rarer, because the sexual activities of elite women are the most closely monitored in nearly all societies. Thus socially defined categories of difference such as race, nation, and class are maintained by sexual restrictions, and these restrictions are gendered, with women's experience different from that of men.

Christian authorities recognized the importance of regulating sexual activity through external controls and internal norms long before the early modern period. Though conversion did not bring the right to divorce a non-believing spouse, unmarried converts were encouraged to marry other converts, and eventually, Christians were prohibited from marrying Jews and Muslims. Such prohibitions appear to have been effective even in areas with significant Jewish and Muslim populations such as medieval Spain, though there were other types of sexual contacts, such as prostitution, between persons of different faiths. Christian groups outside of Europe, such as the Malabar

Christians in India and later the "Hidden Christians" in Japan, were also endogamous – marrying within the group – and missionaries throughout the New World and Asia enforced religious endogamy by refusing to marry a Christian and a non-Christian.

After the Protestant Reformation, secular and religious authorities both in Europe and in colonial areas attempted to prohibit marriages between members of different denominations, or when they occurred, to ensure that the children were raised within the "correct" faith. (This practice continues in some denominations today, with a spouse from outside that tradition required to promise that any children will be raised within it, whether or not the outside spouse also converts.) As in many cultures, such rules some-times involved a sexual double-standard that prohibited women from marrying outside the group while allowing men to do so. Whether gender-specific or not, these regulations varied in their effectiveness. People sometimes crossed not only denominational boundaries to marry and start families, but also physical boundaries, travelling to a different area to find a religious authority who would marry them or baptize their children. Small radical Protestant groups were the most effective at policing intermarriage, as they made out-marriage grounds for expulsion. In such cases, the group itself (or a subset of its members) was the ultimate authority, but the marriage did not bring with it civil penalties as it might in areas where secular authorities enforced prohibitions on intermarriage.

Religious affiliation is a particularly tricky boundary to maintain as it is to some degree volitional, that is, people can change from one religion to another although they cannot change their mother tongue or skin color. Most early modern Christian denominations were, of course, actively seeking conver-sions among both Christians and non-Christians, but these very conversions challenged their categories of self and other. Though on one level conver-sion was desired, on another it was suspect precisely because it was volitional, and the convert could always revert. Converts were often suspected of retaining some loyalties to their original religious affiliation, or of either surreptitiously or openly inserting its traditions into their new religion.

Religious beliefs were often conceptualized physically as blood, with people regarded as having Jewish, Muslim, or Christian blood, and after the Reformation, Protestant or Catholic blood. The most dramatic expression of this occurred in early modern Spain, where "purity of the blood" – having no Jewish or Muslim ancestors – became an obsession, but it was also true elsewhere. A father choosing a wetnurse for his children took care to make sure she was of the same denomination, lest, if he was a Catholic, her Protestant blood turn into Protestant milk and thus infect the child with heretical ideas. Children born of religiously mixed marriages were often slightly mistrusted, for one never knew whether their Protestant or Catholic blood would ultimately triumph.

Of course, "blood" was also a way of talking about class differences in many parts of the world, with those of "noble blood" – or in south Sulawesi "white blood" – prohibited from marrying commoners and taught to be protective of their lineage. Blood was also used to describe national boundaries; those having "French blood" were distinguished from those with "German blood," "English blood", or "Spanish blood." Conceptualizing class status and national identity as "blood" naturalized these and made them appear innate; sexual contacts across such fundamental dividing lines could thus be made to appear threatening and dangerous.

As Europeans developed colonial empires, blood became a way to describe racial distinctions as well as those of religion, class, and nation. In the case of Jews or Jewish converts in Spain and its empire, or the Gaelic Irish in Ireland, religious and racial differences were linked, with religious traditions being viewed as signs of barbarity and racial inferiority. Initially, in colonial areas outside Europe, the spread of Christianity was used to justify the conquest and enslavement of indigenous peoples. As they converted, however, religion became a less persuasive means of differentiation, and race or skin color took its place. As we have seen, Virginia laws regarding fornication distinguished between "christian" and "negroe" in 1662, but by 1691 between "white" men and women and those who were "negroe, mulatto, or Indian." "One drop of [black] blood" made one black in the binary racial classification developing in North America, whether or not one was Christian. Religious affiliation also played an increasingly small role in the more complex racial hierarchies which developed in Latin America and the European colonies in Asia, where crown, church, and company policies about intermarriage vacillated between promotion and prohibition. Churches were important agents in the creation and maintenance of those hierarchies, however. Church officials had the authority to affirm (or alter) one's racial classification for the purposes of marriage, entering a convent, or becoming a priest by assessing the level of European, creole, Indian, or African blood in one's veins.

Religious affiliation and race were not the only significant boundaries for early modern Christians. Religious and secular authorities drew (or attempted to draw) a sharp boundary between marriage and other types of sexual relationships, and to limit sexual activity to married people. These efforts began during the Roman Empire in Europe, as the church preached against concubinage and other non-marital sexual arrangements, and in favor of allowing individuals of any social status, including slaves, to marry. The sharp divide between married and unmarried was accepted only slowly in Europe, and even more slowly when Christianity was exported outside of Europe into cultures in which there was a range of approved sexual relationships, but it was still there. In some situations certain population groups came to be regarded as exempt from the requirement of marriage or were actually prohibited from marrying, and their sexual activities were rarely the concern of church or state authorities. These groups, such as slaves in the southern British colonies of North America or mixed-race people in the Spanish colonies, were thus further marginalized by their exclusion from marriage and the legitimacy it conferred; this in turn was taken as a sign of their moral depravity. In these areas, race became a marker of marital status, with slave or *mestizo* children simply assumed to be illegitimate.

In all early modern societies, marriage was a matter of concern for families and communities as well as religious and secular authorities, for marriage was closely linked with familial and individual honor. At times familial and community interests conflicted with Christian doctrine. At least in theory, the consent of the parties was required for marriage and that of the individual for a vow of celibacy; these conditions put a greater emphasis on individual choice and what some historians have termed "sexual agency." The power of kin and community over these choices was never completely relinquished, however, and at certain times and locations made a resurgence in law as well as practice. On the other hand, some individuals were able to defy family wishes in their choices about marriage, and occasionally enlisted religious authorities as their supporters.

Conflicts over marital choice could be dramatic and protracted, and they have left a historical record no doubt out of proportion to their frequency. In many more cases, familial, community, and church aims supported one another, and young people were socialized effectively enough to choose appropriate marital partners. This pattern in marital choice has often been described as marriage for convenience in contrast to a more modern pattern of marriage for love. In many ways this sets up a false dichotomy, for harmony and companionship – both viewed as aspects of love – were widely regarded among early modern Christians as more easily achieved between spouses whose family backgrounds were similar. Letters and diaries reveal that both men and women expected affection from their spouses and were disappointed when it was lacking.

Christian authors frequently addressed the sexual and emotional elements of marriage in sermons, treatises, and advice manuals as well as private letters, precisely because sex was to be limited to marriage. The glorification of heterosexual married love began in medieval sermons, but it was intensified after the Reformation by Protestants and later by Catholics. Only a handful of Christian authors after 1500, such as a few Orthodox writers from Russia, envisioned the possibility of marriage without sex, for a "chaste marriage" was increasingly defined by both Protestants and Catholics as one in which spouses were sexually faithful to each other and moderate in their sexual activity, not one in which they renounced sex. Marital sexuality still carried with it the taint of sin for many Catholic authors, but most Protestants and some Catholics such as Tomás Sánchez regarded it as morally neutral or even morally good because it increased spousal affection. The inability to have sex in marriage was grounds for annulment, a practice which continues in many states in the United States today, where consummation along with a legal ceremony is required for a marriage to be complete.

The restriction of sexual activity to marriage made a range of sexual activities morally unacceptable, and in many cases illegal, as church and state authorities first in Europe and then elsewhere sought to "criminalize sin." The criminalization of certain sexual activities was not new in the early modern period in Europe; nor was it limited to Christianity. Medieval Christians and non-Christians set punishments for adultery (usually defined as sex with a married women), for marrying someone within a prohibited degree or type of relationship, and for engaging in sexual activites which broke religious taboos. After 1500 such sexual crimes were joined by others, and the mechanisms of investigation and punishment were expanded, in part through technical innovations such as the printing press and institutional innovations such as birth and marriage registers. All sides in the religious controversies which engulfed western and central Europe during the sixteenth and early seventeenth centuries regarded the control of sexual activities as extremely important, for to religious and political authorities order, morality, discipline, hierarchy, propriety, and stable families were all linked and were a mark of divine favor. Both in Europe and beyond, authorities established and supported institutions which attempted to control the sexual activities of their adherents or subjects, and tried to instill attitudes which would encourage discipline and decorum. Control of language was an important part of these efforts, and individuals were punished for denying church doctrines about sex, reciting love charms, using sexual blasphemy, or defaming their neighbors with sexual slander. The most rigorous authorities hoped to shape thoughts along with words and actions, haranguing people in confession or sermons about lascivious thoughts and dreams, attempting to regulate desire as well as conduct. Secular courts adopted procedures and punishments developed by religious bodies, imposing sentences which involved public confession and shaming rituals. As sins were made crimes, crimes were also made sins.

Efforts to control sin generally had a greater effect on elites and urban residents than they did on non-elites and rural dwellers, but they also often excluded those very members of the elite, whose moral and sexual conduct was not subject to the same rules as the rest of the population. Because the consequences of heterosexual activity were visible in the bodies of women, the criminalization of non-marital sexuality discriminated by gender as well as class, and the ones who suffered most were often non-elite women who became pregnant. Undisciplined sexuality in both men and women was portrayed from the pulpit and press as a threat to Christian order, but it was women's lack of discipline that was most often punished, even in cases which authorities recognized as involving coercion or force. Penalties for abortion and infanticide increased; women were required to report all pregnancies, and unmarried women were occasionally subject to bodily searches. Only in cases of purported impotence were male bodies subjected to similar public scrutiny.

The desire to draw a sharp boundary between honorable and dishonorable conduct and character led to stricter controls on women whose sexual lives were in some way irregular. Authorities defined them all as "prostitutes" and attempted to punish or incarcerate them in convents or prisons. Gender shaped the handling of clerical sexuality among Catholics as well. Priests and monks were encouraged to abstain from sex and occasionally incarcerated if their sexual activities led to scandal; nuns and other female religious were physically enclosed to keep them from the temptations of the world as pure "Brides of Christ." In Orthodox Russia, elite lay women were similarly enclosed in special women's quarters to keep them pure, though for an earthly, rather than heavenly, bridegroom.

Race, along with gender and social class, shaped the enforcement of sexual regulations, and the discourse of racial difference was sexualized and gendered. In Europe, the oppositional pair white woman/non-white man was used in literature and art to represent the contrast between purity and evil, while that of white man/non-white woman was used to represent domination and submission. Sexualized conceptualizations of race were more obvious in colonial areas, where in the initial years of conquest, indigenous peoples were often feminized, described or portrayed visually as weak and passive in contrast to their virile and masculine conquerors. Sexual violation was not simply a metaphor in colonial areas, however, for conquest also involved the actual rape of indigenous women and the demands for sexual as well as other types of labor or services. After the immigration of more European women, new discursive elements emerged, and racial hierarchies became linked with those of sexual virtue and purity, especially for women. Again, this was not a matter of language alone; unmarried white women who bore mixed-race children were more harshly treated than those who bore white children, while pregnancy out of wedlock was often ignored or even encouraged among non-white women, who were not pressured to name the father as their white counterparts were.

The boundaries established by religion, race, and marital status were under-girded by an even more fundamental opposition, that between "natural" – which often shaded into godly – and "unnatural" – which shaded into demonic. Sodomy in all its forms – homosexual, bestial, heterosexual anal – was first defined as a "crime against nature" in about 1250, and viewed by some author-ities as heresy and a violation of God's commandments. Causality more often moved in the other direction, however, with persons accused of heresy, such as the Knights Templars in France or *converso* officials in Spain, also charged as sodomites. Racial and ethnic classifications were also a factor in sodomy accusations; the Chinese, Turks, Moors, and Italians, for example, were seen as particularly likely to engage in sodomy and certain Indian tribes to engage in sodomy and other "unnatural" practices such as cannibalism.

The "unnaturalness" of certain activities linked them firmly to the demonic. In the eyes of their neighbors, only the Devil could lead men in Sweden to have sex with animals, or women in Belgium who were pregnant out of wedlock to kill their own children. Contraception was both "unnatural" and "demonic" in the eyes of some authors, as were coital positions other than man-on-top because they overturned the "natural" gender hierarchy and might have contraceptive effects. In Mexico and the Andes, practitioners of indige-nous religions were accused of unnatural sexual practices as well as idolatry. In New England, Anne Hutchinson and Mary Dyer, a Quaker woman, were charged with giving birth to monstrous children as well as monstrous ideas. The link between unnatural sexuality and demons was particularly evident in witchcraft accusations; demonologists were often obsessed with how witches copulated with the devil, while less educated people were more concerned with the practical effects of witchcraft on fertility, such as making men impotent or women miscarry.

The actual ability of religious authorities to maintain boundaries through the control of sexuality varied widely, but nowhere were they as successful as they hoped they would be. Though agents of control in the early modern period were certainly more numerous and powerful than they had been in the Middle Ages, they did not approach the policing possibilities of twentieth-century democratic states, to say nothing of totalitarian regimes. Thus there is an enormous – and sometimes misleading – gap between rhetoric and reality in almost all aspects of sexual regulation.

The gap between learned ideal and lived reality was especially evident in issues surrounding marriage. Particularly in rural areas, people refused to accept the idea that sex between engaged persons was wrong, for it did not upset the marital household as long as the wedding actually took place as planned; thus they continued to engage in it, defend it verbally, and hold fancy weddings despite the obvious pregnancy of the bride. "Trial marriages" continued among the Basques and North American Indian converts, for these practices, too, were viewed as reinforcing the stability of marriage. Despite post-Tridentine demands that weddings be conducted in public, Catholics in Italy continued to hold weddings in secret to ward off evil spells cast by envious neighbors. Christian wedding ceremonies were thought to bring luck and fertility to converts in Africa and Latin America, and they were sometimes added to existing rituals, especially for the first marriage, but they were also avoided so that restrictions on divorce could be ignored. Those restrictions were also less cumbersome in actuality than in theory: abandonment served the function of divorce for many poor people; annulments were frequently possible for the elite; divorces were occasionally granted in Protestant areas on grounds such as severe incompatibility which were socially, though not legally, acceptable. In some places Christians avoided the need for such measures by simply avoiding marriage in the first place. Despite the praise for marriage and the legal advantages which it brought, high rates of births out of wedlock continued in Latin America, for instance, where "concubinage" and other non-marital arrangements were socially useful.

Marriage was not the only sexual matter with a demonstrable gap between theory and practice. In a few cases, such as adultery in Geneva or sodomy in Scotland, punishments were harsher than those set by legal statute, but in most cases the reverse was true. In colonial North America, there were harsh denunciations and stringent laws against adultery and homosexual activity, but almost no cases. Fornication was prohibited, but it was almost never prosecuted in most parts of the world unless it resulted in the birth of a child. Consanguinity – defined differently in various denominations – was forbidden, but the lack of records in Catholic and Orthodox Europe and the colonies made consanguinity rules impossible to enforce except among the elites whose family connections were known. Those elites could generally obtain dispensations to marry their relatives in any case. Brothels were closed, but prostitution continued; popular rituals celebrating or condemning sexual activity, such as maypoles or *charivaris*, were prohibited, but went on; clerical concubinage and solicitation were condemned and punished and probably declined, but did not disappear.

Religious and political authorities recognized the limitations on their abilities actually to shape behavior and to maintain boundaries, and so relied upon other individuals and institutions to assist them, including heads of families, volunteer or paid investigatory agents such as the *familiares*, and even concerned and watchful neighbors. To describe such individuals and groups as "assisting" authorities is, in many cases, misleading, for often they, and not higher authorities, took the lead in policing, denouncing, and investigating sexual conduct. Guilds, confraternities, and neighborhood groups might even be more rigorous than church or state authorities, for they often had more to lose if marriages broke down or their members or neighbors were tainted with dishonor. On a day-to-day basis this informal control of sexuality had more of an impact than written laws or formal courts; the actual policing of boundaries was thus very much a shared task, rather than simply imposed from above. Informal policing was done by women as well as men; women arranged marriages, shaped sexual reputations through conversations with their neighbors, accused other women of witchcraft, or reported people who said fornication was not a sin. In colonial areas, control was also exerted by indigenous or mixed-race people – *dogigues* in Canada, *fiscales* in Mexico, or Proponents in the VOC colonies – as well as Europeans; they catechized, investigated cases, punished those found guilty of moral lapses, examined candidates for marriage, and sometimes even heard confessions.

Individuals also policed their own activities through the internalization of Christian norms communicated to them in sermons, printed materials, schools, and confession. Confession, either to a priest or to a congregation, encouraged people to talk about their sexual sins, with the ultimate goal of repressing the activity deemed sinful. Confession to a priest may have worked more to disseminate sexual information in some areas than to restrict activity, but it is clear many people developed a sense of guilt which was stronger than simply a fear of being discovered or receiving punishment in this world. It is, of course, impossible to measure something as subjective as a sense of guilt, and those who felt most guilty left the most records, for their feelings led them to indict themselves to their neighbors, legal authorities, or religious personnel, or leave behind private writings such as diaries. In some cases these self-indictments were undoubtedly duplicitous, as individuals recognized that expressing contrition was a way to avoid or lessen sentences for such offenses as prostitution or sodomy, but in many cases the sense of guilt appears to have been genuine.

Of all the issues covered in this book, historians disagree the most on how to interpret local and internalized control of sexual norms and activities. Some ignore these aspects, and focus primarily on formal religious institutions such as the Inquisitions, episcopal courts, consistories, or missions, noting the ways in which such institutions narrowed the range of acceptable sexual behavior and promoted hierarchical gender structures. Others view popular control and self-discipline as examples of "false consciousness," and argue that people were deluded into working against their own self-interest and repressing their sexual desires. Others apply Gramschi's idea of hegemony, in which some individuals and groups become convinced through education or other forms of socialization that agreeing with authorities is preferable, and then gain special privileges through their association with the dominant group and its ideas.

These largely negative or dismissive views of internalized and popular control of sexuality are countered by other scholars who point out that in many instances, including colonial ones, the norms of authorities and those of local families and communities actually meshed to a great degree. Yes, families and groups were disciplined, they argue, but they were also disciplining. When the goals of higher authorities did not fit with community standards, they were generally not accomplished, as groups adapted Catholic or Protestant norms to their own situations. The syncretism and selective adoption of Christian values and practices was not an example of "false consciousness," but of actual religious conversion in which people chose to shape their behavior and thoughts in order to follow Orthodox, Catholic, or Protestant norms. These scholars assert that though Christianity introduced a language of repression, individuals and groups created their own meanings for that language and developed a "double-voiced discourse."

As the preceding chapters have shown, there are examples to support all sides of this debate, and historians' positions are determined to a large degree by their general philosophical views on the ability of people to determine their own history. Their arguments are also shaped by the particular situation with which they are most familiar, for the common concerns with boundary setting shared across the early modern Christian world were accompanied by significant local differences in the exact definitions of those boundaries and the ways sex was regulated to establish and preserve them.

First, though I have identified certain ideas and approaches as Catholic, Protestant, or Orthodox, there was wide variation within each of these traditions. Even official theology was not univocal: some Catholics openly doubted the value of celibacy while some Protestants thought it had merit; the morality of sexual enjoyment in marriage was debated in both Protestant and Catholic circles; Jesuits and Jansenists fought over the importance of sexual activities to salvation. Lay people were similarly split: lay Catholics in some places tolerated clerical concubinage, while in others they took the lead in combatting it; lay Calvinists in some places reported their neighbors to authorities but not in others; some lay Orthodox celebrated fertility rituals that were pagan in origin, while others killed themselves as Old Believers in defense of traditional Orthodox doctrines. Uniformity in belief was often invented or pretended when one denomination came into conflict with another or was threatened from the outside, but differences emerged again when the threat had passed.

"Protestant" covers a particularly large spectrum of belief and practice, from state-church Lutherans who emphasized the patriarchal family to radical groups who wanted no connection to a secular government and experimented with family forms. Divorce was possible only by Act of Parliament in the England of Anglicanism, but was available on grounds which went far beyond the traditional Biblical ones in Calvinist Neuchâtel and Lutheran Sweden. Though a few radical groups were sexually freer than magisterial Protestants or Catholics, most of them were more moralistic, using exclusion and excommunication to shape sexual conduct and create a small "sacralized society" within the larger and more sinful society. Groups such as the Quakers and Moravians, in which the entire body made disciplinary decisions, were more egalitarian in their policing of boundaries than those which relied on authorities such as pastors, judges, or inquisitors, and they were also more effective.

In some instances, the differences within Protestantism, Catholicism, and Orthodoxy were caused by factors outside the realm of religion. In some parts of Europe and its colonies, royal or municipal courts gained power over marriage, beginning a process of secularization that would speed up in the eighteenth century. When monarchical interests conflicted with those of the church, as in Peter the Great's Russia or post-Tridentine France, monarchs often won. In both Russia and France, for example, parental consent was required for a marriage to be valid, despite church doctrine about the primacy of spousal consent.

Second, though there are striking similarities among all early modern Christian denominations and, as just noted, striking differences of opinion within them, there are also some basic distinctions between them. Despite doubts about the value of forced celibacy among Catholics and Orthodox, voluntary celibacy and virginity continued to be highly prized and praised. For some Russian Orthodox writers, this included marital virginity, a practice that Luther and other Protestants regarded as grounds for divorce as well as unnatural. Their rejection of celibacy meant Protestants saw stronger links between marriage, honor, and adulthood than did adherents of other denominations. Both Orthodox and Catholic authorities were suspicious of unmarried women who lived on their own and enforced stricter enclosure on female religious, but Protestants were also suspicious of unmarried adult men, ordering them in some places to move in with married couples. The ability of an adult to reject a life which included sexual activity was denied by most Protestants, for whom celibacy also meant an abdication of his or her basic nature as a man or woman. Protestants thus set up a uniform ideal of sexual life, with marriage and parenthood as essential for both sexes, while Catholicism and Orthodoxy endorsed a range of options.

A third line of difference is that between Europe and the colonies. In some colonial settings, such as the Puritan towns of Massachusetts or the Jesuit missions of Canada and Latin America, religious authorities attempted to create disciplined moral and sexual utopias where God's law, as they interpreted it, would be the basis of all social and legal institutions in ways that were impossible in the more decadent Europe. They gathered their co-religionists or converts tightly together in order to supervise their lives and encourage mutual surveillance. For brief periods such places may have been the most sexually disciplined communities in the Christian world, but their isolation was difficult to maintain for long, and those who objected to discipline went elsewhere.

In most parts of the colonial world, opportunities for Christian discipline were less rather than more intense than those in Europe. Christian authorities were generally few in number and widely scattered geographically, so that their ability to shape actual behavior was more limited than it was in Europe where courts and churches were more numerous. Settlements were widely dispersed in many colonial areas, and the opportunities for neighborly surveillance were minimal, as were the opportunities to reinforce one's internal controls by listening to sermons or attending confession. There were more institutions of moral control in colonial cities than in the countryside, but also more opportunities for activities judged immoral, such as prostitution or homosexual relationships. (This is also true of European cities.)

In all parts of the colonial world, whether mission utopia or urban fleshpot, Christian notions were redefined in the face of pre-existing values and norms. This redefinition had also occurred in Europe as Christianity accommodated itself to existing Roman and Germanic practices, but by 1500 it was largely in the past. Accommodation was ongoing in colonial settings: in Asia, for example, ideas about moral debt shaped confessional practices and the development of a sense of guilt; in Latin America, ideas about balance shaped notions of the value of celibacy. In Europe, Catholicism, Protestantism, and Orthodoxy were not static in this period, but the range of possibilities was greater in the colonial world.

It was not infinite, however, and though indigenous people developed their own patterns and served as religious officials, the ultimate authority in most colonial settings was in European hands. Other than in Malabar and Ethiopia, Christianity was initially foreign and imported in the colonial world in ways that it was not, of course, in Europe by 1500. It was also part of a structure of dominance that went primarily in one direction, for the attitudes and expectations of European Christians about the peoples they encountered ultimately had a much greater impact on those peoples than the reverse. Colonization had some impact on the regulation of sexuality in Europe, both in terms of demographic changes such as male outmigration and intellectual changes such as new notions of racial difference, but these cannot compare with the changes in colonial areas. In some parts of the world, colonization also brought European diseases and demographic catastrophe along with Christianity, and these influenced family relations and sexual activities far more than any courts or clergy.

A fourth line of difference occurs among the colonies. Syncretistic adaptation not only made the situation in Europe different from the colonies, but it also made each colony distinct. Such distinctions in Christian forms were added to many other differences: whether the ultimate purpose of the colony was trade, exploitation, or settlement; how many people immigrated; how many of those people were free or slave women; what Christian authorities thought about the local culture; whether clergy saw their most important function as conversion of indigenous peoples or ministering to immigrants. Each of these and many other factors not only made the experience of colonies different from one another, but also created great differences within a single colony.

A final line of difference is one which intersects all of the others: change over time. As we have seen, in each geographic area there were high points of concern with morality and sexual conduct, followed by periods of less intense scrutiny. There was also a slow tendency toward fewer cases and milder punishments of sexual offenses after a high point sometime in the late sixteenth or early seventeenth century in Europe, and the late seventeenth century in the colonies. Executions for sodomy and witchcraft ended; fornication was no longer prosecuted unless a child needed to be supported; infanticide was no longer assumed if a child born out of wedlock died. By 1750, new ideas were beginning to develop about the sexual natures of women and men, the importance of personal and familial privacy, and the proper boundaries between religion and the state. All of these ideas would play a role in the development of "modern" sexuality and create a world where Christianity played a lesser role in its definition and regulation than that we have traced here.

Our modern world has not shaken its history as much as some theorists of sexuality have posited, however. The reactions of my friends and neighbors when I began this study reinforced my sense of its continuing importance. As I finish this conclusion, a sex scandal has just led to the impeachment of the American president, and phrases that have appeared often in these pages – "criminalization of sin," "puritanical zeal," "public confessions," and even "witchhunt" – are used regularly on the evening news. Commentators from outside the United States trying to understand and explain the situation refer often to the distinctive religious history of England's North American colonies and their attempts to create sacralized societies by disciplining sexuality. Any lingering doubts I might have had about the enduring significance of Christianity to contemporary sexual discourse are gone.

INDEX